NELSON'S

Student

Bible

DICTIONARY

A Complete Guide to Understanding
the World of the Bible

NELSON'S

Student

Bible

DICTIONARY

A Complete Guide to Understanding
the World of the Bible

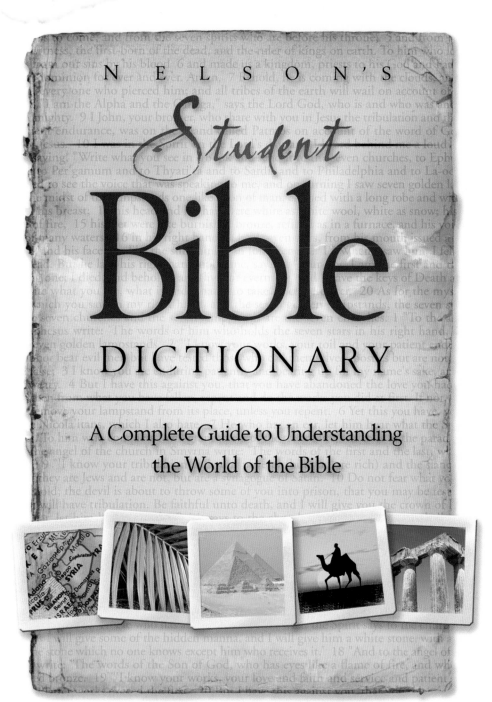

Ronald F. Youngblood, F. F. Bruce, and R. K. Harrison

NELSON REFERENCE & ELECTRONIC

A Division of Thomas Nelson Publishers

Since 1798

www.thomasnelson.com

Published in Nashville, Tennessee, by Thomas Nelson, Inc.

Unless otherwise indicated, all Scripture quotations are from the New King James Version, copyright © 1979, 1980, 1982, 1992 by Thomas Nelson, Inc. All rights reserved.

Verses marked "NASB" are taken from the *New American Standard Bible,* copyright © 1960, 1962, 1963, 1968, 1971, 1972, 1973, 1975 by Lockman Foundation.

Verses marked "NIV" are taken from the *Holy Bible:* New International Version, copyright © 1973, 1978, 1984 by International Bible Society.

Verses marked "RSV" are taken from the *Holy Bible:* Revised Standard Version, second edition, copyright © 1946, 1951, 1972 by the Division of Christian Education of the National Council of the Churches of Christ in the United States of America.

The Scripture quotations contained herein from the New Revised Standard Version of the Bible are © 1989 by the Division of Christian Education of the National Council of the Churches of Christ in the United States of America.

Verses marked "REB" are from the Revised English Bible, copyright © 1989 by the delegates of the Oxford University Press and the Syndics of the Cambridge University Press.

Book composition by *Rainbow Graphics*, Kingsport, Tennessee.

Library of Congress Cataloging-in-Publication Data

Nelson's student Bible dictionary.
        p. cm.
    Includes index.
    ISBN 1-4185-0330-4
    1. Bible—Dictionaries. I. Title: Student Bible dictionary. II. Thomas Nelson (Firm)
    BS440.N3495 2005
    220.3—dc22

                                        2005004472

ISBN 1-4185-0330-4

6 7 8 9—09 08 07 06

Printed in China

Contents

Preface vii
Bible History Chart viii
Dictionary Articles A to Z 1

ARTICLES AND TEACHING OUTLINES ON BOOKS OF THE BIBLE

Old Testament

Genesis	90	Ecclesiastes	62
Exodus	74	Song of Solomon	233
Leviticus	148	Isaiah	116
Numbers	177	Jeremiah	121
Deuteronomy	57	Lamentations	144
Joshua	134	Ezekiel	77
Judges	136	Daniel	52
Ruth	226	Hosea	110
1 Samuel	228	Joel	128
2 Samuel	228	Amos	12
1 Kings	140	Obadiah	179
2 Kings	140	Jonah	132
1 Chronicles	40	Micah	163
2 Chronicles	40	Nahum	172
Ezra	78	Habakkuk	100
Nehemiah	175	Zephaniah	274
Esther	71	Haggai	101
Job	127	Zechariah	272
Psalms	208	Malachi	156
Proverbs	207		

New Testament

Matthew	160	1 Timothy	247
Mark	158	2 Timothy	247
Luke	153	Titus	248
John	131	Philemon	195
Acts	4	Hebrews	103
Romans	224	James	118
1 Corinthians	46	1 Peter	192
2 Corinthians	46	2 Peter	192
Galatians	86	1 John	130
Ephesians	67	2 John	130
Philippians	197	3 John	130
Colossians	42	Jude	135
1 Thessalonians	244	Revelation	221
2 Thessalonians	244		

CONTENTS

CHARTS, TABLES, AND MAPS

Bible History viii
Alexander's Greek Empire 10
Books of the Apocrypha 15
The Twelve Apostles 16
The Jewish Calendar 35
David's Triumphs 54
David's Troubles 54
Jewish Feasts 81
Does the Bible Really Say That? 92
Old Testament Names for God 94
Pagan Gods of Egypt 96
Why Four Gospels? 97
The "I Am" Statements 113
Titles of Christ 125
The Period of the Judges 136
The Levitical Offerings 150
The Miracles of Jesus Christ 166
Monies of the Bible 168
Palestine in Christ's Time 184
The Parables of Jesus Christ 186
Paul's First and Second Missionary Journeys 188
Paul's Third and Fourth Missionary Journeys 189
The Pentateuch 190
Chronology of Israel in the Pentateuch 191
The Ten Plagues on Egypt 199
Chronology of Old Testament Kings and Prophets 204
Fulfilled Prophecies from Isaiah 206
The Preservation of the Remnant 219
The Seven Churches of Revelation 222
Names of Satan 231
Solomon's Empire 234
Solomon's Twelve Districts 235
New Testament Lists of Spiritual Gifts 236
The Plan of the Tabernacle 239
The Furniture of the Tabernacle 239
The Temples of the Bible 242
Weights 263
Measures of Length 263
Dry Measures 264
Liquid Measures 264
Old Testament Women 267
New Testament Women 268

Preface

Nelson's Student Bible Dictionary is a portable and engaging sourcebook of biblical information that is accurate, thorough, dependable, and easy to understand. Entries covering the essential people, places, things, events, and doctrines of the Bible appear in the book, making it the perfect Bible dictionary for students of all ages.

Nelson's Student Bible Dictionary complements the alphabetically-arranged articles and definitions with visual guides to the Bible. Readers will appreciate the full-color photographs throughout; the easy-to-use study and teaching outlines for every book of the Bible; tables, charts, and diagrams that illustrate Bible teachings and life in Bible times; and maps to biblical places.

Users will benefit from the book's extensive cross-reference system, which makes it easy to use with most of the popular English translations of the Bible. The key words in each article are based on the New King James Version of the Bible (NKJV), but variant names from five additional translations—the King James Version (KJV), the New American Standard Bible (NASB), the Revised English Bible (REB), the New International Version (NIV), and the New Revised Standard Version (NRSV)—are fully cross-referenced.

Readers are also referred to related articles in the dictionary for further information. The article on the "Levites," for example, contains a reference to priests (the word appears in small capital letters: "PRIESTS"). This format refers the reader to the article on priests that contributes to a better understanding of the Levites.

The publisher sends forth *Nelson's Student Bible Dictionary* trusting that it will enrich your study of the Word of God.

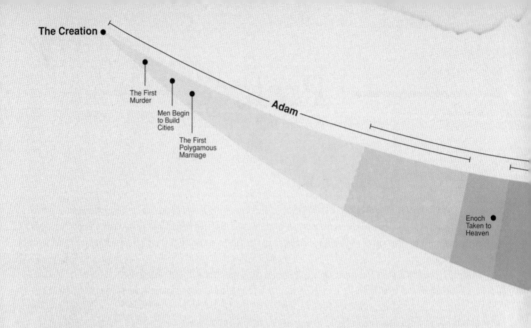

The Creation

The First Murder

Men Begin to Build Cities

The First Polygamous Marriage

Adam

Enoch Taken to Heaven

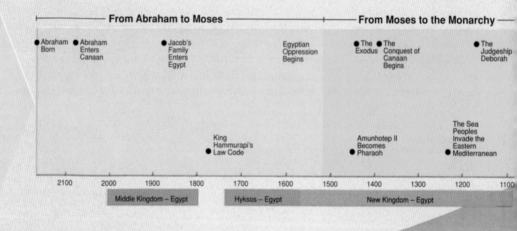

From Abraham to Moses ———————— **From Moses to the Monarchy**

Abraham Born

Abraham Enters Canaan

Jacob's Family Enters Egypt

Egyptian Oppression Begins

The Exodus

The Conquest of Canaan Begins

The Judgeship Deborah

King Hammurapi's Law Code

Amunhotep II Becomes Pharaoh

The Sea Peoples Invade the Eastern Mediterranean

| 2100 | 2000 | 1900 | 1800 | 1700 | 1600 | 1500 | 1400 | 1300 | 1200 | 1100 |

Middle Kingdom – Egypt   Hyksos – Egypt   New Kingdom – Egypt

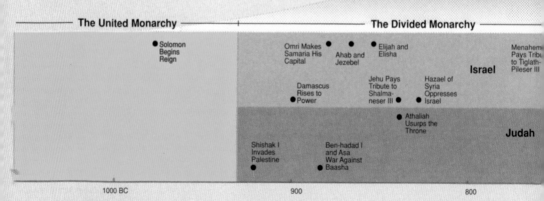

The United Monarchy ———————— **The Divided Monarchy**

Solomon Begins Reign

Omri Makes Samaria His Capital

Ahab and Jezebel

Elijah and Elisha

Menahem Pays Tribute to Tiglath-Pileser III

Israel

Damascus Rises to Power

Jehu Pays Tribute to Shalmaneser III

Hazael of Syria Oppresses Israel

Athaliah Usurps the Throne

Judah

Shishak I Invades Palestine

Ben-hadad I and Asa War Against Baasha

| 1000 BC | 900 | 800 |

Bible history

© Thomas Nelson, Inc.

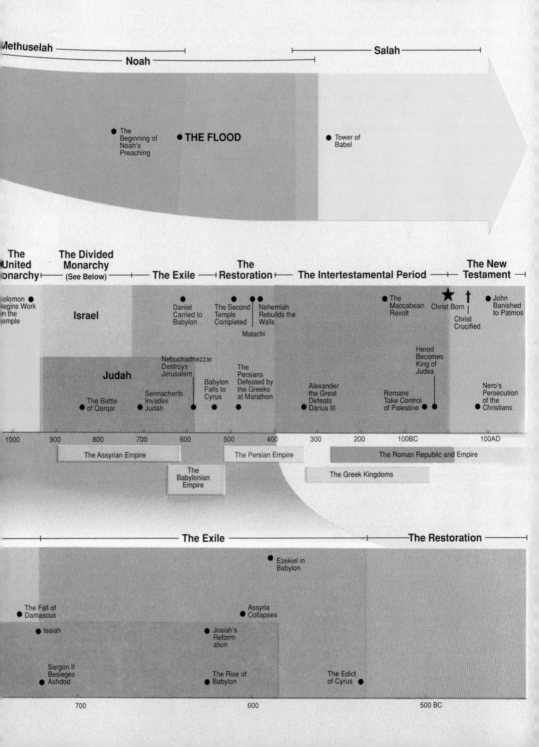

Methuselah — Noah — Salah

- The Beginning of Noah's Preaching
- THE FLOOD
- Tower of Babel

| The United Monarchy | The Divided Monarchy (See Below) | The Exile | The Restoration | The Intertestamental Period | The New Testament |

- Solomon Begins Work on the Temple
- Israel
- Daniel Carried to Babylon
- The Second Temple Completed
- Nehemiah Rebuilds the Walls
- Malachi
- The Maccabean Revolt
- ★ Christ Born
- † Christ Crucified
- John Banished to Patmos

- Judah
- Nebuchadnezzar Destroys Jerusalem
- Babylon Falls to Cyrus
- The Persians Defeated by the Greeks at Marathon
- Herod Becomes King of Judea
- Alexander the Great Defeats Darius III
- Romans Take Control of Palestine
- Nero's Persecution of the Christians
- The Battle of Qarqar
- Sennacherib Invades Judah

1000 900 800 700 600 500 400 300 200 100BC 100AD

- The Assyrian Empire
- The Babylonian Empire
- The Persian Empire
- The Greek Kingdoms
- The Roman Republic and Empire

The Exile — The Restoration

- Ezekiel in Babylon
- The Fall of Damascus
- Assyria Collapses
- Isaiah
- Josiah's Reformation
- Sargon II Besieges Ashdod
- The Rise of Babylon
- The Edict of Cyrus

700 600 500 BC

AARON [a'-ur-un] — brother of Moses and first high priest of the Hebrew nation. He was married to Elisheba, daughter of Amminadab (Ex. 6:23).

When God called Moses to lead the Hebrew people out of slavery in Egypt, Moses protested that he would not be able to speak convincingly to the Pharaoh, so God designated Aaron to be Moses' official spokesman (Ex. 4:14–16).

AARON'S ROD — a rod used by Aaron to perform miracles.

When Moses and Aaron appeared before Pharaoh, Aaron cast down his rod and it became a serpent. When the magicians of Egypt did the same thing, "Aaron's rod swallowed up their rods" (Ex. 7:12). Later, Aaron struck the waters of Egypt with his rod and they turned to blood (7:15–20).

During the wilderness wandering, Aaron's rod was the only staff that produced buds, blossoms, and almonds, indicating God's choice of Aaron and his descendants as priests (Num. 17:1–10).

ABADDON [ab-ad'-dun] *(destruction)* — a term found only once in most English translations of the Bible (Rev. 9:11). Abaddon is a transliteration of a Hebrew word that occurs six other times in the Bible, usually translated "destruction" (Job 26:6; 28:22; 31:12; Ps. 88:11; Prov. 15:11; 27:20).

In the Book of Revelation, Abaddon is not a place—the realm of the dead—but a person—the angel who reigns over the abyss.

ABASE — humble oneself or be humbled; get a right perspective either from within or from another (Phil. 4:12).

ABATE — recede or withdraw (Gen. 8:8, Lev. 27:18).

ABBA [ab'-bah] *(father)* — an Aramaic word that corresponds to our "Daddy" or "Papa." It is found three times in the New Testament, Mark 14:36, Rom. 8:15, and Gal. 4:6. Expresses the approachability of our loving Creator.

ABED-NEGO [ab-ed'-ne-go] *(servant of Nebo)* — the Chaldean name given to Azariah in King Nebuchadnezzar's court when he was chosen as one of the king's servants (Dan. 1:7; 2:49). Abed-Nego was thrown into the fiery furnace, along with Shadrach and Meshach, for refusing to bow down and worship a golden image. The three men were miraculously protected from the fire (Dan. 3:12–30).

ABEL [a'-bel] *(breath, vapor)* — the second son of Adam and Eve (Gen. 4:2) murdered by his jealous brother, Cain (Gen. 4:4–5).

Also, a large stone in the field of Joshua of Beth Shemesh on which the ARK OF THE COVENANT was set by the Philistines (1 Sam. 6:18), as well as a city in northern Israel (2 Sam. 20:14–15, 18).

ABHOR — to hate or reject (Rom. 12:9).

ABIATHAR [ab-i'-uth-ur] *(father of abundance)* — a chief priest in the court of David and the son of Ahimelech.

When Saul massacred the village of Nob for helping David, Abiathar was the only one to escape (1 Sam. 22:6–23). David eventually became king and appointed Abiathar and Zadok as priests in the royal court (2 Sam. 8:17; 1 Chr. 18:16).

During the struggle over who would succeed as king, Abiathar supported Adonijah. When Solomon emerged as the new ruler, Zadok was appointed priest of the royal court, and Abiathar escaped execution only because of his earlier loyalty to David. He and his family were banished to Anathoth, and his rights and privileges as a Jerusalem priest were taken away (1 Kin. 1:7–25; 2:22–35).

ABIDE — stay, continue (1 Sam. 1:22).

ABIGAIL [ab′-e-gul] *(father of joy)* — wife of Nabal the Carmelite and, after Nabal's death, of David (1 Sam. 25:3, 14–42; 2 Sam. 2:2; 1 Chr. 3:1). Also a sister or half–sister of David and mother of Amasa.

ABIHU [a-bi′-hew] *(he is my father)* — second son of Aaron and Elisheba (Ex. 6:23). Abihu was destroyed, along with his brother NADAB, in the Wilderness of Sinai for offering "profane fire" (Lev. 10:1) before the Lord.

ABIMELECH [a-bim′-e-lek] *(my father is king)* — the name of five men in the Old Testament:

1. The king of Gerar in the time of Abraham (Gen. 20:1–18; 21:22–34).

2. The king of Gerar in the time of Isaac (Gen. 26:1–31).

3. The ruler of the city of Shechem during the period of the judges (Judg. 8:30—10:1; 2 Sam. 11:21). Abimelech was a son of Gideon by a concubine from Shechem.

4. A priest in the time of David (1 Chr. 18:16).

5. A Philistine king whom David met while fleeing from King Saul (Psalm 34, title). Abimelech is apparently the royal title of Achish the king of Gath (1 Sam. 21:10–15).

ABLUTION — the ceremonial washing of one's body, vessels, and clothing for the purpose of religious purification.

Ablutions had nothing to do with washing one's body for sanitary or hygienic purposes, but were performed in order to remove ritual defilement (Heb. 9:10, RSV).

ABNER [ab′-nur] *(the father is a lamp)* — the commander-in-chief of Saul's army (1 Sam. 14:50–51; 17:55).

After the death of Saul and his three sons in a battle with the Philistines (1 Sam. 31:1–6), Abner established Saul's son Ishbosheth as king. In the ensuing warfare between the forces of David and Ishbosheth, Abner killed a brother of Joab—one of David's military officers—in self-defense (2 Sam. 2:12—3:1).

Abner was killed by David's commander Joab in an act of vengeance over the death of his brother (2 Sam. 3:22–30).

ABODE — residence, dwelling place (John 14:23).

ABOLISH — terminate (2 Tim. 1:10).

ABOMINABLE, ABOMINATION — anything that offends the spiritual, religious, or moral sense of a person and causes extreme disgust, hatred, or loathing. Among the objects described as an "abomination" were the carved images of pagan gods (Deut. 7:25–26); the sacrifice to God of inferior, blemished animals (Deut. 17:1); the practice of idolatry (Deut. 17:2–5); and the fashioning of a "carved or molded image" of a false god (Deut. 27:15; Is. 44:19).

ABOMINATION OF DESOLATION — a despicable misuse of the temple of the Lord during a time of great trouble—an event foretold by the prophet Daniel.

The phrase is found in Matthew 24:15 and Mark 13:14 as a quotation from Daniel 11:31 and 12:11. In Daniel, the words mean "the abomination that makes desolate." In other words, Daniel prophesied that the temple would be used for an "abominable" purpose at some time in the future. As a result, God's faithful people would no longer worship there—so great would be their moral revulsion, contempt, and abhorrence at the sacrilege—and the temple would become "desolate."

ABOUND — increase, develop abundantly (Prov. 28:20).

ABRAHAM [a′-bra-ham] *(father of a multi-tude)* — originally Abram (*exalted father*) the first great PATRIARCH of ancient Israel and a primary model of faithfulness for Christianity. The accounts about Abraham are found in Genesis 11:26—25:11.

Abraham was the father of the Hebrews and the prime example of a righteous man. In spite of impossible odds, Abraham had faith in the promises of God. Therefore, he is presented as a model for human behavior. Hospitable to strangers (Gen. 18:1–8), he was a God-fearing man (Gen. 22:1–18) who was obedient to God's Laws (Gen. 26:5). The promises originally given to Abraham were passed on to his son Isaac (Gen. 26:3), and to his grandson Jacob (Gen. 28:13; 35:11–12). In later biblical references, the God of Israel is frequently identified as the God of Abraham (Gen. 26:24), and Israel is often called the people "of the God of Abraham" (Ps. 47:9; 105:6). Abraham was such an important figure in the history of God's people that when they were in trouble, Israel appealed to God to remember the covenant made with Abraham (Ex. 32:13; Deut. 9:27; Ps. 105:9).

ABRAHAM'S BOSOM — a figure of speech for the life hereafter. According to the Old Testament, when a person died he went to "be with his fathers" (Gen. 15:15; 47:30; Deut. 31:16; Judg. 2:10).

ABRAM [a′-brum] *(exalted father)* — the original name of ABRAHAM, the great patriarch of Israel (Gen. 17:5).

ABSALOM [ab′-sal-um] *(father of peace)* — the arrogant and vain son of David who tried to take the kingship from his father by force (2 Sam. 15—2 Sam. 18)

Traditional well of Abraham in the plains of Mamre (Gen. 21:22–32). *Photo by Howard Vos*

ABSTAIN, ABSTINENCE — the voluntary, self-imposed, and deliberate denial of certain pleasures, such as food, drink, and sex. The noun "abstinence" is found only once in the KJV (Acts 27:21), where the apostle Paul is described as having experienced "long abstinence." The verb "abstain" is found six times in the KJV (Acts 15:20, 29; 1 Thess. 4:3; 5:22; 1 Tim. 4:3; 1 Pet. 1:11).

ABUNDANCE — much; greater than necessary (John 10:10).

ABUSE — malicious treatment; intentional harm (Heb. 10:33).

ABYSS [a-biss] — the bottomless pit or the chaotic deep. Sumerian in origin, the term referred to a deep mass of waters surrounding the earth. Darkness is said to have been on the face of the deep or abyss (Gen. 1:2).

The term is used in several other ways in the Bible. It describes the prison of disobedient spirits, or the world of the dead (Luke 8:31; Rom. 10:7; Rev. 20:1–3). Terms like "the pit" and "bottomless pit" represent the abode of all the wicked dead.

ACACIA [a-cay′-shih] — large tree that was an excellent source of wood. The ark of the covenant was made from the wood of this tree (Deut. 10:3).

ACCEPT — to receive or treat with favor. In the Bible, a person is accepted by the grace, mercy, or covenant-love of God through faith and repentance (Eph. 1:6).

ACCESS — the privilege of having an audience with one's superior. Access to God is that positive, friendly relationship with the Father in which we have confidence that we are pleasing and acceptable to Him. Jesus is the "new and living way" (Heb. 10:20) who gives us access to God.

ACCOMPLISH — succeed, finish, complete (Is. 55:11).

ACCORD — agreement, conformity, harmony (Acts 2:46; 7:57; 15:25).

ACCOUNT, ACCOUNTABILITY — the biblical principle that we are answerable to our Maker for our thoughts, words, and deeds. The Bible plainly teaches "the whole world [is] accountable to God" (Rom. 3:19, NASB) and that "all have sinned and fall short of the glory of God" (Rom. 3:23).

ACCURSED — under a curse, doomed; anything on which a curse has been pronounced (Josh. 6:17–18; Gal. 1: 8–9).

ACCUSE — to blame; charging with improper actions (Luke 11:54).

ACHAIA [ak-ah′-yah] — in Roman times, the name for the whole of Greece, except Thessaly (Acts 19:21). The Romans gave the region this name when they captured Corinth and destroyed the Achaian League in 146 B.C. Later it comprised several Greek cities, including Athens.

ACHAN [a′-kan] — son of Carmi of the tribe of Judah who unintentionally brought about the Israelites' defeat at Ai (Josh. 7:1, 18–24). He is called Achar in 1 Chronicles 2:7 and is described as the "troubler of Israel, who transgressed in the accursed thing."

ACHOR [a′-kor] *(trouble)* — a valley near Jericho where Achan was stoned to death during the time of Joshua (Josh. 7:24, 26). The prophets used the phrase "the Valley of Achor" (Is. 65:10) to symbolize the idyllic state of contentment and peace of the messianic age (Hos. 2:15).

ACKNOWLEDGE — recognize, agree with, (Deut. 21:17; 1 Cor. 14:37).

ACTS OF THE APOSTLES — the one historical book of the New Testament, which traces the development of the early church after the Ascension of Jesus. Standing between the Gospels and the Epistles, the Book of Acts is a bridge between the life of Jesus and the ministry of the apostle Paul. As such, it offers invaluable information about the development of the early church.

The Acts of the Apostles could justly be entitled "The Acts of the Holy Spirit," for the Spirit is mentioned nearly 60 times in the book. In His parting words, Jesus reminds the disciples of the promise of the Father (1:4–8); ten days later the power of the Spirit descends at PENTECOST (2:1–4). Persons "from every nation under heaven" (2:5) are enabled by the Holy Spirit to hear "the wonderful works of God" (2:11), and so the Christian church was born.

A.D. — abbreviation for *Anno Domini*, which is Latin for in the year of our Lord.

ADAM [ad'-um] *(red, ground)* — the name of the first man, created by God on the sixth day of creation, and placed in the Garden of Eden (Gen. 2:19–23; 3:8–9, 17, 20–21; 4:1, 25; 5:1–5). He and his wife EVE, created by God from one of Adam's ribs (Gen. 2:21–22), became the ancestors of all people now living on the earth. Adam was unique

ACTS:
A Study and Teaching Outline

Part One: The Witness in Jerusalem (1:1—8:3)

I. **The Power of the Church** . . . . .1:1—2:47
  A. Introduction to Acts .1:1—3
  B. Appearances of the Resurrected Christ . . . . .1:4—8
  C. Ascension of Christ .1:9—11
  D. Anticipation of the Holy Spirit . . . . .1:12—14
  E. Appointment of Matthias . . . . .1:15—26
  F. Filling with the Holy Spirit . . . . .2:1—4
  G. Speaking with Other Tongues . . . . .2:5—13
  H. Peter Explains Pentecost . . . . .2:14—39
  I. Practices of the Early Church . . . . .2:40—47
II. **The Progress of the Church** . . . . .3:1—8:3
  A. Peter Heals the Lame Man . . . . .3:1—10
  B. Peter's Second Sermon . . . . .3:11—26
  C. Peter and John Are Arrested . . . . .4:1—4
  D. Peter Preaches to the Jewish Sanhedrin . . .4:5—12
  E. The Sanhedrin Commands Peter
    Not to Preach . . . . .4:13—22
  F. Apostles' Prayer for Boldness . . . . .4:23—31
  G. The Early Church Voluntarily Shares . . . . .4:32—37
  H. Ananias and Sapphira Lie . . . . .5:1—11
  I. The Apostles' Mighty Miracles . . . . .5:12—16
  J. The Apostles' Persecution . . . . .5:17—42
  K. Deacons Are Appointed . . . . .6:1—7
  L. Stephen Is Martyred . . . . .6:8—7:60
  M. Saul Persecutes the Church . . . . .8:1—3

Part Two: The Witness in Judea and Samaria (8:4—12:24)

I. **The Witness of Philip** . . . . .8:4—40
  A. Philip Witnesses to the Samaritans . . . . . . .8:4—25
  B. Philip Witnesses to the Ethiopian . . . . . .8:26—40
II. **The Conversion of Saul** . . . . .9:1—31
  A. Saul Is Converted and Blinded . . . . .9:1—9
  B. Saul Is Filled with the Holy Spirit . . . . . . .9:10—19
  C. Saul Preaches at Damascus . . . . .9:20—22
  D. Saul Witnesses in Jerusalem . . . . .9:23—31
III. **The Witness of Peter** . . . . 9:32—11:18
  A. Peter Heals Aeneas at Lydda . . . . 9:32—35
  B. Peter Raises Dorcas at Joppa . . . . 9:36—43
  C. Peter Witnesses to Cornelius
    at Caesarea . . . . 10:1—11:18
IV. **The Witness of the Early Church** . . . . . 11:19—12:24
  A. The Witness of the Antioch Church . . . . .11:19—30
  B. The Persecution by Herod . . . . .12:1—24

Part Three: The Witness to
the Ends of the Earth
(12:25—28:31)

I. **The First Missionary Journey** . . . . .12:25—14:28
  A. Barnabas and Saul are Sent
     from Antioch .12:25—13:3
  B. Ministry at Cyprus 13:4–12
  C. Ministry at Antioch 13:13–50
  D. Ministry at Iconium . . . . .13:51—14:5
  E. Ministry at Lystra 14:6–20
  F. Ministry on the Return Trip 14:21–25
  G. Report on the First Missionary
     Journey 14:26–28
II. **The Jerusalem Council** 15:1–35
  A. Debate over Gentiles Keeping the Law 15:1–5
  B. Peter Preaches Salvation through Grace . .15:6–11
  C. Paul and Barnabas Testify 15:12
  D. James Proves Gentiles Are Free from
     the Law 15:13–21
  E. The Council Sends an Official Letter 15:22–29
  F. Report to Antioch 15:30–35
III. **The Second Missionary Journey** . . . . . . .15:36—18:22
  A. Disagreement over John Mark 15:36–41
  B. Derbe and Lystra: Timothy Is
     Circumcised 16:1–5
  C. Troas: Macedonian Call 16:6–10
  D. Philippi: Extensive Ministry 16:11–40
  E. Thessalonica: "Turn the World
     Upside Down" 17:1–9
  F. Berea: Many Receive the Word 17:10–15
  G. Athens: Paul's Sermon at the
     Areopagus 17:16–34
  H. Corinth: One-and-a-half Years
     of Ministry 18:1–17
  I. Return Trip to Antioch 18:18–22
IV. **The Third Missionary Journey** . . . . .18:23—21:14
  A. Galatia and Phrygia: Strengthening
     the Disciples 18:23
  B. Ephesus: Three Years of Ministry . . .18:24—19:41
  C. Macedonia: Three Months of Ministry 20:1–6
  D. Troas: Eutychus Falls from Loft 20:7–12
  E. Miletus: Paul Bids Farewell to
     Ephesian Elders 20:13–38
  F. Tyre: Paul Is Warned about Jerusalem 21:1–6
  G. Caesarea: Agabus' Prediction 21:7–14
V. **The Trip to Rome** . . . . .21:15—28:31
  A. Paul Witnesses in Jerusalem . . . . . . .21:15—23:33
  B. Paul Witnesses in Caesarea . . . . .23:34—26:32
  C. Paul Witnesses in Rome . . . . .27:1—28:31

and distinct from the animals in several ways. His creation is described separately from that of the animals and the rest of God's creative acts (Gen. 1:3–25; 1:26–27; 2:7).

ADAR [a′-dar] *(cloudy)* — the name of a town in southern Judah (Josh. 15:3) also called Hazar Addar (Num. 34:4). Also the Babylonian name of the 12th month of the Jewish year (Ezra 6:15; Esth. 3:7, 13; 8:12; 9:1, 15–21).

ADDER — snake; SERPENT (Gen. 49:17).

ADHERE — stick to, obey, show loyalty (2 Kin. 17:34, NIV).

This Greek inscription at Athens contains the text of Paul's speech which he delivered at the Areopagus (Acts 17:22–31). *Photo by Gustav Jeeninga*

ADJURE, ADJURATION — an earnest urging or advising (Matt. 26:63); the action by which a person in authority imposes the obligations of an oath upon another (1 Sam. 14:24; 1 Kin. 22:16; Mark 5:7; Acts 19:13).

ADMONISH — to suggest, encourage, inspire, motivate (Col 3:16; 2 Thess. 3:15).

ADONIJAH [ad-on-i'-jah] *(the Lord is my Lord)* — the name of three men in the Old Testament:

1. The fourth of the six sons born to David while he was at Hebron (2 Sam. 3:4). With the exception of Absalom, David apparently favored Adonijah over his other five sons. When David was old, Adonijah attempted to seize the throne, although he probably knew that his father intended Solomon to succeed him (1 Kin. 1:13).

2. One of the Levites sent by Jehoshaphat to instruct the people of Judah in the law (2 Chr. 17:8).

3. A chieftain who, with Nehemiah, sealed the covenant (Neh. 10:14–16); he is also called Adonikam (Ezra 2:13).

ADULTERY — willful sexual intercourse with someone other than one's spouse. Jesus expanded the meaning of adultery to include the cultivation of lust: "Whoever looks at a woman to lust for her has already committed adultery with her in his heart" (Matt. 5:28).

ADVERSARY — one who opposes or hinders another, enemy. In the Bible, this word is often used of SATAN, the Adversary of God and His plan of righteousness and redemption in the world (1 Pet. 5:8; 1 John 2:1).

ADVERSITY — difficult situation (Prov. 24:10).

ADVOCATE — one who pleads another's cause before a tribunal or judicial court. The word "advocate" is found only once in the NKJV: "If anyone sins, we have an Advocate with the Father, Jesus Christ the righteous" (1 John 2:1). The Greek word translated as "advocate" here is also found four times in the Gospel of John, all referring to the Holy Spirit (John 14:16, 26; 15:26; 16:7; helper, NKJV).

AFFECTION — a feeling; liking (Rom. 1:26).

AFFLICTION — any condition or problem that produces suffering or pain. The Bible speaks of two types of affliction—suffering that represents God's judgment on sin (Is. 53:4; Matt. 24:29; Rom. 2:9), and suffering that brings about the purifying of believers as they identify with Christ (Rom. 5:3–5; 2 Thess. 1:4–7).

AGABUS [ag'-ab-us] — a Christian prophet of Jerusalem who went to Antioch of Syria while

Paul and Barnabas were there, and "showed by the Spirit that there was going to be a great famine throughout all the world" (Acts 11:28).

AGAPE [a-gah'-pay] — a Greek word for love used often in the New Testament (John 13:35; 1 Cor. 13; 1 John 4:7–18). Contrary to popular understanding, the significance of *agape* is not that it is an unconditional love, but that it is primarily a love of the will rather than the emotions.

AGE — an aeon; a specified period of time during which certain related events come to pass. As used in the New Testament, age generally refers to the present era, as opposed to the future age (Col. 1:26).

AGRIPPA I [a-grip'-pah] — Roman ruler of Galilee and eventual ruler of the territory previously governed by his grandfather, Herod the Great. Agrippa persecuted the Christians in Jerusalem (Acts 12:1–23) during his reign in Judea from A.D. 41 until his death in A.D. 44.

AGRIPPA II [a-grip'-pah] — son of Herod Agrippa I and great-grandson of Herod the Great. He was appointed by the Roman Emperor Claudius as ruler of Abilene, part of Galilee, Iturea, and Trachonitis. Shortly before the apostle Paul was taken prisoner to Rome, he appeared before Herod Agrippa II (Acts 25:13—26:32).

AHAB [a'-hab] *(father is brother)* — the name of two men in the Old Testament:

1. The son of Omri and the seventh king of Israel (1 Kin. 16:30). Under the influence of Jezebel his wife, Ahab gave Baal equal place with God. Ahab also built a temple to Baal in which he

Remains of a palace from Ahab's time, uncovered in an excavation at the site of ancient Samaria.
Photo by Howard Vos

erected a "wooden image" of the Canaanite goddess Asherah (1 Kin. 16:33). At Jezebel's urging, Ahab opposed the worship of the Lord, destroyed His altars, and killed His prophets. He reigned over Israel in Samaria for 22 years (873—852 B.C.) (1 Kin. 16:29).

2. The son of Kolaiah, and one of two false prophets denounced by Jeremiah (Jer. 29:21–23). Because Ahab prophesied falsely in God's name, Jeremiah declared that he would die at the hand of Nebuchadnezzar, king of Babylon, and would be cursed by all Babylonian captives from Judah.

AHASUERUS [a-has-u-e'-rus] *(mighty man)* — the name of two kings in the Old Testament:

1. A king of Persia and the husband of Es-THER. Scholars generally agree that Ahasuerus is the same person as Xerxes I (485—464 B.C.).

2. A king of the Medes and the father of DARIUS (Dan. 9:1).

AHAZ [a'-haz] — the name of two men in the Old Testament:

1. A son of Jotham and the eleventh king of Judah (2 Kin. 15:38; 16:1–20; Achaz, KJV). He was an ungodly king who promoted the worship of Molech, with its pagan rites of human sacrifice (2 Chr. 28:1–4).

2. A Benjamite and descendant of King Saul. Ahaz was a son of Micah and the father of Jehoaddah (1 Chr. 8:35–36; 9:42).

AHAZIAH [a-haz-i'-ah] *(the Lord sustains)* — the name of two kings in the Old Testament:

1. The son and successor of Ahab and the ninth king of Israel (1 Kin. 22:40, 49, 51). Ahaziah reigned from 853 to 852 B.C.

The son of JEZEBEL, Ahaziah followed policies that showed evidence of his mother's pagan influence.

2. The son and successor of Joram and the nephew of Ahaziah No. 1 (2 Kin. 8:24–26). Ahaziah is also called Jehoahaz (2 Chr. 21:17; 25:23) and Azariah (2 Chr. 22:6). The sixth king of Judah, Ahaziah reigned for only one year (841 B.C.).

Ahaziah became king at age 22 (2 Kin. 8:26; 2 Chr. 22:1). His wicked reign was heavily influenced by his mother Athaliah. She was the evil power behind his throne: "He walked in the way of the house of Ahab" (2 Kin. 8:27).

AI [a'-i] *(the ruin)* — a Canaanite city (Josh. 10:1) located east of Bethel (Gen. 12:8). Many years before Joshua's time, Abraham pitched his tent at Ai before journeying to Egypt (Gen. 12:8). Also an Ammonite city in Moab (Jer. 49:3).

ALABASTER — smooth stone used to make containers for perfumes and ointments (Matt. 26:7; Mark 14:3; Luke 7:37).

ALAS — expression of sadness or grief; can be used in a warning (Josh. 7:7).

ALEXANDER [al-ex-an'-dur] *(defender of men)* — the name of five or six men in the Bible,

Bust of Alexander the Great, Greek military conqueror. *Photo by Howard Vos*

Alexander's Greek Empire
(Daniel 2, 7, 8, 11)

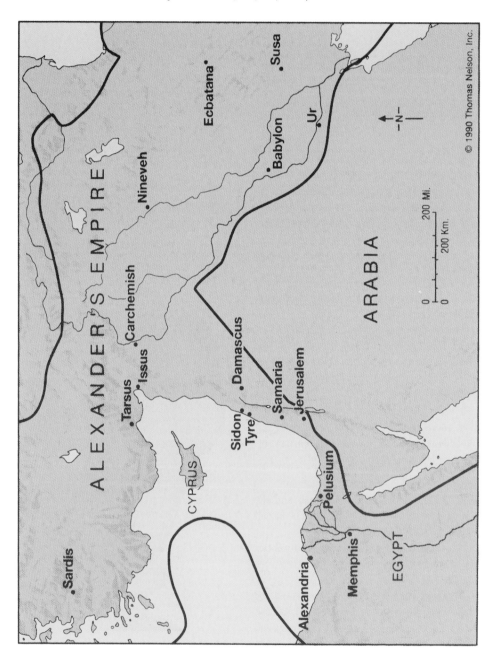

but most notably, Alexander III (the Great), son of Philip II (King of Macedon) and founder of the Hellenistic (Greek) Empire. Also the son of Simon (Mark 15:21), and a brother of Rufus; a member of the family of Annas, the Jewish high priest (Acts 4:6); a Jew who lived at Ephesus during the riot started by Demetrius and the silversmiths who opposed Paul's preaching (Acts 19:21–41); one of two heretical teachers at Ephesus mentioned by the apostle Paul (1 Tim. 1:19–20); and the coppersmith who did Paul "much harm" (2 Tim. 4:14).

ALIEN — a foreigner, sojourner, or stranger from a country other than Israel. Aliens did not enjoy the rights of Israelites (Deut. 14:21; Job 19:15; Ps. 69:8).

ALLEGORY — a symbolic representation of a truth about human conduct or experience. The word "allegory" is found only once in the King James Version. In Galatians 4:24 it translates the Greek verb *allegoreo,* which means to say something different from what the words normally imply. The NKJV translates it by the word "symbolic."

In the New Testament, Jesus' parable of the wheat and the tares (Matt. 13:24–30) is a good example of allegory. The apostle Paul also used allegories when writing. In Ephesians 6:11–17 he urges his readers to "put on the whole armor of God" and then gives the symbolic spiritual designation for each article worn by the Christian soldier. And in 1 Corinthians 10, Paul gives an allegory that compares the experience of Moses and the Israelites to Christian baptism and the Lord's Supper.

ALLELUIA [al-e-loo′-yah] *(praise the Lord)* — a Greek form of the Hebrew word *Hallelujah,* used to express joy, praise, and thanksgiving.

The words, "Praise the Lord," found often in the Psalms, are a translation of the Hebrew *Hallelujah* (Ps. 104:35; 116:19; 147:1). The word was probably a standardized call to worship in the temple, since it usually appears at the beginning or end of a psalm.

ALLOTMENT — in the Old Testament a system of land tenure used in Israel to distribute the land to the tribes, clans and families (Joshua 13—19).

ALMIGHTY — all powerful; possessing complete control (Gen. 17:1).

ALMS — money given out of mercy for the poor (Deut. 15:11).

ALPHA AND OMEGA [al′-fah, oh-may′-guh] — the first and last letters of the Greek alphabet. This title is given to God the Father and God the Son (Rev. 1:8; 21:6). The risen Christ says, "I am the Alpha and the Omega, the Beginning and the End, the First and the Last" (Rev. 22:13). By calling Jesus Christ the Alpha and the Omega, the writer of the Book of Revelation acknowledged that He is the Creator, the Redeemer, and the Final Judge of all things.

ALPHAEUS [al-fe′-us] *(leader or chief)* — the name of two men in the New Testament:

1. The father of the apostle James the Less (Matt. 10:3; Acts 1:13).

2. The father of Levi (or Matthew), the apostle and writer of the first Gospel (Mark 2:14).

ALTAR — a table, platform, or elevated place on which a priest placed a sacrifice as an offering to God (Gen. 8:20). The nature of altars changed considerably during the several centuries of Bible times. In addition to describing altars dedicated to God, the Bible speaks frequently of pagan altars, particularly those associated with the false worship of the Canaanites (2 Chr. 33:3; 1 Kin. 11:5–7).

AMALEK [am′-al-ek] — a grandson of Esau and son of Eliphaz by Timnah, his concubine (Gen. 36:12; 1 Chr. 1:36). A chieftain of an Edomite tribe (Gen. 36:16), Amalek gave his name to the Amalekites.

AMBASSADOR — representative (Eph. 6:19–20).

Excavations at ancient Megiddo, showing the ancient round altar used for pagan sacrifices.
Photo by Gustav Jeeninga

AMEN *(so be it)* — a solemn word by which a person confirms a statement, an oath, or a covenant (Num. 5:22; Neh. 5:13). It is also used in worship to affirm an address, psalm, or prayer.

AMOS [a′-mos] *(burden bearer)* — the famous shepherd-prophet of the Old Testament who denounced the people of the northern kingdom of Israel for their idol worship, graft and corruption, and oppression of the poor. He was probably the earliest of the writing prophets. His prophecies and the few facts known about his life are found in the Book of Amos.

AMOS, BOOK OF — a prophetic book of the Old Testament. The book is named for its author, the prophet Amos, whose name means "burden bearer." Amos lived up to his name as he declared God's message of judgment in dramatic fashion to a sinful and disobedient people.

The nine chapters of the Book of Amos emphasize one central theme: The people of the nation of Israel have broken their COVENANT with God, and His judgment against their sin will be severe.

Following these messages of judgment, the Book of Amos ends on a positive, optimistic note. Amos predicted that the people of Israel would be restored to their special place in God's service after their season of judgment had come to an end (9:11–15).

The Book of Amos is one of the most eloquent cries for justice and righteousness to be found in the Bible. And it came through a humble shepherd who dared to deliver God's message to the wealthy and influential people of his day. His message is just as timely for our world, since God still places a higher value on justice and righteousness than on silver and gold and the things that money will buy.

AMOS: A Study and Teaching Outline

I. Introduction to Amos 1:1–2
II. The Eight Judgments . . . . 1:3—2:16
   A. Judgment on Damascus 1:3–5
   B. Judgment on Gaza 1:6–8
   C. Judgment on Tyre 1:9–10
   D. Judgment on Edom 1:11–12
   E. Judgment on Ammon 1:13–15
   F. Judgment on Moab 2:1–3
   G. Judgment on Judah 2:4–5
   H. Judgment on Israel 2:6–16
III. The Three Sermons of Judgment . . . . 3:1—6:14
   A. The First Sermon: Israel's Present 3:1–15
     1. Israel's Judgment Is Deserved 3:1–10
     2. Israel's Judgment Is Described 3:11–15
   B. The Second Sermon: Israel's Past 4:1–13
     1. Israel's Judgment Is Deserved 4:1–5
     2. Israel's Judgment Is Demonstrated 4:6–11
     3. Israel's Judgment Is Described 4:12–13
   C. The Third Sermon: Israel's Future . . . . . 5:1—6:14
     1. Israel's Judgment Is Deserved 5:1–15
     2. Israel's Judgment Is Described . . . . . 5:16—6:14
       a. The First Woe of Judgment 5:16–27
       b. The Second Woe of Judgment 6:1–14
IV. The Five Visions of Judgment . . . . 7:1—9:10
   A. Vision of the Locusts 7:1–3
   B. Vision of the Fire 7:4–6
   C. Vision of the Plumb Line 7:7–9
   D. Opposition of Amaziah
     (Historical Parenthesis) 7:10–17
   E. Vision of the Summer Fruit 8:1–14
   F. Vision of the Doorposts 9:1–10
V. The Five Promises of the Restoration
  of Israel 9:11–15

ANANIAS [an-an-i′-as] *(the Lord is gracious)* — the name of three New Testament men:

1. A Christian in the early church at Jerusalem (Acts 5:1–11). With the knowledge of his wife, SAPPHIRA, Ananias sold a piece of property and brought only a portion of the proceeds from its sale to Peter. When Peter rebuked him for lying about the amount, Ananias immediately fell down and died. Sapphira later repeated the same falsehood, and she also fell down and died.

2. A Christian disciple living in Damascus at the time of Paul's conversion (Acts 9:10–18; 22:12–16). In a vision the Lord told Ananias of Paul's conversion and directed him to go to Paul and welcome him into the church. Aware of Paul's reputation as a persecutor of Christians, Ananias reacted with alarm. When the Lord informed him that Paul was "a chosen vessel of Mine" (Acts 9:15), Ananias went to Paul and laid his hands upon him. Paul's sight was restored immediately, and he was baptized (Acts 9:18).

3. The Jewish high priest before whom Paul appeared after his arrest in Jerusalem following his third missionary journey, about A.D. 58 (Acts 23:2). Ananias was also one of those who spoke against Paul before the Roman governor Felix (Acts 24:1).

ANATHEMA [a-nath′-em-ah] *(accursed)* — the transliteration of a Greek word that means "accursed" or "separated" (Luke 21:5; Rom. 9:3; Gal. 1:8–9).

ANCIENT OF DAYS — a name for God used by the prophet Daniel, who portrayed God on His throne, judging the great world empires of his day (Dan. 7:9, 13, 22).

ANDREW [an'-drew] *(manly)* — brother of Simon Peter and one of Jesus' first disciples. Both Andrew and Peter were fishermen (Matt. 4:18; Mark 1:16–18) from Bethsaida (John 1:44), on the northwest coast of the Sea of Galilee. They also had a house at Capernaum in this vicinity (Mark 1:29).

At the feeding of the 5,000, Andrew called Jesus' attention to the boy with five barley loaves and two fish (John 6:5–9).

ANGEL — a member of an order of heavenly beings who are superior to human beings in power and intelligence. By nature angels are spiritual beings (Heb. 1:14). Their nature is superior to human nature (Heb. 2:7), and they have superhuman power and knowledge (2 Sam. 14:17, 20; 2 Pet. 2:11). They are not, however, all-powerful and all-knowing (Ps. 103:20; 2 Thess. 1:7).

ANGER — a bold emotion of frustration felt and displayed by God and man. Anger is a result of sin—our own or another's (Ps. 37:8).

ANNA [an'-nah] *(favor)* — a widow, daughter of Phanuel of the tribe of Asher (Luke 2:36). She was at the temple in Jerusalem when Mary and Joseph brought Jesus to be dedicated (Luke 2:27). Anna recognized Jesus as the long-awaited Messiah (Luke 2:37–38).

ANNAS [an'-nas] *(grace of the Lord)* — one of the high priests at Jerusalem, along with Caiaphas, when John the Baptist began his ministry, about A.D. 26 (Luke 3:2). During His trial, Jesus was first taken to Annas, who then sent Jesus to Caiaphas (John 18:13, 24). Both Annas and Caiaphas were among the principal examiners when Peter and John were arrested (Acts 4:6).

ANNIHILATE — completely destroy; eliminate (Esth. 3:13).

ANNUNCIATION — the announcement by the angel Gabriel (Luke 1:26–38) to the Virgin Mary of the forthcoming birth of Jesus. The angel told Mary that the Holy Spirit would cause her to conceive a child, and "that Holy One who is to be born will be called the Son of God" (Luke 1:35).

ANOINT, ANOINTING — to authorize, or set apart, a person for a particular work or service (Is. 61:1). The anointed person belonged to God in a special sense. In the New Testament, all who are Christ's disciples are said to be anointed; they are God's very own, set apart and commissioned for service (2 Cor. 1:21).

ANTICHRIST, THE — a false prophet and evil being who will set himself up against Christ and the people of God in the last days before the Second Coming. The term is used only in the writings of John in the New Testament. It refers to one who stands in opposition to all that Jesus Christ represents (1 John 2:18, 22; 4:3; 2 John 7). John wrote that several antichrists existed already in his day—false teachers who denied the deity and the Incarnation of Christ—but that the supreme Antichrist of history would appear at some future time.

ANTIOCH OF PISIDIA [an'-te-ok, pih-sid'-e-uh] — a city of southern Asia Minor in Phrygia, situated just north of the territory of Pisidia. Antioch was an important first-century commercial center and an important center for the spread of the gospel. Founded by Seleucus I Nicator (about 300 B.C.) and named for his father Antiochus, it became a great center for commerce and was inhabited by many Jews.

ANTIOCH OF SYRIA [an'-te-ok, sihr'-e-uh] — the capital of the Roman province of Syria that played an important part in the first-century expansion of the church. Antioch was situated on the east bank of the Orontes River, about 27 kilometers (16.5 miles) from the Mediterranean Sea and 485 kilometers (300 miles) north of Jerusalem. The city was founded about 300 B.C. by Seleucus I Nicator, one of the three successors to ALEXANDER the Great, and named for his father Antiochus.

APOCRYPHA, THE [a-pock'-rih-fuh] — a group of books written during a time of turmoil in the history of the Jewish people, from about 190 B.C. to about A.D. 210. These books fall into two main divisions, Old Testament apocryphal books and New Testament apocryphal books.

The Old Testament books, fifteen in number, were written during the period from about 190 B.C. to about A.D. 70, when the Jewish people were in rebellion against the repression of foreign military rulers. These books were excluded from some early versions of the Old Testament but included in others. Bibles used by Roman Catholics contain the Old Testament Apocrypha, while they are not included in most Protestant editions of the Bible.

The books known as the New Testament Apocrypha were written during the second and third centuries A.D., long after the death of the apostles and other eyewitnesses to the life and ministry of Jesus. None of these books were included in the New Testament because they were judged as unworthy and not authoritative by officials of the early church.

APOLLOS [a-pol'-os] *(destroyer)* — a learned and eloquent Jew from Alexandria in Egypt and an influential leader in the early church. Well-versed in the Old Testament, Apollos was a disciple of John the Baptist and "taught accurately the things of the Lord" (Acts 18:25). However, while Apollos knew some of Jesus' teaching, "he knew only the baptism of John" (Acts 18:25). When Priscilla and Aquila, two other leaders in the early church, arrived in Ephesus, they instructed Apollos more accurately in the way of God (Acts 18:26).

APOSTLE — a special messenger of Jesus Christ; a person to whom Jesus delegated authority for certain tasks. The word "apostle" is used of those twelve disciples whom Jesus sent out, two by two, during His ministry in Galilee to expand His own ministry of preaching and healing. It was on that occasion, evidently, that they were first called "apostles" (Mark 3:14; 6:30).

APOSTOLIC COUNCIL — the assembly of apostles and elders of the New Testament church in Jerusalem (A.D. 50). This council considered the question of whether Gentiles had to be circumcised and keep certain other laws of the Jewish faith in order to be members of the church (Acts 15). This assembly decided that a Gentile does not first have to become a Jew in order to be a Christian.

APPAREL — clothing, garments worn for a specific reason (1 Tim. 2:9).

APT — likely; probable (Prov. 15:23).

The Order of the Books of the Apocrypha

1. First Esdras
2. Second Esdras
3. Tobit
4. Judith
5. The Additions to Esther
6. The Wisdom of Solomon
7. Ecclesiasticus, or the Wisdom of Jesus, the Son of Sirach
8. Baruch
9. The Letter of Jeremiah
10. The Prayer of Azariah and the Song of the Three Young Men
11. Susanna
12. Bel and the Dragon
13. The Prayer of Manasseh
14. First Maccabees
15. Second Maccabees

The Twelve Apostles

Matthew 10:2–4	Mark 3:16–19	Luke 6:14–16	Acts 1:13
Simon Peter	Simon Peter	Simon Peter	Simon Peter
Andrew	James	Andrew	John
James	John	James	James
John	Andrew	John	Andrew
Philip	Philip	Philip	Philip
Bartholomew	Bartholomew	Bartholomew	Thomas
Thomas	Matthew	Matthew	Bartholomew
Matthew	Thomas	Thomas	Matthew
James	James	James	James
(of Alphaeus)	(of Alphaeus)	(of Alphaeus)	(of Alphaeus)
Thaddaeus[1]	Thaddaeus	Simon (the Zealot)	Simon (the Zealot)
Simon	Simon	Judas	Judas
(the Cananite)[2]	(the Cananite)	(of James)	(of James)
Judas Iscariot	Judas Iscariot	Judas Iscariot	....

Matthew and Mark have the name Thaddaeus while Luke, in his two lists (Luke 6 and Acts 1), has Judas (of James). Some think Judas may have been his original name and that it was changed later to Thaddaeus (meaning perhaps "warm-hearted") in order to avoid the stigma attached to the name Judas Iscariot.

"The Cananite" is a transliteration which probably represents an Aramaic word meaning "Zealous."

It is interesting that all four lists begin with Simon Peter and end with Judas Iscariot (except the Acts 1 list, for Judas had already killed himself). Also, the names would appear to be in groups of four. Peter, Andrew, James, and John are always in the first group—though not always in that order—and Philip, Bartholomew, Thomas, and Matthew are in the second group in all four lists.

In all four lists, Peter's name heads the first group, Philip heads the second, and James (of Alphaeus) heads the third. John's Gospel does not contain a listing of the apostles.

AQUILA [ac′-quil-ah] *(eagle)* — a Jewish Christian living in Corinth with his wife PRISCILLA at the time of Paul's arrival from Athens (Acts 18:2). Aquila was born in Pontus (located in Asia Minor) but lived in Rome until Claudius commanded that all Jews leave the city. He and Priscilla moved to Corinth, where Aquila took up his trade, tentmaking.

ARCHANGEL — in the celestial hierarchy, a spiritual being next in rank above an angel. The word "archangel" occurs several times in the Bible. In the New Testament the voice of an archangel and the sounding of the trumpet of God will signal the coming of Christ for His people (1 Thess. 4:16). Michael, the archangel, disputed with the devil about the body of Moses (Jude 9). In the Old Testament, Michael is described as having great power and authority (Dan. 10:13) and is the guardian of Israel (Dan. 10:21), especially in the "time of trouble" in the last days (Dan. 12:1).

AREOPAGUS [a-re-op′-a-gus] *(hill of the god Ares)* — a limestone hill in Athens between the Acropolis and the Agora. Also the council that met near or on the hill (Acts 17: 16–34).

ARIMATHEA [ar-im-ath-e′-ah] *(height)* — a city in the Judean hills northwest of Jerusalem. It was the home of Joseph, a member of the Jewish SANHEDRIN in Jerusalem, who placed the body of Jesus in his new tomb (Luke 23:50).

The Areopagus (Mars' Hill) is a little hill near the acropolis in Athens where Paul may have been brought before the philosophers of this city (Acts 17:16–34). *Photo by Gustav Jeeninga*

ARK OF THE COVENANT — a sacred portable chest which—along with its two related items, the MERCY SEAT and CHERUBIM—was the most important sacred object of the Israelites during the wilderness period. It was also known as the ark of the Lord (Josh. 6:11), the ark of God (1 Sam. 3:3), and the ark of the Testimony (a synonym of covenant; Ex. 25:22).

ARK OF MOSES — a small basket-like container in which Moses was hidden by his mother to save him from the slaughter of Hebrew children by the Egyptian Pharaoh (Ex. 2:3–6). The basket was made of woven BULRUSHES and sealed with a tar-like pitch. The lid on the basket kept insects and the sun off the child so he could sleep. The ark was discovered by the daughter of Pharaoh when she came to bathe at the river.

ARK, NOAH'S — a vessel built by Noah to save him, his family, and animals from the Flood (Gen. 6:14—9:18). God commanded Noah to make the ark of gopherwood (Gen. 6:14). Many scholars believe gopherwood is cypress, which was noted for its lightness and durability and therefore was used extensively in shipbuilding by the Phoenicians.

In the New Testament, Jesus spoke of the Flood and of Noah and the ark, comparing "the days of Noah" with the time of "the coming of the Son of Man" (Matt. 24:37–38; Luke 17:26–27). The ark is a striking illustration of salvation through Christ, who preserves us from the flood of divine judgment.

ARMAGEDDON [ar-mag-ed′-don] *(mountain of Megiddo)* — the site of the final battle of this age in which God intervenes to destroy the armies of Satan and to cast Satan into the bottomless pit (Rev. 16:16). Scholars disagree about the exact location of this place, but the most likely possibility is the valley between Mount Carmel and the city of Jezreel. This valley (known as the Valley of Jezreel and sometimes

A stone carving that may represent the Ark of the Covenant, discovered at the excavation of a synagogue in Capernaum. *Photo: Levant Photo Service*

referred to as the Plain of Esdraelon) was the crossroads of two ancient trade routes and thus was a strategic military site and the scene of many ancient battles.

Because of this history, Megiddo became a symbol of the final conflict between God and the forces of evil. According to the Book of Revelation, at Armageddon "the cup of the wine of the fierceness of His [God's] wrath" (Rev. 16:19) will be poured out, and the forces of evil will be overthrown and destroyed.

ART — the conscious use of skill and creative imagination, especially in the creation of beautiful objects. Also Old English verb form for *are*, Matt. 6:9. Bible students find it difficult to gain a clear picture of the art of the Hebrew people. Except for the descriptions of the tabernacle and the temple in the Bible, art is really not discussed at all in the Scriptures. Most of what is known on this subject has been gathered from the work of archaeologists.

ASCENSION OF CHRIST — the dramatic departure of the risen Christ from His earthly, bodily ministry among His followers (Mark 16:19; Luke 24:50–51; Acts 1:9–11).

ASHER [ash'-ur] *(happy)* — the name of a man and a city in the Bible:

1. The eighth son of Jacob, the second by Leah's maidservant, Zilpah (Gen. 30:13). On his deathbed Jacob blessed Asher: "Bread from Asher shall be rich, and he shall yield royal dainties" (Gen. 49:20).

2. A city situated east of Shechem on the road to Beth Shean, in the half-tribe of Manasseh west of the Jordan River (Josh. 17:7).

ASHERAH [ash-er'-ah] — pagan goddess (Judg. 3:7).

A fine example of mosaic art, this map shows Palestine in the sixth century A.D. Note the city of Jericho in the lower part of the mosaic. *Photo by Gustav Jenninga*

ASHTAROTH [ash′-ta-roth] — the plural form of Ashtoreth, a pagan goddess. First Samuel 31:10 connects her with the Philistines, and 1 Kings 11:5 connects her with the Sidonians. She was often considered the companion or partner of the male god BAAL (Judg. 2:13).

ASHTORETH [ash′-to-reth] — the singular form of ASHTAROTH.

ASLEEP — a reference to death as well as the term for actual sleep (1 Thess. 4:13; Matt. 8:24).

ASP — snake, SERPENT (Is. 11:8).

ASS — donkey (Num. 22:21).

ASSEMBLY — a group united by a common cause (Joel 1:14).

ASSURANCE — the state of being assured; freedom from doubt and uncertainty. As a theological concept, assurance is one of the richest doctrines of the Bible. It refers to the believers' full confidence and conviction that the penalty of their sins has been paid and that heaven has been secured as their eternal destiny by Christ's death and Resurrection (1 John 5:12).

ASSYRIA [as-sir′-e-ah] — a kingdom between the Tigris and Euphrates Rivers that often dominated the ancient world. After defeating the northern kingdom of Israel in 722 B.C., the Assyrians carried away thousands of Israelites and resettled them in other parts of the Assyrian Empire. This was a blow from which the nation of Israel never recovered (Gen. 10:22).

ASTROLOGER — one who sought answers by studying the sun, moon, planets, and stars (Is. 47:13).

ASUNDER — a division or separation, usually a negative context (Acts 15:39).

ATONEMENT — the act by which God restores a relationship of harmony and unity between Himself and human beings. The word can be broken into three parts that express this great truth in simple but profound terms: "at–one–ment." Through God's atoning grace and forgiveness, we are reinstated to a relationship of at–one–ment with God, in spite of our sin (Rom. 5:11).

ATONEMENT, DAY OF — a Jewish holy FEAST day known today by its Hebrew name, Yom Kippur (Leviticus 16). The tenth day of the seventh month was set aside as a day of public fasting and humiliation. On this day the nation of Israel sought atonement for its sins (Lev. 23:27; 16:29; Num. 29:7). The Day of Atonement was the only fasting period required by the law (Lev. 16:29, 23:31), and it was a solemn, holy day accompanied by elaborate ritual.

The high priest first sancitifed himself by taking a ceremonial bath and putting on white garments (Lev. 16:4). Then he made atonement for himself and other priests by sacrificing a bullock (Num. 29:8). After sacrificing the bullock, the HIGH PRIEST chose a goat for a sin offering and sacrificed it, sprinkling the blood on and about the MERCY SEAT in the sanctuary (Lev. 16:12, 14, 15). Finally, the SCAPEGOAT bearing the sins of the people was sent into the wilderness (Lev. 16:20–22).

AUGUSTUS [aw-gus′-tus] *(consecrated, holy, sacred)* — a title of honor bestowed upon Octavian, the first Roman emperor (27 B.C.—A.D. 14). Luke refers to him as "Caesar Augustus" (Luke 2:1). Octavian eventually became the sole ruler of Rome and reigned as emperor for more than 44 years, until his death in A.D. 14. It was during his reign that Jesus was born (Luke 2:1).

AUTHORITIES — those in a position of power both physical and spiritual (Luke 12:11; Eph. 3:10).

Bust of Augustus Caesar, first emperor of the Roman Empire.

AUTHORITY — the power or right to do something, particularly to give orders and see that they are followed. The word "authority" as used in the Bible usually means a person's right to do certain things because of the position or office held by that person. This word emphasizes the legality and right, more than the physical strength, needed to do something (Rom. 13:1).

AVENGE — provide complete justice (Jer. 46:10).

AWAKE — revive (Dan. 12:2).

AWE — admiration, amazement (Ps. 33:8).

AZARIAH [az-a-ri′-ah] *(the Lord has helped)* — the Hebrew name of ABED-NEGO, whom Nebuchadnezzar placed in the fiery furnace (Dan. 1:6–7, 11, 19; 2:17).

AZAZEL [az′-a-zel] — NRSV, KJV word for SCAPEGOAT (Lev. 16:8, 10).

BAAL [ba′-al] *(lord, master)* — the name of one or more false gods, a city in the tribe of Simeon (1 Chr. 4:33), and two men in the Bible (1 Chr. 5:5–6), (1 Chr. 8:30; 9:36).

BABEL, TOWER OF [ba′-bel] — an ancient tower symbolizing human pride and rebellion. It was built during the period after the FLOOD.

The narrative of the Tower of Babel appears in Genesis 11:1–9 as the climax to the account of early mankind found in Genesis 1—11. The geographical setting is a plain in the land of Shinar (Gen. 11:2). In the light of information contained in Genesis 10:10, Shinar probably refers to Babylonia.

BABYLON, CITY OF [bab′-i-lun] — ancient walled city between the Tigris and Euphrates Rivers and capital of the Babylonian Empire. The leading citizens of the nation of Judah were carried to this city as captives in 586 B.C. after Jerusalem fell to the invading Babylonians. Biblical writers often portrayed this ancient capital of the Babylonian people as the model of paganism and idolatry (Jer. 51:44; Dan. 4:30).

BABYLONIA [bab-i-low′-nih-uh] — ancient pagan empire between the Tigris and Euphrates Rivers in southern Mesopotamia. The Babylonians struggled with the neighboring Assyrians for domination of the ancient world during much of their history. At the height of their power, the Babylonians overpowered the nation of Judah, destroyed Jerusalem, and carried God's covenant people into captivity in 586 B.C.

BACKBITE — to speak slanderously or spitefully about a person (Ps. 15:3; Rom. 1:30).

BACKSLIDE — to revert to sin or wrongdoing; to lapse morally or in the practice of religion. "Backsliding" is a term found mainly in the Book of Jeremiah (2:19; 31:22; 49:4). It refers to the lapse of the nation of Israel into paganism and idolatry.

BALAAM [ba′-la-am] — a magician or soothsayer (Josh. 13:22) who was summoned by the Moabite king Balak to curse the Israelites before they entered Canaan (Num. 22:5—24:25; Deut. 23:4–5). The exact meaning of the account of Balaam's "stubborn" donkey is not clear. After telling Balaam it was all right to go,

This drawing of Babylon shows the main avenue of the city, passing through the Gate of Ishtar in the city wall.

21

God either tried to forbid him from going or wanted to impress upon him that he should speak only what he was told to say. When the angel of the Lord blocked their way, the donkey balked three times and was beaten by Balaam, who had not seen the angel. Finally, after the third beating, the donkey spoke, reproving Balaam.

BALANCES — devices to measure weight. At the time of the Exodus and following, the Israelites probably used the common balances of Egypt. These balances consisted of a vertical stand and a horizontal crossbeam, from each end of which a pan was suspended.

In the Bible, "balances" are often used in a figurative way. The Lord told the Israelites, "You shall have just balances, just weights" (Lev. 19:36; Ezek. 45:10). The "just balances" symbolize honesty, righteousness, justice, and fair dealing (Job 31:6; Ps. 62:9; Prov. 16:11). "False balances" symbolize evil and bring the displeasure and judgment of God (Prov. 11:1; Mic. 6:11).

BALM — plant-based ointment used for medicinal purposes (Jer. 51:8).

BAPTISM — a ritual practiced in the New Testament church (Rom. 6:1–4) that is still used in various forms by different denominations and branches of the Christian church. Baptism involves the application of water to the body of a person. It is frequently thought of as an act by which the believer enters the fellowship of a local congregation or the universal church. Widely differing interpretations of the act exist among Christian groups. They have different views on the nature of baptism, who should be baptized, and the appropriate method by which baptism should be administered.

A baptistry, or bath, used for purification ceremonies in the Essene community at Qumran.

Photo by Gustav Jeeninga

A baptistry in the form of a cross in the Church of St. John at Ephesus. *Photo by Howard Vos*

BAPTISM OF FIRE — a concept used by John the Baptist to describe the work of Christ: "He [Christ] will baptize you with the Holy Spirit and fire" (Matt. 3:11; Luke 3:16). Some scholars believe that two different baptisms are mentioned here: "the baptism of the Holy Spirit" (the baptism that brings mercy, forgiveness, and life) and "the baptism of fire" (the baptism that brings judgment, condemnation, and death). When this interpretation is followed, the baptism of the Holy Spirit belongs to the present age of grace and the baptism of fire belongs to a future age of judgment.

BAPTIST — one who baptizes such as John (Mark 1:4–5); also a Christian denomination.

BARABBAS [ba-rab′-bas] — a "robber" (John 18:40) and "notorious prisoner" (Matt. 27:16) who was chosen by the mob in Jerusalem to be released instead of Jesus.

BARBARIAN — a person who is different from the dominant class or group. Originally, this term

(*barbaros*) had no negative connotation. The Greeks used it to describe anyone who did not speak the Greek language (Rom. 1:14). Later, when Rome conquered Greece and absorbed its culture, the word "barbarian" signified those whose lives were not ordered by Greco-Roman culture.

BAR-JESUS [bar-je′-sus] *(son of Jesus)* — a false prophet who opposed Barnabas and Paul at Paphos, a town on the island of Cyprus (Acts 13:4–12). He is also called Elymas, which means "magician" or "sorcerer." Bar-Jesus was temporarily struck blind because of his opposition to the gospel.

BARNABAS [bar′-na-bus] *(son of encouragement)* — an apostle in the early church (Acts 4:36–37; 11:19–26) and Paul's companion on his first missionary journey (Acts 13:1—15:41). A LEVITE from the island of Cyprus, Barnabas' given name was Joseph, or Joses (Acts 4:36). When he became a Christian, he sold his land and gave the money to the Jerusalem apostles (Acts 4:36–37).

BARREN — the condition of being unable to bear children. In the Bible, the term is also applied figuratively to anything that is unproductive, such as land (2 Kin. 2:19) or a nation (Is. 54:1).

The tomb of Barnabas on the island of Cyprus in the Mediterranean Sea. *Photo by Gustav Jenninga*

BARTHOLOMEW [bar-thol'-o-mew] *(son of Tolmai)* — one of the twelve apostles of Jesus, according to the four lists given in the New Testament (Matt. 10:3; Mark 3:18; Luke 6:14; Acts 1:13). Many scholars equate Bartholomew with NATHANAEL (John 1:45–49), but no proof of this identification exists, except by inference. According to church tradition, Bartholomew was a missionary to various countries, such as Armenia and India. He is reported to have preached the gospel along with Philip and Thomas. According to another tradition, he was crucified upside down after being flayed alive.

BASE — as an adjective, humble or lowly (Ezek. 29:15); as a noun, pedestal (Ezra 3:3).

BASHAN [ba'-shan] — the territory east of the Jordan River and the Sea of Galilee (Deut. 32:14).

BATH — a liquid measure, approximately 5.8 gallons (1 Kin. 7:38).

BATHSHEBA [bath-she'-buh] *(daughter of oath)* — a wife of Uriah the Hittite and of King David (2 Sam. 11; 12:24). David saw the beautiful Bathsheba bathing on the roof of a nearby house. With his passion aroused, David committed adultery with Bathsheba and they had a child.

David tried to trick Uriah into having relations with his wife so he would believe the child was his, but Uriah refused to engage in marital relations with his wife while his companions were involved in battle. When David's attempt failed, he sent Uriah back into battle. This time, David ordered that Uriah be placed at the front of the battle and that his fellow soldiers retreat from him, so that he might be killed. After a period of mourning, Bathsheba became David's wife (2 Sam. 11:27). But the child conceived in adultery died.

B.C. — a time reference meaning *Before Christ*.

BEATITUDES, THE — the eight declarations of blessedness made by Jesus at the beginning of the Sermon on the Mount (Matt. 5:3–12), each beginning with "Blessed are…" Some scholars speak of seven, nine, or ten beatitudes, but the number appears to be eight (verses 10–12 of Matthew 5 being one beatitude).

Chapel on the Mount of Beatitudes, the site where Jesus delivered His Sermon on the Mount, according to many scholars. *Photo: Levant Photo Service*

BEELZEBUB [be-el′-ze-bub] — Greek form of Baal-Zebub (Matt. 12:24).

BEERSHEBA [be-ur′-she-ba] *(well of the seven or well of the oath)* — the chief city of the Negev. Beersheba was situated in the territory of Simeon (Josh. 19:1–2) and was "at the limits of the tribe of the children of Judah, toward the border of Edom in the South" (Josh. 15:21, 28). Midway between the Mediterranean Sea and the southern end of the Dead Sea, Beersheba was considered the southern extremity of the Promised Land, giving rise to the often-used expression, "from Dan [in the north] to Beersheba" (Judg. 20:1) or "from Beersheba to Dan" (1 Chr. 21:2).

BEGET — to cause; usually in reference to fathering (1 Cor. 4:15).

BEGOTTEN, ONLY — a New Testament phrase that describes Christ as the only, or unique, Son of His heavenly Father (John 1:14, 18; 3:16–18; 1 John 4:9, one and only, NIV). The Greek word expresses the idea of distinctiveness—"one of a kind." As the unique, sinless Son, Jesus accomplished our salvation through His death on the Cross.

BELIAL [be′-le-al] *(worthlessness)* — an Old Testament term designating a person as godless or lawless. The NKJV translates corrupt (1 Sam. 2:12), perverted (Judg. 19:22), rebel (2 Sam. 20:1), scoundrel (1 Kin. 21:10, 13), worthless men (1 Sam. 30:22), and worthless rogues (2 Sam. 16:7). A "daughter of Belial" (1 Sam. 1:16, KJV) means a wicked woman (NKJV, NIV), one who is worthless (NASB, NRSV).

Belial sometimes takes the form of a proper name (or a personification), applied to a demon or to Satan (Nah. 1:15; 2 Cor. 6:15). Many scholars believe that Belial is another name for SATAN.

BELIEVE, BELIEVER — to place one's trust in God's truth; one who takes God at His word and trusts in Him for salvation (John 14:1; 20:31).

Abraham's Well at the ancient city of Beersheba. *Photo: Levant Photo Service*

BELSHAZZAR [bel-shaz'-ar] *(Bel, protect the king)* — the oldest son of Nabonidus and the last king of the Neo-Babylonian Empire (Dan. 5:1–2; 7:1; 8:1).

BELTESHAZZAR [bel-te-shaz'-ar] — the Hebrew form of the Babylonian name given to DANIEL by the chief of Nebuchadnezzar's EUNUCHS (Dan. 1:7; 5:12). This name should not be confused with BELSHAZZAR.

BENJAMIN [ben'-jam-min] *(son of the right hand* or *son of the south)* — the name of three or four men in the Old Testament:

1. Jacob's youngest son, born to his favorite wife, RACHEL (Gen. 35:18, 24).

2. A son of Bilhan, a Benjamite (1 Chr. 7:10).

3. A son of Harim who lived in Jerusalem following the return from the Captivity. Benjamin divorced his pagan wife at Ezra's urging (Ezra 10:31–32).

4. A priest during the time of Nehemiah (Neh. 12:34) who helped repair and dedicate the wall of Jerusalem (Neh. 3:23). He may be the same person as No. 3.

BEREA [be-re'-ah] — a city of Macedonia about 73 kilometers (45 miles) west of Thessalonica (modern Salonika). On his first missionary journey, the apostle Paul preached at Berea (Acts 17:10) with much success. The Bereans were "more fair-minded than those in Thessalonica," because they "searched the Scriptures daily to find out whether these things were so" (Acts 17:11).

BERYL — a gem stone that was usually green or bluish green (Ezek. 1:16; 10:9).

BESEECH — to strongly appeal or beg; ask intently (Rom. 12:1).

BESIEGE — close in, usually military (Deut. 20:19).

BETHANY [beth'-a-ny] — the name of two villages in the New Testament:

1. A village on the southeastern slopes of the MOUNT OF OLIVES about three kilometers (two miles) east of Jerusalem near the road to Jericho (Mark 11:1).

2. A village in Transjordan where John the Baptist was baptizing (John 1:28, NIV; Bethabara, KJV, NKJV).

BETHEL [beth'-el] *(house of God)* — the name of two cities in the Old Testament:

1. A city of Canaan about 19 kilometers (12 miles) north of Jerusalem. Bethel is mentioned more often in the Bible than any other city except Jerusalem. It is first mentioned in connection with Abraham, who "pitched his tent with Bethel on the west and … built an altar to the LORD" (Gen. 12:8; 13:3). The region around Bethel is still suitable for grazing by livestock.

2. A city in the territory of Simeon (1 Sam. 30:27). Scholars believe this Bethel is a variant reading for Bethul (Josh. 19:4) or Bethuel (1 Chr. 4:30).

BETHLEHEM [beth'-le-hem] *(house of bread* or *house of* [the god] *Lahmu)* — the name of two cities and possibly one man in the Bible:

1. The birthplace of Jesus Christ. Bethlehem was situated about eight kilometers (five miles) south of Jerusalem in the district known as Ephrathah in Judah (Mic. 5:2), a region known for its fertile hills and valleys.

2. A town in the land of Zebulun (Josh. 19:15).

3. A son of Salma, a descendant of Caleb (1 Chr. 2:51). As the "father" of Bethlehem, Salma may have been the founder of Bethlehem rather than being the father of a son named "Bethlehem."

BETHSAIDA [beth-sa'-da] *(house of fishing)* — the name of one or possibly two cities in the New Testament:

1. Bethsaida, which was later called Julias, was situated three kilometers (two miles) north of the Sea of Galilee and east of the Jordan River.

2. The Gospels of Mark, Luke, and John seem to speak of another Bethsaida which was the home of Philip, Andrew, and Peter (John 1:44)

Bethlehem, in the hill country of Judah—the home of David and the birthplace of Jesus (1 Sam. 16:1, 4; Luke 2:11). *Photo by Gustav Jenninga*

and perhaps of James and John (Luke 5:10). This city was situated northwest of the Sea of Galilee in the fertile plain of Gennesaret (Mark 6:45, 53) near Capernaum (John 6:17) in the province of Galilee (John 12:21).

BETROTHAL, BETROTHED — a mutual promise or contract for a future marriage; an engagement. (Deut. 20:7; Jer. 2:2; Luke 1:27).

The betrothal was celebrated by a feast. In some instances, it was customary for the bridegroom to place a ring, a token of love and fidelity, on the bride's finger. In Hebrew custom, betrothal was actually part of the marriage process. A change of intention by one of the partners after he or she was betrothed was a serious matter, subject in some instances to penalty by fine.

A Jewish betrothal could be dissolved only by the man's giving the woman a certificate of divorce. A betrothal usually lasted for one year. During that year the couple were known as husband and wife, although they did not have the right to be united sexually.

Betrothal was much more closely linked with marriage than our modern engagement. But the actual marriage took place only when the bridegroom took the bride to his home and the marriage was consummated in the sexual union.

BEWRAY — to divulge, betray, reveal, or disclose (Matt. 26:73).

BIBLE, THE — the sacred Book, or collection of books, accepted by the Christian church as uniquely inspired by God, and thus authoritative, providing guidelines for belief and behavior.

The Bible contains two major sections known as the Old Testament and the New Testament. The books of the Old Testament were written over a period of about 1,000 years in the Hebrew language, except for a few selected passages, which were written in Aramaic. The Old Testament tells of the preparation that was made for Christ's coming.

The New Testament was written in Greek over a period of about 60 years. This portion of the Bible tells of Christ's coming, His life and ministry, and the growth of the early church.

BIBLE VERSIONS AND TRANSLATIONS — The Bible was written across a period of

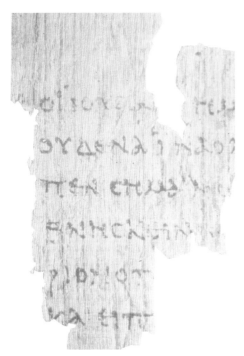

Papyrus fragments of portions of John 18 that date from about A.D. 125—150. *Photo by Howard Vos*

several centuries in the languages of Hebrew and Aramaic (Old Testament) and Greek (New Testament). With the changing of nations and cultures across the centuries, these original writings have been translated many times to make the Bible available in different languages.

BILDAD [bil′-dad] — the second of the "friends" or "comforters" of Job. In his three speeches to Job (Job 8:1–22; 18:1–21; 25:1–6), Bildad expressed the belief that all suffering is the direct result of one's sin. He had little patience with the questionings and searchings of Job. He is called "Bildad the Shuhite" (Job. 2:11), which means he belonged to an Aramean nomadic tribe that lived in the Transjordan area southeast of Canaan.

BIRTHRIGHT — a right, privilege, or possession to which a person, especially the firstborn son, was entitled by birth in Bible times. In Israel,

as in the rest of the ancient world, the firstborn son enjoyed a favored position. His birthright included a double portion of his father's assets upon his death (Deut. 21:17) as well as a special blessing from the father (Gen. 27:27) and the privilege of leadership of the family (Gen. 43:33).

BISHOP — an overseer, elder, or pastor charged with the responsibility of spiritual leadership in a local church in New Testament times (Acts 20:17, 28; Titus 1:5, 7).

BISHOPRICK — the office held by a bishop; his responsibilities (Acts 1:20, KJV).

BITTER HERBS — herbs eaten by the Israelites during the celebration of PASSOVER. Those herbs helped them remember their bitter experience as an enslaved people in Egypt (Ex. 1:14; 12:8; Num. 9:11). These herbs may have included such plants as sorrel, dandelions, and horseradish.

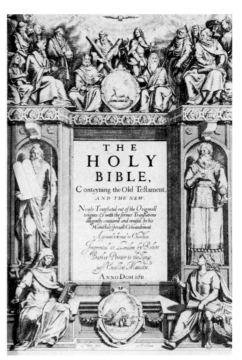

Title page from an early copy of the King James Version of the Bible, published originally in 1611.

BLASPHEME, BLASPHEMY — the act of cursing, slandering, reviling or showing contempt or lack of reverence for God. In the Old Testament, blaspheming God was a serious crime punishable by death (Lev. 24:15–16). It was a violation of the third Commandment, which required that the name and reputation of the Lord be upheld (Ex. 20:7).

BLESS, BLESSING — the act of declaring, or wishing, favor and goodness upon others. The blessing is not only the good effect of words; it also has the power to bring them to pass. In the Bible, important persons blessed those with less power or influence. The patriarchs pronounced benefits upon their children, often near their own deaths (Gen. 49:1–28). Even if spoken by mistake, once a blessing was given it could not be taken back (Gen. 27:33).

BLOOD — the red fluid circulating in the body that takes nourishment to the body parts and carries away waste. The word "blood" is often used literally in Scripture. Sometimes the word refers to the blood of animals (Gen. 37:31); at other times it refers to human blood (1 Kin. 22:35). The word is also used figuratively in the Bible. It may mean "blood red" (Joel 2:31) or murder (Matt. 27:24). The phrase "flesh and blood" means humanity (Heb. 2:14).

BLOODGUILTINESS — guilt that occurs after murder (Ps. 51:14).

BOAST — in a positive sense, it means to praise something or someone (Ps. 44:8); and in a negative sense, it refers to bragging about wrongdoing and showing false pride (Ps. 52:1).

BOAZ [bo′-az] *(in him is strength)* — the name of a prominent man and an object in the temple:

1. A wealthy and honorable man of Bethlehem from the tribe of Judah. He was a kinsman of Elimelech, Naomi's husband, and he became the husband of RUTH, Naomi's widowed daughter-in-law (Ruth 2—4). Through their son Obed, Boaz and Ruth became ancestors of King David and of the Lord Jesus Christ (Matt. 1:5; Booz, KJV).

The fields of Boaz, near the city of Bethlehem (Ruth 2:1—4). *Photo by Howard Vos*

2. One of the two bronze pillars that stood in front of King Solomon's magnificent temple (2 Chr. 3:17). The name of the other was Jachin.

BODY — the material or physical part of a person, whether alive or dead. Some religions consider the body evil or inferior to the soul, but the Bible teaches that the body is God's good gift to us (Gen. 1:31). It is a necessary ingredient for a fully human existence (Gen. 2:7). In the Old Testament the word "body" sometimes means "corpse" (Num. 6:6). Occasionally the reference is to the body as that part of a person that is involved in reproduction (Deut. 28:4). The word body is also used to symbolize the church (Rom. 12:4–5; 1 Cor. 12:12–14; Col. 1:18).

BOND, BONDS — an obligation or restraint of any kind. In the Bible, the word is used literally, of the fetters and chains of prisoners (Judg. 15:14). In a figurative sense, it refers to the bonds of sin and wickedness (Is. 58:6), covenant obligation (Ezek. 20:37), and peace and love (Eph. 4:3).

BONDAGE — physical slavery or a reference to life prior to knowing Jesus Christ (Rom. 8:15; Gal. 4:7–9).

BONES — the skeletal framework of the human body. The bones of Joseph were revered by the Israelites (Ex. 13:19). In the prophet Ezekiel's vision of the valley of dry bones (Ezek. 37:1–14), the dead bones came to life, showing that the Jews would be restored as a nation after their years of CAPTIVITY in Babylon.

BOOK — In Bible times a book was almost anything in written form, usually preserved on a scroll, a roll of papyrus, leather, or parchment (Jer. 36:2).

BOOK OF LIFE — a heavenly book in which the names of the righteous (the redeemed or saved) are written. The concept of God's having a "Book of Life" was probably first enunciated by Moses, who prayed that God would blot him out

of God's book rather than dooming his fellow Israelites (Ex. 32:32–33). This concept likely arose from the practice of registering people by genealogy (Jer. 22:30; Neh. 7:5, 64) and keeping a record of priests and Levites (Neh. 12:22–23).

At the end of time (Rev. 20:11–15), those whose names are not written in the Book of Life will be "cast into the lake of fire" (Rev. 20:15). But those whose names appear there (Rev. 21:27) will be allowed to enter the New Jerusalem. (see JERUSALEM, NEW.)

BOOTHS, FEAST OF — also known as Feast of TABERNACLES (Lev. 23:34–36).

BOOTY — plunder and spoils of war. Booty consisted of everything of value taken in battle—gold and silver, clothing, food, household items, weapons, implements of agriculture, camels, sheep, cattle, and men, women, and children to be used as slaves (Gen. 14:11–12; Jer. 49:32).

BORN AGAIN — a spiritual birth (John 3:3).

BORNE — carried (Matt. 23:4).

BOSOM — another word for the chest of the human body, usually used symbolically in the Bible to suggest closeness or intimacy. Receiving something into the bosom means accepting it completely (Is. 40:11). The word "bosom" may also imply a person's inner thoughts (Ps. 35:13, KJV; heart, NKJV). "Abraham's bosom" symbolizes a place of honor (Luke 16:22–23). Bosom also suggests the intimacy between Jesus and His heavenly Father (John 1:18).

BOUNTY — abundance, blessing (2 Cor. 9:5).

BOWELS — the internal parts of a person's body. Symbolically, the bowels were considered the seat of emotions and feelings, much like the use of the word "heart." Hence "bowels" means pity, compassion, and tenderness (Job 30:27; 1 John 3:17).

BRANCH — a secondary stem or limb growing from the trunk of a tree. The arms of the golden lampstand made for the tabernacle are also described as branches (Ex. 37:17–22). But the most significant use of this word in the Bible is a symbolic title for the MESSIAH.

BREACH — exposed, vulnerable place (2 Kin. 22:5).

BREAD — a staple food made from flour or meal and mixed with a liquid, usually combined with leaven and kneaded into dough, then shaped into loaves and baked.

Bread played an important role in Israel's worship as well as being a crucial part of trade and commerce.

Satan tempted Jesus by saying, "If You are the Son of God, command that these stones become bread." But Jesus answered, "It is written, 'Man shall not live by bread alone, but by every word that proceeds from the mouth of God' " (Matt. 4:3–4).

In the Lord's Prayer, Jesus taught His disciples to pray, "Give us this day our daily bread" (Matt. 5:11). In the Gospel of John, Jesus called Himself "the true bread from heaven" (5:32), "the bread of God" (5:33), "the bread of life" (5:34), and "the bread which came down from heaven" (5:41).

On the night before His Crucifixion, Jesus instituted the Lord's Supper: "And as they were eating, Jesus took bread, blessed it and broke it, and gave it to the disciples and said, 'Take, eat; this is My body' " (Matt. 26:26). By His sacrifice, Christ became the Bread of Life for His people that they may eat of Him and find forgiveness of sin and eternal life.

BREASTPLATE — armor (Eph. 6:14), a religious garment (Ex. 28:15–30).

BREECHES — KJV word for trousers (Ex. 28:42).

BRETHREN — refers to brothers in one's physical family (Gen. 47:1) as well as their spiritual family (Acts 20:32).

BRIDE — a woman who has recently been married or is about to be married. In biblical times, it

was customary for fathers to select wives for their sons (Gen. 38:6). Occasionally, a son might express his preference for a bride to his father, and his father would negotiate with the parents or guardians of the young woman in question (Gen. 34:4, 8). The father of the young woman also might initiate wedding proposals (Ex. 2:21).

BRIDEGROOM — a man who has recently been married or is about to be married. The term is applied symbolically to the MESSIAH. John the Baptist called Jesus the "bridegroom" (John 3:29). Jesus referred to Himself as the "bridegroom" (Matt. 9:15). Jesus' bride, of course, is the church—those who are spiritually united with Him by faith.

BRIMSTONE — a bright yellow mineral usually found near active volcanoes. Highly combustible, it burns with a disagreeable odor. The Hebrew and Greek words for "brimstone" denote divine fire (Gen. 19:24; Ezek. 38:22; Luke 17:29). Another word for brimstone used in various Bible translations is sulphur.

BROOD — young birds in the nest (Luke 13:34).

BUCKLER — a shield (1 Chr. 5:18), also symbolic of God's protection (Ps. 18:2).

BULL, BULLOCK — animal used for sacrifice (Heb. 10:4; Ex. 29:11).

BULRUSH — Gigantic hollow-stemmed grasses that grew along river banks and in moist areas of Egypt and Palestine. Moses' basket was woven from bulrushes (Ex. 2:3–6).

BULWARKS — towers built along city walls from which defenders shot arrows and hurled large stones at the enemy (Ps. 48:13; Is. 26:1).

BURDEN — a heavy load or weight. This weight can be a literal burden (Ex. 23:5) or a figurative burden (Num. 11:11, 17). The prophets frequently spoke of their messages as burdens. A prophetic utterance or oracle usually was ominous and foreboding, a denouncing of evil and a pronouncing of judgment against a place or a people (Is. 13:1; Ezek. 12:10; Hos. 8:10).

BURIED — placed in a grave (Num. 20:1), also used symbolically in reference to baptism (Rom. 6:4).

BURN — to consume with fire. The words are used often in a literal way, as in the case of the burning bush (Ex. 3:2) and the fiery furnace (Dan. 3:20–25). They are also used figuratively, of anger (Ex. 32:10–11), jealousy (Ps. 79:5), and strong emotion (Luke 24:32).

BURNING BUSH — the flaming shrub at Mount Horeb through which Moses became aware of the presence of God (Ex. 3:2–4). Attracted by the phenomenon, Moses turned aside to see why the bush did not burn. Some scholars believe the burning bush symbolized Israel, which had endured and survived the "fiery trial" of Egyptian bondage. The bush may have been a thornbush.

C

CAESAR [se'-zur] — a title applied to several emperors of the Roman Empire, beginning with Augustus (Matt. 22:17).

CAESAREA [ses-a-re'-ah] *(pertaining to Caesar)* — an important biblical seaport located south of modern Haifa. Built at enormous expense by HEROD the Great between 25 and 13 B.C., and named in honor of Caesar Augustus. This is the place where Paul was imprisoned for two years (Acts 23:33).

CAESAREA PHILIPPI [ses-a-re'-ah fil'-a-pi] *(Caesar's city of Philip)* — a city on the southwestern slope of Mount Hermon and at the northernmost extent of Jesus' ministry (Matt. 16:13; Mark 8:27).

The present–day village of Baniyas is built on the same site. It was near Caesarea Philippi that Jesus asked His disciples who He was and received the inspired answer from Simon Peter: "You are the Christ, the Son of the living God" (Matt. 16:16).

CAIAPHAS [cah'-ya-fus] — the high priest of Israel appointed about A.D. 18 by the Roman procurator, Valerius Gratus. Caiaphas and his father–in–law, Annas, were high priests when John the Baptist began his preaching (Matt. 26:3, 57; Luke 3:2). Caiaphas also was a member of the Sadducees.

After Jesus raised LAZARUS from the dead, the Jewish leaders became alarmed at Jesus' increasing popularity. The SANHEDRIN quickly called a meeting, during which Caiaphas called for Jesus'

Ruins of the palaces of the Caesars, emperors of the Roman Empire, in the capital city of Rome.

Photo by Howard Vos

These man–made breakwaters built by the Romans turned Caesarea into a major Mediterranean port city.

death. As high priest, Caiaphas' words carried great authority, and his counsel was followed (John 11:49–53). Subsequently, Caiaphas plotted the arrest of Jesus (Matt. 26:3–4) and was a participant in the illegal trial of Jesus (Matt. 26:57–68).

CAIN *(metalworker)* — the oldest son of Adam and Eve and the brother of Abel (Gen. 4:1–25).

Cain was the first murderer. A farmer by occupation, Cain brought fruits of the ground as a sacrifice to God. His brother Abel, a shepherd, sacrificed a lamb from his flock. The Lord accepted Abel's offering but rejected Cain's (Gen. 4:7). The proof of Cain's wrong standing before God is seen in his impulse to kill his own brother Abel when his own offering was rejected (Gen. 4:8). Cain was the ancestor of a clan of metalworkers (Gen. 4:18–19, 22).

CALDRON — a ceramic or metal container for boiling meat, either for ceremonial or domestic purposes (2 Chr. 35:13; Mic. 3:3). Metallic pots for cooking have been found in Egypt and Mesopotamia.

CALEB [ca´-leb] *(dog)* — the name of two men in the Old Testament:

1. One of the twelve spies sent by Moses to investigate the land of Canaan (Num. 13:6, 30; 14:6, 24, 30, 38). Ten of the twelve spies frightened the Israelites with reports of fortified cities and gigantic peoples. Compared to the giants in the land, they saw themselves as "grasshoppers" (Num. 13:33).

Joshua and Caleb also saw the fortified cities in the land, but they reacted in faith rather than fear. They advised Moses and Aaron and the Israelites to attack Canaan immediately (Num. 13:30). The Israelites listened to the spies rather than the two, and the Lord viewed their fear as a lack of faith and judged them for their spiritual timidity. Of all the adults alive at that time, only Caleb and Joshua would live to possess the land (Josh. 14:6–15).

2. A son of Hezron of the family of Perez of the tribe of Judah (1 Chr. 2:18–19, 42).

CALENDAR — a system of reckoning time, usually based on a recurrent natural cycle (such as the sun through the seasons or the moon through its phases); a table, or tabular register, of days according to a system usually covering one year and referring the days of each month to the days of the week.

From the beginning of recorded history, the calendar has been used to keep records and predict the time for the changing of the seasons. The calendar provided a framework in which people could plan their work. It was an effective timetable for marking various religious festivals that were to be celebrated at regular intervals.

The Jewish Calendar

The Jews used two kinds of calendars:
  Civil Calendar—official calendar of kings, childbirth, and contracts.
  Sacred Calendar—from which festivals were computed.

NAMES OF MONTHS	CORRESPONDS WITH	NO. OF DAYS	MONTH OF CIVIL YEAR	MONTH OF SACRED YEAR
TISHRI	Sept.–Oct.	30 days	1st	7th
HESHVAN	Oct.–Nov.	29 or 30	2nd	8th
CHISLEV	Nov.–Dec.	29 or 30	3rd	9th
TEBETH	Dec.–Jan.	29	4th	10th
SHEBAT	Jan.–Feb.	30	5th	11th
ADAR	Feb.–Mar.	29 or 30	6th	12th
NISAN	Mar.–Apr.	30	7th	1st
IYAR	Apr.–May	29	8th	2nd
SIVAN	May–June	30	9th	3rd
TAMMUZ	June–July	29	10th	4th
AB	July–Aug.	30	11th	5th
***ELUL**	Aug.–Sept.	29	12th	6th

The Jewish day was from sunset to sunset, in 8 equal parts:

FIRST WATCH . . . . .SUNSET TO 9 P.M.
SECOND WATCH . . . . .9 P.M. TO MIDNIGHT
THIRD WATCH . . . . .MIDNIGHT TO 3 A.M.
FOURTH WATCH . . . . .3 A.M. TO SUNRISE

FIRST HOUR . . . . .SUNRISE TO 9 A.M.
THIRD HOUR . . . . .9 A.M. TO NOON
SIXTH HOUR . . . . .NOON TO 3 P.M.
NINTH HOUR . . . . .3 P.M. TO SUNSET

*Hebrew months were alternately 30 and 29 days long. Their year, shorter than ours, had 354 days. Therefore, about every three years (7 times in 19 years) an extra 29-day month, VEADAR, was added between ADAR and NISAN.

CALL, CALLING — an important theological idea with several different meanings in the Bible:

1. God's call of individuals to SALVATION, made possible by the sacrifice of Jesus Christ on the Cross (Rom. 8:28–30; 1 Thess. 2:12).

2. To call on God for help, or to pray (Ps. 55:16–17).

3. To name or to call by name (Gen. 17:5; Luke 1:13).

CALVARY [cal'-va-ry] (from the Latin word *calvaria,* "the skull") — the name used in the KJV and NKJV for the place outside Jerusalem where the Lord Jesus was crucified (Luke 23:33; the Skull, NIV).

CANA [ca'-nah] *(place of reeds)* — a village of Galilee where Jesus performed His first miracle—turning water into wine (John 2:1, 11). Cana was the home of Nathanael, one of the Twelve (John 21:2). Its probable location, Kfar Kanna, is about 13 kilometers (8 miles) northeast of Nazareth.

CANAAN [ca'-na-an] *(land of purple)* — the name of a man and a land or region in the Old Testament:

1. The fourth son of Ham and the grandson of Noah (Gen. 9:18–27; 10:6, 15).

2. The region along the Mediterranean Sea occupied by the Canaanites before it was taken and settled by the Israelite people (Gen. 11:31; Josh. 5:12).

CANAANITES [ca'-na-an-ites] — an ancient tribe that lived in the land of Canaan before they were displaced by the nation of Israel.

CANON — rule, standard, guide. Although this word is not used in the Bible, it is a reference to the books recognized as inspired by God.

CANOPY — any high, overarching covering. The word is used figuratively twice. Elihu proclaimed God's majesty by referring to "the thunder from his canopy" (Job 36:29). The psalmist, in speaking of God the sovereign Creator, declared, "His canopy around Him was dark waters" (Ps. 18:11).

Cana of Galilee, the village where Jesus performed His first miracle. *Photo by Gustav Jeeninga*

CAPERNAUM [ca-pur'-na-um] *(village of Nahum)* — the most important city on the northern shore of the Sea of Galilee in New Testament times and the center of much of Jesus' ministry (Matt. 4:13–15; 9:1). Capernaum is not mentioned in the Old Testament, and the Nahum after whom it was named is probably not the prophet Nahum. In all likelihood, Capernaum was founded sometime after the Jews returned from captivity.

CAPTIVE — a person taken and held as a prisoner, especially by an enemy in war (2 Sam. 8:2; 1 Kin. 20:32; 2 Kin. 25:7).

CAPTIVITY — the state or condition of being in bondage to one's enemies, especially if this involves deportation to a foreign land. The term "captivity" is commonly used to describe two periods when the nations of Israel (722 B.C.) and Judah (605 B.C. and later) were taken away from their native lands and into Exile.

CAREFUL — being worried, anxious, or afraid (Luke 10:41). Modern day usage is the state of being cautious, caring, concerned and attentive to detail (Phil. 4:10; Titus 3:8).

CARMEL [car'-mel] *(garden/orchard of God)* — the name of a mountain range and a town in the Old Testament:

1. A town in the hill country of Judah (Josh. 15:55; 1 Sam. 25:2, 5, 7, 40). It has been identified as present-day Khirbet el-Kermel, about 13 kilometers (8 miles) southeast of Hebron. Carmel, near Maon, was the home of a very rich and very foolish man named Nabal.

2. A mountain range stretching about 21

Aerial view of the ruins of ancient Capernaum, a city on the shore of the Sea of Galilee.
Photo by Werner Braun

In prehistoric times, families lived in some of these caves in the vicinity of Mount Carmel.
Photo by E. B. Trovillion

kilometers (13 miles) from the Mediterranean coast southeast to the Plain of Dothan. At the Bay of Accho (Acre), near the modern city of Haifa, this mountain range juts out into the Mediterranean Sea in a promontory named Mount Carmel. It rises sharply from the seacoast to a height of 143 meters (470 feet) near Haifa. The mountain range as a whole averages over 1,000 feet above sea level, with 530 meters (1,742 feet) being the summit.

CARNAL — sensual, worldly, nonspiritual; relating to or given to the crude desires and appetites of the FLESH or body. The apostle Paul contrasts "spiritual people"—that is, those who are under the control of the Holy Spirit—with those who are "carnal"—those under the control of the flesh (1 Cor. 3:1–4; Rom. 8:5–7). The word "carnal" is usually reserved in the New Testament to describe worldly Christians.

CENSER — a container, probably a ladle or shovel-like device, used for carrying live coals of fire, in which incense was burned (Num. 16:6, 17–18, 37–39, 46). The censers of the tabernacle were of bronze (Ex. 27:3; Lev. 16:12); those of the temple were "of pure gold" (1 Kin. 7:50; 2 Chr. 4:22).

CENSUS — an official counting and registration of citizens; a property evaluation for tax purposes in early Rome (Luke 2:1–5).

CENTURION — leader of one hundred soldiers in a Roman army (Matt. 8:5–10; Acts 10).

CEPHAS [se′-fas] *(rock)* — the Aramaic name of Simon the son of Jonah (John 1:42), given to him by Jesus.

CEREAL OFFERING — an offering to God (Leviticus 2; Num. 15:1–9).

CHAFF — the fine, dry material, such as husks (seed coverings) and other debris, that is separated from the seed in the process of threshing grain. In the Bible, chaff symbolizes worthless, evil, or wicked persons (or things) that are about to be destroyed (Ps. 1:4; Matt. 3:12; Luke 3:17). It is a fitting figure of speech to describe complete destruction by judgment. "The ungodly," said the psalmist, "are like the chaff which the wind drives away" (Ps. 1:4).

CHARITY — KJV word for LOVE (Col. 3:14).

CHASTE — inwardly pure. While this purity is inward in nature, it also affects a person's conduct (1 Pet. 3:2). As commonly understood, the word "chaste" is applied to sexuality; the chaste person is innocent of sexual impurity, in desire, imagination, and action (2 Cor. 11:2; Titus 2:5). Some modern translations use the word "pure" where the KJV uses "chaste."

CHASTEN — correct with the intent of teaching (1 Cor. 11:32).

CHASTISEMENT — an infliction of punishment (as by whipping or beating). In the Bible the term chastisement usually refers to punishment or discipline brought by God for the purpose of (1) education, instruction, and training (Job 4:3); (2) corrective guidance (2 Tim. 2:25); and (3) discipline, in the sense of corrective physical punishment (Prov. 22:15; Heb. 12:5–11; Rev. 3:19).

CHEBAR [ke'-bar] *(great)* — a "river" of Chaldea. The Jewish captives, including the prophet Ezekiel, lived along the banks of this river at the village of Tel Abib (Ezek. 1:1, 3; 3:15, 23). It was here that Ezekiel saw several of his remarkable visions (Ezek. 10:15, 20, 22; 43:3; Kebar, NIV). The Chebar was most likely not a river at all, but the famous Grand Canal of Nebuchadnezzar that connected the Tigris and Euphrates Rivers.

CHERUB [chair'-ub] — a place in Babylonia where some Jewish citizens lived during the Captivity. The persons who returned to Judah from this place could not prove their Israelite descent (Ezra 2:59; Neh. 7:61; Kerub, NIV).

CHERUBIM [chair'-oo-bim] — winged angelic beings, often associated with worship and praise

of God. The cherubim are first mentioned in the Bible in Genesis 3:24. When God drove Adam and Eve from the Garden of Eden, He placed cherubim at the east of the garden, "and a flaming sword which turned every way, to guard the way to the tree of life." They were similar in appearance to the statues of winged sphinxes that flanked the entrances to palaces and temples in ancient Babylonia and Assyria.

CHINNERETH, CHINNEROTH, CINNEROTH [kin'-ne-reth, kin'-ne-roth, sin'-e-roth] *(lute, harp)* — most notably the early name of the Sea of GALILEE (Num. 34:11; Josh. 12:3; 13:27; Kinnereth, NIV). It was also called the "Lake of Gennesaret" (Luke 5:1) and the "Sea of Tiberias" (John 6:1; 21:1). The lake is shaped like the outline of a harp.

CHOOSE, CHOSEN — to appoint, select, call; one who is appointed, selected or called out (Matt. 20:16; Deut. 7:6–11).

CHOSEN PEOPLE — a name for the people of Israel, whom God chose as His special instruments. As a holy people set apart to worship God, they were to make His name known throughout the earth (Ex. 19:4–6; Deut. 7:6–8; Ps. 105:43). In the New Testament, Peter describes Christians as members of a "chosen generation" (1 Pet. 2:9; chosen people, NIV).

CHRIST *(anointed one)* — a name for Jesus that showed that He was the long-awaited king and deliverer. For centuries the Jewish people had looked for a prophesied Messiah, a deliverer who would usher in a kingdom of peace and prosperity (Ps. 110; Is. 32:1–8; 61:1–3; Amos 9:13). Jesus was clearly identified as this Messiah in Peter's great confession, "You are the Christ, the Son of the living God" (Matt. 16:16).

CHRISTIAN — an adherent or follower of Christ. The word occurs three times in the New Testament: "The disciples were first called Christians in Antioch" (Acts 11:26); Agrippa said to Paul, "You almost persuade me to be a Christian"

FIRST CHRONICLES:

A Study and Teaching Outline

Part One: From Adam to Saul (1:1—9:44)

I. **The Family of Adam** 1:1–27
   A. From Adam to Noah 1:1–4
   B. From Noah to Abraham 1:5–27

II. **The Family of Abraham** 1:28–54
   A. From Abraham to Isaac 1:28–34
   B. From Isaac to Israel 1:35–54

III. **The Family of Israel** 2:1–55
   A. The Sons of Israel 2:1–2
   B. The Sons of Judah 2:3–55

IV. **The Family of David** 3:1–24
   A. The Sons of David 3:1–9
   B. The Sons of Solomon 3:10–24

V. **The Descendants of the Israelite Tribes** . . . . 4:1—8:40
   A. The Family of Judah 4:1–23
   B. The Family of Simeon 4:24–43
   C. The Family of Reuben 5:1–10
   D. The Family of Gad 5:11–22
   E. The Family of Manasseh 5:23–26
   F. The Family of Levi 6:1–81
   G. The Family of Issachar 7:1–5
   H. The Family of Benjamin 7:6–12
   I. The Family of Naphtali 7:13
   J. The Family of Manasseh 7:14–19
   K. The Family of Ephraim 7:20–29
   L. The Family of Asher 7:30–40
   M. The Family of King Saul 8:1–40

VI. **The Descendants of the Remnant** 9:1–34
   A. The Family of the Tribes Who Returned 9:1–9
   B. The Family of the Priests Who Returned . . 9:10–13
   C. The Family of the Levites Who Returned . 9:14–34

VII. **The Family of Saul** 9:35–44

Part Two: The Reign of David (10:1—29:30)

I. **David Becomes King** . . . . 10:1—12:40
   A. Death of Saul 10:1–14
   B. Anointing of David as King 11:1–3
   C. Conquest of Jerusalem 11:4–9
   D. Account of David's Mighty Men . . . . . 11:10—12:40

II. **The Removal of the Ark
of the Covenant** . . . . 13:1—17:27
   A. Improper Transportation of the Ark 13:1–14
   B. Prosperity of David's Reign 14:1–17
   C. Proper Transportation of the Ark 15:1–29
   D. Celebration of the Ark in Jerusalem 16:1–43
   E. Institution of the Davidic Covenant 17:1–27

III. **The Military Victories of King David** . . . . 18:1—20:8
   A. David's Early Victories Summarized 18:1–17
   B. David's Latter Victories Summarized . . 19:1—20:8

IV. **The Preparation and Organization of Israel
for the Temple** . . . . 21:1—27:34
   A. Sinful Census of David 21:1–30
   B. Material Provisions for Building the
      Temple 22:1–5
   C. Leaders Are Charged to Build the Temple . 22:6–19
   D. Organization of the Temple Leaders . . 23:1—26:32
   E. Organization of the Leaders of Israel 27:1–34

V. **The Last Days of David** . . . . 28:1—29:30
   A. Final Exhortations of David 28:1–10
   B. Final Provisions for the Temple . . . . . 28:11—29:9
   C. David's Final Prayer of Thanksgiving 29:10–19
   D. Coronation of Solomon 29:20–25
   E. Death of King David 29:26–30

(Acts 26:28); Peter exhorted, "If anyone suffers as a Christian, let him not be ashamed" (1 Pet. 4:16). In each instance, the word Christian assumes that the person called by the name was a follower of Christ. Christians were loyal to Christ, just as the Herodians were loyal to Herod (Matt. 22:16; Mark 3:6; 12:13).

CHRONICLES, BOOKS OF FIRST AND SECOND — two historical books of the Old Testament that may be characterized as "books of hope." In broad, selective strokes, these books trace the history of humankind from Adam to the CAPTIVITY and Restoration. Much of this material is a repetition of that found in the Books of 1 and 2 Samuel and 1 and 2 Kings. But the writer of Chronicles apparently wrote his history to encourage the exiles who had returned to Jerusalem after 70 years of captivity in Babylon. This selective history reminded them of Israel's glorious days from the past and gave them hope for the future as they pondered God's promises to His covenant people.

CHRYSOLITE — a yellow stone used in description of the new heaven and new earth (Rev. 21:20).

CHURCH — a local assembly of believers (1 Cor. 4:17) as well as the redeemed of all the ages who follow Jesus Christ as Savior and Lord (1 Cor. 10:32).

CIRCUMCISION — the surgical removal of the foreskin of the male sex organ. This action served as a sign of God's COVENANT relation with His people.

Moses and the prophets used the term "circum-

SECOND CHRONICLES: A Study and Teaching Outline

Part Two: The Reigns of Selected Kings of Judah (10:1—36:23)

Part One: The Reign of Solomon (1:1—9:31)

I. The Succession of Solomon as King 1:1–17
II. The Completion of the Temple . . . . 2:1—7:22
III. The Glory of the Reign of Solomon . . . . . 8:1—9:28
IV. The Death of Solomon 9:29–31

I. The Reign of Rehoboam . . . . 10:1—12:16
II. The Reign of Abijah. 13:1–22
III. The Reign of Asa . . . . 14:1—16:14
IV. The Reign of Jehoshaphat . . . . 17:1—20:37
V. The Reign of Jehoram 21:1–20
VI. The Reign of Ahaziah 22:1–9
VII. The Reign of Athaliah . . . . 22:10—23:15
VIII. The Reign of Joash . . . . 23:16—24:27
IX. The Reign of Amaziah 25:1–28
X. The Reign of Uzziah 26:1–23
XI. The Reign of Jotham 27:1–9
XII. The Reign of Ahaz. 28:1–27
XIII. The Reign of Hezekiah . . . . 29:1—32:33
XIV. The Reign of Manasseh 33:1–20
XV. The Reign of Amon 33:21–25
XVI. The Reign of Josiah. . . . . 34:1—35:27
XVII. The Reign of Jehoahaz 36:1–3
XVIII. The Reign of Jehoiakim 36:4–8
XIX. The Reign of Jehoiachin 36:9–10
XX. The Reign of Zedekiah. 36:11–21
XXI. The Proclamation by Cyrus to Return to Jerusalem. 36:22–23

cised" as a symbol for purity of heart and readiness to hear and obey. Through Moses the Lord challenged the Israelites to submit to "circumcision of the heart," a reference to their need for repentance. "If their uncircumcised hearts are humbled, and they accept their guilt," God declared, "then I will remember My covenant" (Lev. 26:41–42; also Deut. 10:16). Jeremiah characterized rebellious Israel as having "uncircumcised" ears (6:10) and being "uncircumcised in the heart" (9:26).

CISTERN — an artificial reservoir for storing liquids (especially water); specifically, an underground tank for catching and storing runoff rainwater.

Most references to cisterns in the Bible are symbolic. In writing of the peril of adultery, Proverbs 5:15 says, "Drink water from your own cistern, and running water from your own well." Jeremiah 2:13 describes God as a "fountain of living waters"—a cool, pure, natural spring. But Judah's unfaithfulness amounted to "broken cisterns that can hold no water."

CITIES OF REFUGE — six Levitical cities set aside to provide shelter and safety for those guilty of manslaughter. Of the 48 cities assigned to the Levites, six were designated as cities of refuge, three on either side of the Jordan River (Num. 35:6–7; Josh. 20:7–8).

CITY — an inhabited place of greater size, population, or importance than a town or village; a center of population, commerce, and culture. In biblical times the thing that distinguished a city from a town or village was not the size of its population but whether it had walls for defense (Lev. 25:29–31; Ezek. 38:11). But most cities also became known by their size and the magnificence of their buildings.

CITY OF DAVID — the name of two cities in the Bible:

1. The stronghold of ZION, the fortified city of the Jebusites, later known as Jerusalem. King David and his men captured it (2 Sam. 5:7, 9).

2. Bethlehem, the birthplace or home of David (1 Sam. 16:1, 13; Luke 2:4, 11; John 7:42) and of Jesus, David's greatest descendant.

CLEAVE — cling to intently; become inseparable with one's mate (Gen. 2:24;25) and with God (Deut. 11:22).

CLOVEN — divided, split; usually in reference to an animal hoof (Deut. 14:7).

COLLECTION — money gathered for two distinctive purposes:

1. In the Old Testament, the word "collection" refers to a nonvoluntary religious tax collected from the people of Israel by the Levites (2 Chr. 24:6, 9). The Mosaic Law also referred to this tax as "ransom" (Ex. 30:12) and "atonement money" (Ex. 30:16).

2. In the New Testament, "collection" refers to a voluntary contribution gathered from the churches of Gentile territories for distribution to needy Christians in Jerusalem. In his letters to the churches at Corinth and Rome, the apostle Paul explained the need for this collection and encouraged the Gentile Christians to give liberally for this worthy cause (Rom. 15:25–27; 1 Cor. 16:1–4; 2 Cor. 8:1–15).

COLOSSE — a city in the Roman province of Asia (western Turkey), situated in the Lycus River Valley about 160 kilometers (100 miles) east of Ephesus. The apostle Paul wrote a letter to the church at Colosse (Col. 1:2; Colossae, NASB, REB, NRSV).

COLOSSIANS, EPISTLE TO THE — one of four shorter epistles written by Paul while he was in prison, the others being Philippians, Ephesians, and Philemon. The Epistle to the Colossians focuses on the person and work of Jesus Christ. It reaches heights of expression that rival anything said of Christ elsewhere in Scripture. Colossians shares many similarities in style and content with Ephesians. Colossians probably was written as a companion to the brief letter to Philemon (compare Col. 4:7–13 and Philem. 12, 24).

COMELINESS — beauty (Is. 53:2).

The mound of ancient Colosse, a city in Asia Minor where a church was established during the days of the apostle Paul. *Photo: Levant Photo Service*

COMMEND — to praise (Luke 16:8), entrust (Luke 23:46).

COMMUNION — sharing with an intimacy implied (1 Cor. 10:16). (see LORD'S SUPPER).

COMPASSION — feel along with another (Lam. 3:22).

CONCUBINE [con′-cue-bine] — in Old Testament times, a female slave or mistress with

COLOSSIANS:
A Study and Teaching Outline

Part One: Supremacy of Christ in the Church (1:1—2:23)

I. Introduction 1:1–14
   A. Paul's Greeting to the Colossians 1:1–2
   B. Paul's Thanksgiving for the Colossians 1:3–8
   C. Paul's Prayer for the Colossians 1:9–14
II. The Preeminence of Christ . . . . 1:15—2:3
   A. Christ Is Preeminent in Creation 1:15–18
   B. Christ Is Preeminent in Redemption 1:19–23
   C. Christ Is Preeminent in the Church . . . . 1:24—2:3
III. The Freedom in Christ 2:4–23
   A. Freedom from Enticing Words 2:4–7
   B. Freedom from Vain Philosophy 2:8–10
   C. Freedom from Human Judgment 2:11–17
   D. Freedom from Improper Worship 2:18–19
   E. Freedom from Human Doctrine 2:20–23

Part Two: Submission to Christ in the Church (3:1—4:18)

I. The Position of the Believer 3:1–4
II. The Practice of the Believer . . . . 3:5—4:6
   A. Put Off the Old Nature 3:5–11
   B. Put On the New Nature 3:12–17
   C. Personal Commands for Holiness . . . . . . 3:18—4:6
      1. Holiness in Family Life 3:18–21
      2. Holiness in Work Life . . . . 3:22—4:1
      3. Holiness in Public Life 4:2–6
III. Conclusion 4:7–18
   A. Commendation of Tychicus 4:7–9
   B. Greetings from Paul's Friends 4:10–14
   C. Various Matters Regarding the Epistle 4:15–18

whom a man was lawfully permitted to have sexual intercourse (Gen. 25:6).

CONDEMN, CONDEMNATION — to declare a person guilty and worthy of punishment. Condemn and condemnation are judicial terms, the opposite of Justify and JUSTIFICATION (Matt. 12:37; Rom. 5:16, 18). God alone is the judge of people; in His demand for righteousness, sin leads invariably to condemnation and death.

CONFESS — to admit (Matt. 3:6), proclaim, declare (Phil. 2:11).

CONFESSION — an admission of sins (1 John 1:9); the profession of belief in the doctrines of a particular faith. In the Bible most of the uses of the word "confession" fall into one of these two categories. Examples of confession of sin may be found in Joshua's words to Achan (Josh. 7:19), in the confession during the Passover during Hezekiah's reign (2 Chr. 30:22), and in Ezra's call to the people to admit wrongdoing in marrying pagan wives (Ezra 10:11).

The Bible also uses the word "confession" to describe an open, bold, and courageous proclamation of one's faith. The apostle Paul wrote: "If you confess with your mouth the Lord Jesus and believe in your heart that God has raised Him from the dead, you will be saved. For with the heart one believes to righteousness, and with the mouth confession is made to salvation" (Rom. 10:9–10).

CONFOUND — confuse (Gen. 11:7, 9).

CONGREGATION — a gathering or assembly of persons for worship and religious instruction; a religious community, such as the people of Israel or the Christian church (Acts 13:43).

CONGREGATION, MOUNT OF — the place where God is enthroned, whether in heaven or on earth (Is. 14:13; mount of assembly, NIV).

CONSCIENCE — a person's inner awareness of conforming to the will of God or departing from it, resulting in either a sense of approval or condemnation (Rom. 2:14–15).

CONSECRATE — to set apart for God's use (2 Chr. 29:31–33).

CONSECRATION — the act of setting apart, or dedicating, something or someone for God's use. In the Old Testament, the temple and its trappings were the most important objects consecrated to God (2 Chr. 7:5–9; Ezra 6:16–17); and Aaron and his sons were consecrated to the priesthood (Ex. 29; Lev. 8). But even such items as the spoils of battle (Josh. 6:19; Mic. 4:13) and cattle could be consecrated (Lev. 27:28). Before the beginning of the priesthood in Israel's history, the firstborn of men and animals alike were consecrated (Ex. 13:2). But after the priesthood began, the tribe of Levi served as a substitute in this consecration (Num. 3:12).

CONTENTMENT — freedom from anxiety or worry (1 Tim. 6:6). The idea of contentment comes from a Greek word that means "independence" or "self-sufficiency." But the apostle Paul used the word in a Christian sense to show that real satisfaction or sufficiency comes from God: "I can do all things through Christ who strengthens me" (Phil. 4:13).

CONTRITE — the kind of spirit, or heart, pleasing and acceptable to God (Ps. 34:18; crushed, NRSV, NIV, REB, NASB; Ps. 51:17). People who have a contrite spirit weep over wrongdoing and express genuine sorrow for their sins (see also Matt. 5:4; Luke 6:21; 2 Cor. 7:10).

CONVERSATION — communication from one person to another. The word is used only twice in the NKJV (Jer. 38:27; Luke 24:17). But conversation is used often in the KJV to describe one's conduct, behavior, or way of life. Thus, the writer of the Book of Hebrews declared, "Let your conversation be without covetousness" (Heb. 13:5, KJV).

CONVERSION, CONVERT — the initial change of attitude and will that brings a person into right relationship with God. The word "conversion" appears as a noun only once in the New

Testament, referring to the conversion of the Gentiles (Acts 15:3). But the Bible is filled with examples of persons who experienced conversion.

The fullest description of conversion occurs in the words spoken to Saul of Tarsus at his own conversion: "To open their eyes, and to turn them from darkness to light, and from the power of Satan to God, that they may receive forgiveness of sins and an inheritance among those who are sanctified by faith in me" (Acts 26:18).

Conversion involves turning away from evil deeds and false worship and turning toward serving and worshiping the Lord. Conversion marks a person's entrance into a new relationship with God, forgiveness of sins, and new life as a part of the fellowship of the people of God.

CONVICT OF SIN, CONVICTION — the process of being condemned by one's own conscience as a sinner because of God's demands. The idea of conviction is a major theme of Scripture, although the word is rarely used (Ps. 32; 51; Acts 2:37; Rom. 7:7–25). The agent of conviction is the Holy Spirit (John 16:7–11); and the means of conviction is either the Word of God (Acts 2:37) or God's general revelation of His demands through nature and people's inborn consciousness of a sense of right and wrong (Rom. 1:18–20; 2:15). The purpose of conviction is to lead people to repent of their sins (Acts 2:37–38; Rom. 2:1–4) and to turn to God for salvation and eternal life.

CORBAN [cor'-ban] *(an offering brought near)* — a word applied to a gift or offering in the temple that declared that gift dedicated to God in a special sense (Mark 7:11). Once a gift was offered under the special declaration of Corban, it could not be withdrawn or taken back; it was considered totally dedicated for the temple's special use.

CORINTH [cor'-inth] — ancient Greece's most important trade city (Acts 18:1; 19:1; 1 Cor. 1:2; 2 Cor. 1:1, 23; 2 Tim. 4:20). Ideally situated on the

The ruins of Corinth, one of the wealthiest and most immoral of ancient cities (1 Cor. 5:1; 6:9–11). *Photo by Gustav Jeeninga*

Isthmus of Corinth between the Ionian Sea and the Aegean Sea, Corinth was the connecting link between Rome, the capital of the world, and the East. At Corinth the apostle Paul established a flourishing church, made up of a cross section of the worldly minded people who had flocked to Corinth to participate in the gambling, legalized temple prostitution, business adventures, and amusements available in a first–century port city (1 Cor. 6:9–11).

FIRST CORINTHIANS:
A Study and Teaching Outline

Part One: In Answer to Chloe's Report of Divisions (1:1—4:21)

I.   Introduction 1:1–9
II. Report of Divisions 1:10–17
III. Reasons for Division . . . . 1:18—4:21
   A. Misunderstanding of the Gospel Message. . . . . 1:18—3:4
   B. Misunderstanding of the Gospel Messenger. . . . . 3:5—4:5
   C. Misunderstanding of Paul's Ministry 4:6–21

Part Two: In Answer to Reports of Immorality (5:1—6:20)

I.   On Incest . . . . 5:1—13
   A. Deliver the Fornicators for Discipline 5:1–8
   B. Separate Yourselves from Immoral Believers 5:9–13
II. Concerning Litigation Between Believers 6:1–11
III. Warning Against Sexual Immorality 6:12–20

Part Three: In Answer to the Letter of Questions (7:1—16:24)

I.   Counsel Concerning Marriage. 7:1–40
   A. Principles for Married Life. 7:1–9
   B. Principles for the Married Believer 7:10–16
   C. Principle of Abiding in God's Call 7:17–24
   D. Principles for the Unmarried 7:25–38
   E. Principles for Remarriage 7:39–40
II. Counsel Concerning Spiritual Liberty. . . . . . 8:1—11:1
   A. Principles of Liberty and the Weaker Believer 8:1–13
   B. Illustration of Paul and His Liberty 9:1–27
   C. Warning Against Forfeiting Liberty 10:1–13
   D. Exhortation to Use Liberty to Glorify God . . . . 10:14—11:1
III. Counsel Concerning Public Worship . . . . 11:2—14:40
   A. Principles of Public Prayer. 11:2–16
   B. Rebuke of Disorders at the Lord's Supper. 11:17–34
   C. Principles of Exercising Spiritual Gifts . . . . 12:1—14:40
IV. Counsel Concerning the Resurrection 15:1–58
   A. Fact of Christ's Resurrection 15:1–11
   B. Importance of Christ's Resurrection 15:12–19
   C. Order of the Resurrections. 15:20–28
   D. Moral Implications of Christ's Resurrection 15:29–34
   E. Bodies of the Resurrected Dead 15:35–50
   F. Bodies of the Translated Living 15:51–58
V.   Counsel Concerning the Collection for Jerusalem. 16:1–4
VI. Conclusion 16:5–24

CORINTHIANS, EPISTLES TO THE — two letters of the apostle Paul addressed to the church in Corinth. First Corinthians is unique among the Pauline letters because of the variety of its practical concerns. Second Corinthians is one of Paul's most personal letters, containing a wealth of insights into the heart of Paul the pastor. Both letters reveal the degree to which Paul identified with his churches, suffering in their shortcomings and celebrating their victories. The

SECOND CORINTHIANS:
A Study and Teaching Outline

Part One: Paul's Explanation of His Ministry (1:1—7:16)

I. Introduction 1:1–11
II. Paul's Explanation of His Change
    of Plans . . . . 1:12—2:13
    A. Paul's Original Plan 1:12–22
    B. Paul's Change of Plans . . . . 1:23—2:4
    C. Paul's Appeal to Forgive 2:5–13
III. Paul's Philosophy of Ministry . . . . 2:14—6:10
    A. Christ Causes Us to Triumph 2:14–17
    B. Changed Lives Prove Ministry 3:1–5
    C. New Covenant Is the Basis of Ministry 3:6–18
    D. Christ Is the Theme of Ministry 4:1–7
    E. Trials Abound in Ministry 4:8–15
    F. Motivation in Ministry . . . . 4:16—5:21
    G. Giving No Offense in Ministry 6:1–10
IV. Paul's Exhortations to the Corinthians . . . . 6:11—7:16
    A. Paul's Appeal for Reconciliation 6:11–13
    B. Paul's Appeal for Separation from
       Unbelievers . . . . 6:14—7:1
    C. Paul's Meeting with Titus 7:2–7
    D. Corinthians' Response to Paul's Letter 7:8–16

Part Two: Paul's Collection for the Saints (8:1—9:15)

I. Example of the Macedonians 8:1–6
II. Exhortation to the Corinthians . . . . 8:7—9:15
    A. Example of Christ 8:7–9
    B. Purpose of Giving 8:10–15
    C. Explanation of the Delegation . . . . 8:16—9:5
    D. Exhortation to Giving 9:6–15

Part Three: Paul's Vindication of His Apostleship (10:1—13:14)

I. Paul Answers His Accusers 10:1–18
    A. The Charge of Cowardice Is Answered 10:1–2
    B. The Charge of Worldliness Is Answered 10:3–9
    C. The Charge of Personal Weakness Is
       Answered 10:10–18
II. Paul Defends His Apostleship . . . . 11:1—12:13
    A. Paul's Declaration of His Apostleship 11:1–15
    B. Paul's Sufferings Support His
       Apostleship 11:16–33
    C. Paul's Revelations Support His
       Apostleship 12:1–10
    D. Paul's Signs Support His Apostleship 12:11–13
III. Paul Announces His Forthcoming Visit . . 12:14—13:10
    A. Paul's Concern Not to Be a Financial
       Burden 12:14–18
    B. Paul's Concern Not to Find Them
       Carnal 12:19–21
    C. Paul's Warning to Examine Themselves . . . 13:1–10
IV. Conclusion 13:11–14

Corinthian correspondence draws us into a world much like our own. Paul the anxious pastor wrote to young Christians who were concerned with problems involved in living the Christian life in a non-Christian environment.

First and Second Corinthians bear unmistakable marks of Pauline authorship (1 Cor. 1:1; 2 Cor. 2:1). The first epistle was written from Ephesus (1 Cor. 16:8) during Paul's third missionary journey, perhaps in A.D. 56. The second letter followed some 12 to 15 months later from Macedonia, where Paul met Titus and received news of the church's repentance (2 Cor. 2:12–17).

The problems Paul faced in the church at Corinth were complex and explosive. The correspondence that resulted is rich and profound in theological insight. While addressing the problems in Corinth, the apostle reaches some of the most sublime heights in all New Testament literature.

CORRUPTIBLE, CORRUPTION — perishable, (Rom. 1:23), decay of the body (Acts 2:27, 31) and degradation of human life through the power of sin (2 Pet. 1:4). But because of the Resurrection of Christ our bodies, sown in corruption (subject to the decay and dissolution of organic matter), will be raised in incorruption (1 Cor. 15:42, 50–54).

COUNCIL — an assembly of people who meet to discuss important matters and to make decisions (Acts 25:12). The Greek words usually translated as council can refer to the place where a council meets, the group itself, or the meeting. In the New Testament, council is a technical term that often refers to the supreme Jewish council, the SANHEDRIN.

COUNSEL — as a verb, to advise (John 18:14), as a noun, advice (Dan. 4:27).

COUNSELOR — one who gives counsel or advises (Prov. 11:14), especially the king's adviser (2 Sam. 15:12; 1 Chr. 27:33), or one of the chief men of the government (Job 3:14; Is. 1:26). In Mark 15:43 (KJV) and Luke 23:50 (KJV), the word designates a "council member" (of the SANHEDRIN).

The HOLY SPIRIT is also called "the Counselor" in the NRSV and NIV (John 14:16, 26; 15:26; 16:7).

COUNTENANCE — look, appearance (1 Sam. 16:7), honor (Ex. 23:3).

COURAGE — the strength of purpose that enables one to withstand fear or difficulty. Physical courage is based on moral courage—a reliance on the presence and power of God and a commitment to His commandments (Josh. 1:6–7, 9, 18; 23:6; 2 Chr. 19:11).

COVENANT — an agreement between two people or two groups that involves promises on the part of each to the other. The Hebrew word for "covenant" probably means "betweenness," emphasizing the relational element that lies at the basis of all covenants. Human covenants or treaties were either between equals or between a superior and an inferior. Divine covenants, however, are always of the latter type, and the concept of covenant between God and His people is one of the most important theological truths of the Bible. Indeed, the word itself has come to denote the two main divisions of Christian Scripture: Old Covenant and New Covenant (traditionally, Old Testament and New Testament).

COVERING THE HEAD — the practice among women of wearing a head covering in early Christian worship services. The apostle Paul argued that a woman participating in the services ought to have her head covered (1 Cor. 11:5–16).

According to Paul, it was a "symbol of authority" (1 Cor. 11:10). The Christian woman had received a new freedom and spiritual authority from Christ (Gal. 3:28). Thus she was able to pray and prophesy in the services. By wearing the head covering, however, she would show that her authority had come from God; she had not seized it herself. Without the covering she might offend recent Jewish converts or others who held to the ancient tradition that women ought to always have their heads covered in public as a sign of modesty.

COVETOUSNESS — an intense desire to possess something (or someone) that belongs to another person. The Ten Commandments prohibit this attitude (Ex. 20:17; Deut. 5:21). Covetousness springs from a greedy self-centeredness and an arrogant disregard of God's Law. The Bible repeatedly warns against this sin (Josh. 7:21; Rom. 7:7; 2 Pet. 2:10).

CREATE, CREATION — God's action in bringing the natural universe into being. The writer of the Epistle to the Hebrews in the New Testament declared, "By faith we understand that the world was framed by the word of God, so that the things which are seen were not made of things which are visible" (Heb. 11:3).

CREATURE — any created being, humans included, brought into existence as a result of God's power and authority. The Bible declares that the Redeemer God is the sovereign Creator of all things. Through His might and power He brought the universe into existence (Gen. 1:3–24; Ps. 33:6; Heb. 11:3). Therefore, all beings, even angels, are His creatures (John 1:3; 1 Cor. 8:6). The creaturely status of all finite beings and things reveals the sovereign rule of God and the dependence of humankind and the world on Him.

CRIMSON — bold red color, also symbolizes sin (Is. 1:18).

CROSS — an upright wooden stake or post on which condemned people were executed (John 19:17). Before the manner of Jesus' death caused the cross to symbolize the very heart of the Christian faith, the Greek word for cross referred primarily to a pointed stake used in rows to form the walls of a defensive stockade.

CROWN OF THORNS — a mock symbol of authority fashioned by the Roman soldiers and

God the Creator, from a painting by Michelangelo in the Sistine Chapel in Rome. *Photo by Howard Vos*

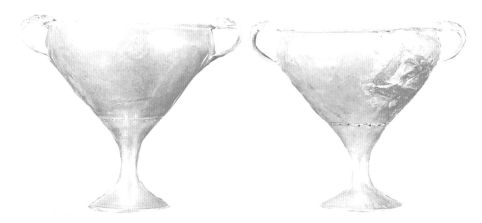

Gold cups discovered by archaeologists in tombs at the ancient city of Mycene on the island of Crete. *Photo by Howard Vos*

placed on Jesus' head shortly before His Crucifixion (Matt. 27:29; Mark 15:17; John 19:2, 5). Crowns were symbols of honor and authority in the Greek and Roman worlds. Jesus' crown of thorns was probably meant to make Him an object of mockery and ridicule. "Hail, King of the Jews!" (Matt. 27:29; Mark 15:18; John 19:2) they scoffed, as they engaged in their cruel and brutal sport. But Jesus' love was so strong that He patiently endured this mockery to accomplish His mission on earth.

CRUCIFIXION — the method of torture and execution used by the Romans to put Christ to death. At a crucifixion the victim usually was nailed or tied to a wooden stake and left to die.

CUBIT — the distance from the elbow to the fingertip—about 45 centimeters (18 inches) (Gen. 6:15). (see WEIGHTS AND MEASURES).

CUMMIN — plant used for seasoning (Is. 28:25, 27).

CUP — a small container used for drinking water (Matt. 10:42), wine (Jer. 35:5), and other liquids. The cup is spoken of often in the Bible in a literal sense. Figuratively, the image of a cup also expresses several important ideas.

D

DAGON [day'-gun] — pagan god of the Philistines (Judg. 16:23–30).

DAMASCUS [da-mas'-cus] — the oldest continually inhabited city in the world and capital of Syria (Is. 7:8), located northeast of the Sea of Galilee.

DAN *(a judge)* — the name of a man and a city in Israel named after him:

1. The fifth son of Jacob and the first born to Rachel's handmaid Bilhah (Gen. 30:1–6).

2. A city in the northern territory of the tribe of Dan identified as the modern ruin or archaeological site known as Tell el-Qadi. This city was located farther north than any other village in Israel during much of the Old Testament period. This explains the phrase, "from Dan to Beersheba" (Judg. 20:1), used to describe the entire territory of the Israelites from north to south.

DANIEL *(God is my judge)* — the name of three or four men in the Bible:

An altar for pagan worship at the city of Dan. Portions of the altar were constructed by King Ahab of Israel. *Photo by Howard Vos*

DANIEL:
A Study and Teaching Outline

Part One: The Personal History of Daniel (1:1–21)

I. Daniel Carried Away to Babylon 1:1–7
II. The Faithfulness of Daniel in Babylon 1:8–16
III. Daniel's Reputation in Babylon 1:17–21

**Part Two:
The Prophetic Plan
for the Gentiles
(2:1—7:28)**

I. Nebuchadnezzar's Dream. 2:1–49
   A. Nebuchadnezzar Conceals His Dream. 2:1–13
   B. God Reveals the Dream. 2:14–23
   C. Daniel Interprets the Dream 2:24–45
   D. Nebuchadnezzar Promotes Daniel. 2:46–49
II. Nebuchadnezzar's Image of Gold 3:1–30
   A. Nebuchadnezzar's Image is Set Up 3:1–7
   B. Daniel's Friends Refuse to Worship. 3:8–12
   C. Daniel's Friends Trust God 3:13–18
   D. Daniel's Friends Are Protected in the
      Furnace. 3:19–25
   E. Daniel's Friends Are Promoted 3:26–30
III. Nebuchadnezzar's Vision of a Great Tree. 4:1–37
   A. Nebuchadnezzar's Proclamation 4:1–3
   B. Nebuchadnezzar's Vision. 4:4–18
   C. Daniel's Interpretation of the Vision 4:19–27
   D. Nebuchadnezzar's Humiliation 4:28–33
   E. Nebuchadnezzar's Restoration 4:34–37
IV. Belshazzar and the Handwriting on the Wall . . 5:1–31
   A. Belshazzar Defiles the Temple Vessels. 5:1–4
   B. Belshazzar Sees the Handwriting 5:5–9
   C. Daniel Interprets the Handwriting 5:10–29
   D. Belshazzar Is Killed. 5:30–31
V. Darius' Decrees 6:1–28
   A. Daniel Is Promoted 6:1–3
   B. Darius Signs a Foolish Decree 6:4–9
   C. Daniel Prays Faithfully 6:10–15
   D. Daniel in the Lion's Den 6:16–17
   E. Daniel Is Saved from the Lions 6:18–24
   F. Darius' Wise Decree 6:25–28
VI. Daniel's Vision of the Four Beasts. 7:1–28
   A. The Revelation of the Vision 7:1–14
   B. The Interpretation of the Vision 7:15–28

**Part Three:
The Prophetic Plan
for Israel
(8:1—12:13)**

I. Daniel's Vision of the Ram and Male Goat 8:1–27
   A. The Revelation of the Vision 8:1–12
   B. The Length of the Vision. 8:13–14
   C. The Interpretation of the Vision 8:15–27
II. Daniel's Vision of the Seventy Weeks 9:1–27
   A. The Understanding of Daniel 9:1–2
   B. The Intercession of Daniel 9:3–19
   C. The Intervention of Gabriel. 9:20–23
   D. The Revelation of the Seventy Weeks 9:24–27
III. Daniel's Vision of Israel's Future . . . . 10:1—12:13
   A. The Preparation of Daniel 10:1–21
   B. The Kings of the South and North 11:1–35
   C. The King Who Magnifies Himself. . . . 11:36—12:3
   D. The Conclusion of the Visions of Daniel . . 12:4–13

1. A son of David and Abigail (1 Chr. 3:1). He is also called Chileab (2 Sam. 3:3).

2. A priest of the family of Ithamar who returned with Ezra from the Captivity (Ezra 8:2). Daniel sealed the covenant in the days of Nehemiah (Neh. 10:6).

3. A wise (Ezek. 28:3) and righteous man (perhaps non-Israelite), mentioned together with Noah and Job (Ezek. 14:14, 20), to be identified with an ancient Canaanite worthy named Daniel or equated with No. 4.

4. A prophet during the period of the Captivity of God's covenant people in Babylon and Persia (Dan. 1:6–12:9; Matt. 24:15). Daniel is the central figure in the book in the Old Testament that bears his name.

DANIEL, BOOK OF — a major prophetic book of the Old Testament that emphasizes the truth that God is in control of world history. The book is named for Daniel, its central personality, who was rescued miraculously from a den of lions after he refused to bow down and worship a pagan king.

The Book of Daniel belongs to that period among God's covenant people known as the Babylonian CAPTIVITY. Nebuchadnezzar took captives from Judah on four separate occasions, beginning in 605 B.C. Among this first group taken were Daniel and his companions. Their courageous acts must have been a great encouragement to the other captives.

The major contribution of the Book of Daniel arises from its nature as apocalyptic prophecy. Highly symbolic in language, the prophecy was related to the events of Daniel's near future, but even today it contains a message for the future.

DARIUS [da-ri'-us] — the name of several rulers of ancient Persia such as Darius I, the Great, who reigned from about 522 to 485 B.C., Darius II Ochus, the son of Artaxerxes I, who ruled over Persia from about 424 to 405 B.C. (Neh. 12:22), and Darius III Codomannus, the king of Persia from 336 to 330 B.C. This Darius is probably the "fourth" king of Persia mentioned by the prophet Daniel (Dan. 11:2).

Tombs of Darius I and Artaxerxes I at the royal city of Persepolis in ancient Persia.
Photo by Howard Vos

DARKNESS — the absence of light. Darkness existed before the light of creation (Gen. 1:2). Since darkness was associated with the chaos that existed before the creation, it came to be associated with evil, bad luck, or affliction (Job 17:12; 21:17). Darkness was also equated with death. In SHEOL, the land of the dead, there is only darkness (Job 10:21–22; 38:17). Darkness symbolizes human ignorance of God's will and, thus, is associated with sin (Job 24:13–17).

Darkness also describes the condition of those who have not yet seen the light concerning Jesus (John 1:4–5; 12:35; Eph. 5:14) and those who deliberately turn away from the light (John 3:19–20). Hating the light will bring condemnation (Col. 1:13; 2 Pet. 2:17). Living in extreme darkness describes those who at the end of time have not repented (Rev. 16:10; 18:23).

DAUGHTER — the female offspring of a husband and wife. The term "daughter" is also used in the Bible to designate a stepsister, niece, or any female descendant (Gen. 20:12; 24:48; granddaughter, NIV). Sometimes the word is used in an even more general sense to refer to the female branch of a family or the female portion of a community (Is. 23:10, 12), as in "the daughters of Levi" (Num. 26:59; descendant, NIV).

DAVID *(beloved)* — second king of the United Kingdom of Israel, ancestor of Jesus Christ, and

David's Triumphs

David was a man after God's own heart (1 Sam. 13:14), that is, his will was completely committed to the will of his Lord. As a dedicated servant of God, he was used by God to perform mighty acts for the sake of His chosen people Israel.	King of Judah (2:4) King of Israel (5:3) Conquers Jerusalem (5:7) Returns ark (6:12) Davidic covenant (7:16) Defeats Philistines (8:1) Defeats Moab (8:2) Defeats Ammon (10:16) Defeats Syria (10:19)

David's Troubles

Causes	Effects
Adultery (11:4)	Bathsheba bears a son (11:5)
Murder of Uriah (11:17)	Accused, repents, but the child dies (12:10, 13, 19)
Amnon's incest (13:14)	Amnon murdered (13:28, 29)
Absalom usurps throne (16:15, 16)	Absalom murdered (18:14, 15)
The census (24:2)	Plague (24:15)
Consistently illustrated in the life of David's household is the principle that a disobedient life is a troubled life.	

Oasis at En Gedi where David hid from King Saul during his years as a fugitive (1 Sam. 23:29; 24:1). *Photo by Howard Vos*

writer of numerous psalms. The record of David's life is found in 1 Samuel 16—31; 2 Samuel 1—24; 1 Kings 1—2; and 1 Chronicles 10—29. An Aramaic inscription including the words "house [dynasty] of David" was found in 1993 in the ruins of the city of Dan. It dates to the 9th century B.C. and is the only known mention of David in ancient contemporary writings outside of the Old Testament itself.

DAY OF THE LORD, THE — a special day at the end of time when God's will and purpose for humanity and His world will be fulfilled (Phil. 1:6, 10). Many Bible students believe the Day of the Lord will be a long period of time rather than a single day—a period when Christ will reign throughout the world before He cleanses heaven and earth in preparation for the eternal state of all mankind. But others believe the Day of the Lord will be an instantaneous event when Christ will return to earth to claim His faithful believers while consigning unbelievers to eternal damnation.

DEACON — a servant or minister; an ordained lay officer in many Christian churches (1 Tim. 3:8–13).

DEAD SEA — a large lake in southern Israel at the lowest point on earth. In the Old Testament it is called the Salt Sea (Gen. 14:3; Josh. 3:16); the Sea of the Arabah (Deut. 3:17); and the Eastern Sea (Ezek. 47:18; Joel 2:20).

DEAD SEA SCROLLS — the popular name for about 800 scrolls and fragments of scrolls that were found in 11 caves near Khirbet ("ruin of") QUMRAN on the northwest shore of the Dead Sea in 1947 and shortly thereafter. Taken together, these leather and PAPYRUS (primitive paper) manuscripts were a find without precedent in the history of modern archaeology. The Dead Sea Scrolls have helped scholars to: (1) establish the date of a Hebrew Bible no later than A.D. 70; (2) reconstruct various details of the history of the Holy Land from the fourth century B.C. to A.D.

135; and (3) clarify the relationship between Jewish religious traditions and early Christianity.

DEATH — a term that, when applied to the lower orders of living things such as plants and animals, means the end of life. With reference to human beings, however, death is not the end of life. The Bible teaches that we are more than physical creatures; we are also spiritual beings. For humans, therefore, physical death does not mean the end of existence but the end of life as we know it and the transition to another dimension in which our conscious existence continues (Matt. 25:46; 1 John 3:14; Rom. 6:4–8; Rev. 20:6).

DEBAUCHERY — bad behavior including drunkenness and lust (Gal. 5:19; 1 Pet. 4:13, NIV).

DEBORAH [deb'-o-rah] *(bee)* — the name of two women in the Old Testament:

1. A nurse to Rebekah, Isaac's wife (Gen. 24:59; 35:8). Deborah accompanied Rebekah when she left her home in Mesopotamia to become Isaac's wife and lived with Jacob and Rebekah. She probably spent her years caring for their sons, Jacob and Esau. Deborah died at an advanced age. She was buried below Bethel under a tree that Jacob called Allon Bachuth (literally "oak of weeping")—a fitting name for the burial place of one who had served so long and so faithfully (Gen. 35:8).

2. The fifth judge of Israel, a prophetess and the only female judge (Judg. 4–5).

DECAPOLIS [de-cap'-o-lis] *(ten cities)* — a district of northern Palestine, with a large Greek population, mostly on the east side of the Jordan River and embracing ten cities. Early in his ministry, Jesus was followed by "great multitudes," including people from Decapolis (Matt. 4:25). When Jesus healed the demon-possessed man from GADARA, he "began to proclaim in Decapolis all that Jesus had done for him" (Mark 5:20). Later, Jesus traveled through the midst of the region (Mark 7:31).

DECREE — an official order, command, or edict issued by a king or other person of authority. The decrees of kings were often delivered to distant towns or cities by messengers and publicly announced at city gates or other public places (Ezra 1:1; Amos 4:5). The Bible also refers to God's decrees, universal laws or rules to which the entire world is subject (Ps. 148:6).

DEDICATE, DEDICATION — set apart, make holy (Eph. 5:26); a religious ceremony in which a person or a thing is set aside or consecrated to God's service. In Bible times, many different things were included in such services: the temple (2 Chr. 2:4), a field (Lev. 27:16), a house (Lev. 27:14), articles of precious metal (2 Sam. 8:10), even spoils won in battle (1 Chr. 26:27).

In one of the most beautiful passages in the Bible, Hannah presented her young son Samuel to God in an act of child dedication (1 Sam. 1:19–28). Hannah's prayer of thanksgiving to God (1 Sam. 2:1–10) is a model of praise and dedication for all who seek to honor God through their lives.

DEDICATION, FEAST OF — This feast, also known as Hanukkah and the Feast of Lights, is mentioned only once in the Bible (John 10:22). It celebrated the cleansing of the temple in 165 B.C. after its desecration by Antiochus Epiphanes. The Feast of Dedication is observed on the 25th day of the ninth month.

DEEP, THE — a vast space, expanse, or abyss. The term is used in Scripture in several ways. The first use occurs in Genesis 1:2: "The earth was without form, and void; and darkness was on the face of the deep" (Gen. 1:2). The term is elsewhere used to refer to the oceans and to the volume of water that burst forth at the Flood (Gen. 7:11; 8:2). Jonah spoke of God's casting him "into the deep" (Jon. 2:3), or the Mediterranean Sea.

The deep also refers to the ABYSS, the abode of the dead (Rom. 10:7) and evil spirits (Luke 8:31; Rev. 9:1–2, 11; 20:1). All of these references to the "bottomless pit" translate a Greek word for unfathomable depth.

Figuratively, the deep means that which is profound or mighty: the great judgments of God (Ps. 36:6; 92:5; Rom. 11:33) or the "deep things of God" (1 Cor. 2:10).

DEFILE — to make unclean or impure. At least five types of defilement are mentioned in the Old Testament: (1) ceremonial (Lev. 15:19); (2) ethical (Ezek. 37:23); (3) physical (Song 5:3); (4) religious (Jer. 3:1); and (5) sexual (Lev. 15:24). The purpose of the Old Testament laws about defilement was to preserve the holiness of God's chosen people. But these laws became a legalistic system that emphasized ceremonial cleanliness while ignoring spiritual purity. Jesus reversed this situation by emphasizing the need for moral purity and ethical living (Mark 7:1–23).

DEITY — a god, also God.

DELILAH [de-li′-lah] — the woman loved by Samson, the mightiest of Israel's judges. She was probably a Philistine. She betrayed Samson to the lords of the Philistines for 1,100 pieces of silver (Judg. 16:5). Deluding Samson into believing she loved him, Delilah persuaded him to tell her the secret of his strength—his long hair, which was the symbol of his Nazirite vow. While Samson slept at her home in the Valley of Sorek, the Philistines entered and cut his hair. With his strength gone, Samson was easily captured and imprisoned, then blinded.

DEMAS [de′-mas] — a friend and coworker of the apostle Paul at Rome. Demas later deserted Paul, "having loved this present world" (2 Tim. 4:10; Col. 4:14; Philem. 24).

DEMETRIUS [dah-me′-tre-us] — the name of two men in the New Testament:

1. A silversmith at Ephesus (Acts 19:24, 38) who made and sold silver models of the city's famed temple of the goddess Diana (Artemis). Alarmed at what the spread of the gospel would do to his business, Demetrius incited a riot against the apostle Paul. For two hours, the mob cried, "Great is Diana of the Ephesians!" (Acts

19:28, 34). The mob was quieted by the city clerk (Acts 19:35–40). Later, Paul left Ephesus for Macedonia (Acts 20:1).

2. A Christian commended by John because he had "a good testimony from all" (3 John 12).

DEMONIAC — a person who is possessed by demons (Matt. 8:22–33; Mark 5:15–16).

DEMONS — another name for fallen angels who joined the kingdom of Satan in rebellion against God (Luke 10:17).

DENARIUS [de-nar′-e-us] — silver coin (Matt. 20:1–16). (see MONEY OF THE BIBLE).

DENY — to be untrue or to disown. This word is used often in the Bible to express one's faithfulness to God or Christ. A person may deny God in word or deed. Denial in word often involves disowning or rejecting a relationship with, or knowledge of, God or Christ (Josh. 24:27; Matt. 10:33; 2 Pet. 2:1). Denial in deed especially refers to withholding something from someone (Prov. 30:7; 1 Tim. 5:8). It may even refer to self-denial—abstaining from the pleasures of the world for the sake of Christ (Matt. 16:24).

DERBE [der′-by] — a city in the southeastern part of Lycaonia, a province of Asia Minor, to which Paul and Barnabas retreated when driven from Lystra (Acts 14:6–20), while on their first missionary journey. Paul also visited Derbe on his second missionary journey (Acts 16:1). Derbe is twice mentioned with Lystra; it was situated southeast of that city (Acts 14:6; 16:1).

DESOLATE — deserted, unoccupied (Jer. 33:12).

DEUTERONOMY, BOOK OF — an Old Testament book commonly identified as the farewell speech of Moses to the people of Israel just before his death. The title of the book, from the Greek word *Deuteronomion*, means "second law" and comes from the SEPTUAGINT text of Deuteronomy 17:18 ("a copy of this law"). In his

The unexcavated mound of Derbe, a city visited by the apostle Paul (Acts 14:20; 16:1).
Photo by Howard Vos

address, Moses underscored and repeated many of the laws of God that the people received at Mount Sinai about 40 years earlier. He also challenged the people to remain faithful to their God and His commands as they prepared to enter the Promised Land.

Some people look upon the laws of God in the Old Testament as burdensome and restrictive. The Book of Deuteronomy, however, teaches that God's Laws are given for our own good to help us stay close to Him in our attitudes and behavior. Thus, Moses called on the people to keep God's statutes, "which I command you today for your good" (10:13). The intention of God's Law is positive; passages in the New Testament that seem to condemn the law must be interpreted in this light. It is the misuse of the law—trusting it rather than God's mercy as the basis of our salvation—that we should avoid. God's Law is actually fulfilled in the person of our Lord and Savior Jesus Christ (Matt. 5:17, 20).

DEVICE — thought (Prov. 19:21).

DEVIL *(accuser, slanderer)* — the main title for the fallen angelic being who is the supreme en-

emy of God and humankind (1 Cor. 10:20). Satan is his most common name, and devil is what he is—the accuser or deceiver. The term comes from a Greek word that means "a false witness" or "malicious accuser."

DIADEM [di´-a-dem] — a band or wrapping around the turban of a king or his queen signifying royal authority. Rulers of the ancient Near East did not wear rigid gold crowns but cloth turbans wound around the head and decorated in turn with cloth diadems studded with gems. The New Testament also makes a clear distinction between a diadem and a CROWN. A crown was a garland or a wreath awarded for faithfulness in service, such as a crown of righteousness (2 Tim. 4:8), while a diadem always symbolized royal authority.

DIDYMUS [did´-ih-mus] *(twin)* — the Greek name of THOMAS, one of the twelve disciples of Christ (John 11:16; 20:24; 21:2).

DISCERN — determine good from bad (Job 6:30; Heb. 5:14).

DISCIPLE — a student, learner, or pupil. In the Bible the word is used most often to refer to a fol-

DEUTERONOMY:
A Study and Teaching Outline

Part One: Moses' First Speech
What God Has Done for Israel (1:1—4:43)

I. Preamble of the Covenant 1:1–5
II. Historical Review of God's Acts for Israel . . . 1:6—4:43
    A. From Mount Sinai to Kadesh Barnea 1:6–18
    B. At Kadesh Barnea 1:19–46
    C. From Kadesh Barnea to Moab 2:1–23
    D. Conquest of Transjordan . . . . 2:24—3:20
    E. Change of Leadership 3:21–29
    F. Summary of the Covenant 4:1–43

Part Two: Moses' Second Speech
What God Expects of Israel (4:44—26:19)

I. Introduction to the Law of God 4:44–49
II. Explanation of the Covenant Stipulations . . 5:1—11:32
    A. The Covenant of the Great King 5:1–33
    B. The Command to Teach the Law 6:1–25
    C. The Command to Conquer Canaan 7:1–26
    D. The Command to Remember the Lord 8:1–20
    E. Commands about Self-Righteousness . . . . 9:1—10:11
    F. Commands Regarding Blessings and Cursings . . . . 10:12—11:32
III. Explanation of the Additional Laws . . . . . . 12:1—26:19
    A. Explanation of the Ceremonial Laws . . . . 12:1—16:17
    B. Explanation of the Civil Laws . . . . . . 16:18—20:20
    C. Explanation of the Social Laws . . . . . . 21:1—26:19

Part Three: Moses' Third Speech
What God Will Do for Israel (27:1—34:12)

I. Confirming the Covenant . . . . 27:1—28:68
II. Establishing the Covenant . . . . 29:1—30:20
III. Changing the Covenant Mediator . . . . 31:1—34:12
    A. Moses Charges Joshua and Israel 31:1–13
    B. God Charges Israel 31:14–21
    C. The Book of the Law Is Deposited 31:22–29
    D. The Song of Moses . . . . 31:30—32:47
    E. The Death of Moses . . . . 32:48—34:12
        1. Moses Is Ordered to Mount Nebo . . . 32:48–52
        2. Moses Blesses the Tribes 33:1–29
        3. Moses Views the Promised Land 34:1–4
        4. Moses Dies and Is Mourned 34:5–8
        5. Moses Is Replaced by Joshua 34:9
        6. Moses Is Praised in Israel 34:10–12

lower of Jesus. The word is rarely used in the Old Testament. Isaiah used the term "disciples" to refer to those who are taught or instructed (Is. 8:16).

DISCIPLESHIP — the life and training of a disciple.

DISCIPLINE — to train by instruction and control (1 Cor. 9:27). The biblical concept of discipline has both a positive side (instruction, knowledge, and training) and a negative aspect (correction, punishment, and reproof). Those who refuse to submit to God's positive discipline by obeying His laws will experience God's negative discipline through His wrath and judgment.

DISOBEDIENCE — unwillingness to comply with the guidance of authority, especially refusal to follow God's will. The first and most crucial act of disobedience occurred when Adam and Eve ate of the forbidden fruit (Genesis 3). Like all later human disobedience, that act involved setting the desire of the flesh above the will of God. As a result of this, all people became "sons of disobedience" (Eph. 2:2). Christians have no choice, therefore, but to engage in a kind of spiritual warfare against their own natural tendency to disobey God (2 Cor. 10:5–6). They should aim to be as obedient to God's will as Christ was when He "became obedient to the point of death" (Phil. 2:8).

DISPENSATION — a period of time under which mankind is answerable to God for how it has obeyed the revelation of God that it has received. The term "dispensation" is found twice in the NKJV: "The dispensation of the fullness of the times" (Eph. 1:10) and "the dispensation of the grace of God" (Eph. 3:2; administration, NIV). The KJV uses the term four times (1 Cor. 9:17; Eph. 1:10; 3:2; Col. 1:25).

DISPERSE — scatter, spread (Prov. 15:7; Ezek. 12:15).

DISPERSION — a scattering of the Jewish people among other nations. Throughout their history, the Hebrew people have experienced many dispersions—a term which comes from a Greek word meaning "to scatter." Some of these dispersions have been voluntary, while others have been forced upon them.

DIVERS — various (Mark 1:34 KJV).

DIVINATION — fortune-telling (Deut. 18:10; Ezek. 21:21; Acts 16:16).

DIVINE — of or relating to God (Heb. 9:1).

DIVORCE — the legal dissolution of a marriage (Deut. 24:1–4).

DOCTRINE — a body of beliefs about God, humankind, Christ, the church, and other related concepts considered authoritative and thus worthy of acceptance by all members of the community of faith (Prov. 4:2).

DOMINION — rule (Gen. 1:26).

DOOM — calamity (Deut. 32:35).

DOOR — the covering over an entrance into a tent (Gen. 18:1), a permanent house (Judg. 19:22), or a public building (Ezek. 47:1). The doors of Bible times were made of a wide variety of material, ranging from animal hides to wood and metal. Doors are also spoken of symbolically in the Bible. In speaking of Himself as the Good Shepherd, Jesus declared, "I am the door of the sheep" (John 10:7).

DOORKEEPER — a guard, not military (Ps. 84:10).

DOORPOSTS — the two sides of a doorway, similar to a doorframe. The Hebrews were ordered by the Lord to spread the blood of a sacrificial lamb on the doorposts of their houses during the PASSOVER while in captivity in Egypt. This was a sign of their loyalty to the Lord; it also was a sign for the destroying angel to pass over the houses of the Hebrews when the firstborn of Egypt were killed in the tenth and final plague that struck the land (Ex. 12:7). The Hebrews were later told to write sacred words on the doorposts of their houses as a reminder of God's commands (Deut. 6:9; 11:20).

DORCAS [dor'-cas] *(gazelle)* — a Christian woman from Joppa known for befriending and helping the poor (Acts 9:36–43); Tabitha was her Aramaic name (it also means "gazelle"). She was raised from the dead by the apostle Peter. The Bible tells us little about her background, but it is possible that she was a woman of some wealth, or at least had connections with the wealthy. Dorcas may well have been one of the early converts of Philip the evangelist, who established a Christian church at Joppa.

DOUBLE-TONGUED — without integrity (1 Tim. 3:8).

DOVE — small bird used for sacrifice (John 2:14).

DOWRY — a gift given to the father of one's bride. In the ancient world, when a man married, he was expected to give something to the woman's father. This was not considered a payment or a purchase price for a wife, but compensation to the father for the loss of her help as a daughter. The dowry could be money or goods (Gen. 34:12; Ex. 22:16–17), service to make up for the loss (Gen. 29:15–30), or the performance of some assigned task (1 Sam. 18:25–27; Judg. 1:12). Through the trickery of Laban, JACOB was forced to give 14 years of labor as a dowry for Laban's daughter, Rachel (Gen. 29:15–30).

DOXOLOGY — a declaration of praise to God or a brief hymn expressing His power and glory. The word itself does not appear in the Bible, but the concept is certainly present. Several passages in the Bible are called doxologies because of their clear declaration of praise to God.

DRACHMA [drock'-ma] — silver coin similar to a Roman denarius, not mentioned in KJV.

DREAD — fear (1 Chr. 22:13).

DREAM — a state of mind in which images, thoughts, and impressions pass through the mind of a person who is sleeping. Dreams have had a prominent place in the religious literature of ancient peoples. In ancient times, dreams—especially those of kings and priests—were thought to convey messages from God (Num. 12:6; Gen. 31:10–13). In the Bible these were sometimes prophetic in nature. Elihu stated clearly his belief that God speaks through dreams (Job 33:14–15).

DRUNK, DRUNKENNESS — a drugged or deranged condition that results from drinking intoxicating beverages (1 Cor. 5:11; 6:10; Eph. 5:18). Drunkenness regularly appears in lists of vices in the New Testament (Luke 21:34; Rom. 13:13; Gal. 5:21).

DULCIMER — musical instrument. The exact nature of the dulcimer is unknown. Some scholars believe it may have been similar to a Greek instrument known as the symphonia, which consisted of two pipes thrust through a leather sack (Dan. 3:5, 10, 15).

DULL — slow to learn (Heb. 5:11).

DUMB — silent, mute (Mark 7:37).

DUNG — literally, waste produced by humans and animals as a part of the process of digesting food (Ex. 29:14; Lev. 4:11; Job 20:7). The word is also used in a general or symbolic way to describe what is useless, rejected, or despised (Jer. 16:4; refuse, NIV). It is in this sense that Paul evaluates the accomplishments of his life before Christ (Phil. 3:8; rubbish, NIV), and the fate of Jezebel is described (2 Kin. 9:37).

DUNG HILL — KJV phrase for a heap or pit of human and animal wastes, used to fertilize plants in Bible times (Is. 25:10; refuse heap, NKJV; manure, NIV).

DURST — dared (Esth. 7:5; Luke 20:40).

DUST — loose earth. God fashioned Adam out of the dust of the earth (Gen. 2:7). Because he led people to sin, the serpent was cursed to eat dust as he crawled on his belly (Gen. 3:14). Dust was poured upon the head as a sign of mourning. Dust is also used as a symbol for a numberless multitude (Gen. 13:16), for death (Gen. 3:19; Job 10:9; Eccl. 12:7), and the grave (Dan. 12:2).

EARNEST — a down payment or first installment given by a buyer to a seller to bind a contract, as a promise that the full amount will be paid at a later time. Paul wrote, God has "given us the Spirit in our hearts as a deposit" (2 Cor. 1:22; earnest, KJV)—that is, as a guarantee of our inheritance (2 Cor. 5:5; Eph. 1:14; earnest, KJV; deposit, NIV; pledge, NASB, REB).

EARTH, EARTHLY — the planet on which mankind lives. "The earth is the LORD's," wrote the psalmist, "and all its fullness" (Ps. 24:1). God is sovereign over the earth. All its living creatures, including human beings, are subject to His rule. The Israelites were promised that if they obeyed God's will and kept His laws, the earth would produce fruitful harvests; if they were disobedient, however, the crops would fail and famine would come (Deuteronomy 28).

EAST, MEN OF — people east of Palestine (Job 1:3).

EAST WIND — destructive desert wind (Gen. 41:27).

EBED-MELECH [e'-bed-me'-lek] *(servant of the king)* — an Ethiopian EUNUCH who served Zedekiah, king of Judah. Ebed-Melech rescued the prophet Jeremiah from a dungeon (Jer. 38:7–13). Later, Jeremiah informed him that he would be spared when the Babylonians captured Jerusalem (Jer. 39:15–18).

EBENEZER [eb-en-e'-zer] *(stone of help)* —a place where Israel was defeated by the Philistines and the ARK OF THE COVENANT was captured (1 Sam. 5:1), and a stone erected by Samuel to commemorate Israel's victory over the Philistines. (1 Sam. 7:12).

ECCLESIASTES, BOOK OF — a wisdom book of the Old Testament that wrestles with the question of the meaning of life. It takes its name from the Greek word, *ekklesiastes,* meaning "convener of an assembly." The book is often referred to by its Hebrew name, *qoheleth,* which means "preacher" or "speaker."

The Book of Ecclesiastes has a powerful message for our selfish, materialistic age. It teaches that great accomplishments and earthly possessions alone do not bring lasting happiness. True satisfaction comes from serving God and following His will for our lives.

But another important truth from Ecclesiastes is that life is to be enjoyed. The Preacher repeats this truth several times so it does not escape our attention: "There is nothing better for them than to rejoice, and to do good in their lives, and also that every man should eat and drink and enjoy the good of all his labor—it is the gift of God" (3:12–13). Our grateful acceptance of God's daily blessings can bring a sense of joy and fulfillment to our lives.

EDEN [e'-dun] *(delight)* —the first home of Adam and Eve, the first man and woman (Genesis 2—3).

EDICT — official order (Esth. 1:20; Heb. 11:23).

EDIFY, EDIFICATION — build up, strengthen (Eph. 4:12, 29).

EDOM [e'-dum] *(red)* —an alternate name for Esau, who traded his BIRTHRIGHT to his brother

ECCLESIASTES:

A Teaching and Study Outline

Part One: All Is Vanity" (1:1–11)

I. Introduction: All Is Vanity. 1:1–3
II. Illustrations of Vanity. 1:4–11

Part Two: The Proof that "All Is Vanity" (1:12—6:12)

I. Proof of "All Is Vanity" from
   Experience. . . . . 1:12—2:26
   A. Vanity of Wisdom. 1:12–18
   B. Vanity of Pleasure 2:1–3
   C. Vanity of Great Accomplishments 2:4–17
   D. Vanity of Hard Labor 2:18–26
II. Proof of "All Is Vanity" from Observation . . . 3:1—6:12
   A. Unchangeable Nature of God's Program . . . 3:1–22
      1. God Predetermines the Events of Life. . . . 3:1–8
      2. God Predetermines the Conditions
         of Life 3:9–15
      3. God Judges All 3:16–22
   B. Inequalities of Life. 4:1–16
      1. Evil Oppression. 4:1–3
      2. Folly of Hard Work 4:4–12
      3. Fleeting Nature of Popularity 4:13–16
   C. Insufficiencies of Human Religion. 5:1–7
   D. Insufficiencies of Wealth 5:8–20
      1. Wealth Does Not Satisfy 5:8–12
      2. Wealth Brings Difficulties. 5:13–17
      3. Wealth Comes Ultimately from God . . . 5:18–20
   E. Inescapable Vanity of Life. 6:1–12
      1. No Satisfaction in Wealth 6:1–2
      2. No Satisfaction in Children. 6:3–6
      3. No Satisfaction in Labor 6:7–8
      4. No Satisfaction in the Future 6:9–12

Part Three: The Counsel for Living with Vanity (7:1—12:14)

I. Coping in a Wicked World . . . . 7:1—9:18
   A. Wisdom and Folly Contrasted 7:1–14
   B. Wisdom of Moderation. 7:15–18
   C. Strength of Wisdom. 7:19–29
   D. Submit to Authority. 8:1–9
   E. Inability to Understand All God's Doing. . . 8:10–17
   F. Judgment Comes to All 9:1–6
   G. Enjoy Life While You Have It. 9:7–12
   H. Value of Wisdom 9:13–18
II. Counsel for the Uncertainties of Life . . . . . 10:1—12:8
   A. Wisdom's Characteristics 10:1–15
   B. Wisdom Related to the King 10:16–20
   C. Wisdom Related to Business 11:1–6
   D. Wisdom Related to Youth . . . . 11:7—12:8
      1. Rejoice in Your Youth 11:7–10
      2. Remember God in Your Youth 12:1–8
III. Conclusion: Fear God and Keep His
   Commandments. 12:9–14

Petra, situated in ancient Edom, is the site of numerous buildings carved from red sandstone cliffs by the Nabateans about 300 B.C. *Photo by Gustav Jeeninga*

Jacob for a meal, which consisted of a red stew (Gen. 25:29–34). Also the land inhabited by the descendants of Edom, or Esau (Gen. 32:3; 36:8).

EDOMITES [e'-dum-ites] — descendants of Edom, or Esau—an ancient people who were enemies of the Israelites. During the days of Abraham, the region which later became the home of the Edomites was occupied by more than one tribe of non-Israelite peoples. When Esau moved to this region with his family and possessions, the Horites already lived in the land (Gen. 36:20).

EGYPT [e'-jipt] — the country in the northeast corner of Africa that extended from the Mediterranean Sea on the north to the first waterfall on the Nile River in the south—a distance of about 880 kilometers (540 miles). The Israelites spent 430 years in this land (Ex. 12:40) between the time of Joseph and Moses. Jesus lived temporarily in Egypt during His infancy (Matt. 2:13–15).

The Sphinx and the Great Pyramid, timeless symbols of the land of Egypt and its people.
Photo by Howard Vos

The step pyramid (right) of the Pharaoh Zoser at Saqqarah near Cairo—the oldest known Egyptian pyramid (2700 B.C.)—with accompanying temple. *Photo by Howard Vos*

ELAM [e′-lam] *(highland)* — the name of eight or nine men but most notably a son of Shem and grandson of Noah (Gen. 10:22). He was the ancestor of the Elamites (Ezra 4:9). Also, a geographical region east of the Tigris River. It was bounded on the north by Media and Assyria, on the east and southeast by Persia, and on the south by the Persian Gulf.

ELDER — a term used throughout the Bible but designating different ideas at various times in biblical history. The word may refer to age, experience, and authority, as well as specific leadership roles (Gen. 27:42).

ELEAZAR [el-e-a′-zar] *(God is helper)* — the name of seven men in the Bible but most notably Aaron's third son by his wife, Elisheba (Ex. 6:23). Eleazar was the father of Phinehas (Ex. 6:25). Consecrated a priest, he was made chief of the Levites after his elder brothers, Nadab and Abihu, were killed for offering unholy fire (Lev. 10:1–7). Also the son of Abinadab who was charged with keeping watch over the ark while it stayed in Abinadab's house in Kirjath Jearim (1 Sam. 7:1).

ELECTION — the gracious and free act of God by which He calls those who become part of His kingdom and special beneficiaries of His love and blessings (2 Pet. 1:10). The Bible describes the concept of election in three distinct ways. Election sometimes refers to the choice of Israel and the church as a people for special service and privileges. Election may also refer to the choice of a specific individual to some office or to perform some special service. Still other passages of the Bible refer to the election of individuals to be children of God and heirs of eternal life.

ELI [e′-li] *(the Lord is high)* — a judge and high priest with whom the prophet Samuel lived during his childhood (1 Sam. 1—4; 14:3).

ELI, ELI, LAMA SABACHTHANI [e′-li, e′-li, la′-ma, sa-bock′-tan-ni′] — the bitter, central, anguished cry of Jesus from the Cross (Matt. 27:46). The first two words, Eli, Eli ("My God, My God"), are in Hebrew, while the final words ("why have You forsaken me?") are in Aramaic. Mark 15:34 quotes the entire expression in Aramaic, beginning with "Eloi, Eloi" (see also an alternate reading in Matt. 27:46). With these words, Jesus identified with sinners, took their sins upon Himself, and experienced the righteous judgment of God against sin. In this moment of loneliness and despair, He cried out to His Father God by quoting these words from the Hebrew Old Testament (Ps. 22:1). Yet, even His cry ("My God") portrayed His ultimate faith in God's deliverance.

ELIEZER [el-e-e'-zer] *(My God is helper)* — the name of eleven men in the Bible, notably Abraham's chief servant (Gen. 15:2). If Abraham had never had a son, Eliezer of Damascus would have been his heir.

Another Eliezer of importance, Moses' second son by Zipporah (Ex. 18:4; 1 Chr. 23:15).

ELIJAH [e-li'-jah] *(the Lord is my God)* — the name of three or four men in the Old Testament:

1. A Benjamite, the son of Jeroham (1 Chr. 8:27).

2. An influential prophet who lived in the ninth century B.C. during the reigns of Ahab and Ahaziah in the northern kingdom of Israel. Elijah shaped the history of his day and dominated Israelite thinking for centuries afterward.

3. A son of Harim (Ezra 10:21). Elijah divorced his foreign wife following the Captivity in Babylon.

4. An Israelite who divorced his foreign wife (Ezra 10:26). He may be the same as No. 3.

ELISHA [e-li'-shah] *(my God saves)* — an early Hebrew prophet who succeeded the prophet Elijah when Elijah's time on earth was finished (1 Kin. 19:16). Elisha ministered for about 50 years in the northern kingdom of Israel, serving God during the reigns of Jehoram, Jehu, Jehoahaz, and Joash. The period of his ministry dates from about 850–800 B.C. Elisha's work consisted of presenting the Word of God through prophecy, advising kings, anointing kings, helping the needy, and performing several miracles.

ELIZABETH [e-liz'-a-beth] *(God is my oath)* — the mother of John the Baptist (Luke 1). Of the priestly line of Aaron, Elizabeth was the wife of the priest ZACHARIAS. Although both "were ... righteous before God, they had no child, because

Elizabeth was barren" (Luke 1:6–7). But God performed a miracle, and Elizabeth conceived the child who was to be the forerunner of the Messiah. Also spelled Elisabeth.

EMMANUEL [em-man'-uel] — a form of IMMANUEL (Is. 7:14; Matt. 1:23).

EMMAUS [em'-ma-us] *(warm wells)* — a village in Judea where Jesus appeared to two disciples after His Resurrection. The disciples, Cleopas and an unidentified companion, encountered Jesus on the road to Emmaus, but they did not recognize Him. Jesus accompanied them to Emmaus, and they invited Him to stay there with them. As He blessed and broke bread at the

Statue of the prophet Elijah at the Muhraqah on Mount Carmel, commemorating his victory over the pagan worshipers of Baal.

Photo: Levant Photo Service

evening meal, the disciples' "eyes were opened and they knew Him" (Luke 24:31). The modern location of ancient Emmaus is uncertain. Luke reported the village was 11 kilometers (7 miles) from Jerusalem, but he did not specify in which direction.

ENCHANTMENT — the practice of magic or sorcery. In the Bible, enchantment is used as a general word that can refer to several different types of supernatural experiences, including fortune telling, calling up demons, and controlling evil spirits. Most ancient civilizations believed in such magical approaches to religion, but the Mosaic Law referred to such practices as "abominations," forbidding them to the Hebrews (Deut. 18:10–12). The Law also provided that practitioners of such "black magic" should be stoned (Lev. 20:27).

EN GEDI [en-ghe'-di] *(spring of a kid)* — an oasis on the barren western shore of the Dead Sea about 54 kilometers (35 miles) southeast of Jerusalem. It lay on the eastern edge of the

The spring at En Gedi, where David hid from King Saul (1 Sam. 24:1). *Photo by Gustav Jeeninga*

rugged Wilderness of Judah, which contained many hideouts where David sometimes hid when he was fleeing from King Saul (1 Sam. 23:29—24:1).

ENMITY — deep–seated animosity or hatred. The apostle Paul declared that the human mind in its natural state is in "enmity against God" (Rom. 8:7). This enmity can be changed only through the redemptive power of Christ.

ENOCH [e'-nok] *(initiated or dedicated)* — the name of two men and one city in the Bible:

1. The firstborn son of Cain (Gen. 4:17–18).

2. A city built by Cain in the land of Nod and named after his son (Gen. 4:17).

3. A son of Jared and the father of Methuselah (Gen. 5:18–24; Henoch; 1 Chr. 1:3, KJV). After living for 365 years, Enoch was "translated," or taken directly into God's presence without experiencing death (Gen. 5:24; Heb. 11:5–6).

ENSAMPLE — model (Phil. 3:17).

ENVY — a feeling of resentment and jealousy toward others because of their possessions or good qualities. James linked envy with self–seeking (James 3:14, 16; selfish ambition, NIV, NRSV). Christians are warned to guard against the sin of envy (Rom. 13:13; 1 Pet. 2:1).

EPHAH [e'-fah] — a unit for measuring volume (Judg. 6:19), as well as the name of two men, one woman, and a tribe.

EPHESIANS [e-fe'-zheuns] — natives or inhabitants of EPHESUS (Acts 19:35). Trophimus, one of Paul's coworkers, was an Ephesian (Acts 21:29).

EPHESIANS, EPISTLE TO THE — one of four shorter epistles written by the apostle Paul while he was in prison, the others being Philippians, Colossians, and Philemon. Ephesians shares many similarities in style and content with Colossians; it may have been written about the same time and delivered by the same person.

In the Epistle to the Ephesians, Paul is transported to the limits of language in order to

EPHESIANS:
A Study and Teaching Outline

Part One: The Position of the Christian (1:1—3:21)

I. **Praise for Redemption** 1:1–14
  A. Salutation from Paul 1:1–2
  B. Chosen by the Father 1:3–6
  C. Redeemed by the Son 1:7–12
  D. Sealed by the Spirit 1:13–14
II. **Prayer for Revelation** 1:15–23
III. **Position of the Christian** . . . . 2:1—3:13
  A. The Christian's Position Individually 2:1–10
    1. Old Condition: Dead to God 2:1–3
    2. New Condition: Alive to God 2:4–10
  B. The Christian's Position Corporately . . 2:11—3:13
    1. Reconciliation of Jews and
       Gentiles 2:11–22
    2. Revelation of the Mystery of the
       Church 3:1–13
IV. **Prayer for Realization** 3:14–21

Part Two: The Practice of the Christian (4:1—6:24)

I. **Unity in the Church** 4:1–16
  A. Exhortation to Unity 4:1–3
  B. Explanation of Unity 4:4–6
  C. Means for Unity: The Gifts 4:7–11
  D. Purpose of the Gifts 4:12–16
II. **Holiness in Life** . . . . 4:17—5:21
  A. Put Off the Old Nature 4:17–22
  B. Put On the New Nature 4:23–29
  C. Grieve Not the Holy Spirit . . . . 4:30—5:12
  D. Walk as Children of Light 5:13–17
  E. Be Filled with the Spirit 5:18–21
III. **Responsibilities in the Home and at
    Work** . . . . 5:22—6:9
  A. Wives: Submit to Your Husbands 5:22–24
  B. Husbands: Love Your Wives 5:25–33
  C. Children: Obey Your Parents 6:1–4
  D. Servants: Submit to Your Masters 6:5–9
IV. **Conduct in the Conflict** 6:10–24
  A. Put On the Armor of God 6:10–17
  B. Pray for Boldness 6:18–20
  C. Conclusion 6:21–24

describe the enthroned Christ who is Lord of the church, the world, and the entire created order. As the ascended Lord, Christ is completing what He began in His earthly ministry, by means of His now "extended body," the church. Christ's goal is to fill all things with Himself and bring all things to Himself.

The theme of Ephesians is the relationship between the heavenly Lord Jesus Christ and His earthly body, the church. Christ now reigns "far above all principality and power and might and dominion" (1:21) and has "put all things under His feet" (1:22). Exalted though He is, He has not drifted off into the heavens and forgotten His people. Rather, so fully does He identify with the church that He considers it His body, which He fills with His presence (1:23; 3:19; 4:10).

EPHESUS [ef'-e-sus] — a large and important city on the west coast of Asia Minor where the apostle Paul founded a church.

EPHOD OF HIGH PRIEST [e'-fod] — a vest worn by the HIGH PRIEST when he presided at the altar (Ex. 28:4–14; 39:2–7). Worn over a blue robe (Ex. 28:31–35), the ephod was made of fine linen interwoven with some threads of pure gold and other threads that were blue, purple, and scarlet in color. The ephod consisted of two pieces joined at the shoulders and bound together at the bottom by a woven band of the same material as the ephod.

Upon the shoulders of the ephod, in settings of gold, were two onyx stones, upon which were engraved the names of the twelve tribes of Israel. The front of the vest, or the breastplate, was fastened to the shoulder straps by two golden chains (Ex. 28:14) and by a blue cord (Ex. 28:28).

In later years, ephods were worn by associate priests as well as the high priest (1 Sam. 22:18). Even the boy Samuel, dedicated to serve in the Shiloh Sanctuary, wore an ephod (1 Sam. 2:18). David, although not a priest, wore an ephod when he brought the ark to Jerusalem (2 Sam. 6:14; 1 Chr. 15:27).

EPHRAIM [e′-fra-im] *(doubly fruitful)* — the second son of Joseph by Asenath.

When Ephraim was born to Joseph in Egypt, he gave him his name meaning "fruitful" because "God has caused me to be fruitful in the land of my affliction" (Gen. 41:52). Even though Joseph was a foreigner (a Hebrew) in Egypt, he had been blessed by God as he rose to a high position in the Egyptian government and fathered two sons. Later this same theme of fruitfulness and blessing was echoed by Joseph's father, Jacob, as he accepted Ephraim as his grandson (Gen. 48:5). Eventually Ephraim's thousands of descendants settled in the land of Canaan as one of the most numerous of the tribes of Israel (Gen. 48:19; Num. 1:10).

EPICUREANS [ep-i-cu-re′-ans] — Greek philosophers who belonged to a school founded by Epicurus about 306 B.C. The Epicureans were concerned with the practical results of philosophy in everyday life. Their chief aim in life was pleasure. They believed they could find happiness by seeking that which brought physical and mental pleasure, and by avoiding that which brought pain (Acts 17:16–33).

The great theater of the city of Ephesus, showing the marble boulevard leading to the nearby harbor, now silted in because of erosion. *Photo by Ben Chapman*

EPISTLE — a letter of correspondence between two or more parties; the form in which several books of the New Testament were originally written (2 Pet. 3:1). Epistle is generally synonymous with letter, although epistle sometimes is regarded as more formal correspondence, and letter as more personal.

ER [ur] — the name of three men in the Bible:

1. A son of Judah (Gen. 38:3, 6–7).

2. A son of Shelah, the youngest son of Judah (1 Chr. 4:21).

3. An ancestor of Jesus who lived between the time of David and Zerubbabel (Luke 3:28).

ESAU [e'-saw] — a son of Isaac and Rebekah and the twin brother of Jacob. Also known as Edom, Esau was the ancestor of the Edomites (Gen. 25:24–28; Deut. 2:4–8).

Most of the biblical narratives about Esau draw a great contrast between him and his brother, Jacob. Esau was a hunter and outdoorsman who was favored by his father, while Jacob was not an outdoors type and was favored by Rebekah (Gen. 25:27–28).

Even though he was a twin, Esau was considered the oldest son because he was born first. By Old Testament custom, he would have inherited most of his father's property and the right to succeed him as family patriarch. But in a foolish, impulsive moment, he sold his BIRTHRIGHT to Jacob in exchange for a meal (Gen. 25:29–34). This determined that Jacob would carry on the family name in a direct line of descent from Abraham and Isaac, his grandfather and father.

Esau in many ways was more honest and dependable than his scheming brother Jacob. But he sinned greatly by treating his birthright so casually and selling it for a meal (Heb. 12:16–17). To the ancient Hebrews, one's birthright actually represented a high spiritual value. But Esau did

An epistle, or letter, in the Greek language from the third century A.D., written to a person named Aphrodite. *Photo: Pacific School of Religion*

Reverse side of the letter to Aphrodite, showing how two pieces of papyrus were pressed together in crisscross fashion to produce a piece of writing material. *Photo: Pacific School of Religion*

not have the faith and farsightedness to accept his privileges and responsibilities. Thus, the right passed to his younger brother.

ESCHATOLOGY [es-ca-tol′-ogy] — the study of what will happen when all things are consummated at the end of history, particularly centering on the event known as the Second Coming of Christ. The word comes from two Greek words, *eschatos* (last) and *logos* (study)—thus its definition as "the study of last things."

ESTABLISH — strengthen, confirm (Prov. 8:28; Heb. 13:9).

ESTHER [es′-tur] *(star)* — the Jewish queen of the Persian king AHASUERUS (Xerxes). Esther saved her people, the Jews, from a plot to eliminate them. A daughter of Abihail (Esth. 2:15; 9:29) and a cousin of Mordecai (Esth. 2:7, 15), Esther was raised by Mordecai as his own daugh-ter after her mother and father died. Esther was a member of a family carried into captivity in Babylon that later chose to stay in Persia rather than return to Jerusalem. Her Jewish name was Hadassah, which means "myrtle" (Esth. 2:7).

ESTHER, BOOK OF — a historical book of the Old Testament that shows how God preserved His chosen people. The book is named for its main personality, Queen Esther of Persia, whose courage and quick thinking saved the Jewish people from disaster.

The Book of Esther is a major chapter in the struggle of the people of God to survive in the midst of a hostile world. Beginning with the Book of Genesis, God had made it clear that he would bless His covenant people and bring a curse upon those who tried to do them harm (Gen. 12:1, 3). The Book of Esther shows how God has kept this promise at every stage of

ESTHER:
A Study and Teaching Outline

Part One: The Threat to the Jews (1:1—4:17)

I. **The Selection of Esther as Queen** . . . . .1:1—2:20
  A. The Divorce of Vashti. 1:1–22
    1. The Feasts of Ahasuerus. 1:1–8
    2. Refusal of Queen Vashti 1:9–12
    3. Removal of Vashti. 1:13–22
  B. The Marriage to Esther 2:1–20
    1. Decree to Search for Vashti's
      Replacement. 2:1–4
    2. Preparation of Esther. 2:5–14
    3. Selection of Queen Esther 2:15–20
II. **The Formulation of the Plot by Haman.** . . . 2:21—4:17
  A. Mordecai Reveals the Plot to Murder
    the King. 2:21–23
  B. Haman Plots to Murder the Jews . . . . . . 3:1—4:17
    1. Haman Is Promoted. 3:1
    2. The Reason for Haman's Plot. 3:2–6
    3. Ahasuerus' Decree to Destroy the
      Jews. . . . . 3:7—4:17

Part Two: The Triumph of the Jews (5:1—10:3)

I. **The Triumph of Mordecai over Haman** . . . . . 5:1—8:3
  A. Setting for the Triumph . . . . 5:1—6:3
    1. Esther's First Feast. 5:1–8
    2. Haman Plots to Kill Mordecai 5:9–14
    3. King Ahasuerus' Plan to Honor
      Mordecai 6:1–3
  B. Mordecai Is Honored 6:4–14
    1. Haman's Plan to Honor Himself 6:4–9
    2. Haman Is Forced to Honor
      Mordecai. 6:10–14
  C. Haman Dies on Gallows Prepared for
    Mordecai 7:1–10
    1. Esther's Second Feast. 7:1–4
    2. Haman Is Indicted 7:5–8
    3. Haman Is Hanged. 7:9–10
  D. Mordecai Is Given Haman's House 8:1–3
II. **The Triumph of Israel Over Her Enemies** . . . 8:4—10:3
  A. Preparation for the Victory of Israel. 8:4–17
    1. Esther's Petition to King Ahasuerus. 8:4–6
    2. King Ahasuerus' Counter-Decree 8:7–14
    3. Many Gentiles Are Converted 8:15–17
  B. Israel's Victory over Her Enemies 9:1–16
    1. Victories on the First Day. 9:1–11
    2. Victories on the Second Day. 19:12–16
  C. Israel's Celebration . . . . 9:17—10:3
    1. The Feast of Purim. 9:17–32
    2. The Fame of Mordecai 10:1–3

history. Just as Haman met his death by execution, we can trust God to protect us from the enemy, Satan, and to work out His ultimate purpose of redemption in our lives.

One unusual fact about this book is that it never mentions the name of God. For this reason, some people believe Esther has no place in the Bible. They see it as nothing but a fiercely patriotic Jewish book that celebrates the victory of the Jews over their enemies.

This harsh criticism is unfair to Esther. A careful reading will reveal that the book does have a spiritual base. Queen Esther calls the people to fasting (4:16), and God's protection of His people speaks of His providence (4:14). The book also teaches a valuable lesson about the sovereignty of God: although the enemies of the covenant people may triumph for a season, He holds the key to ultimate victory.

ESTRANGE, ESTRANGED — make unknown (Jer. 19:4).

ETERNAL LIFE — a person's new and redeemed existence in Jesus Christ that is granted by God as a gift to all believers. Eternal life refers to the quality or character of our new existence in Christ as well as the unending character of that life. The phrase, "everlasting life," is found in the Old Testament only once (Dan. 12:2). But the idea of eternal life is implied by the prophets in their pictures of the glorious future promised to God's people.

ETHIOPIA [e-the-o'-pe-ah] *(burnt face)* — the Greek name for the ancient nation south of Egypt, comprising the upper Nile region of Africa (Acts 8:26–40). Its Hebrew name was Cush. Modern Ethiopia (Abyssinia), in the horn of East Africa, is hundreds of miles away from ancient Ethiopia.

ETHIOPIAN — occupant of Ethiopia (Jer. 13:23).

EUNUCH [yu'-nuk] — a male servant of a royal household in Bible times. Such servants were often emasculated by castration as a precautionary measure, especially if they served among the women in a ruler's harem (2 Kin. 9:32; Esth. 2:15). The New Testament reported the conversion of a eunuch from Ethiopia under the ministry of PHILIP the evangelist (Acts 8:26–38).

EUPHRATES [yu-fra'-teze] — the longest river of Western Asia and one of two major rivers in Mesopotamia. The river begins in the mountains of Armenia in modern-day Turkey. It then heads west toward the Mediterranean Sea, turns to the south, swings in a wide bow through Syria, and then flows some 1,000 miles southeast to join the Tigris River before it empties into the Persian Gulf.

EUTYCHUS [yu'-tik-us] *(fortunate)* — a young man of Troas who fell asleep while listening to a sermon by the apostle Paul and "fell down from the third story." When his friends reached him, he was "taken up dead." Paul miraculously brought Eutychus back to life (Acts 20:9–10).

EVANGELIST, EVANGELIZE — a person authorized to proclaim the gospel of Christ. In a more narrow sense, the word refers to one of the Gospel writers: Matthew, Mark, Luke, or John. Literally, however, the word means, "one who proclaims good tidings" (Eph. 4:11; 2 Tim. 4:5).

EVE [eev] *(life-giving)* — the first woman (Gen. 3:20; 4:1), created from one of Adam's ribs to be "a helper comparable to him" (Gen. 2:18–22).

EVERLASTING — lasting forever; eternal. The Greek word translated as everlasting in the New Testament means "age-lasting," as contrasted with what is brief and fleeting. The Bible speaks of the everlasting God (Is. 40:28), Father (Is. 9:6), King (Jer. 10:10), and Redeemer (Is. 63:16). The Lord is a God of everlasting kindness (Is. 54:8), love (Jer. 31:3), and mercy (Ps. 100:5; 103:17) who has established an everlasting covenant with His people (Heb. 13:20). His kingdom is everlasting (2 Pet. 1:11), as is His salvation (Ps. 45:17).

EVIL — a force that opposes God and His work of righteousness in the world (Rom. 7:8–19). The word is also used for any disturbance to the harmonious order of the universe, such as disease (Ps. 41:8). But the Bible makes it plain that even these so-called "physical evils" are the result of a far more serious moral and spiritual evil that began with the FALL of Adam and Eve in the Garden of Eden (Genesis 3).

EVIL ONE — Satan, the devil (John 17:15; 1 John 3:12).

EWE — female sheep (Lev. 14:10).

EXALT — to lift up (Ex. 15:2).

EXCEEDING — abundant (Eph. 1:19).

EXECRATION — an oath or curse (Jer. 42:18; 44:12).

EXHORT, EXHORTATION — a message of warning or encouragement, designed to motivate persons to action. The apostle Paul often exhorted his fellow Christians to live out their calling as ministers of the Lord Jesus (Rom. 12:8; 2 Cor. 8:17).

EXILE — to place in captivity and remove from one's homeland.

EXODUS, THE — the departure of the Israelites from captivity in Egypt under the leadership of Moses. The actual Exodus was the final event in a series of miracles by which God revealed Himself to His people in bondage, humbled the pride of the Pharaoh who opposed the Israelites, and enabled Jacob's descendants to live in freedom once again.

EXODUS, BOOK OF — key Old Testament book about Israel's beginning and early years as a nation. It takes its name from the event known as the EXODUS, the dramatic deliverance of the Hebrew people from enslavement in Egypt under the leadership of Moses. Throughout Exodus we meet a God who is the Lord of history and the Redeemer of His people. These themes, repeated throughout the rest of the Bible, make Exodus one of the foundational books of the Scriptures.

The Book of Exodus has exercised much influence over the faith of Israel, as well as Christian theology. The Bible's entire message of redemption grows out of the covenant relationship between God and His people first described in this book. In addition, several themes in the book can be clearly traced in the life and ministry of Jesus. Moses received the Law on Mt. Sinai; Jesus delivered the sermon on the mount. Moses lifted up the serpent in the wilderness to give life to the people; Jesus was lifted up on the Cross to bring eternal life to all who trust in Him (John 3:14).

The rugged Sinai Desert, through which the Israelites passed during the Exodus from Egypt.
Photo by Howard Vos

The Book of Exodus is a dramatic testimony to the power of God. The signs and plagues sent by God to break Pharaoh's stubbornness are clear demonstrations of His power. In addition to setting the Israelites free, they also dramatize the weakness of Egypt's false gods. The puny idols of Egypt are powerless before the mighty God of Israel.

EXORCIST — one who drives away demons (Acts 19:13).

EXPEDIENT, EXPEDIENCY — doing what is necessary in a given circumstance to achieve a certain goal. During the plot to kill Jesus, Caiaphas the high priest declared, "It is expedient that one man [Jesus] should die for the people, and not that the whole nation should perish" (John 11:50; also 18:14). His argument was that it was better for an innocent man to be crucified than to give the Romans cause to destroy the whole nation.

EXODUS:
A Study and Teaching Outline

Part One: Redemption from Egypt (1:1—18:27)

I. **The Need for Redemption from Egypt.** 1:1–22
   A. Israel's Rapid Multiplication 1:1–7
   B. Israel's Severe Affliction. 1:8–14
   C. Israel's Planned Destruction 1:15–22
II. **The Preparation of the Leaders of the Redemption** . . . . 2:1—4:31
   A. Moses Is Saved. 2:1–10
   B. Moses Avenges a Wrong. 2:11–22
   C. Israel Calls upon God. 2:23–25
   D. God Calls Moses . . . . 3:1—4:17
   E. Moses Accepts the Call. 4:18–26
   F. Israel Accepts the Call of Moses as Deliverer 4:27–31
III. **The Redemption of Israel from Egypt by God.** . . . . 5:1—15:21
   A. Moses Confronts Pharaoh by Word . . . . . . 5:1—6:9
   B. Moses Confronts Pharaoh with Miracles. 6:10—7:13
   C. Moses Confronts Pharaoh Through Plagues . . . . 7:14—11:10
      1. First Plague: Blood. 7:14–25
      2. Second Plague: Frogs. 8:1–15
      3. Third Plague: Lice 8:16–19
      4. Fourth Plague: Flies. 8:20–32
      5. Fifth Plague: Disease on Livestock. 9:1–7
      6. Sixth Plague: Boils. 9:8–12
      7. Seventh Plague: Hail 9:13–35
      8. Eighth Plague: Locusts 10:1–20
      9. Ninth Plague: Darkness 10:21–29
      10. Tenth Plague: Death Announced 11:1–10
   D. Israel Redeemed by Blood through the Passover . . . . 12:1—13:16
   E. Israel Redeemed from Egypt by God's Power. . . . . 13:17—15:21
IV. **The Preservation of Israel in the Wilderness.** . . . . 15:22—18:27
   A. Preserved from Thirst 15:22–27
   B. Preserved from Hunger 16:1–36
   C. Preserved from Thirst Again 17:1–7
   D. Preserved from Defeat 17:8–16
   E. Preserved from Chaos 18:1–27

Part Two: Revelation from God (19:1—40:38)

I. **The Revelation of the Old Covenant**..... 19:1—31:18
    A. The Preparation of the People 19:1–25
    B. The Revelation of the Covenant......... 20:1–26
        1. The Ten Commandments.......... 20:1–17
        2. The Response of Israel 20:18–21
        3. Provision for Approaching God 20:22–26
    C. The Judgments .... 21:1—23:33
        1. Social Regulations............. 21:1—22:15
        2. Moral Regulations............. 22:16—23:9
        3. Religious Regulations 23:10–19
        4. Conquest Regulations 23:20–33
    D. The Formal Renewal of the Covenant 24:1–11
        1. The Covenant Is Renewed through
            Blood 24:1–8
        2. The God of the Covenant Is
            Revealed....................... 24:9–11
    E. The Tabernacle .... 24:12—27:21
        1. The Revelation Is Given on
            Mount Sinai.................... 24:12–18
        2. The Offering for the Tabernacle 25:1–7
        3. The Revelation of the Tabernacle . 25:8—27:21
    F. The Priests .... 28:1—29:46
        1. The Clothing of the Priests 28:1–43
        2. The Consecration of the Priests...... 29:1–37
        3. The Continual Offerings of the
            Priests 29:38–46
    G. Institution of the Covenant......... 30:1—31:18
        1. Instructions for Using the
            Tabernacle 30:1–38
        2. Instructions for Building the
            Tabernacle 31:1–11
        3. Sign of the Covenant: The
            Sabbath 31:12–17
        4. Two Tablets Are Presented 31:18

II. **The Response of Israel to the
    Covenant**.......................... 32:1—40:38
    A. Israel Willfully Breaks the Covenant 32:1–6
    B. Moses Intercedes for Israel's Salvation ... 32:7–33
    C. Moses Convinces God Not to Abandon
        Israel........................ 32:34—33:23
    D. God Renews the Covenant with Israel.... 34:1–35
    E. Israel Willingly Obeys the Covenant .. 35:1—40:33
    F. God Fills the Tabernacle with His
        Glory 40:34–38

EXTOL — to exalt (Ps. 68:4).

EYESERVICE — the outward show of service, in order to impress others—a form of deception condemned by the apostle Paul (Eph. 6:6; Col. 3:22).

EZEKIEL [ih-zeek'-e-uhl] *(God will strengthen)* — a prophet of a priestly family carried captive to Babylon in 597 B.C. when he was about 25 years old. His call to the prophetic ministry came five years later. Ezekiel prophesied to the captives who dwelt by the River Chebar at Tel Abib. He is the author of the Book of Ezekiel.

Ezekiel shows us just how ugly and serious our sin is. Perhaps this is why God acted so dramatically in dealing with the human condition—

by sending His Son Jesus to die in our place and set us free from the bondage of sin.

EZEKIEL, BOOK OF — a prophetic book of the Old Testament with vivid, symbolic language much like that in the Book of Revelation in the New Testament. The Book of Ezekiel is named for its author, the prophet Ezekiel, who received his prophetic messages from God in a series of visions. He addressed these prophecies to the

EZEKIEL:
A Study and
Teaching Outline

Part One: The Commission of Ezekiel (1:1—3:27)

I.   **Ezekiel Sees the Glory of God** 1:1–28
II. **Ezekiel Is Commissioned to Proclaim the Word of God**. . . . . 2:1—3:27

Part Two: Judgment on Judah (4:1—24:27)

I.   **Four Signs of Coming Judgment** . . . . 4:1—5:17
    A. Sign of the Clay Tablet 4:1–3
    B. Sign of Ezekiel's Lying on His Side 4:4–8
    C. Sign of the Defiled Bread 4:9–17
    D. Sign of the Razor and Hair. 5:1–4
    E. Explanation of the Signs 5:5–17
II. **Two Messages of Coming Judgment** . . . . . . 6:1—7:27
    A. Destruction Because of Idolatry 6:1–14
    B. Description of the Babylonian Conquest . . . 7:1–27
III. **Four-part Vision of Coming Judgment.** . . . . 8:1—11:25
    A. Vision of the Glory of God 8:1–4
    B. Vision of the Abominations in the Temple 8:5–18
    C. Vision of the Slaying in Jerusalem 9:1–11
    D. Departure of the Glory of God to the Threshold. 10:1–8
    E. Vision of the Wheels and Cherubim 10:9–22
    F. Vision of the Twenty-five Wicked Rulers. 11:1–12
    G. Promise of the Restoration of the Remnant. 11:13–21
    H. Departure of the Glory of God to the Mount of Olives 11:22–25
IV. **Signs, Parables, and Messages of Judgment** . . . . 12:1—24:27
    A. Sign of Judah's Captivity 12:1–16
    B. Sign of Trembling. 12:17–28
    C. Message against the False Prophets 13:1–23
    D. Message against the Elders. 14:1–23
    E. Parable of the Vine 15:1–8
    F. Parable of Israel's Marriage 16:1–63
    G. Parable of the Two Eagles. 17:1–24
    H. Message of Personal Judgment for Personal Sin. 18:1–32
    I. Lament for the Princes of Israel. 19:1–9
    J. Parable of the Withered Vine 19:10–14
    K. Messages of Judgment on Jerusalem . . . . 20:1—24:27

Part Three: **Judgment on the** **Nations (25:1—32:32)**	**I. Judgment on Ammon** . . . . 25:1–7 **II. Judgment on Moab** . . . . 25:8–11 **III. Judgment on Edom.** . . . . 25:12–14 **IV. Judgment on Philistia.** . . . . 25:15–17 **V. Judgment on Tyre** . . . . 26:1—28:19 **VI. Judgment on Sidon** . . . . 28:20–26 **VII. Judgment on Egypt** . . . . 29:1—32:32

Part Four: Restoration of
Israel (33:1—48:35)
	I. The Return of Israel to the Land . . . . 33:1—39:29
	  A. The Appointment of Ezekiel as
	    Watchman 33:1–33
	  B. The Message to the Shepherds 34:1–31
	  C. The Judgment of Edom 35:1–15
	  D. Prophecies Concerning Israel . . . . 36:1—37:28
	  E. Prophecies Concerning Gog and
	    Magog . . . . 38:1—39:29
	II. The Restoration of Israel in the
	Kingdom . . . . 40:1—48:35
	  A. The New Temple . . . . 40:1—43:27
	  B. The New Worship . . . . 44:1—46:24
	  C. The New Land . . . . 47:1—48:35

Jewish exiles in Babylonia, where he lived among them.

EZRA [ez'-rah] ([God is] *a help*) — the name of three men in the Old Testament:

1. A descendant of Judah (1 Chr. 4:17; Ezrah, NIV, NRSV; perhaps Ezer, 1 Chr. 4:4).

2. A scribe and priest who led the returned captives in Jerusalem to make a new commitment to God's Law. A descendant of Aaron through Eleazar, Ezra was trained in the knowledge of the Law while living in captivity in Babylon with other citizens of the nation of Judah. Ezra gained favor during the reign of Artaxerxes, king of Persia. This king commissioned him to return to Jerusalem about 458 B.C. to bring order among the people of the new community. Artaxerxes even gave Ezra a royal letter (Ezra 7:11–16), granting him civil as well as religious authority, along with the finances to furnish the temple, which had been rebuilt by the returned captives.

3. One of the priests who returned from the Captivity with Zerubbabel (Neh. 12:1, 13).

EZRA, BOOK OF — a historical book of the Old Testament that describes the resettlement of the Jewish people in their homeland after their long exile in Babylonia. The book is named for its author and central figure, Ezra the priest, who led the exiles in a new commitment to God's Law after their return.

The theme of the Book of Ezra is the restoration of the remnant of God's covenant people in Jerusalem in obedience to His Law. The book shows clearly that God had acted to preserve His people, even when they were being held captives in a pagan land. But in their absence, the people had not been able to carry on the true form of temple worship. Only in their temple in Jerusalem, they believed, could authentic worship and sacrifice to their Redeemer God be offered. This is why the rebuilding of the temple was so important. Here they could restore their worship of God and find their true identity as God's people of destiny in the world.

The Book of Ezra also teaches a valuable lesson about the providence of God. Several different Persian kings are mentioned in this book.

Each king played a significant role in returning God's covenant people to their homeland and helping them restore the temple as the center of their religious life. This shows that God can use pagans as well as believers to work His ultimate will in the lives of His people.

EZRA:
A Study and
Teaching Outline

**Part One: The Restoration
of the Temple of God
(1:1—6:22)**

I. The First Return to Jerusalem Under
    Zerubbabel . . . . 1:1—2:70
    A. Decree of Cyrus 1:1–4
    B. Gifts from Israel and Cyrus 1:5–11
    C. Census of the Returning People. 2:1–63
        1. The People of Known Descent 2:1–58
        2. The People of Unknown Descent 2:59–63
    D. The Return Completed. 2:64–70
        1. The People Who Returned 2:64–67
        2. The Gifts the People Gave 2:68–70
II. The Construction of the Temple . . . . 3:1—6:22
    A. Construction of the Temple Foundation . . . 3:1–13
        1. Spiritual Preparation of the People 3:1–6
        2. Completion of the Temple
            Foundation. 3:7–13
    B. Interruption of the Temple Construction . . 4:1–24
        1. Present Opposition Under Darius. 4:1–5
        2. Later Opposition Under Ahasuerus 4:6
        3. Later Opposition Under Artaxerxes. 4:7–23
        4. Present Interruption of Construction
            Under Darius 4:24
    C. Completion of the Temple. . . . . 5:1—6:18
        1. Resumption of the Temple
            Construction 5:1–2
        2. Opposition to the Temple Construction . 5:3–17
        3. Confirmation of the Temple
            Construction 6:1–12
        4. Completion of the Temple 6:13–15
        5. Dedication of the Temple 6:16–18
    D. Celebration of the Passover 6:19–22

**Part Two: The Reformation
of the People of God
(7:1—10:44)**

I. The Second Return to Jerusalem Under
    Ezra . . . . 7:1—8:36
    A. The Decree of Artaxerxes 7:1–28
        1. Ezra's Qualifications. 7:1–10
        2. Artaxerxes' Letter 7:11–26
        3. Ezra's Response 7:27–28
    B. Census of the Returning Israelites. 8:1–14
    C. Spiritual Preparation for the Return 8:15–23
        1. Acquisition of Temple Leadership. 8:15–20
        2. Proclamation of a Fast 8:21–23
    D. The Return Is Completed. 8:24–36
II. The Restoration of the People . . . . 9:1—10:44
    A. Israel Intermarries. 9:1–2
    B. Ezra Intercedes with God 9:3–15
        1. Lamentation of Ezra. 9:3–4
        2. Confession of Ezra 9:5–15
    C. Reformation of Israel 10:1–44
        1. Israel Laments 10:1–2
        2. The Covenant Is Instituted. 10:3–5
        3. Solution for Intermarriage. 10:6–44

FACE — that part of the human body that contains a person's unique, identifying characteristics; a term used in a symbolic way in the Bible to express the presence of God. In the Garden of Eden, Adam and Eve "hid themselves from the presence [literally, face] of the Lord God" (Gen. 3:8). Jacob said, "I have seen God face to face, and my life is preserved" (Gen. 32:30). God's presence and glory have been revealed fully in the face, or the person, of Jesus Christ (2 Cor. 4:6). In the future many things that are now puzzling to Christian believers will be made clear: "For now we see in a mirror, dimly, but then face to face" (1 Cor. 13:12).

FAINT — weak (Is. 40:30).

FAITH — a belief in or confident attitude toward God, involving commitment to His will for one's life.

FAITHFUL — true (Prov. 20:6); unwavering (Acts 16:15).

FAITHFULNESS — dependability, loyalty, and stability, particularly as it describes God in His relationship to human believers. The faithfulness of God and His Word is a constant theme in the Bible. It is particularly prominent in Psalms 89 and 119. God is "the faithful God who keeps covenant" (Deut. 7:9) and chooses Israel (Is. 49:7); great is His faithfulness (Lam. 3:23).

FALL, THE — the disobedience and sin of Adam and Eve that caused them to lose the state of innocence in which they had been created. This event plunged them and all of mankind into a state of sin and corruption. The account of the Fall is found in Genesis 3.

FALLOW — a deer (Deut. 14:5), unplowed ground (Jer. 4:3).

FALSE, FALSEHOOD — lie (Deut. 5:20).

FAMILY — a group of persons related by marriage and blood ties and generally living together in the same household (Ex. 12:21).

FAMINE — the lack of a supply of food or water. This word occurs often in the Bible in both literal and figurative senses. Since the line between famine and plenty in Palestine depends mainly on the rains coming at the right time and in the proper supply, famine was an ever-present threat. In the face of famine, Abraham migrated to Egypt (Gen. 12:10), Isaac went to Gerar in Philistine territory (Gen. 26:1), and Jacob moved to Egypt (Gen. 41—47).

FARE — peace, prosperity (1 Sam. 17:18).

FAST, FASTING — going without food or drink voluntarily, generally for religious purposes. Fasting, however, could also be done for other reasons. It was sometimes done as a sign of distress, grief, or repentance. The Law of Moses specifically required fasting for only one occasion–the Day of ATONEMENT. This custom resulted in calling this day "the day of fasting" (Jer. 36:6) or "the Fast" (Acts 27:9).

FATHER — the male parent of a household in Bible times (Gen. 2:24), charged with the responsibility of providing for the family and giving religious instruction to the children.

FATHOM — unit of measure for water, approximately six feet (Acts 27:28).

FATLING — a grain-fed lamb, calf, or kid raised for meat (1 Sam. 15:9). Because of the expense of feed, these animals were very valuable in Bible times and were probably a luxury not available to the poor.

FAULT — error, sin (Dan. 6:4; Gal. 6:1).

FAVOR — grace (Esth. 2:15).

FEAR — a feeling of reverence, awe, and respect (Acts 2:43), or an unpleasant emotion caused by a sense of danger. Fear may be directed toward God or humankind, and it may be either healthful or harmful.

FEASTS AND FESTIVALS — the holy convocations, the regular assemblies of the people of Israel for worship of the Lord.

The feasts and festivals of the nation were scheduled at specific times in the annual calendar and they were both civil and religious in nature. Some feasts and festivals marked the beginning or the end of the agricultural year, while others commemorated historic events in the life of the nation. All of the feasts were marked by thanksgiving and joyous feasting.

FEET-WASHING — (see FOOT-WASHING).

FELIX [fe'-lix] *(happy)* — Roman governor of Judea before whom the apostle Paul appeared (Acts 24:27).

FELLOWSHIP — sharing things in common with others (Gal. 2:9). In the New Testament, fellowship has a distinctly spiritual meaning. Fellowship can be either positive or negative.

FESTUS, PORCIUS [fes'-tus por'-shih-us] — the successor of FELIX as Roman procurator, or governor, of Judea (Acts 24:27). After Festus arrived at Caesarea, he went to Jerusalem and met with the high priest and other Jewish leaders.

Jewish Feasts

Feast of	Month on Jewish Calendar	Day	Corresponding Month	References
Passover	Nisan	14	Mar.–Apr.	Ex. 12:1–14; Matt. 26:17–20
*Unleavened Bread	Nisan	15–21	Mar.–Apr.	Ex. 12:15–20
Firstfruits	Nisan or Sivan	16 6	Mar.–Apr. May–June	Lev. 23:9–14; Num. 28:26
*Pentecost (Harvest or Weeks)	Sivan	6 (50 days after barley harvest)	May–June	Deut. 16:9–12; Acts 2:1
Trumpets, *Rosh Hashanah*	Tishri	1, 2	Sept.–Oct.	Num. 29:1–6
Day of Atonement, *Yom Kippur*	Tishri	10	Sept.–Oct.	Lev. 23:26–32; Heb. 9:7
*Tabernacles (Booths or Ingathering)	Tishri	15–22	Sept.–Oct.	Neh. 8:13–18; John 7:2
Dedication (Lights), *Hanukkah*	Chislev	25 (8 days)	Nov.–Dec.	John 10:22
Purim (Lots)	Adar	14, 15	Feb.–Mar.	Esth. 9:18–32

*The three major feasts for which all males of Israel were required to travel to the Temple in Jerusalem (Ex. 23:14–19).

They informed him of Paul's confinement in prison. Paul had been left in prison when Felix was removed as procurator by the Roman authorities.

FETTERS — shackles or chains attached to the ankles of prisoners to restrain movement (Ps. 105:18). Fetters were usually made of iron or bronze.

FIDELITY — faithfulness, loyalty. The word occurs only once (Titus 2:10). The apostle Paul wrote to Titus instructing him to exhort slaves to show "all good fidelity" to their own masters.

FIG, FIG TREE — A fruit-producing plant that could be either a tall tree or a low-spreading shrub. The size of the tree depended on its location and soil. The blooms of the fig tree always appear before the leaves in spring. When Jesus saw leaves on a fig tree, He expected the fruit (Mark 11:12–14, 20–21). There were usually two crops of figs a year.

Figs were eaten fresh (2 Kin. 18:31), pressed into cakes (1 Sam. 25:18), and used as a poultice (Is. 38:21). Jeremiah used the fig tree as a symbol of desolation (Jer. 8:13). It also signified security and hope for Adam and Eve (Gen. 3:7), the twelve spies (Num. 13:23), and the poets and prophets. Sycamore figs were similar to the fig but were smaller and of poorer quality (Amos 7:14). They were eaten by poor people who could not afford the better variety.

FILLETS — fasteners (Ex. 27:10).

FILTH, FILTHINESS — in a literal sense, foul or dirty matter; in a figurative sense, ceremonial uncleanness or spiritual corruption. "All our righteousnesses," declared the prophet Isaiah, "are like filthy rags" (Is. 64:6). But God will forgive and cleanse the sinner who repents and believes in Christ (1 John 1:7–9).

FIRE — In the Bible, fire often appears as a symbol of God's presence and power (Gen. 15:17–18).

FIRM — strong and stable (Heb. 3:6).

FIRMAMENT — the expanse of sky and space in which the stars and planets are set. God made the firmament on the second day of creation to divide the waters that covered the earth from those that were above it (Gen. 1:7). But the firmament includes more than the atmospheric region between the seas of earth and the rain clouds of the sky; it is far more vast. In fact, on the fourth day of creation God placed the stars, the sun, and the moon in the "firmament of the heavens" (Gen. 1:15–18).

FIRSTBORN — the first offspring of human beings or animals (Gen. 27:19; Matt. 1:25).

FIRSTFRUITS — the firstborn of the flocks and the first vegetables and grains to be gathered at harvest time. The Hebrew people thought of these as belonging to God in a special sense. They were dedicated or presented to God on the day of the firstfruits, a part of the celebration of PENTECOST (Num. 28:26; 2 Chr. 31:5).

FIRSTLING — the firstborn of animals or the first of the harvest from a crop. Abel brought the firstlings of his flock as an offering to God (Gen. 4:4). The law of the FIRSTBORN is recorded in Exodus 13:11–16.

FISH GATE — a gate in Jerusalem, place for a fish market (2 Chr. 33:14).

FLAGON [flag'-gon] — KJV word for raisin cake.

FLATTER — compliment for selfish reasons (Prov. 28:23).

FLEE — leave hurriedly with the intention of getting away from someone or something (Gen. 16:8; Matt. 2:13).

FLESH, FLESHLY — the physical bodies of humans or animals. When God removed a rib from Adam with which he created Eve, he closed up the place with flesh (Gen. 2:21). The apostle Paul spoke of the flesh of men, beasts, fish, and birds (1 Cor. 15:39).

The imagery of flesh expresses several different ideas in the Bible. Rather than only the "fleshy" parts of the body, the word could also refer to the entire body (Gal. 5:13). From this idea, the concept of a fleshly or human bond between people follows. A man and his wife "shall become one flesh" (Gen. 2:24), while a man can tell his family that "I am your own flesh and bone" (Judg. 9:2). "Flesh" is even used occasionally to describe all of mankind, and even animals (Gen. 6:3).

FLINT — rock used for tool and weapon making (Deut. 8:15).

FLOCK — a herd of animals that consisted of a mixture of sheep and goats in Bible times. Both kinds of animals grazed and traveled together (Gen. 30:31–32). The animals in such mixed flocks were difficult to tell apart except at close range. This explains Jesus' teaching about separating sheep from goats at the last judgment (Matt. 25:32). In Old Testament times, the size of one's flocks and herds was a measure of wealth (1 Sam. 25:2; Job 1:3).

FLOOD, THE — the divinely-sent deluge that destroyed all sinful humankind by water during the time of Noah (Genesis 6—8).

FOLD — a place for animals (Num. 32:16), also means flock (John 10:16).

FOOD — nourishing substances eaten by people and animals. Palestine, the land of the Bible, was called a land of "milk and honey" (Ex. 13:5). Food was plentiful, although hard labor was required for its production. Lack of rainfall or other weather conditions sometimes resulted in meager crops.

Inscribed stone tablet from Babylon that describes a great flood. Unlike the Babylonian stories, the biblical account of the Flood emphasizes the sin of people and the power and moral judgment of God. *Photo by Howard Vos*

FOOL, FOOLISHNESS — a stupid person or a senseless act. In the Bible, the most foolish person of all is one who denies the reality of God the Father: "The fool has said in his heart, 'There is no God'" (Ps. 14:1; 53:1). Like the Book of Proverbs, where "fool" denotes a person who is morally and spiritually deficient, Jesus contrasted wise and foolish persons. Persons who keep His sayings are wise; those who do not are foolish (Matt. 7:24–27). The use of the word "fool" in Matthew 5:22 is a special case. Jesus warned against using the word fool as a form of abuse. This word expressed hatred in one's heart toward others; therefore, Jesus condemned the use of the word in this way.

FOOT-WASHING — an expression of hospitality extended to guests in Bible times. People traveling dusty roads in Palestine needed to wash their feet for comfort and cleanliness. Foot-washing was generally performed by the lowliest servant in the household (Luke 7:44). Guests were often offered water and vessels for washing their own feet (Gen. 18:4; Judg. 19:21).

At the Last Supper, Jesus washed His disciples' feet. He explained that this act was an example of the humble ministry that they must always be ready to perform for one another (John 13:5–17). First Timothy 5:10 suggests that the early church followed Christ's example in observing the ritual of foot-washing. But many churches reject this because the other duties mentioned in the verse are household tasks. Churches of some denominations continue to practice foot-washing today.

FORBEAR, FORBEARANCE — tolerate (Eph. 4:2); tolerance or mercy. Although human sin deserves punishment, God in His forbearance, or longsuffering patience, gives an opportunity for REPENTANCE (Rom. 2:4).

FORD — a shallow place that provides easy passage across a body of water (Josh. 2:7; Judg. 3:28).

FOREFATHERS — ancestors (Jer. 11:10).

FOREIGNER — a person whose citizenship and loyalty belong to a different country (Deut. 15:3). The "foreigner" (or "outsider") mentioned often in the Bible was distinct from the "sojourner." The sojourner belonged to another nation; but, unlike the foreigner, he came to live (or sojourn) for a period of time away from his home country, perhaps taking on some obligations and enjoying some privileges in his new land.

FOREKNOW, FOREKNOWLEDGE — the unique knowledge of God that enables Him to know all events, including the free acts of people, before they happen.

FORESKIN — skin covering the end of the male sex organ. The foreskin was cut off in the rite of CIRCUMCISION, the sign of the Abrahamic covenant (Gen. 17:10–25). Males had their foreskin removed eight days after birth (Lev. 12:3). Because circumcision was a sign of the covenant with God, the word "foreskin" symbolically represented rebellion against God. Thus, the Israelites were told to "circumcise the foreskin of your heart" (Jer. 4:4), or to give up their disobedience.

FORGIVE, FORGIVENESS — the act of excusing or pardoning others in spite of their slights, shortcomings, and errors. As a theological term, forgiveness refers to God's pardon of the sins of human beings.

FORM — to create, bring forth (Gen. 2:7).

FORNICATION — sexual relationships outside the bonds of marriage. The technical distinction between fornication and ADULTERY is that adultery involves married persons while fornication involves at least one person who is unmarried. But the New Testament often uses the term in a general sense for any unchastity. Of the seven lists of sins found in the writings of Paul, the word "fornication" is found in five of them (Rom. 13:13; 1 Cor. 5:11; Gal. 5:19; Eph. 5:3; Col. 3:5). In the Book of Revelation, fornication is symbolic of how idolatry and pagan religion defile true worship of God (Rev. 14:8; 17:4).

FORSAKE — to abandon (Matt. 19:27).

FORTRESS — safe place (Is. 25:12; Ps. 18:2).

FOUL — offensive, unclean (Mark 9:25).

FOUNDATION — the strong, stable base on which a building is constructed. When moral foundations are destroyed, a society is in danger of collapse (Ps. 11:3). Jesus taught that believers should build their faith on the strong foundation of practicing His teachings (Matt. 7:24–27). The apostle Paul also referred to Christ as a foundation for believers (1 Cor. 3:11).

FOWL — bird (Gen. 1:21).

FRAME — as a verb, establish (Jer. 18:11); as a noun, a form (Ps. 103:14).

FRANKINCENSE — fragrant substance made from tree resin (Matt. 2:11).

FREE, FREEDOM — the absence of slavery; the ability to do and go as one desires (John 8:36; Rom. 6:18).

FREEWILL OFFERING — voluntary offering (Lev. 22:18).

FRONTLET — small container which held scripture (Deut. 6:8).

FROWARD — corrupt (Prov. 2:15).

FRUIT — food (Gen. 1:11), also symbolic for children (Ex. 21:22), and spiritually speaking, good characteristics (Gal. 5:22).

FRUSTRATE — put aside (Gal. 2:21).

FUGITIVE — a runaway or escapee (Gen. 4:14).

FULFILL — complete (Matt. 3:15).

FULLNESS OF TIME — exact time (Gal. 4:4).

FUNERAL — a burial ceremony. The Bible provides few details about the actual rituals involved in burying the dead in ancient Palestine. Corpses were generally buried (Gen. 23:4, 6, 8), but only Joseph is said to have been embalmed and put in a coffin (Gen. 50:26). Mourners at funerals included family members (Gen. 37:34), acquaintances (1 Sam. 15:35) and, at times, professional mourners (Eccl. 12:5).

Mourning customs included weeping (Gen. 23:2), wearing sackcloth (Is. 15:3), cutting one's hair (Jer. 7:29), fasting (2 Sam. 1:11), and throwing ashes on oneself (Ezek. 27:30). A procession of mourners usually carried the corpse to the burial site (2 Sam. 3:31–34).

FURNACE — an oven (Dan. 3:6).

FURY — violent and intense anger; rage. The Bible speaks often of the "fury of the Lord" (Is. 51:13, 22)—a phrase referring to the judgment of a holy God against the sinful rebellion of human beings.

FUTURE — the time that is yet to come (Ps. 37:37–38). After the archangel Gabriel interpreted Daniel's vision, he said to Daniel, "Seal up the vision, for it refers to many days in the future" (Dan. 8:17–26). The Christian believer is confident of the future because he belongs to Jesus Christ.

GABRIEL [ga'-bre-el] *(God is great)* — an ARCHANGEL who acts as the messenger of God; he appeared to Daniel (Dan. 8:16), Zacharias (Luke 1:19), and the Virgin Mary (Luke 1:26–38).

All appearances of Gabriel recorded in the Bible are connected with the promise about the coming of the Messiah. But one passage may link Gabriel with Christ's return. In Christian tradition, Gabriel is sometimes identified as the archangel whose voice is heard at the Second Coming of Christ (1 Thess. 4:16). Although Gabriel is not mentioned by name in this passage, he is sometimes depicted as the trumpeter of the Last Judgment.

GAD *(good fortune)* — the name of the founder of a tribe in Israel, a prophet, and a pagan god:

1. The seventh of Jacob's twelve sons. Gad was the firstborn of ZILPAH (Leah's maid) and a brother of Asher (Gen. 30:11). Moses praised Gad for his bravery and faithfulness to duty (Deut. 33:20–21). With the possible exception of Ezbon, Gad's seven sons all founded tribal families (Num. 26:15–18).

2. A prophet described as David's "seer" (1 Chr. 21:9). Gad commanded David to buy the threshing floor of Araunah the Jebusite, which became the site of the TEMPLE. Gad the prophet also helped arrange the tabernacle music (2 Chr. 29:25) and is credited with writing an account of David's reign (1 Chr. 29:29).

3. The name of a pagan god (Is. 65:11, NKJV; Fortune, NIV). The name "Gad" appears in compound names, such as Baal Gad (Josh. 11:17) and Migdal Gad (Josh. 15:37).

GADARA [gad'-ar-a] *(walls)* — a city of Transjordan about ten kilometers (six miles) south-east of the Sea of Galilee. Gadara was primarily a Greek city, one of the cities of the DECAPOLIS. It also was the capital city of the Roman province of Perea. The ruins of Gadara, present-day Um Qeis, include two theaters, a basilica, baths, and a street lined with columns. They indicate that at one time Gadara was a large and beautiful city.

GADARENES [gad-a-renes'] — the inhabitants of GADARA, the capital of the Roman province of Perea. The Gadarenes are mentioned in the account of Jesus' healing of the demon-possessed man (Mark 5:1–20) (or men) (Matt. 8:28–34, NIV, NAS, NRSV, REB). The city was on the east side of the Jordan River, about ten kilometers (six miles) from the Sea of Galilee, opposite Tiberias. Variant readings of this name in different English versions are Gergesenes and Gerasenes.

GALATIA [ga-la'-she-a] — a region in central Asia Minor (modern Turkey) bounded on the east by Cappadocia, on the west by Asia, on the south by Pamphylia and Cilicia, and on the north by Bithynia and Pontus. The northern part of the region was settled in the third century B.C. by Celtic tribes that had been driven out of Gaul (France). From these tribes, the region derived its name, Galatia.

GALATIANS [ga-la'-she-ans] — the inhabitants of GALATIA (Gal. 3:1).

GALATIANS, EPISTLE TO THE — a brief but energetic letter from the apostle Paul to the Christians of Galatia. Galatians is one of Paul's most commanding epistles; its importance far exceeds its size. It provides valuable information

Remains of a church at ancient Gergesa which memorialized Jesus' healing of the demoniac (Matt. 8:28–34). This region east of the Sea of Galilee was also known as Gadara and Gerasa.
Photo by Howard Vos

about Paul's life between his conversion and missionary journeys (1:11—2:14). Beyond its autobiographical value, however, Galatians ranks as one of Paul's great epistles; in it he forcefully proclaims the doctrine of justification by faith alone. Martin Luther, the Reformer, claimed Galatians as "my epistle." So wedded was Luther to Galatians, both in interest and temperament, that, together, they shaped the course of the Reformation. Galatians has been called the "Magna Charta of Christian Liberty." The peals of its liberating truth have thundered down through the centuries, calling people to new life by the grace of God.

Galatians falls into three sections, each two chapters long. The first third of the letter is a defense of Paul's apostleship and gospel (chs. 1—2). The middle section (chs. 3—4) is devoted to the question of salvation. In it Paul uses a variety of means—logic (3:15–20), quotations from the Old Testament (3:7–14), metaphor (4:1–6), personal authority (4:12–20), and allegory

(4:21–31) —to argue that salvation comes not through obeying the Mosaic Law, but by receiving the grace of God through faith. The third section of Galatians concerns the consequences of saving faith (chs. 5—6). Christians are free to love (5:1–15); the Holy Spirit produces fruit in their lives (5:16–26); and the needs of others lay a rightful claim on them (6:1–10). Paul concludes by summing up the main points of the letter (6:11–16), along with a closing admonition that he bears the marks of Jesus in his body (6:17), and a blessing (6:18).

The letter to the Galatians was written in a spirit of inspired agitation. For Paul, the issue was not whether a person was circumcised, but whether he had become "a new creation" (6:15). If Paul had not been successful in his argument for justification by faith alone, Christianity would have remained a sect within Judaism, rather than becoming the universal way of salvation. Galatians, therefore, is not only Luther's epistle; it is

GALATIANS:
A Study and Teaching Outline

I. The Gospel of Grace Defended . . . . 1:1—2:21
   A. Introduction 1:1–9
   B. The Gospel of Grace Is Given by Divine
      Revelation 1:10–24
   C. The Gospel of Grace Is Approved by
      Jerusalem Leadership 2:1–10
   D. The Gospel of Grace Is Vindicated by
      Rebuking Peter 2:11–21

II. The Gospel of Grace Explained. . . . . 3:1—4:31
   A. The Holy Spirit Is Given by Faith, Not
      by Works 3:1–5
   B. Abraham Was Justified by Faith, Not
      by Works 3:6–9
   C. Justification Is by Faith, Not by
      the Law . . . . 3:10—4:11
      1. Christ Redeems Us from the Curse
         of the Law 3:10–14
      2. The Abrahamic Covenant Is Not
         Voided by the Law 3:15–18
      3. Law Is Given to Drive Us to Faith 3:19–22
      4. Believers Are Free from the Law. . . 3:23—4:11
   D. Galatians Receive Blessings by Faith,
      Not by the Law 4:12–20
   E. Law and Grace Cannot Co-exist 4:21–31

III. The Gospel of Grace Applied . . . . 5:1—6:18
   A. Position of Liberty: Stand Fast 5:1–12
   B. Practice of Liberty: Love One Another . . . 5:13–15
   C. Power for Liberty: Walk in the Spirit 5:16–26
      1. Conflict between the Spirit and the
         Flesh 5:16–18
      2. Works of the Flesh. 5:19–21
      3. Fruit of the Spirit 5:22–26
   D. Performance in Liberty: Do Good to All . . . 6:1–10
      1. Bear One Another's Burdens 6:1–5
      2. Do Not Be Weary While Doing
         Good 6:6–10
   E. Conclusion 6:11–18
      1. Motives of the Circumcised 6:11–13
      2. Motives of the Apostle Paul 6:14–18

the epistle of every believer who confesses with Paul:

"I have been crucified with Christ; it is no longer I who live, but Christ lives in me; and the life which I now live in the flesh I live by faith in the Son of God, who loved me and gave Himself for me" (Gal. 2:20).

GALILEE [gal′-i-lee] *(circle or circuit)* — a Roman province of Palestine during the time of Jesus. Measuring roughly 80 kilometers (50 miles) north to south and about 58 kilometers (30

miles) east to west, Galilee was the most northerly of the three provinces of Palestine—Galilee, Samaria, and Judea. Covering more than a third of Palestine's territory, Galilee extended from the base of Mount Hermon in the north to the Carmel and Gilboa ranges in the south. The Mediterranean Sea and the Jordan River valley were its western and eastern borders, respectively.

GALILEE, SEA OF — a freshwater lake, fed by the Jordan River, which was closely connected

The Sea, or Lake, of Galilee, at the point where the Jordan River flows into the northern end of the lake. *Photo by Willem A. VanGemeren*

with the earthly ministry of Jesus. This "sea" is called by four different names in the Bible: the "Sea of Chinnereth" [or "Chinneroth"] (the Hebrew word for "harp-shaped," the general outline of the lake; Num. 34:11; Josh. 12:3; 13:27); the "Lake of Gennesaret" (Luke 5:1), taking the name from the fertile Plain of Gennesaret that lies on the northwest (Matt. 14:34); the "Sea of Tiberias" (John 6:1; 21:1), because of its association with the capital of Herod Antipas; and the "Sea of Galilee" (Matt. 4:18; Mark 1:16).

GALL — a bitter thing (Job 20:14; Matt. 27:34).

GAMALIEL [gam-a′-le-el] *(God is my recompense)* — the name of two men in the Bible:

1. A leader of the tribe of Manasseh chosen to help take the census during Israel's wandering in the wilderness (Num. 1:10).

2. A famous member of the Jewish SANHEDRIN and a teacher of the Law. Gamaliel, who had

taught the apostle Paul (Acts 22:3), advised the Sanhedrin to treat the apostles of the young Christian church with moderation. Gamaliel's argument was simple. If Jesus was a false prophet, as many others had been, the movement would soon fade into obscurity. If, however, the work was "of God," he pointed out, "you cannot overthrow it" (Acts 5:39).

GARMENT — piece of clothing (Matt. 9:16).

GARRISON — a fort or a company of soldiers stationed in a fort. During Saul's reign as king of Israel, the Philistines had garrisons deep inside Israel—at Geba (1 Sam. 13:3) and Bethlehem (2 Sam. 23:14; 1 Chr. 11:16). In later years, David drove out the Philistines and placed his own garrisons in Damascus (2 Sam. 8:6) and Edom (2 Sam. 8:14; 1 Chr. 18:13).

In the New Testament, the word "garrison" always refers to a detachment of Roman soldiers who were stationed in Palestine (Matt. 27:27) or in one of the surrounding nations visited by the apostle Paul (2 Cor. 11:32). Paul was once rescued from an angry mob by a garrison of soldiers (Acts 21:31).

GATE — an entrance (Acts 3:10).

GAZA [ga'-za] *(stronghold)* — one of the five principal cities of the Philistines. The southernmost city of Canaan, Gaza was situated on the great caravan route between Mesopotamia and Egypt, at the junction of the trade route from Arabia. This location made Gaza an ideal rest stop and a commercial center for merchants and travelers.

GEHENNA [ge-hen'-na] — used in reference to hell (Deut. 32:22).

GENEALOGY — a list of a person's ancestors that normally contains the members of each generation in succession. When compiled in the form of a "family tree," it begins at the bottom with the rootstock from which the family came, then advances and branches out as the "tree" grows. When the genealogy records descent from ancestors by generations, the originating stock is listed first and all subsequent descendants are derived from it.

GENERATION — a word with two distinct meanings in the Bible:

1. A body of people who live at the same time in a given period of history. Generation is used in this sense in, for example, Deuteronomy 32:5, where Moses calls his contemporaries "a perverse and crooked generation." Applied in this way, generation is roughly synonymous with the word "age," as in this sentence: "Our age is characterized by its love of technology." See Matthew 11:16 and Luke 9:41 for further examples of this usage.

2. A single succession, made up of a set of individuals who share a common ancestor, in the line of descent. In this sense (Gen. 17:7; Ex. 1:6; Matt. 1:17), the word generation usually occurs when the Bible gives a genealogical or historical account of a family or tribe. First Chronicles 5:6–7, for instance, is the account of Beerah, his brothers, and "the genealogy of their generations."

GENESIS, BOOK OF — the first book of the Bible. Placed at the opening of the Hebrew Scriptures, Genesis is the first of the five books of Moses, known as the PENTATEUCH.

Genesis is the book of beginnings. The word Genesis means "the origin, source, creation, or coming into being of something." The Hebrew name for the book is *bereshith,* the first word in the Hebrew text, which is translated as "in the beginning" (Gen. 1:1). Genesis describes such important beginnings as the Creation, the Fall of man, and the early years of the nation of Israel.

The Book of Genesis is a primary source for several basic doctrines of the Bible. The book focuses on God primarily in two areas: He is the Creator of the universe, and He is the One who initiates covenant with His people. Genesis ties creation and covenant together in a stunning manner: the God who initiates covenant is the same God who has created the entire universe. The eternal God and almighty Creator enters into covenant with His people (Gen. 1:1; John 1:1).

GENNESARET [ghen-nes'-a-ret] — the name of a lake, a district, and a city in the New Testament:

1. The town Gennesaret, on the west shore of the lake of the same name. This town was a fortified city of Naphtali (Josh. 19:35) commonly referred to as Chinnereth.

2. The district of Gennesaret, identified in the Bible as "the land of Gennesaret" (Mark 6:53). This district was a plain extending two kilometers (one mile) from the Sea of Galilee along a five-kilometer (three mile) section of Galilee's north shore. Figs, olives, palms, and a variety of other types of trees were grown in this region's rich, loamy soil.

3. The "Lake of Gennesaret" (Luke 5:1). This lake is more commonly known as the Sea of Galilee (Matt. 4:18) and is sometimes simply referred to as "the lake" (Luke 5:2).

GENESIS:
A Study and
Teaching Outline

Part One:
Primeval History
(1:1—11:9)

I. **The Creation** .... 1:1—2:25
   A. Creation of the World. .... 1:1—2:3
   B. Creation of Man 2:4–25
II. **The Fall.** .... 3:1—5:32
   A. The Fall of Man. 3:1–24
   B. After the Fall: Conflicting Family
      Lines .... 4:1—5:32
III. **The Judgment of the Flood.** .... 6:1—9:29
   A. Causes of the Flood. 6:1–5
   B. Judgment of the Flood 6:6–22
   C. The Flood. .... 7:1—8:19
   D. Results of the Flood .... 8:20—9:17
   E. After the Flood: The Sin of the
      Godly Line. 9:18–29
IV. **The Judgment on the Tower of Babel.** ..... 10:1—11:9
   A. Family Lines after the Flood. 10:1–32
   B. Judgment on all the Family Lines. 11:1–9

Part Two:
Patriarchal History
(11:10—50:26)

I. **The Life of Abraham** .... 11:10—25:18
   A. Introduction of Abram 11:10–32
   B. The Covenant of God with Abram ... 12:1—25:18
      1. Initiation of the Covenant 12:1–20
      2. Separation to the Covenant ..... 13:1—14:24
      3. Ratification of the Covenant ..... 15:1—16:16
      4. Sign of the Covenant:
         Circumcision. 17:1–27
      5. Testing of the Covenant .... 18:1—20:18
      6. Consummation of the
         Covenant. .... 21:1—25:18
II. **The Life of Isaac** .... 25:19—26:35
   A. The Family of Isaac. 25:19–34
   B. The Failure of Isaac. 26:1–33
   C. The Failure of Esau. 26:34–35
III. **The Life of Jacob.** .... 27:1—36:43
   A. Jacob Gains Esau's Blessing .... 27:1—28:9
   B. Jacob's Life at Haran .... 28:10—31:55
   C. Jacob's Return .... 32:1—33:20
   D. Jacob's Residence in Canaan. .... 34:1—35:29
   E. The Family Line of Esau. 36:1–43
IV. **The Life of Joseph.** .... 37:1—50:26
   A. The Corruption of Joseph's
      Family .... 37:1—38:30
   B. The Exaltation of Joseph .... 39:1—41:57
   C. The Salvation of Jacob's Family ..... 42:1—50:26

GENTILES — a term used by Jewish people to refer to foreigners, or any other people who were not a part of the Jewish race (Rom. 9:24).

GERGESENES [ghur′-ghes-enes′] — a variant reading for GADARENES (Matt. 8:28).

GETHSEMANE [geth-sem′-a-ne] *(olive press)* — the garden where Jesus often went alone or with His disciples for prayer, rest, or fellowship, and the site where He was betrayed by Judas on the night before His Crucifixion (Luke 21:37; John 18:1–2).

GIANTS — human beings of abnormal size and strength. Races of giants are first mentioned in the Old Testament in Genesis 6:4, where giant

Saying or Phrase	Meaning Today	Original Context or Meaning
A Garden of Eden.	A paradise of unspoiled beauty and unlimited resources.	The place where God originally put Adam and Eve, before their sin (Gen. 2:8, 15).
Forbidden fruit.	A pleasure or delight that we ought not to enjoy, but which is also more attractive because it is off-limits; often refers to sexual gratification.	The fruit of the tree of the knowledge of good and evil, which Adam and Eve were told not to eat (Gen. 2:17; 3:3).
Adam's apple.	The hard lump of cartilage that is often prominent in a man's throat.	The tradition that a piece of the forbidden fruit (popularly thought of as an apple) became stuck in Adam's throat (Gen. 3:6).
Fig leaf.	In art, a small covering for the genitalia; figuratively, any means of protecting oneself from embarrassment.	The coverings that Adam and Eve made after they sinned and became aware of their nakedness (Gen. 3:7).
Am I my brother's keeper?	A rhetorical question often posed to evade responsibility in regard to someone else.	The question with which Cain replied when the Lord asked him where Abel was, whom Cain had murdered (Gen. 4:9).
Forty days and forty nights.	A long passage of time.	The duration of the downpour that caused the flood of Noah's time (Gen. 7:12).
Babel, or a Tower of Babel.	A symbol of confusion and chaos.	The place where God confused the languages of the nations in order to disperse them throughout the earth (Gen. 11:1–9).
The Promised Land.	An image of ultimate freedom, happiness, and self-determination.	The phrase used to describe the land that God promised to give Abraham's descendants, the land of Canaan, said to be flowing with milk and honey (Gen. 12:7; 15:18–21).
A mess of pottage.	An allusion to being cheated or shortchanged.	The bargain by which Jacob gained the family birthright from his elder brother Esau in exchange for a bowl of red stew called "pottage" in some translations (Gen. 25:27–34).

godlike beings were produced by the union of "the sons of God" and "the daughters of men." These abnormal unions displeased God (Gen. 6:5–6). The giants, or NEPHILIM, became "mighty men ... men of renown," perhaps a reference to their tremendous height.

GIDEON [ghid'-e-on] — a military hero and spiritual leader who delivered Israel from the oppression of the Midianites (Judg. 6:13–14).

GIFT, GIVING — the act of bestowing a favor or an item on another person without expecting anything in return. The purpose of a gift may be to honor (2 Sam. 8:2; Dan. 2:48), celebrate (Rev. 11:10), or simply to bestow favor or help (Esth. 9:22). God is the giver of every good and perfect gift (Matt. 7:11; James 1:5, 17), including eternal life (Rom. 6:23), salvation (Eph. 2:8), the necessities of life (Matt. 6:11), ability to work (Eccl. 3:13; 5:19; Deut. 8:18), the Holy Spirit (Acts 2:38; 5:32), spiritual abilities (1 Cor. 12:4), and above all His indescribable gift (2 Cor. 9:15), His Son (John 3:16).

GIFTS, SPIRITUAL — special abilities given by God (1 Cor. 7:7).

GILEAD [ghil′-e-ad] — the name of three men, two mountains, and one city in the Old Testament:

1. A son of Machir and grandson of Manasseh (Josh. 17:1). He founded a tribal family, the Gileadites.

2. A mountain region east of the Jordan River 915 meters (3,000 feet) above sea level. Extending about 97 kilometers (60 miles) from near the south end of the Sea of Galilee to the north end of the Dead Sea, Gilead is about 32 kilometers (20 miles) wide. It is bounded on the west by the JORDAN River, on the south by the land of Moab, on the north by the Yarmuk River, and on the east by the desert.

3. A mountain on the edge of the Jezreel valley (Judg. 7:3). Gideon and his men were camped here when Gideon ordered a reduction in his troops before he fought the Midianites.

4. The father of Jephthah, a judge of Israel (Judg. 11:1—12:7).

5. A chief of the family of Gad (1 Chr. 5:14).

6. A city in the region of Gilead condemned by the prophet Hosea (Hos. 6:8). The name Gilead in this passage is probably a poetic shortening of Ramoth Gilead or Jabesh Gilead, two of the cities of Gilead.

GILGAL [gil′-gal] *(circle)* — the name of a campsite and two cities in the Old Testament:

1. A village from which the prophet Elijah ascended into heaven (2 Kin. 2:1).

2. The first campsite of the people of Israel after they crossed the Jordan River and entered the Promised Land (Josh. 4:19–20). They took stones from the Jordan and set them up at Gilgal as a memorial to God's deliverance. Many important events in Israel's history are associated with this city. The first Passover in Canaan was held at Gil-

The Garden of Gethsemane, where Jesus agonized in prayer on the night before His crucifixion (Matt. 26:36–46). The roots of these giant olive trees may date from the time of Christ or before.

gal (Josh. 5:9–10). It also became the base of military operations for Israel during the conquest of Canaan. From Gilgal Joshua led Israel against the city of Jericho (Josh. 6:11, 14) and conducted his southern campaign (Joshua 10). It was there that he began allotting the Promised Land to the tribes.

In later years, Gilgal was the site of King Saul's coronation as well as his rejection by God as king (1 Sam. 11:15; 13:4–12; 15:12–33). After

Absalom's revolt, the people of Judah gathered at Gilgal to welcome David back as their king (2 Sam. 19:15, 40). But during the days of later kings, Gilgal became a center of idolatry. Like Bethel, it was condemned by the prophets (Hos. 4:15; Amos 5:5). The presumed site of Gilgal is about two kilometers (one mile) northeast of Old Testament Jericho (Josh. 4:19).

3. A town between Dor and Tirzah (Josh. 12:23), probably Jiljulieh, a little town north of the brook Kanah and eight kilometers (five miles) northeast of Antipatris.

GIRD — put on and fasten (Acts 12:8).

GIRDLE — a belt (2 Kin. 1:8; Mark 1:6); also called loincloth.

GLEAN, GLEANING — the process of gathering grain or other produce left in the fields by reapers (Judg. 8:2; Ruth 2; Is. 17:6). The Old Testament Law required that property owners leave the gleanings of their produce in the fields so they might be gathered by "the poor and the stranger" (Lev. 19:9–10; 23:22).

GLORIFICATION — process of making holy and pure.

GLORIFY — praise (Ps. 86:9).

GLORY — beauty, power, or honor; a quality of God's character that emphasizes His greatness and authority (Acts 7:2; James 2:1).

GLUTTON — a person who is debased and excessive in his or her eating habits. Gluttony is more than overeating. In its association with drunkenness (Prov. 23:21; Deut. 21:20), it describes a life given to excess. When Jesus was called a "gluttonous man" (Matt. 11:19), His critics were accusing Him of being loose and excessive by associating with tax collectors and sinners.

GNASH, GNASHING OF TEETH — to grate or grind one's teeth together as an expression of hatred and scorn (Job 16:9). Jesus used the phrase to portray the futility of the wicked who will be judged by God at the end of time (Matt. 13:42, 50).

GNAT — tiny insect (Matt. 23:24).

GNOSTICISM [nos'-ti-siz-im] — a system of false teachings that existed during the early centuries of Christianity. Its name came from *gnosis,* the Greek word for knowledge. The Gnostics believed that knowledge was the way to salvation. For this reason, Gnosticism was condemned as

Old Testament Names for God	
1. Elohim, "God," i.e., His power and might	Gen. 1:1; Ps. 19:1
2. El-Elyon, "The most high God"	Gen. 14:17-20; Is. 14:13,14
3. El-Olam, "The everlasting God"	Is. 40:28-31
4. El-Roi, "The strong one who sees"	Gen. 16:13
5. El-Shaddai, "God Almighty"	Gen. 17:1; Ps. 91:1
6. Adonai, "Lord," i.e., the Lordship of God	Mal. 1:6
7. Jehovah (Yahweh), "The LORD," i.e., God's eternal nature	Gen. 2:4
8. Jehovah-Jireh, "The LORD will provide"	Gen. 22:13,14
9. Jehovah-Maccaddeshem, "The LORD your sanctifier"	Ex. 31:13
10. Jehovah-Nissi, "The LORD our banner"	Ex. 17:15
11. Jehovah-Rapha, "The LORD our healer"	Ex. 15:26
12. Jehovah-Rohi, "The LORD my shepherd"	Ps. 23:1
13. Jehovah-Sabbaoth, "The LORD of Hosts"	Is. 6:1-3
14. Jehovah-Shalom, "The LORD is peace"	Judg. 6:24
15. Jehovah-Shammah, "The LORD who is present"	Ezek. 48:35
16. Jehovah-Tsidkenu, "The LORD our righteousness"	Jer. 23:6

false and heretical by several writers of the New Testament.

GOD — the creator and sustainer of the universe who has provided humankind with a revelation of Himself through the natural world and through His Son, Jesus Christ.

God may be described in terms of attributes. An attribute is an inherent characteristic of a person or being. While we cannot describe God in a comprehensive way, we can learn about Him by examining His attributes as revealed in the Bible.

GOD, NAMES OF — the titles or designations given to God throughout the Bible. In the ancient world, knowing another's name was a special privilege that offered access to that person's thought and life. God favored His people by revealing Himself by several names that offered special insight into His love and righteousness.

GODS, PAGAN — the false gods and idols worshiped by people during Bible times—especially the false gods of Egypt, Mesopotamia (Assyria and Babylon), Canaan, Greece, and Rome.

GOD'S WILL — God's plan and desire for us (Matt. 6:10; Mark 3:35).

GOLGOTHA [gol'-gath-a] *(place of a skull)* — the place where Jesus was crucified, a hill just outside the walls of Jerusalem (Mark 15:22).

GOLIATH [go-li'-ath] — a Philistine giant whom David felled with a stone from his sling (1 Sam. 17:4–51). Goliath, who lived in the Philistine city of Gath, was probably a descendant of a tribe of giants known as the Anakim, or descendants of Anak (Num. 13:33). These giants probably served in a capacity similar to that of a foreign mercenary or soldier of fortune.

GOMORRAH [go-mor'-rah] *(submersion)* — one of the five "cities of the plain" located in the Valley of Siddim (Salt Sea or Dead Sea). The other cities were Sodom, Admah, Zeboiim, and Zoar (Gen. 14:2–3). Gomorrah is associated closely with its twin city, Sodom. Because these cities became the site of intolerable wickedness, they were destroyed by fire (Gen. 19:24, 28). The destruction of Sodom and Gomorrah is often referred to in the Bible as a clear example of divine judgment against the vilest of sinners (Is. 13:19; Jer. 49:18; Amos 4:11; Matt. 10:15; 2 Pet. 2:6; Jude 7).

GOOD — a word with two distinct meanings in the Bible:

1. As an adjective, "good" means "pleasant" (Prov. 15:23), "in full measure" (Gen. 30:20), "kind" and "gracious" (1 Sam. 25:15).

2. As a noun, "good" means primarily God Himself (Mark 10:18). The Bible also speaks of God's works, gifts, and commands as good.

GOPHERWOOD — wood used for building Noah's ark; probably similar to cypress wood (Gen. 6:14).

A bust of Zeus in the Ephesus Museum. Zeus was the chief god of the ancient Greeks.

Photo by Howard Vos

Pagan Gods of Egypt

Name	Responsibility	Form or Sacred Animal
Aker	Earth-god • Helper of the dead	Two lion heads
Amon	Wind-god • God of Thebes • Helper of the pious	Human (ram and goose sacred)
Anubis	Glorifier of the dead	Jackal-headed, black-skinned
Apis	Ensures fertility	Bull
Aton	Sun-god	
Atum	Primordial creature-god	Serpent-human
Bes	Protection at birth • Dispenser of virility	Group of demons
Edjo	Goddess of Delta/Lower Egypt	Uraeus serpent
Geb	Earth-god • Consort of Nut • Begetter of Osiris	Human
Hathor	Sky-goddess • Goddess of love, dance, alcohol	Cow
Heket	Primordial goddess	Frog
Horus	Sky-god	Falcon
Isis	Goddess of life, healing • Daughter of Geb Consort/sister of Osiris • Mother of Horus	Human
Khepri	Primordial god • Rising sun	Scarabaeus
Khnum	Giver of the Nile • Creator of mankind	Human with ram's head
Khons	Moon-god	Human
Maat	Justice • Daughter of Ra	Human
Meskhenet	Goddess protector of newborns and of destiny	
Min	God of virility and reproduction	
Mut	"Eye of the sun," consort of Amon	Vulture or human
Nekhbet	Goddess of Upper Egypt	
Nut	Sky-goddess • Consort of Geb Mother of Osiris and Seth • Mother of heavenly bodies	
Osiris	Dead pharoahs • Ruler of dead, life, vegetation	
Ptah	Creator-god • Lord of artisans	
Ra	God of sun, earth and sky • Father of Maat • National god	Human with falcon head
Sekhmet	Goddess of war and sickness	Human with lion head
Selket	Guardian of life • Protector of dead	Scorpion
Seshat	Goddess of writing and books	
Seth	God of chaos, desert and storm, crops • Brother of Osiris	
Shu	God of air, bearer of heaven	
Sobek	Creator-god	Crocodile
Sothis	God of Nile floodwaters	
Thermuthis	Goddess of fertility and harvest; fate	Serpent
Thoth	God of wisdom, moon, chronology • Messenger of gods	Ibis or baboon
Thoueris	Goddess of fertility and women in labor	Hippopotamus

GOSHEN [go'-shen] — the name of two areas and one city in the Old Testament but most notably, the northeastern territory of the NILE Delta in Egypt, known today as the area of the Wadi Tumilat. Jacob and his family were granted permission to settle in this fertile section during Joseph's rule as prime minister of Egypt (Gen. 46:28).

During the time of the Exodus, Goshen was protected from the plagues of flies (Ex. 8:22) and hail (Ex. 9:26) that engulfed the rest of Egypt. The district was not large, containing perhaps 900 square miles, and it had two principal cities: Rameses and Pithom.

GOSPEL — the joyous Good News of salvation in Jesus Christ. The Greek word translated as "gospel" means "a reward for bringing good news" or simply "good news." In Isaiah 40:9, the prophet proclaimed the "good tidings" that God would rescue His people from captivity. In His famous sermon at the synagogue in Nazareth, Jesus quoted Isaiah 61:1 to characterize the spirit of His ministry: "The Spirit of the Lord is upon Me, because He has anointed Me to preach the gospel [good news] to the poor" (Luke 4:18).

GOSPELS — the four accounts at the beginning of the New Testament about the saving work of God in His Son Jesus Christ. The writers of the four Gospels introduced a new literary category into literature. The Gospels are not true biographies, because apart from certain events surrounding His birth (Matt. 1—2; Luke 1—2) and one from His youth (Luke 2:41–52), they record only the last two or three years of Jesus' life.

Why Four Gospels?

Gospel	Matthew	Mark	Luke	John
Audience	Jews	Romans	Hellenists	Greek World
Portrait of Jesus	Jesus is the **Messiah/King** who fulfills Old Testament prophecy and expectations	Jesus is the authoritative Son of God	Jesus is the perfect **Son of Man** who came to save and minister to all people through the power of the Holy Spirit and prayer	Jesus is the fully **divine Son of God** in whom we should believe to receive eternal life (the "I AM" of God)
Key Verses	Matthew 1:1; 16:16; 20:28	Mark 1:1; 8:27; 10:45; 15:34	Luke 19:10	John 20:31
Key Words	Fulfilled	Immediately	Son of Man	Believe; Eternal Life

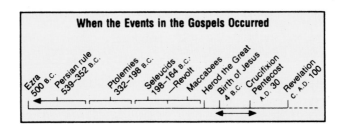

When the Events in the Gospels Occurred

Ezra 500 B.C. · Persian rule 539–352 B.C. · Ptolemies 332–198 B.C. · Seleucids 198–164 B.C. · Maccabees–Revolt · Herod the Great · Birth of Jesus 4 B.C. · Crucifixion A.D. 30 · Pentecost · Revelation C. A.D. 100

Moreover, the material included is not written as an objective historical survey of Jesus' ministry. The Gospels present Jesus in such a way that the reader realizes that God acted uniquely in Him. The authors of the Gospels wrote not only to communicate knowledge about Jesus as a person, but also to call us to commitment to Him as Lord.

The Gospels produce four distinctive portraits of Jesus rather than exact photographic likenesses. Thus, there are four Gospels (accounts) of the one Gospel (the Good News of salvation in Jesus Christ).

GOVERNMENT — earthly authority; those who rule over others in order to keep society stable and orderly (2 Pet. 2:10).

GOVERNOR — a regional agent or officer for the Roman emperor during New Testament times (Luke 2:2).

GRACE — favor or kindness shown without regard to the worth or merit of the one who receives it and in spite of what that person deserves. Grace is one of the key attributes of God. The Lord God is "merciful and gracious, long-suffering, and abounding in goodness and truth" (Ex. 34:6). Therefore, grace is almost always associated with mercy, love, compassion, and patience.

GRANT — to give, allow (Ps. 85:7; Rev. 3:21).

GRAVE — a place where the dead are buried. In general, the Hebrew people buried their dead in graves much as today, except that they were not as deep. In towns and cities the burial grounds were situated outside the city limits (Luke 7:12; John 11:30). Evidence of this may be seen today in the many graves in the Kidron Valley east of Jerusalem and at the Essene community overlooking the Dead Sea. Plain stones or a stone slab were used to cover the grave as a safeguard against animals and to mark the burial place (2 Sam. 18:17). In some instances hewn stones were used. Occasionally expensive pillars were used as memorials (2 Kin. 23:17); thus, Jacob erected a pillar over Rachel's grave (Gen. 35:20), which today is marked by a building over the traditional site.

GREECE — a region or country of city-states in southeastern Europe between Italy and Asia Minor. Greece was bounded on the east by the Aegean Sea, on the south by the Mediterranean Sea, on the west by the Adriatic Sea and Ionian Sea, and on the north by Mount Olympus and adjacent mountains. The Old Testament name for Greece was Javan (Gen. 10:2, 4; Is. 66:19).

In the early years of its history, Greece was a country of self-governing city-states. Politically and militarily, the Greek city-states were weak. Their varied backgrounds led to frictions and rivalries that kept them from becoming one unified nation.

Greece is important to Christianity because of its language. In New Testament times Greek was the language spoken by the common people of the ancient world, as far west as Rome and the Rhone Valley in southeastern France. Most of the New Testament was written originally in Greek, a precise and expressive language.

GREEK — language spoken in Greece.

GREEKS — natives of Greece or people of Greek descent. In the New Testament, "Greeks" is sometimes used as a general term for all who are not Jews.

GRIEF — an emotion of sorrow; the experience of emotional distress or pain. Today the word grief is usually used to express what a person feels in periods of intense sadness, as in the time of death. But the Bible uses the word more freely and, more often than not, in reference to things other than death. Grief is a response to the trouble one's enemies cause (Ps. 6:7; 31:10) or to the foolishness of a child (Prov. 10:1).

GROPE — clumsily feel, search (Job 12:25).

GROW — mature, can be used in reference to the physical and spiritual (Gen. 21:20; Luke 2:40).

GUARANTEE — a promise or assurance; something given or held as security. The apostle Paul declared that the Holy Spirit, who lives in our hearts, is the guarantee that we shall receive our full inheritance from God (2 Cor. 5:5).

GUILT, GUILTY — bearing responsibility for an offense or wrongdoing; remorseful awareness of having done something wrong (Lev. 4:3; Ezra 9:6, 13, 15). Although the word "guilt" is not specifically used, some classic examples of guilt in the Bible are: Adam and Eve (Gen. 3:7–8), Cain (Gen. 4:8–9), and David (2 Sam. 11; Ps. 51). One Greek word in the New Testament translated as "guilty" means "under justice," or answerable to the judgment and condemnation of God.

HABAKKUK [hab′-ak-uk] — a courageous Old Testament prophet and author of the Book of Habakkuk. The Scriptures say nothing of his ancestry or place of birth. A man of deep emotional strength, Habakkuk was both a poet and a prophet. His hatred of sin compelled him to cry out to God for judgment (Hab. 1:2–4). His sense of justice also led him to challenge God's plan to judge the nation of Judah by the pagan Babylonians (Hab. 1:12—2:1). His deep faith led him to write a beautiful poem of praise in response to the mysterious ways of God (Habakkuk 3).

HABAKKUK, BOOK OF — a short prophetic book of the Old Testament that deals with the age-old problems of evil and human suffering. The book is named for the prophet Habakkuk.

Habakkuk's book contains only three short chapters, but they present a striking contrast. In the first two, Habakkuk protests, complains, and questions God. But the final chapter is a beautiful psalm of praise. Habakkuk apparently used this complaining and questioning technique to drive home his powerful message about the approaching judgment of God.

The question-and-answer technique of the prophet Habakkuk teaches a valuable lesson about the nature of God. That God allows Himself to be questioned by one of His followers is an indication of His long-suffering mercy and grace.

HABITATION — a dwelling place. Solomon referred to the temple as God's "house of habitation" (2 Chr. 6:2, KJV). The church is also called "a habitation of God in the Spirit" (Eph. 2:22).

HADES [ha′-dees] — place of the dead, does not appear in the KJV (Matt. 16:18, NIV).

HAGAR [ha′-gar] — the Egyptian bondwoman of Sarah who bore a son, ISHMAEL, to Abraham (Gen. 16:1–16). After waiting ten years for God to fulfill his promise to give them a son, Sarah presented Hagar to Abraham so he could father a child by her, according to the custom of the day. Sarah's plan and Abraham's compliance demonstrated a lack of faith in God.

HAGGAI [hag′-ga-i] *(festive)* — an Old Testament prophet and author of the Book of Haggai. As God's spokesman, he encouraged the captives who had returned to Jerusalem to complete the reconstruction of the temple. This work had started shortly after the first exiles returned from

HABAKKUK:
A Study and
Teaching Outline

I. **The Questions of Habakkuk** . . . . 1:1—2:20
  A. The First Question 1:1–4
  B. God's First Reply. 1:5–11
  C. The Second Question of Habakkuk . . . . . 1:12—2:1
  D. God's Second Reply. 2:2–20
II. **The Praise of Habakkuk.** 3:1–19
  A. Habakkuk Prays for God's Mercy. 3:1–2
  B. Habakkuk Remembers God's Mercy 3:3–15
  C. Habakkuk Trusts in God's Salvation 3:16–19

Babylon in 538 B.C. But the building activity was soon abandoned because of discouragement and oppression. Beginning in 520 B.C., Haggai and his fellow prophet, Zechariah, urged the people to resume the task. The temple was completed five years later, about 515 B.C. (Ezra 5:1).

HAGGAI, BOOK OF — a short prophetic book of the Old Testament written to encourage the people of Israel who had returned to their native land after the Captivity in Babylon.

The two short chapters of Haggai contain four important messages, each dated to the very month and day it was delivered. He called on the people to rebuild the temple, to remain faithful to God's promises, to be holy and enjoy God's great provisions, and to keep their hope set on the coming of the MESSIAH and the establishment of His kingdom.

Haggai urged the people to put rebuilding the temple at the top of their list of priorities. This shows that authentic worship is a very important matter. The rebuilt temple in Jerusalem was important as a place of worship and sacrifice. Centuries later, at the death of Jesus "the veil of the temple was torn in two" (Luke 23:45), demonstrating that He had given Himself as the eternal sacrifice on our behalf.

The Book of Haggai ends with a beautiful promise of the coming of the Messiah. Meanwhile, God's special servant, ZERUBBABEL, was to serve as a "signet ring" (2:23), a sign or promise of the glorious days to come. As the Jewish governor of Jerusalem under appointment by the Persians, Zerubbabel showed there was hope for the full restoration of God's covenant people in their native land.

HAIL — a greeting that involves a wish for the good health and peace of the person addressed. Judas greeted Jesus hypocritically when he went up to Him in the Garden of Gethsemane and said, "Greetings [Hail, KJV], Rabbi!" and then kissed Him (Matt. 26:49). After His Resurrection, Jesus met His disciples and said to them, "Rejoice!" (Matt. 28:9; All hail, KJV).

HALF-TRIBE — a term used in the Old Testament to refer to the two separate settlements of the tribe of Manasseh—one east of the Jordan River and the other in central Palestine west of the Jordan. During the days of Moses, half of the people of the tribe of Manasseh requested permission to settle the territory east of the Jordan after the land was conquered. Moses agreed to this request, on the condition that the entire tribe assist in the conquest of Canaan (Num. 32:33–42; Deut. 3:12–13; Josh. 1:12–18).

HALLELUJAH — a form of ALLELUIA.

HALLOWED — holy, set apart (Matt. 6:9).

HAGGAI: A Study and Teaching Outline

I. **The Completion of the Latter Temple** 1:1–15
   A. The Temple Is Not Complete 1:1–6
   B. The Temple Must Be Completed 1:7–15
II. **The Glory of the Latter Temple** 2:1–9
   A. The Latter Temple Is Not as Glorious as
      the First 2:1–3
   B. The Latter Temple Will Be More Glorious
      than the First 2:4–9
III. **The Blessings of Obedience** 2:10–19
   A. The Problem: The Disobedience of the
      Remnant 2:10–14
   B. The Solution: The Obedience of the
      Remnant 2:15–19
IV. **The Future Blessings through Promise** 2:20–23
   A. The Future Destruction of the Nations 2:20–22
   B. The Future Recognition of Zerubbabel 2:23

HAMAN [ha'-man] — the evil and scheming prime minister of Ahasuerus (Xerxes I), king of Persia (485—464 B.C.). When MORDECAI refused to bow to Haman, Haman plotted to destroy Mordecai and his family, as well as all of the Jews in the Persian Empire. But ESTHER intervened and saved her people. Haman was hanged on the very gallows he had constructed for Mordecai (Esth. 3:1—9:25). This shows that God is always in control of events, even when wickedness and evil seem to be winning out.

HANANIAH [han-a-ni'-ah] *(The Lord is gracious)* — the name of 15 men in the Old Testament but most notably the Hebrew name given to Shadrach (Dan. 1:6–7).

HANDMAID — female slave or servant (Luke 1:38).

HANNAH [han'-nah] *(gracious)* — a wife of Elkanah, a Levite of the Kohathite branch of the priesthood (1 Sam. 1:1—2:21). Unable to bear children, Hannah suffered ridicule from Elkanah's other wife Peninnah, who bore him several children. Hannah vowed that if she were to give birth to a son, she would devote him to the Lord's service. The Lord answered her prayers, and to her was born the prophet Samuel.

Hannah was faithful to her promise. Making what must have been a heart-rending sacrifice, Hannah took Samuel to the temple after he was weaned, there to "remain forever" (1:21). God rewarded Hannah's piety and faithfulness with three more sons and two daughters. Hannah's beautiful thanksgiving prayer (2:1–10) is similar to the song that Mary sang when she learned she would be the mother of Jesus (Luke 1:46–55).

HANUKKAH [han'-na-ka] — same as the Feast of Dedication or the Feast of Lights (John 10:22).

HARAN [ha'-ran] — the name of three men and one city in the Old Testament:
1. The third son of Terah, Abraham's father, and the younger brother of Abraham. Haran was the father of Lot, Milcah, and Iscah (Gen. 11:26–31).
2. A son of Caleb by Ephah, Caleb's concubine. Haran was the father of Gazez (1 Chr. 2:46).
3. A Levite from the family of Gershon and a son of Shimei. Haran lived during David's reign (1 Chr. 23:9).
4. A city of northern Mesopotamia. Abraham and his father Terah lived there for a time (Gen. 11:31–32; 12:4–5). The family of Abraham's brother Nahor also lived in this city for a time, as did Jacob and his wife Rachel (Gen. 28:10; 29:4–5). The city was on the Balikh, a tributary of the Euphrates River, 386 kilometers (240 miles) northwest of Nineveh and 450 kilometers (280 miles) northeast of Damascus. Haran lay on one of the main trade routes between Babylonia and the Mediterranean Sea. Like the inhabitants of Ur of the Chaldeans, Haran's inhabitants worshiped Sin, the moon-god. Second Kings 19:12 records that the city was captured by the Assyrians. Today Haran is a small Arab village, Harran, a spelling that preserves the two *r*'s of the original place name and helps to distinguish it from the personal name Haran. The city name is also spelled Charran (Acts 7:2, 4; KJV).

HARD BY — close to (Lev. 3:9).

HARDHEARTED, HARDHEARTEDNESS — stubbornness in opposition to God's will (1 Sam. 6:6; Job 38:30). The classic case in the Bible of such disobedience was the Pharaoh of Egypt, who refused to release the Hebrew people in spite of repeated displays of God's power (Ex. 4:21; 7:3; 14:4, 17).

HARLOT — a prostitute. The term "harlot" is often used in a symbolic way in the Old Testament to describe the wicked conduct of the nation of Israel in worshiping false gods (Is. 1:21; Jer. 2:20; Ezek. 16).

HASTE — extreme hurry (Ex. 12:11).

HAUGHTY — arrogant, proud (Ezek. 16:50).

HEAP — to place upon (Prov. 25:22).

HEARKEN — to pay attention (Acts 27:21).

HEART — the inner self that thinks, feels, and decides. In the Bible the word "heart" has a much broader meaning than it does to the modern mind. The heart is that which is central to a person. Nearly all the references to the heart in the Bible refer to some aspect of human personality (Acts 1:24).

HEARTH — a dug-out depression in a house or tent where fires were built for heating or cooking. The smoke from the fire was let out through a hole in the wall, usually translated as "chimney" (Hos. 13:3).

HEATHEN — one of several words used for the non-Jewish peoples of the world. The distinction between the Israelites and the other nations was important because God's relationship with Israel was unique. He chose Israel, rescued the people from Egypt, entered into a COVENANT with them, and gave the nation His laws. God actually planned to bring light and salvation to all nations through Israel (Gen. 12:3; Is. 2:1–3), but this required that they keep separate from the sinful ways of the surrounding nations (Lev. 18:24).

HEAVEN — a word that expresses several distinct concepts in the Bible:

1. As used in a physical sense, heaven is the expanse over the earth (Gen. 1:8). The tower of Babel reached upward to heaven (Gen. 11:4). God is the possessor of heaven (Gen. 14:19). Heaven is the location of the stars (Gen. 1:14; 26:4) as well as the source of dew (Gen. 27:28).

2. Heaven is also the dwelling place of God (Gen. 28:17; Rev. 12:7–8). It is the source of the new Jerusalem (Rev. 21:2, 10). Because of the work of Christ on the Cross, heaven is, in part, present with believers on earth as they obey God's commands (John 14:2, 23).

3. The word "heaven" is also used as a substitute for the name of God (Luke 15:18, 21; John 3:27). The kingdom of God and the kingdom of heaven are often spoken of interchangeably (Matt. 4:17; Mark 1:15).

At the end of time a new heaven will be created to surround the new earth. This new heaven will be the place of God's perfect presence (Is. 65:17; 66:22; Rev. 21:1). Then there will be a literal fulfillment of heaven on earth.

HEBREW [he′-broo] — a descendant of Abraham (Gen. 14:13); the language the Old Testament is written in.

HEBREWS, EPISTLE TO THE — the nineteenth book in the New Testament. Hebrews is a letter written by an unknown Christian to show how Jesus Christ had replaced Judaism as God's perfect revelation of Himself. Hebrews begins with a marvelous tribute to the person of Christ (1:1–3), and throughout the epistle the author weaves warning with doctrine to encourage his readers to hold fast to Jesus as the great High Priest of God. The author makes extensive use of Old Testament quotations and images to show that Jesus is the supreme revelation of God and the all-sufficient Mediator between God and humankind. Because of its literary style and the careful way it develops its argument, Hebrews reads more like an essay than a personal letter.

HEBRON [he′-brun] *(alliance)* — the name of two cities and two men in the Bible:

1. A city situated 31 kilometers (19 miles) southwest of Jerusalem on the road to Beer-sheba. Although it lies in a slight valley, the city is 927 meters (3,040 feet) above sea level, which makes it the highest town in Palestine. Originally Hebron was called Kirjath Arba (Gen. 23:2). Numbers 13:22 speaks of Hebron being built seven years before Zoan in Egypt. This probably refers to the rebuilding of the city by the Hyksos rulers of Egypt. The 12 Hebrew spies viewed Hebron on their mission to explore the Promised Land.

2. The third son of Kohath, the son of Levi (Ex. 6:18). Hebron was an uncle of Moses, Aaron, and Miriam. His descendants were called Hebronites (Num. 3:27).

Peasants appear before an Egyptian nobleman in this painting from a royal tomb. In their early history, the Hebrew people were enslaved by the Egyptians.

Modern Hebron, successor to the ancient city of the same name where Abraham bought a burial cave for Sarah and his descendants (Genesis 23). *Photo by Howard Vos*

HEBREWS:

A Study and Teaching Outline

Part One: The Superiority of Christ's Person (1:1—4:13)

Part Two: The Superiority of Christ's Work (4:14—10:18)

Part Three: The Superiority of the Christian's Walk of Faith (10:19—13:25)

I. The Superiority of Christ over the Prophets 1:1–3
II. The Superiority of Christ over the Angels . . . . 1:4—2:18
   A. Christ Is Superior because of His Deity 1:4–14
   B. First Warning: Danger of Neglect 2:1–4
   C. Christ Is Superior because of His Humanity 2:5–18
III. The Superiority of Christ over Moses . . . . . . 3:1—4:13
   A. Christ Is Superior to Moses in His Work 3:1–4
   B. Christ Is Superior to Moses in His Person 3:5–6
   C. Second Warning: Danger of Unbelief . . . . 3:7—4:13

I. The Superiority of Christ's Priesthood . . . . . 4:14—7:28
   A. Christ Is Superior in His Position 4:14–16
   B. Christ Is Superior in His Qualifications 5:1–10
   C. Third Warning: Danger of Not Maturing . . . . 5:11—6:20
   D. Christ Is Superior in His Priestly Order 7:1–28
II. The Superiority of Christ's Covenant 8:1–13
   A. A Better Covenant 8:1–6
   B. A New Covenant 8:7–13
III. The Superiority of Christ's Sanctuary and Sacrifice . . . . 9:1—10:18
   A. Old Covenant's Sanctuary and Sacrifice 9:1–10
   B. New Covenant's Sanctuary and Sacrifice . . . . 9:11—10:18

I. A Call to Full Assurance of Faith . . . . . . 10:19—11:40
   A. Hold Fast the Confession of Faith 10:19–25
   B. Fourth Warning: Danger of Drawing Back 10:26–39
   C. Definition of Faith 11:1–3
   D. Examples of Faith 11:4–40
     1. Abel 11:4
     2. Enoch 11:5–6
     3. Noah 11:7
     4. Abraham and Sarah 11:8–19
     5. Isaac 11:20
     6. Jacob 11:21
     7. Joseph 11:22
     8. Moses' Parents 11:23
     9. Moses 11:24–29
    10 Joshua and Rahab 11:30–31
    11. Many Other Heroes of Faith 11:32–40
II. Endurance of Faith 12:1–29
   A. Example of Christ's Endurance 12:1–4
   B. A Call to Endure God's Chastening 12:5–24
   C. Fifth Warning: Danger of Refusing God 12:25–29
III. A Call to Love 13:1–17
   A. Love in the Social Realm 13:1–6
   B. Love in the Religious Realm 13:7–17
IV. Conclusion 13:18–25

3. A descendant of Caleb (1 Chr. 2:42–43).

4. A town in Asher (Josh. 19:28, KJV; Ebron, NRSV, NKJV). This may be the same town as Abdon (Josh. 21:30).

HEIFER — young cow (Gen. 15:9).

HEIR — one who inherits (Rom. 8:17). (see INHERITANCE).

HELL — the place of eternal punishment for the unrighteous. The NKJV and KJV use this word to translate Sheol and Hades, the Old and New Testament words, respectively, for the abode of the dead (Matt. 5:22, 29–30).

HELLENISM — a style of Greek civilization associated with the spread of Greek language and culture to the Mediterranean world after the conquests of Alexander the Great.

In the Hellenistic period, Greek became the common language throughout the ancient world. So many Jews spoke Greek that an authorized Greek translation of the Old Testament, the SEPTUAGINT, was made at Alexandria, Egypt. In the Bible, the word "Hellenists" (NKJV) or "Grecians" (KJV) in Acts 6:1 and 9:29 (Grecian Jews, NIV) refers to Greek-speaking Jews.

HELMET — a protective head covering worn in battle (1 Sam. 17:5); also symbolic for salvation (Eph. 6:17).

HEMORRHAGE — uncontrolled bleeding (Mark 5:25).

HENCEFORTH, HENCEFORWARD — from now on (John 15:15).

HERALD — an officer sent by a king or other high official to proclaim a message or announce good news (Dan. 3:4).

HERB — grass, plant (Luke 11:42).

HEREAFTER — the future or possible reference to life in heaven (Mark 11:14).

HERITAGE — something inherited (Ex. 6:8; 1 Pet. 5:3); can be spiritual or material.

HERMENEUTICS [hur-me-newt'-ics] — the principles and methods used to interpret Scripture. Bible scholars believe a biblical text must be interpreted according to the language in which it was written, its historical context, the identity and purpose of the author, its literary nature, and the situation to which it was originally addressed.

HEROD [her'-od] — the name of several Roman rulers in the Palestine region during Jesus' earthly ministry and the periods shortly before His birth and after His Resurrection.

The Herodian dynasty made its way into Palestine through Antipater, an Idumean by descent. The Idumeans were of Edomite stock as descendants of Esau. Antipater was installed as procurator of Judea by Julius Caesar, the emperor of Rome, in 47 B.C. He appointed two of his sons to ruling positions. One of these was Herod, known as "Herod the Great," who was appointed governor of Judea.

HERODIANS [he-ro'-de-ans] — Jews of influence and standing who were favorable toward Greek customs and Roman law in New Testament times. Although the Herodians should not be equated with the SADDUCEES, they sided with the Sadducees in their pro-Roman sympathies and opposed the PHARISEES, who were anti-Roman. The Herodians joined forces with the Pharisees, however, in their opposition to Jesus.

HERODIAS [he-ro'-de-as] — the queen who demanded John the Baptist's head on a platter (Matt. 14:1–12). The granddaughter of Herod the Great, Herodias first married her father's brother, Herod Philip I. One child was born to this union. Philip's half-brother, the tetrarch Herod Antipas, wanted Herodias for his own wife, so he divorced his wife and married Herodias while Philip was still living.

Excavated remains of a structure in Jerusalem built by Herod the Great. This Herod was known as a builder of many magnificent buildings, including a temple for use by Jewish worshipers.

HESHBON [hesh'-bon] — the former capital of Sihon, king of the Amorites. Situated in Transjordan about 80 kilometers (50 miles) east of Jerusalem and approximately 23 kilometers (14 miles) southwest of modern Amman, Jordan, Heshbon was captured by the Israelites (Josh. 12:1–2), then rebuilt and populated by the tribes of Reuben (Josh. 13:17) and Gad (1 Chr. 6:81). Later, it was captured by Mesha, King of Moab, and was denounced by the prophets (Is. 15:4; 16:8–9).

HEW — to cleave or cut with blows from a heavy cutting instrument, as in chopping firewood (2 Chr. 2:10) or quarrying and cutting stone for building purposes (Amos 5:11).

HEZEKIAH [hez-e-ki'-ah] *(the Lord is my strength)* — the name of three or four men in the Old Testament:

1. The 13th king of Judah. Born the son of Ahaz by Abi, daughter of Zechariah, Hezekiah be-came known as one of Judah's godly kings. That an ungodly man like Ahaz could have such a godly son can only be attributed to the grace of God. Hezekiah's father had given the kingdom over to idolatry; but upon his accession to the throne, Hezekiah decisively and courageously initiated religious reforms (2 Kin. 18:4).

2. A descendant of David's royal line, a son of Neariah (1 Chr. 3:23).

3. A head of a family who returned from the Captivity in Babylon (Neh. 7:21).

4. The great-great-grandfather of the prophet Zephaniah (Zeph. 1:1; Hizkiah, KJV, perhaps the same as No. 1).

HIGH PLACES — elevated or hilltop sites dedicated to worship of pagan gods. Ancient peoples often built their shrines on hilltops. In Mesopotamia, where the land is flat, they built artificial mountains in the shape of step pyramids called Ziggurats. The Tower of BABEL (Gen. 11:1–9) was probably such a ziggurat.

HIGH PRIEST — highest religious position among the Hebrews (2 Chr. 24:11). Aaron was the first.

HILKIAH [hil-ki′-ah] *(the Lord is my portion)* — the name of seven or eight Old Testament men. The two most notable are:

1. A high priest during the reign of King Josiah of Judah (2 Kin. 22:4–14). Hilkiah assisted Josiah in reforming Judah's backslidden people.

2. A priest who helped Ezra read the Book of the Law to the people (Neh. 8:4; 11:11).

HIN — liquid unit of measure (Ex. 30:24).

HINNOM [hin′-nom] — an unknown person, perhaps the original Jebusite owner, whose name appears only in the phrase, "the Valley of Hinnom" (Josh. 15:8; Neh. 11:30)—a valley outside Jerusalem.

HIRAM [hi′-ram] *(my brother is exalted)* — the name of two Old Testament men:

1. A king of Tyre and friend of both David and Solomon (2 Sam. 5:11; 1 Kin. 10:11, 22; 2 Chr. 8:2, 18).

2. A skilled laborer who worked on Solomon's temple (1 Kin. 7:13, 40, 45). He worked in bronze on the pillars, the laver, the basins, and the shovels. The title "father" given to him probably means he was a master workman. His name is also spelled Huram (2 Chr. 2:13–14; Huram-Abi, NIV).

HIRE — employ but also can mean bribe (Ezek. 16:33).

HISS, HISSING — to expel the air between the tongue and the teeth to express contempt, insult, and scorn (Job 27:23). Hissing often was accompanied by clapping the hands, wagging the head, and grinding the teeth (Lam. 2:15–16).

HITHER — here (Gen. 15:16).

HITHERTO — until now (John 16:24).

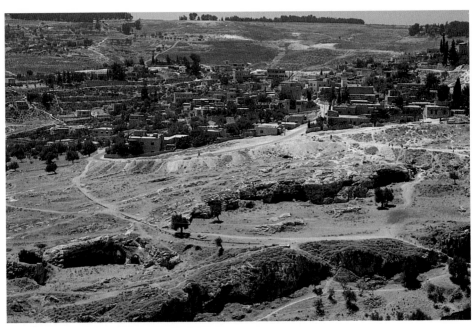

The Valley of Hinnom west and south of Jerusalem. In Jeremiah's time this valley was associated with worship of the pagan god Molech in rites that required child sacrifices (Jer. 19:1–9).

Photo by Howard Vos

HITTITES [hit'-tites] — a people of the ancient world who flourished in Asia Minor between about 1900 and 1200 B.C. The name Hittite comes from Hatti, another name for Anatolia, the capital of which was Hattusha. Later the Hittites spread into northern Syria and populated such cities as Aleppo, Carchemish, and Hamath. The Old Testament contains many references to the Hittites (Gen. 15:20; Num. 13:29; 1 Kin. 10:29; Ezra 9:1; Ezek. 16:3, 45).

HOLY — moral and ethical wholeness or perfection; freedom from moral evil. Holiness is one of the essential elements of God's nature required of His people. Holiness may also be rendered "sanctification" or "godliness." The Hebrew word for "holy" denotes that which is "sanctified" or "set apart" for divine service (Deut. 7:6).

HOLY GHOST — common KJV translation of Holy Spirit (Matt. 1:18).

HOLY OF HOLIES — KJV term for Most HOLY PLACE.

HOLY PLACE — KJV term for the most sacred inner room in the TABERNACLE and the TEMPLE, where only the HIGH PRIEST was allowed to go. This room, separated from the rest of the worship area by a sacred veil, represented the presence of God in all His power and holiness. In this room was the ARK OF THE COVENANT, covered by the sacred MERCY SEAT (Ex. 25:10–22). Once a year on the DAY OF ATONEMENT, the high priest entered the Holy Place with sacrificial blood and made ATONEMENT before God for the sins of the people (Leviticus 16).

HOLY SPIRIT — the third person of the Trinity, who exercises the power of the Father and the Son in creation and redemption (John 14:16–17). Because the Holy Spirit is the power by which believers come to Christ and see with new eyes of faith, He is closer to us than we are to ourselves. Like the eyes of the body through which we see physical things, He is seldom in focus to be seen directly because He is the one through whom all

else is seen in a new light. This explains why the relationship of the Father and the Son is more prominent in the Gospels, because it is through the eyes of the Holy Spirit that the Father-Son relationship is viewed.

HOMER — standard unit for dry measure (Ezek. 45:11–14; Hos. 3:2). This unit contained about 220 liters (6 1/4 bushels). It was a large measure weighing the equivalent of the normal load a donkey could carry (the Hebrew word for "donkey" is *hamor*). In Leviticus 27:16, a homer of barley is worth 50 shekels of silver. (see WEIGHTS AND MEASURES OF THE BIBLE).

HOMOSEXUALITY — the state or condition of directing sexual desire toward another of the same sex. Homosexual behavior is prohibited in Scripture (Lev. 20:13) and is widely believed to have been a major cause of the divine judgment against Sodom and Gomorrah (Gen. 19:4–5, 12–13). The apostle Paul listed those who practice homosexual behavior among "the unrighteous" who would not inherit the kingdom of God (1 Cor. 6:9), and declared that God's wrath stands against such behavior, whether practiced by men or women (Rom. 1:26–27).

HONOR — esteem and respect. To honor God is to give Him reverence and homage, for God alone is worthy of our highest honor (1 Chr. 16:27; Rev. 4:9–11). Jesus makes it plain that one cannot honor the Father unless he also honors the Son (John 5:23). Esteem, honor, and respect should also be given to our spiritual leaders in the church "Let the elders who rule well be counted worthy of double honor, especially those who labor in the word and doctrine," (1 Tim. 5:17; Heb. 13:7, KJV).

HOPE — confident expectancy. In the Bible, the word "hope" stands for both the act of hoping (Rom. 4:18; 1 Cor. 9:10) and the thing hoped for (Col. 1:5; 1 Pet. 1:3). Hope does not arise from the individual's desires or wishes but from God, who is Himself the believer's hope: "My hope is in You" (Ps. 39:7). Genuine hope is not wishful thinking, but a firm assurance about things that are unseen and still in the future (Rom. 8:24–25; Heb. 11:1, 7).

HOR, MOUNT [hoer] — the name of two mountains in the Old Testament:

1. The mountain on the border of the Edomites where Aaron died and was buried (Num. 20:22–29; Deut. 32:50). Numbers 20:23 indicates that Mount Hor was situated by the border of the land of Edom. This was the place where the Hebrew people stopped after they left Kadesh (Num. 20:22; 33:37).

2. A mountain in northern Palestine between the Mediterranean Sea and the approach to Hamath (Num. 34:7–8).

HOREB, MOUNT [ho'-reb] *(waste)* — the "mountain of God" (Ex. 18:5) in the Sinai Peninsula where Moses heard God speaking through the burning bush (Ex. 3:1) and where the law was given to Israel. "Horeb" is the favored name for Mt. Sinai in the Book of Deuteronomy, where the word occurs more often than in the rest of the entire Old Testament.

HOSANNA [ho'-san-na] *(save us now)* — the shout of the multitude at the time of Jesus' triumphal entry into Jerusalem (Matt. 21:9, 15; Mark 11:9–10; John 12:13). The word originally was a prayer requesting God's help (Ps. 118:25), but it had become a cry of joy or a shout of welcome by this time in Jewish history.

HOSEA [ho-zay'-ah] *(deliverance)* — an Old Testament prophet and author of the Book of Hosea. The son of Beeri (Hos. 1:1), Hosea ministered in the northern kingdom of Israel during the chaotic period just before the fall of this nation in 722 B.C. The literary features within Hosea's book suggest he was a member of the upper class. The tone and contents of the book also show he was a man of deep compassion, strong loyalty, and keen awareness of the political events taking place in the world at that time. As a prophet, he was also deeply committed to God and His will as it was being revealed to His covenant people.

HOSEA, BOOK OF — a prophetic book of the Old Testament that emphasizes God's stead-

The barren mountain traditionally identified as Mount Hor, the place where Aaron was buried along the border of ancient Edom (Num. 20:22–29). *Photo: Levant Photo Service*

HOSEA:
A Study and Teaching Outline

I. **The Adulterous Wife and Faithful Husband. . . 1:1—3:5**
  A. The Introduction to the Book of Hosea. 1:1
  B. The Prophetic Marriage of Hosea to
    Gomer. . . . . 1:2—2:1
    1. Hosea's Marriage to Gomer 1:2
    2. The Children of Hosea and Gomer 1:3–9
    3. The Application of Future
      Restoration . . . . 1:10—2:1
  C. The Application of the Adultery of
    Gomer 2:2–23
    1. Israel's Sin of Spiritual Adultery 2:2–5
    2. Judgment of God 2:6–13
    3. Restoration of Israel. 2:14–23
  D. The Restoration of Gomer to Hosea 3:1–5
II. **The Adulterous Israel and Faithful Lord . . . . 4:1—14:9**
  A. The Spiritual Adultery of Israel . . . . 4:1—6:3
    1. The Sins of Israel. 4:1–19
      a. Rejection of the Knowledge of God 4:1–10
      b. Idolatry of Israel 4:11–19
    2. Judgment on Israel 5:1–14
    3. Eventual Restoration of Israel. . . . . 5:15—6:3
  B. The Refusal of Israel to Repent of Its
    Adultery . . . . 6:4—8:14
    1. Willful Transgression of the Covenant. . . . 6:4–11
    2. Willful Refusal to Return to the Lord 7:1–16
    3. Willful Idolatry 8:1–14
  C. The Judgment of Israel by God. . . . . 9:1—10:15
    1. Judgment of Dispersion. 9:1–9
    2. Judgment of Barrenness 9:10–17
    2. Judgment of Barrenness 9:10–17
  D. The Restoration of Israel to the
    Lord . . . . 11:1—14:9
    1. God's Love for Israel 11:1–11
    2. Israel's Continuing Sin . . . . 11:12—13:16
    3. God's Promise to Restore Israel. 14:1–9

fast love for His covenant people, in spite of their continuing sin and rebellion. The book is named for its author, the prophet Hosea, who demonstrated God's steadfast love in dramatic fashion through his devotion to his own unfaithful wife.

Through his marriage and prophetic message, Hosea presents a vivid picture of the steadfast love of God for His people. Because they have sinned and broken the covenant, God's people deserve His certain judgment. But because of His undying love for them, His mercy and lovingkindness will prevail. Many people believe the Old Testament portrays God's wrath, while the New Testament pictures his love. But the Book of Hosea includes tender expressions of deep love

among this prophet's descriptions of judgment. Hosea ranks with Deuteronomy and the Gospel of John as major biblical treatises on the love of God. This love is not mere sentiment; it is rooted in compassion and bound in holiness. God's love makes demands, but it is also willing to forgive.

HOSPITALITY — the practice of entertaining strangers graciously. Hospitality was a very important trait in Bible times. In the New Testament, the Greek word translated "hospitality" literally means "love of strangers" (Rom. 12:13). In the Old Testament, Abraham was the host to angels unaware; he invited strangers into his house, washed their feet, prepared fresh meat, had Sarah bake bread, and later accompanied them as they left (Gen. 18:1–15). Even today a traditional greeting to the guests among the Bedouin people of the Middle East is "You are among your family."

HOST — a person who entertains guests in his home and shows HOSPITALITY to strangers. Perhaps because of their own history as wanderers in the desert, hospitality was important to the Hebrew people. Guests were welcomed and provided for (Gen. 18:1–8; 2 Kin. 4:8–17). A host would go to great lengths to protect his guests (Judg. 19:16–24). This was considered a sign of faithfulness to God (Job 31:32; Is. 58:7).

HOUSE — any dwelling place, whether the hut of a peasant, the palace of a king, or the temple of God. Many different kinds and sizes of houses existed in biblical times. The style and size was dictated by tradition and the resources of the family. Those with money usually had two-story homes with a number of rooms. Local customs and available materials dictated the construction techniques used to build houses.

HUMILITY — a freedom from arrogance that grows out of the recognition that all we have and are comes from God. The Greek philosophers despised humility because to them it implied inadequacy, lack of dignity, and worthlessness. This is not the meaning of humility as defined by the Bible. Jesus is the supreme example of humility (Matt. 11:29; Mark 10:45; John 13:4–17; Phil. 2:5–8), and He is completely adequate and of infinite dignity and worth. Biblical humility is not a belittling of oneself (Matt. 6:16–18; Rom. 12:3), but an exalting or praising of others, especially God and Christ (John 3:30; Phil. 2:3). Humble people focus more on God and others than on themselves.

HYPOCRITE — a person who puts on a false appearance of virtue or religion (Matt. 6:2, 5, 16).

HYSSOP — a small, bushy plant (Ex. 12:22; John 19:29).

I AM (see God, Names of).

ICONIUM [i-co'-ne-um] — the capital of the province of Lycaonia in central Asia Minor. Iconium was visited by Paul and Barnabas when they were expelled from Antioch of Pisidia (Acts 13:51). Paul's ministry at Iconium was blessed by the salvation of many Jews and Gentiles (Acts 14:1). But persecution overtook them, and they had to flee for their lives (Acts 14:6; 19, 21). Iconium is known today as Konya, or Konia.

IDLE — useless, inactive, lazy. The Bible declares that the idle person will come to poverty and suffer hunger (Prov. 14:23; 19:15).

IDOL, IMAGE — a representation or symbol of an object of worship; a false god. In a few places in the Bible, the word "image" appears in a neutral sense, not referring to a man-made object of worship. Adam, created in the image of God (Gen. 1:26), or Christ, the visible image of the invisible God (2 Cor. 4:4; Col. 1:15), are examples of this.

IDOLATRY — the worship of something created as opposed to the worship of the Creator Himself. Scores of references to idolatry appear in the Old Testament. This shows that idolatry probably was the greatest temptation our spiritual forefathers faced. While we find bowing down to a statue no temptation, they apparently slipped into idolatry constantly. So serious was this sin that the prohibition against the making and worshiping of images was included near the beginning of the Ten Commandments (Ex. 20:4–6).

IMAGE — likeness (Gen. 1:26).

IMAGE OF GOD — the characteristics of humankind with which God endowed them at creation, distinguishing them from the rest of God's creatures.

IMMANUEL [im-man'-u-el] *(with us is God)* — a symbolic name from the prophecy of Isaiah applied in later years to Jesus the Messiah (Is. 7:14; Matt. 1:23).

The "I AM" Statements

Twenty-three times in all we find our Lord's meaningful "I AM" (*ego eimi*, Gk.) in the Greek text of John's Gospel (4:26; 6:20, 35, 41, 48, 51; 8:12, 18, 24, 28, 58; 10:7, 9, 11, 14; 11:25; 13:19; 14:6; 15:1, 5; 18:5, 6, 8). In several of these He joins His "I AM" with seven tremendous metaphors which are expressive of His saving relationship toward the world.

"I AM the Bread of life" (6:35, 41, 48, 51).
"I AM the Light of the world" (8:12).
"I AM the Door of the sheep" (10:7, 9).
"I AM the Good Shepherd" (10:11, 14).
"I AM the Resurrection and the Life" (11:25).
"I AM the Way, the Truth, the Life" (14:6).
"I AM the true Vine" (15:1, 5).

IMMORALITY — behavior contrary to established moral principles. The word is used to describe Israel's worship of pagan gods (Ezek. 23:8, 17), an adulterous woman (Prov. 2:16), and sexual impurity (1 Cor. 5:1).

IMMORTALITY — exemption from death; the state of living forever. Thus, immortality is the opposite of mortality, or being subject to death. In the Bible, the word "immortality" refers primarily to the spirit, but is also used of the resurrected or transformed body.

IMPART — to give (Rom. 1:11).

IMPORTUNITY — KJV word for persistence in making a request or demand. In Jesus' parable of the persistent friend (Luke 11:5–8), a man was rewarded for his importunity (persistence, NKJV, NASB; boldness, NIV; persistence, REB) because he kept knocking on the door. Jesus applied this truth to the need for persistence in prayer.

IMPUTE, IMPUTATION — charging or reckoning something to a person's account.

INCARNATION — a theological term for the coming of God's Son into the world as a human being. The term itself is not used in the Bible, but it is based on clear references in the New Testament to Jesus as a person "in the flesh" (Rom. 8:3; Eph. 2:15; Col. 1:22).

INCENSE — a sweet-smelling substance that was burned as an offering to God on the altar in the tabernacle and the temple. The purpose of this incense offering was to honor God. Incense symbolized and expressed the prayers of the Hebrew people, which were considered a pleasant aroma offered to God.

INCREASE — as a noun, fruit (Lev. 26:4); as a verb, to grow, multiply (Prov. 1:5; Acts 6:7).

INDIGNATION — anger (Ps. 69:24; Rev. 14:10).

INFINITY — a theological term implying that God is not bound by time and space (Col. 1:15; Heb. 1:3).

INFIRMITY — sickness, weakness (John 5:5).

INHABITANT — one who dwells in a place (Gen. 19:25; Rev. 17:2).

INHERITANCE — the receipt of property as a gift or by legal right, usually upon the death of one's father (Gen. 15:7; Luke 10:25; Deut. 21:16).

To the Hebrew mind, the term "inheritance" had strong spiritual and national associations extending far beyond the family estate. The land of Canaan was regarded as an inheritance from the Lord because God had promised the land to Abraham and his descendants (Num. 33:53). Both Moses and Joshua were told by the Lord to divide the land of Canaan among the tribes "as an inheritance" (Num. 26:52–53; Josh. 13:6). God directed that the land be distributed to each tribe by lot according to its population.

This incense burner, decorated with sacred serpents, was discovered in the excavation of the Canaanite temple at Beth Shan.

INIQUITY — unrighteousness, lawlessness. The Bible often uses this word to describe evil and wickedness. Iniquity can suggest different types of evil, such as transgressions of spiritual law and crimes against God (2 Pet. 2:16; Rev. 18:5), moral or legal wrongs (1 Cor. 13:6) or depravity and sin in general (Gen. 15:16; Ps. 51:1, 5, 9).

INJUSTICE — a wrong, an injury (Job 16:17).

INNOCENCE — blamelessness; freedom from sin and guilt (Gen. 20:5; Ps. 26:6; Hos. 8:5). Since the Fall, when Adam and Eve brought disobedience into the world (Gen. 3:1–24), no one except Jesus has been totally sinless and blameless (Rom. 3:9–18; 2 Cor. 5:21). People may be called "innocent" only because they have been forgiven of sin and been declared new creations through faith in Christ.

INNOCENT — without guilt (Matt. 27:4).

INSPIRATION — a technical term for the Holy Spirit's supernatural guidance of those who received special revelation from God as they wrote the books of the Bible. The end result of this inspiration is that the Bible conveys the truths that God wanted His people to know and to communicate to the world (2 Tim. 3:16).

INSTRUCT — train, teach (2 Tim. 2:25).

INSURRECTION — an act of rebellion against the established government (Ezra 4:19; Ps. 64:2; Acts 21:38). Barabbas, the criminal who was released by Pilate before Jesus' Crucifixion, was guilty of insurrection against the Roman government (Mark 15:7).

INTEGRITY — honesty, sincerity, singleness of purpose. In the Old Testament, Noah (Gen. 6:9), Abraham (Gen. 17:1), Jacob (Gen. 25:27), David (1 Kin. 9:4), and Job (Job 1:1, 8; 2:3, 9; 4:6; 27:5; 31:6) were called people of integrity. Although Jesus did not use the word "integrity," he called for purity of heart (Matt. 5:8), singleness of purpose (Matt. 6:22), and purity of motive (Matt. 6:1–6).

INTERCESSION — the act of petitioning God or praying on behalf of another person or group (Is. 53:12; Heb. 7:25). The sinful nature of this world separates human beings from God. It has always been necessary, therefore, for righteous individuals to go before God to seek reconciliation between Him and His fallen creation.

INTEREST — additional payment, a fee, especially used in reference to loans.

ISAAC [i'-zak] ([God] *laughs*) — the only son of Abraham by his wife Sarah; father of Jacob and Esau. God promised to make Abraham's descendants a great nation that would become God's chosen people. But the promised son was a long time in coming. Isaac was born when Abraham was 100 years old and Sarah was 90 (Gen. 17:17; 21:5). Both Abraham and Sarah laughed when they heard they would have a son in their old age (Gen. 17:17–19; 18:9–15). This partially explains why they named their son Isaac.

ISAIAH [i'-za-ah] *(the Lord has saved)* — a famous Old Testament prophet who predicted the

Michelangelo's painting of the prophet Isaiah in the Sistine Chapel in Rome. *Photo by Howard Vos*

coming of the Messiah; the author of the Book of Isaiah. Isaiah was probably born in Jerusalem of a family that was related to the royal house of Judah. He recorded the events of the reign of King Uzziah of Judah (2 Chr. 26:22). When Uzziah died (740 B.C.), Isaiah received his prophetic calling from God in a stirring vision of God in the temple (Isaiah 6). The king of Judah had died; now Isaiah had seen the everlasting King in whose service he would spend the rest of his life.

ISAIAH, BOOK OF — a major prophetic book of the Old Testament, noted for its description of the coming Messiah as God's Suffering Servant. Because of its lofty portrayal of God and His purpose of salvation, the book is sometimes called "the fifth gospel," implying it is similar in theme to the Gospels of the New Testament. The book is named for its author, the great prophet Isaiah, whose name means "The Lord has saved."

ISCARIOT [is-car′-e-ot] *(man of Kerioth)* — the surname of Judas, one of the Twelve, who betrayed Jesus (John 6:71; 12:4; 13:2, 26).

ISHMAEL [ish′-ma-el] *(God hears)* — the name of six men in the Old Testament:

1. The first son of Abraham, by his wife's Egyptian maidservant, Hagar. Although God had promised Abraham an heir (Gen. 15:4), Abraham's wife, Sarah, had been unable to bear a child. When Abraham was 85, Sarah offered her maid to him in order to help fulfill God's promise (Gen. 16:1–2).

After Hagar learned that she was pregnant, she grew proud and began to despise Sarah. Sarah complained to Abraham, who allowed her to discipline Hagar. Sarah's harsh treatment of Hagar caused her to flee into the wilderness. There she met the angel of God, who told her to return to Sarah and submit to her authority. As an encouragement, the angel promised Hagar that her son, who would be named Ishmael, would have uncounted descendants. Hagar then returned to Abraham and Sarah and bore her son (Gen. 16:4–15).

2. The son of Nethaniah and a member of the house of David.

3. A descendant of Jonathan, son of Saul (1 Chr. 8:38; 9:44).

4. The father of Zebadiah, ruler of the house of Judah and the highest civil authority under King Jehoshaphat (2 Chr. 19:11).

5. A son of Jehohanan. Ishmael was one of five army officers recruited by Jehoiada to help overthrow Queen Athaliah of Judah in favor of the rightful heir, Joash (2 Chr. 23:1).

6. A priest of the clan of Pashhur who divorced

ISAIAH:
A Study and Teaching Outline

Part One: Prophecies of Condemnation (1:1—35:10)

I.   Prophecies Against Judah . . . . 1:1—12:6
II. Prophecies Against Other Nations . . . . . . 13:1—23:18
III. Prophecies of the Day of the Lord . . . . . . 24:1—27:13
IV. Prophecies of Judgment and Blessing . . . 28:1—35:10

Part Two: Historical Material (36:1—39:8)

I.   Hezekiah's Deliverance from Assyria. . . . 36:1—37:38
II. Hezekiah's Deliverance from Sickness . . . . . 38:1—22
III. Hezekiah's Sin . . . . 39:1—8

Part Three: Prophecies of Comfort (40:1—66:24)

I.   Prophecies of Israel's Deliverance . . . . . 40:1—48:22
II. Prophecies of Israel's Deliverer . . . . 49:1—57:21
III. Prophecies of Israel's Glorious Future . . . 58:1—66:24

The famous Isaiah Scroll is one of the best-preserved manuscripts discovered among the Dead Sea scrolls. It contains the entire text of the Book of Isaiah. *Photo by John C. Trever*

his foreign wife after the Babylonian Captivity (Ezra 10:22).

ISRAEL [iz′-ra-el] *(he strives with God)* — the name given to Jacob after his great struggle with God at Peniel near the brook Jabbok (Gen. 32:28; 35:10). The name Israel has been interpreted by different scholars as "prince with God," "he strives with God," "let God rule," or "God strives." The name was later applied to the descendants of Jacob. The twelve tribes were called "Israelites," "children of Israel," and "house of Israel," identifying them as the descendants of Israel through his sons and grandsons.

ISRAELITE [iz′-ra-el-ite] — a descendant of Israel, or Jacob (Lev. 23:42–43). Israelites were considered to be children of the Covenant, faithful servants of the Lord, and heirs to the promises made to Abraham (Rom. 9:4; 11:1).

JACOB [ja′-cub] *(he supplants)* — one of the twin sons of Isaac and Rebekah. The brother of Esau, he was known also as Israel (Gen. 32:28).

Jacob was born in answer to his father's prayer (Gen. 25:21), but he became the favorite son of his mother (25:28). He was named Jacob because, at the birth of the twins, "his hand took hold of Esau's heel" (25:26). According to the accounts in Genesis, Jacob continued to "take hold of" the possessions of others—his brother's birthright (25:29–34), his father's blessing (27:1–29), and his father-in-law's flocks and herds (30:25–43; 31:1).

JAIRUS [ja-i′-rus] — a ruler of a synagogue near Capernaum and the Sea of Galilee. Jairus' daughter was miraculously raised from the dead by Jesus (Mark 5:21–23, 35–43).

JAMES — five men in the New Testament. The two most notable are:

1. James, the son of Zebedee, one of Jesus' twelve apostles. James' father was a fisherman; his mother, Salome, often cared for Jesus' daily needs (Matt. 27:56; Mark 15:40–41). In lists of the twelve apostles, James and his brother John always form a group of four with two other brothers, Peter and Andrew. The four were fishermen on the Sea of Galilee. Their call to follow Jesus is the first recorded event after the beginning of Jesus' public ministry (Matt. 4:18–22; Mark 1:16–20).

2. James, the son of Alphaeus. This James was also one of the twelve apostles. In each list of the apostles he is mentioned in ninth position (Matt. 10:3; Mark 3:18; Luke 6:15; Acts 1:13).

JAMES, EPISTLE OF — a book characterized by its hard-hitting, practical religion. The epistle reads like a sermon and, except for a brief introduction, has none of the traits of an ancient letter. Each of the five chapters is packed with pointed illustrations and reminders designed to motivate the wills and hearts of believers to grasp a truth once taught by Jesus: "A tree is known by its fruit" (Matt. 12:33).

JAMES:
A Study and Teaching Outline

I. **The Test of Faith**. 1:1–18
  A. The Purpose of Tests 1:1–12
  B. The Source of Temptations 1:13–18
II. **The Characteristics of Faith**. . . . . 1:19—5:6
  A. Faith Obeys the Word 1:19–27
  B. Faith Removes Discriminations. 2:1–13
  C. Faith Proves Itself by Works 2:14–26
  D. Faith Controls the Tongue. 3:1–12
  E. Faith Produces Wisdom. 3:13–18
  F. Faith Produces Humility 4:1–12
  G. Faith Produces Dependence on God . . . . 4:13—5:6
III. **The Triumph of Faith** 5:7–20
  A. Faith Endures, Awaiting Christ's Return . . . 5:7–12
  B. Faith Prays for the Afflicted. 5:13–18
  C. Faith Confronts the Erring Believer 5:19–20

The Epistle of James is a sturdy, compact letter on practical religion. For James, the acid test of true religion is in the doing rather than in the hearing, "believing," or speaking. James exalts genuineness of faith, and is quick to encourage the lowly that God gives grace to the humble (4:6), wisdom to the ignorant (1:5), salvation to the sinner (1:21), and the kingdom to the poor (2:5). He is equally quick to condemn counterfeit religion that would substitute theory for practice, and he does so with biting sarcasm. True religion is moral religion and social religion. True religion is doing the right thing in one's everyday affairs. In this respect James echoes clearly the ethical teaching of Jesus, especially as it is recorded in the Sermon on the Mount (Matthew 5—7). "Not everyone who says to Me, 'Lord, Lord,' shall enter the kingdom of heaven, but he who does the will of My Father in heaven" (Matt. 7:21).

JAPHETH [ja´-feth] — one of the three sons of Noah, usually mentioned after his two brothers Shem and Ham (Gen. 5:32; 6:10; 1 Chr. 1:4). Japheth and his wife were two of the eight people who entered the ark and were saved from the destructive waters of the Flood (Gen. 7:7; 1 Pet. 3:20).

Japheth's descendants spread over the north and west regions of the earth: "The sons of Japheth were Gomer, Magog, Madai, Javan, Tubal, Meshech, and Tiras" (1 Chr. 1:5). The Medes, Greeks, Romans, Russians, and Gauls are often referred to as his descendants.

JEBUSITES [jeb´-u-site] — the name of the original inhabitants of the city of Jebus, their name for ancient Jerusalem (Judg. 19:10–11; 1 Chr. 11:4–6).

JEHOIACHIN [je-hoy´-a-kin] *(the Lord establishes)* — the son and successor of Jehoiakim as king of Judah, about 598 or 597 B.C. (2 Chr. 36:8–9; Ezek. 1:2). Jehoiachin did evil in the sight of the Lord, like his father. But he had little opportunity to influence affairs of state, since he reigned only three months. His brief reign ended when the armies of Nebuchadnezzar of Babylon besieged Jerusalem. When the city surrendered, Jehoiachin was exiled to Babylonia (2 Kin. 24:6–15).

JEHOIADA [je-hoy´-a-dah] *(the Lord knows)* — the name of six men in the Old Testament, most notably a priest during the reigns of Ahaziah, Athaliah, and Joash of Judah (2 Kin. 11:1—12:16) who helped hide the young king Joash from the wrath of Queen Athaliah (2 Chr. 22:10–12). By his courageous action, Jehoiada was instrumental in preserving the line of David, since Joash was a descendant of David and an ancestor of Jesus.

JEHOIAKIM [je-hoy´-a-kim] *(the Lord raises up)* — an evil king of Judah whose downfall was predicted by the prophet Jeremiah.

JEHORAM [je-ho´-ram] *(the Lord is exalted)* — the name of three men in the Old Testament:

1. The fifth king of Judah, Jehoram was also called Joram.

2. The ninth king of Israel, Jehoram was also called Joram.

3. A priest sent by King Jehoshaphat to instruct the people in the law (2 Chr. 17:8).

JEHOSHAPHAT [je-hosh´-a-fat] *(the Lord is judge)* — the name of five men in the Old Testament, most notably a son of Asa who succeeded his father as king of Judah (1 Kin. 15:24). Jehoshaphat was 35 years old when he became king, and he reigned 25 years in Jerusalem (2 Chr. 20:31), from about 873 B.C. to about 848 B.C.

JEHU [je´-hu] *(the Lord is He)* — the name of five men in the Old Testament, namely the 11th king of Israel (2 Chr. 22:7–9). Jehu was anointed by Elisha the prophet as king; he later overthrew Joram (Jehoram), King Ahab's son and successor, and reigned for 28 years (841—813 B.C.). His corrupt leadership weakened the nation. He is known for his violence against all members of the "house of Ahab" as he established his rule throughout the nation.

King Jehu of Israel bows before Shalmaneser III of Assyria, in this obelisk, or stone monument, discovered in ancient Assyria. *Photo by Howard Vos*

A woven tapestry that portrays the prophet Jeremiah, from the Church of San Vitale in Ravenna, Italy. *Photo by Howard Vos*

JEREMIAH [jer-e-mi'-ah] *(the Lord hurls)* — the name of nine men in the Old Testament, most notably the major prophet during the decline and fall of the southern kingdom of Judah and author of the Book of Jeremiah. He prophesied during the reigns of the last five kings of Judah.

JEREMIAH, BOOK OF — a major prophetic book of the Old Testament directed to the southern kingdom of Judah just before that nation fell to the Babylonians. The book is named for its author and central personality, the great prophet Jeremiah, who faithfully delivered God's message of judgment in spite of fierce opposition from his countrymen.

Jeremiah's greatest theological contribution was his concept of the new COVENANT (31:31–34). A new covenant between God and His people was necessary because the people had broken the Old Covenant; the captivity of God's people by a foreign power was proof of that. Although the Old Covenant had been renewed again and again throughout Israel's history, the people still continued to break the promises they had made to God. What was needed was a new type of covenant between God and His people—a covenant of grace and forgiveness written on the human heart, rather than a covenant of law engraved in stone.

JERICHO [jer'-ik-o] — one of the oldest inhabited cities in the world. Situated in the wide plain of the Jordan Valley (Deut. 34:1, 3) at the foot of the ascent to the Judean mountains, Jericho lies about 13 kilometers (8 miles) northwest of the site where the Jordan River flows into the Dead Sea, some 8 kilometers (5 miles) west of the Jordan.

JEREMIAH:
A Study and Teaching Outline

Part One: The Call of Jeremiah (1:1–19)

  I. Jeremiah's Call 1:1–10
 II. Jeremiah's Signs 1:11–16
III. Jeremiah's Assurance 1:17–19

Part Two: The Prophecies to Judah (2:1—45:5)

  I. The Condemnation of Judah . . . . 2:1—25:38
 II. The Conflicts of Jeremiah . . . . 26:1—29:32
III. The Future Restoration of Jerusalem . . . 30:1—33:26
IV. The Present Fall of Jerusalem . . . . 34:1—45:5

Part Three: The Prophecies to the Gentiles (46:1—51:64)

   I. Prophecies against Egypt 46:1–28
  II. Prophecies against Philistia 47:1–7
 III. Prophecies against Moab 48:1–47
  IV. Prophecies against Ammon 49:1–6
   V. Prophecies against Edom 49:7–22
  VI. Prophecies against Damascus 49:23–27
 VII. Prophecies against Kedar and Hazor 49:28–33
VIII. Prophecies against Elam 49:34–39
  IX. Prophecies against Babylonia . . . . 50:1—51:64

Part Four: The Fall of Jerusalem (52:1–34)

  I. The Capture of Jerusalem 52:1–11
 II. The Destruction of Jerusalem 52:12–23
III. The Exile to Babylonia 52:24–30
IV. The Release of Jehoiachin 52:31–34

The mound of ancient Jericho, believed by many archaeologists to be the oldest settlement in Palestine and possibly the oldest city in the ancient world. *Photo by Gustav Jeeninga*

Since it is approximately 244 meters (800 feet) below sea level, Jericho has a climate that is tropical and at times is very hot. Only a few inches of rainfall are recorded at Jericho each year; but the city is a wonderful oasis, known as "the city of palm trees" (Deut. 34:3) or "the city of palms" (Judg. 3:13). Jericho flourishes with date palms, banana trees, balsams, sycamores, and henna (Song 1:14; Luke 19:4).

JEROBOAM [jer-o-bo'-am] *(let the kinsman plead)* — the name of two kings of the northern kingdom of Israel:

1. Jeroboam I, the first king of Israel (the ten northern tribes, or the northern kingdom), a state established after the death of Solomon (1 Kin. 11:26—14:20). The son of Nebat and Zeruah, Jeroboam reigned over Israel for 22 years (1 Kin. 14:20), from 931/30 to 910/09 B.C.

2. Jeroboam II, the 14th king of Israel, who reigned for 41 years (793—753 B.C.). Jeroboam was the son and successor of Joash (or Jehoash); he was the grandson of Jehoahaz and the great-grandson of Jehu (2 Kin. 13:1, 13; 1 Chr. 5:17). The Bible declares that Jeroboam "did evil in the sight of the LORD" (2 Kin. 14:24).

JERUBBAAL [je-rub'-ba-al] *(let Baal plead)* — a name given to GIDEON, one of the judges of Israel, by his father after Gideon destroyed the altar of Baal at Ophrah (Judg. 6:32).

JERUSALEM [je-ru'-sa-lem] *(city of peace)* — sacred city and well-known capital of Palestine during Bible times. The earliest known name for Jerusalem was Urushalem. Salem, of which Melchizedek was king (Gen. 14:18), was a natural abbreviation for Jerusalem. Thus, Jerusalem appears in the Bible as early as the time of Abraham, although the city had probably been inhabited for centuries before that time.

The city of Jerusalem is mentioned directly in the Bible for the first time during the struggle of Joshua and the Israelites to take the land of Canaan (Josh. 10:1–4). Their efforts to take the city were unsuccessful, although the areas surrounding it were taken and the land was given to

The modern city of Jerusalem, showing the Dome of the Rock and the hill on which Solomon's temple was built. The hill in the distance is the site of the Mount of Olives. *Photo by Ben Chapman*

An artist's sketch of what Jerusalem might have looked like in New Testament times. The beautiful temple built by Herod appears within the square wall structure in the foreground.

Photo Amsterdam Bible Museum

Traditional site of the baptism of Jesus in the Jordan River at the beginning of His public ministry (Matt. 3:13–17). *Photo by Howard Vos*

the tribe of Judah. Still remaining in the fortress of the city itself were the Jebusites. Thus, the city was called Jebus.

JERUSALEM, NEW — the holy city described by John in Revelation 21—22; God's perfect and eternal order of the future. This New Jerusalem is not built by human hands; it is a heavenly city—one built and provided by God Himself (Rev. 21:2).

JESSE [jes'-se] *(meaning unknown)* — the father of King David (1 Sam. 16:18–19) and an ancestor of Jesus. Jesse was the father of eight sons—Eliab, Abinadab, Shimea (Shammah), Nethanel, Raddai, Ozem, Elihu, and David—and two daughters, Zeruiah and Abigail (1 Chr. 2:13–16). He is called a "Bethlehemite" (1 Sam. 16:1, 18).

JESUS CHRIST — the human-divine Son of God born of the Virgin Mary; the great High Priest who intercedes for His people at the right hand of God; founder of the Christian church and central figure of the human race.

JETHRO [je'-thro] *(his excellency)* — the father-in-law of Moses (Ex. 3:1), also called Reuel (Ex. 2:18), Hobab (Judg. 4:11), and Raguel (Num. 10:29; Reuel, NIV).

JEWS — a name applied first to the people living in Judah (when the Israelites were divided into the two kingdoms of Israel and Judah); after the Babylonian Captivity, all the descendants of Abraham were called "Jews." The term is used in the New Testament for all Israelites as opposed to the "Gentiles," or those of non-Jewish blood. Since a num-

The Sea, or Lake, of Galilee, scene of many of Jesus' miracles and teachings (Matt. 14:13–33).
Photo by Gustav Jeeninga

Titles of Christ

Name or Title	Significance	Biblical Reference
Adam, Last Adam	First of the new race of the redeemed	1 Cor. 15:45
Alpha and Omega	The beginning and ending of all things	Rev. 21:6
Bread of Life	The one essential food	John 6:35
Chief Cornerstone	A sure foundation for life	Eph. 2:20
Chief Shepherd	Protector, sustainer, and guide	1 Pet. 5:4
Firstborn from the Dead	Leads us into resurrection and eternal life	Col. 1:18
Good Shepherd	Provider and caretaker	John 10:11
Great Shepherd of the Sheep	Trustworthy guide and protector	Heb. 13:20
High Priest	A perfect sacrifice for our sins	Heb. 3:1
Holy One of God	Sinless in His nature	Mark 1:24
Immanuel (God With Us)	Stands with us in all life's circumstances	Matt. 1:23
King of Kings, Lord of Lords	The Almighty, before whom every knee will bow	Rev. 19:16
Lamb of God	Gave His life as a sacrifice on our behalf	John 1:29
Light of the World	Brings hope in the midst of darkness	John 9:5
Lord of Glory	The power and presence of the living God	1 Cor. 2:8
Mediator between God and Men	Brings us into God's presence redeemed and forgiven	1 Tim. 2:5
Only Begotten of the Father	The unique, one-of-a-kind Son of God	John 1:14
Prophet	Faithful proclaimer of the truths of God	Acts 3:22
Savior	Delivers from sin and death	Luke 1:47
Seed of Abraham	Mediator of God's covenant	Gal. 3:16
Son of Man	Identifies with us in our humanity	Matt. 18:11
The Word	Present with God at the creation	John 1:1

An excavated area in ancient Jerusalem known as The Pavement, identified by some scholars as the place where Pilate rendered judgment against Jesus (John 19:13). *Photo by Howard Vos*

A menorah, or seven-branched lampstand, symbolizes Judaism and the Jewish state of Israel. *Photo by Ben Chapman*

ber of Jews (especially the Jewish leaders) were hostile toward Jesus' ministry, the New Testament sometimes speaks simply of "the Jews" (John 6:41), when it really means "those Jews who did not believe in Jesus." This is especially true in John's Gospel (John 5:16, 18; 6:41, 52; 7:1).

JEZEBEL [jez'-e-bel] *(there is no prince)* — the name of two women in the Bible:

1. The wife of Ahab, king of Israel, and mother of Ahaziah, Jehoram, and Athaliah (1 Kin. 16:31). Jezebel was a tyrant who corrupted her husband, as well as the nation, by promoting pagan worship.

2. A prophetess of Thyatira who enticed the Christians in that church "to commit sexual immorality and to eat things sacrificed to idols" (Rev. 2:20). John probably called this woman "Jezebel" because of her similarity to Ahab's idolatrous and wicked queen.

JEZREEL [jez'-re-el] *(God scatters)* — the name of two people, two cities, and a valley or plain in the Old Testament:

1. A man of the tribe of Judah (1 Chr. 4:3).

2. A symbolic name given by the prophet Hosea to his oldest son (Hos. 1:4).

3. A city in the hill country of Judah, near Jokdeam and Zanoah (Josh. 15:56). Apparently David obtained one of his wives from this place (1 Sam. 25:43).

4. A city in northern Israel, on the Plain of Jezreel about 90 kilometers (56 miles) north of Jerusalem. The city was in the territory of Issachar, but it belonged to the tribe of Manasseh (Josh. 19:18). It was between Megiddo and Beth Shean (1 Kin. 4:12) and between Mount Carmel and Mount Gilboa. The palace of King Ahab of Israel was situated in Jezreel. Here Jezebel and all the others associated with Ahab's reign were assassinated by the followers of Jehu (2 Kings 9—10). The city of Jezreel has been identified with modern Zer'in.

5. The Old Testament name of the entire valley that separates Samaria from Galilee (Josh. 17:16).

JOAB [jo'-ab] *(the Lord is father)* —one of the three sons of Zeruiah (2 Sam. 2:13; 8:16; 14:1; 17:25; 23:18, 37; 1 Kin. 1:7; 2:5, 22; 1 Chr. 11:6, 39; 18:15; 26:28; 27:24) who was David's sister (or half sister). Joab was the "general" or commander-in-chief of David's army (2 Sam. 5:8; 1 Chr. 11:6; 27:34).

JOASH, JEHOASH [jo'-ash, je-ho'-ash] *(the Lord supports)* — the name of eight men in the Old Testament but most notably the eighth king of Judah; he was a son of King Ahaziah (2 Kin. 11:2) by Zibiah of Beersheba (2 Kin. 12:1). Joash was seven years old when he became king, and he reigned 40 years in Jerusalem (2 Chr. 24:1), from about 835 B.C. until 796 B.C. He is also called Jehoash (2 Kin. 11:21).

Another Joash is the 13th king of Israel; he was the son and successor of Jehoahaz, king of Israel, and was the grandson of Jehu, king of Israel. He is also called Jehoash (2 Kin. 13:10, 25; 14:8–17). Joash reigned in Samaria for 16 years (2 Kin. 13:9–10), from about 798 B.C. to 782/81 B.C.

JOB [jobe] — the name of two men in the Old Testament:

1. The third son of Issachar, and founder of a tribal family, the Jashubites (Gen. 46:13). He is also called Jashub (Num. 26:24; 1 Chr. 7:1).

2. The central personality of the Book of Job. He was noted for his perseverance (James 5:11) and unwavering faith in God, in spite of his suffering and moments of frustration and doubt. All the facts known about Job are contained in the Old Testament book that bears his name. He is described as "a man in the land of Uz" (Job 1:1) and "the greatest of all the people of the East" (Job 1:3). Uz is probably a name for a region in Edom (Jer. 25:20; Lam. 4:21).

JOB, BOOK OF — an Old Testament book, written in the form of a dramatic poem, that deals with several age-old questions, among

JOB:
A Study and Teaching Outline

Part One: The Dilemma of Job (1:1—2:13)

  I. The Circumstances of Job 1:1–5
 II. The First Assault of Satan 1:6–22
III. The Second Assault of Satan 2:1–10
 IV. The Arrival of Job's Friends 2:11–13

Part Two: The Debates of Job (3:1—37:24)

  I. The First Cycle of Debate . . . . 3:1—14:22
      A. Job's First Speech 3:1–26
      B. Eliphaz's First Speech . . . . 4:1—5:27
      C. Job's Response to Eliphaz . . . . 6:1—7:21
      D. Bildad's First Speech 8:1–22
      E. Job's Response to Bildad . . . . 9:1—10:22
      F. Zophar's First Speech 11:1–20
      G. Job's Response to Zophar . . . . 12:1—14:22
 II. The Second Cycle of Debate . . . . 15:1—21:34
      A. Eliphaz's Second Speech 15:1–35
      B. Job's Response to Eliphaz . . . . 16:1—17:16
      C. Bildad's Second Speech 18:1–21
      D. Job's Response to Bildad 19:1–29
      E. Zophar's Second Speech 20:1–29
      F. Job's Response to Zophar 21:1–34
III. The Third Cycle of Debate . . . . 22:1—26:14
      A. Eliphaz's Third Speech 22:1–30
      B. Job's Response to Eliphaz . . . . 23:1—24:25
      C. Bildad's Third Speech 25:1–6
      D. Job's Response to Bildad 26:1–14
 IV. The Final Defense of Job . . . . 27:1—31:40
      A. Job's First Monologue . . . . 27:1—28:28
      B. Job's Second Monologue . . . . 29:1—31:40
  V. The Solution of Elihu . . . . 32:1—37:24
      A. Elihu Intervenes in the Debate 32:1–22
      B. Elihu's First Rebuttal 33:1–33
      C. Elihu's Second Rebuttal 34:1–37
      D. Elihu's Third Rebuttal 35:1–16
      E. Elihu's Conclusion . . . . 36:1—37:24

Part Three: The Deliverance of Job (38:1—42:17)

  I. The First Controversy of God with Job . . . . 38:1—40:5
      A. God's First Challenge to Job . . . . 38:1—40:2
      B. Job's First Answer to God 40:3–5
 II. The Second Controversy of God with Job . 40:6—42:6
      A. God's Second Challenge to Job . . . . . . 40:6—41:34
      B. Job's Second Answer to God 42:1–6
III. The Deliverance of Job and His Friends 42:7–17

them the question of why the righteous suffer. The book takes its name from the main character in the poem, the patriarch Job. Because Job deals with a number of universal questions, it is classified as one of the Wisdom Books of the Old Testament. Other books of this type are Proverbs, Ecclesiastes, and the Song of Solomon.

The Book of Job teaches us to trust God in all circumstances. When we suffer, it usually is a fruitless effort to try to understand the reasons for the difficulty. Sometimes the righteous must suffer without knowing the reason why; that is why it is important to learn to trust God in everything.

The Book of Job also teaches us that God is good, just, and fair in His dealings. He restored Job's fortunes and gave him more than he had ever enjoyed. God always replaces the darkness of our existence with the light of His presence when we remain faithful to Him.

JOEL [jo′-el] *(the Lord is God)* — the name of 14 men in the Old Testament, most notably an Old Testament prophet and author of the Book of Joel. A citizen of Jerusalem, he spoke often of the priests and their duties (Joel 1:9, 13–14, 16). For this reason, many scholars believe he may have been a temple prophet. He also had an ear for nature (Joel 1:4–7), and included imagery from

A mosaic of the prophet Joel, who prophesied about the outpouring of God's Spirit in the latter days (Joel 2:28).

agriculture and the natural world in his messages.

JOEL, BOOK OF — a brief prophetic book of the Old Testament that predicted the outpouring

JOEL:

A Study and Teaching Outline

I. **The Day of the Lord in the Past**............. 1:1–20
  A. The Past Day of the Locust............. 1:1–12
  B. The Past Day of the Drought........... 1:13–20
II. **The Day of the Lord in the Future**........ 2:1—3:21
  A. The Coming Day of the Lord............ 2:1–27
    1. Prophecy of the Coming Invasion of
      Judah........................... 2:1–11
    2. Conditional Promise of the Salvation
      of Judah....................... 2:12–27
  B. The Ultimate Day of the Lord........ 2:28—3:21
    1. Last Events Before the Terrible Day
      of the Lord..................... 2:28–32
    2. Events of the Terrible Day of the Lord. . 3:1–21
      a. Judgment on the Gentiles........ 3:1–17
      b. Restoration of Judah 3:18–21

Traditional tomb of the apostle John in the Church of St. John at Ephesus. *Photo by Howard Vos*

of the spirit of God on all people—a prophecy fulfilled several centuries later on the Day of PEN-TECOST (Joel 2:28–32; Acts 2:14–21). The title of the book comes from its author, the prophet Joel.

The Book of Joel is remarkable because it shows that a message from God can often come packaged in the form of a natural disaster. The truth of the book is rooted in the disastrous invasion of locusts, which Joel describes in such vivid language. This prophet teaches us that the Lord may use a natural disaster to stir in His people a renewed awareness of His will. Any traumatic event of nature—flood, fire, storm, or earth-quake—should motivate the sensitive ear to listen again to the words of the Lord.

JOHN THE APOSTLE — one of Jesus' disciples, the son of Zebedee, and the brother of James. Before his call by Jesus, John was a fisherman, along with his father and brother (Matt. 4:18–22; Mark 1:16–20). His mother was probably Salome (Matt. 27:56; Mark 15:40), who may have been a sister of Mary (John 19:25), the mother of Jesus.

JOHN THE BAPTIST — forerunner of Jesus; a moral reformer and preacher of messianic

Remains of Machaerus, fortress of King Herod, where John the Baptist was beheaded, according to the Jewish historian Josephus.

hope. According to Luke 1:36, Elizabeth and Mary, the mothers of John and Jesus, were either blood relatives or close kinswomen. Luke adds that both John and Jesus were announced, set apart, and named by the angel Gabriel even before their birth.

JOHN, EPISTLES OF — three epistles—one longer (1 John) and two shorter (2 and 3 John)— written by the author of the Gospel of John. These epistles read like a love letter from an elderly saint who writes from long years of experience with Christ and His message. Although unnamed, the author addresses his readers intimately as "little children" (1 John 2:1, 18, 28; 3:7, 18; 4:4; 5:21) and "beloved" (1 John 3:2, 21; 4:1, 7, 11). His tone changes, however, when he bears down on his opponents for making light of

FIRST JOHN:
A Study and Teaching Outline

Part One: The Basis of Fellowship (1:1—2:27)

Part Two: The Behavior of Fellowship (2:28—5:21)

I. Introduction 1:1–4
II. The Conditions for Fellowship . . . . 1:5—2:14
   A. Walk in the Light 1:5–7
   B. Confession of Sin . . . . 1:8—2:2
   C. Obedience to His Commandments 2:3–6
   D. Love for One Another 2:7–14
III. The Cautions to Fellowship 2:15–27
   A. Love of the World 2:15–17
   B. Spirit of the Antichrist 2:18–27

I. Characteristics of Fellowship . . . . 2:28—5:3
   A. Purity of Life . . . . 2:28—3:3
   B. Practice of Righteousness 3:4–12
   C. Love in Deed and Truth 3:13–24
   D. Testing the Spirits 4:1–6
   E. Love as Christ Loved . . . . 4:7—5:3
II. Consequences of Fellowship 5:4–21
   A. Victory over the World 5:4–5
   B. Assurance of Salvation 5:6–13
   C. Guidance in Prayer 5:14–17
   D. Freedom from Habitual Sin 5:18–21

SECOND JOHN:
A Study and Teaching Outline

I. Abide in God's Commandments 1–6
   A. Salutation 1–3
   B. Walk in Truth 4
   C. Walk in Love 5–6
II. Abide Not with False Teachers 7–13
   A. Doctrine of the False Teachers 7–9
   B. Avoid the False Teachers 10–11
   C. Benediction 12–13

THIRD JOHN:
A Study and Teaching Outline

I. The Commendation of Gaius 1–8
   A. Salutation 1
   B. Godliness of Gaius .2–4
   C. Generosity of Gaius 5–8
II. The Condemnation of Diotrephes 9–14
   A. Pride of Diotrephes 9–11
   B. Praise for Demetrius .12
   C. Benediction 13–14

the bodily existence of Jesus (1 John 2:18–23; 4:1–3, 20).

Like the Gospel of John, the epistles of John are built on the foundation blocks of love, truth, sin, world, life, light, and Paraclete. It emphasizes the great themes of knowing, believing, walking, and abiding. These words seem simple on the surface. But in the hands of one who had pondered the mystery and meaning of Jesus' existence in human form, they yield many deep truths.

JOHN, GOSPEL OF — the fourth and most theological of the Gospels of the New Testament. The first three Gospels portray mainly what Jesus did and how He taught, but the Gospel of John is different. It moves beyond the obvious facts of Jesus' life to deeper, more profound meanings. Events and miracles are kept to a minimum in the Gospel of John. They are used as springboards or "signs" for lengthy discussions that reveal important truths about Christ. On the other hand, John uses a host of key words that symbolize who Jesus

JOHN:
A Study and Teaching Outline

Part One: The Incarnation of the Son of God (1:1–18)

I. The Deity of Christ 1:1–2
II. The Preincarnate Work of Christ 1:3–5
III. The Forerunner of Christ 1:6–8
IV. The Rejection of Christ 1:9–11
V. The Acceptance of Christ 1:12–13
VI. The Incarnation of Christ 1:14–18

Part Two: The Presentation of the Son of God (1:19—4:54)

I. The Presentation of Christ by John the Baptist 1:19–34
II. The Presentation of Christ to John's Disciples 1:35–51
III. The Presentation of Christ in Galilee 2:1–12
IV. The Presentation of Christ in Judea . . . . . . 2:13—3:36
V. The Presentation of Christ in Samaria 4:1–42
VI. The Presentation of Christ in Galilee 4:43–54

Part Three: The Opposition to the Son of God (5:1—12:50)

I. The Opposition at the Feast in Jerusalem 5:1–47
II. The Opposition during Passover Time in Galilee 6:1–71
III. The Opposition at the Feast of Tabernacles in Jerusalem . . . . 7:1—10:21
IV. The Opposition at the Feast of Dedication in Jerusalem 10:22–42
V. The Opposition at Bethany . . . . 11:1—12:11
VI. The Opposition at Jerusalem 12:12–50

Part Four: The Preparation of the Disciples (13:1—17:26)

I. The Preparation in the Upper Room . . . . . 13:1—14:31
II. The Preparation on the Way to the Garden . . . . 15:1—17:26

Part Five: The Crucifixion and Resurrection (18:1—21:25)

I. The Rejection of Christ . . . . 18:1—19:16
II. The Crucifixion of Christ 19:17–37
III. The Burial of Christ 19:38–42
IV. The Resurrection of Christ 20:1–10
V. The Appearances of Christ . . . . 20:11—21:25

This ancient papyrus fragment, written in the Greek language, contains verses 1–14 of the first chapter of John's Gospel. It dates from about A.D. 200. *Photo by Howard Vos*

is and how we may know God. John is a "spiritual" gospel—not because it is more spiritual than the other three—but because it expresses spiritual ideas in spiritual language. Among the gospels, therefore, John offers a unique portrait of Christ that has been cherished by believers through the centuries.

John writes with a modest vocabulary, but his words are charged with symbolism. Terms like believe, love, truth, world, light and darkness, above and below, name, witness, sin, judgment (eternal) life, glory, bread, water, and hour are the key words of this Gospel. In John 3:16–21, a passage of less than 150 words in Greek, seven of these terms occur.

JONAH [jo'-nah] *(a dove)* — the prophet who was first swallowed by a great fish before he obeyed God's command to preach repentance to the Assyrian city of Nineveh. Jonah was not always a reluctant spokesman for the Lord. He is the same prophet who predicted the remarkable expansion of Israel's territory during the reign of Jeroboam II (ruled about 793—753 B.C.; 2 Kin. 14:25). This passage indicates that Jonah, the son of Amittai, was from Gath Hepher, a town in Zebulun in the northern kingdom of Israel.

JONAH, BOOK OF — a short Old Testament book that emphasizes God's love for all people—pagans and Gentiles as well as his chosen people, the Israelites. The book is named for its central figure, the prophet Jonah, who learned about God's universal love as he struggled with God's call to service.

One of the great truths emphasized by this book is that God can use people who do not want to be used by Him. Jonah was practically driven to Nineveh against his will, but his grudging

JONAH:
A Study and Teaching Outline

I. **The First Commission of Jonah** . . . . 1:1—2:10
  A. The Disobedience to the First Call 1:1–3
  B. The Judgment on Jonah 1:4–17
    1. The Great Storm 1:4–16
    2. The Great Salvation of Jonah by the Fish . . 1:17
  C. The Prayer of Jonah 2:1–9
  D. The Deliverance of Jonah 2:10
II. **The Second Commission of Jonah.** . . . . 3:1—4:11
  A. The Obedience to the Second Call 3:1–4
  B. The Repentance of Nineveh   3:5–10
    1. The Great Fast 3:5–9
    2. The Great Salvation of Nineveh by God . . . 3:10
  C. The Prayer of Jonah 4:1–3
  D. The Rebuke of Jonah by God 4:4–11

message still struck a responsive chord in the Assyrians. This shows that revival and repentance are works of God's Spirit. Our task is to proclaim His message.

But the greatest insight of the book is that God desires to show mercy and grace to all the peoples of the world. No one nation or group can claim exclusive rights to His love. The task of the Hebrew people was to preach this message about God's universal love to all the world (Gen. 12:1–3). But they forgot this missionary purpose and eventually claimed God and His blessings as theirs alone. The Book of Jonah cries out against this narrow-minded interpretation of God and His purpose. In the last verse of the book, God makes it plain to Jonah that His mercy and compassion are as wide as the world itself: "And should I not pity Nineveh, that great city, in which are more than one hundred and twenty thousand persons who cannot discern between their right hand and their left, and also much livestock?" (4:11).

JONATHAN [jon'-a-than] *(the Lord has given)* — the name of 14 men in the Old Testament with the most notable being the oldest son of King Saul and a close friend of David (1 Sam. 14:1).

JOPPA [jop'-pah] *(beautiful)* — an ancient seaport city on the Mediterranean Sea, about 56 kilometers (35 miles) northwest of Jerusalem.

A walled city, Joppa was built about 35 meters (116 feet) high on a rocky ledge overlooking the Mediterranean. It supposedly received its name "beautiful" from the sunlight that its buildings reflected.

JORAM [jo'-ram] *(the Lord is exalted)* — the name of four men in the Old Testament, most notably the tenth king of Israel, slain by Jehu (2 Kin. 8:16–29; 9:14–29). The son of Ahab and Jezebel, Joram succeeded his brother, Ahaziah, as king. He was also called Jehoram (2 Kin. 1:17). His 12-year reign was characterized as an evil time, although he did manage to restrain Baal worship (2 Kin. 3:3).

JORDAN [jor'-dan] *(descending, flowing)* — the name of the longest and most important river in Palestine (Josh. 1:2; Mark 1:9). The river is part of the great rift valley that runs north to south into Africa. This rift valley is one of the lowest depressions on earth.

JOSEPH [jo'-zef] *(may he add)* — the name of several men in the Bible. The two most notable are:

1. The 11th son of Jacob (Gen. 30:24). Joseph was sold into slavery and later rose to an important position in the Egyptian government. The account of Joseph's life is found in Genesis 37—50.

2. The husband of Mary, mother of Jesus (Matt. 1:16–24; 2:13; Luke 1:27; 2:4).

JOSHUA [josh'-u-ah] *(the Lord is salvation)* — the successor to Moses and the man who led the nation of Israel to conquer and settle the Promised Land.

Joshua was born in Egypt. He went through the great events of the Passover and the Exodus with Moses and all the Hebrew people who escaped from slavery in Egypt at the hand of their Redeemer God. In the Wilderness of Sinai, Moses took his assistant Joshua with him when he went

Traditional tomb of Joseph at Shechem (Ex. 13:19). *Photo by Howard Vos*

into the mountains to talk with God (Ex. 24:13). Moses also gave Joshua a prominent place at the TABERNACLE. As Moses' servant, Joshua would remain at the tabernacle as his representative while the great leader left the camp to fellowship with the Lord (Ex. 33:11).

JOSHUA, BOOK OF — an Old Testament book that describes the conquest and division of the land of Canaan by the Hebrew people. The book is named for its central figure, Joshua, who succeeded Moses as leader of Israel.

One important message of the Book of Joshua is that true and false religions do not mix. Joshua's orders were to destroy the Canaanites because of their pagan and immoral worship practices. But these people never were totally subdued or destroyed. Traces of their false religion remained to tempt the Israelites. Again and again throughout their history, the Hebrew people departed from worship of the one true God. This tendency toward false worship was the main reason for Joshua's moving farewell speech. He warned the people against worshiping these false gods and challenged them to remain faithful to the Lord, who had delivered them. The point of Joshua's message: You cannot worship these false gods and remain faithful to the Lord. "But as for me and my house, we will serve the Lord" (24:15).

JOSIAH [jo-si´-ah] — the name of two men in the Old Testament:

1. The 16th king of Judah, the son of Amon, and the grandson of Manasseh (2 Kin. 21:23–23:30). The three decades of Josiah's reign were characterized by peace, prosperity, and reform. Hence, they were among the happiest years experienced by Judah. King Josiah devoted himself to pleasing God and reinstituting Israel's observance of the Mosaic Law. That a wicked king like

JOSHUA:
A Study and Teaching Outline

Part One: T.he Conquest of Canaan (1:1—13:7)

Part Two: The Settlement in Canaan (13:8—24:33)

I. **Israel Is Prepared for the Conquest.** . . . . . . 1:1—5:15
  A. Joshua Replaces Moses. 1:1–18
  B. Joshua Prepares Israel Militarily . . . . 2:1—5:1
  C. Joshua Prepares Israel Spiritually 5:2–12
  D. The Commander of the Lord Appears. 5:13–15
II. **The Conquest of Canaan by Israel** . . . . 6:1—13:7
  A. Conquest of Central Canaan . . . . 6:1—8:35
  B. Conquest of Southern Canaan. . . . . 9:1—10:43
  C. Conquest of Northern Canaan 11:1–15
  D. Conquest of Canaan Summarized . . . 11:16—12:24
  E. Unconquered Parts of Canaan 13:1–7

I. **The Settlement East of the Jordan** 13:8–33
  A. Geographical Boundaries 13:8–13
  B. Tribal Boundaries 13:14–33
II. **The Settlement West of the Jordan** . . . . . 14:1—19:51
  A. The First Settlement Done at Gilgal . . 14:1—17:18
  B. The Second Settlement Done at
    Shiloh . . . . 18:1—19:51
III. **The Settlement of the Religious**
  Community . . . . 20:1—21:45
  A. Six Cities of Refuge 20:1–9
  B. Selection of the Levitical Cities 21:1–42
  C. The Settlement of Israel Is Completed . . . 21:43–45
IV. **The Conditions for Continued**
  Settlement . . . . 22:1—24:33
  A. The Altar of Witness. 22:1–34
  B. Blessings of God Come Only Through
    Obedience . . . . 23:1—24:28
  C. Joshua and Eleazar Die 24:29–33

Amon could have such a godly son and successor is a tribute to the grace of God. The Bible focuses almost exclusively on Josiah's spiritual reform, which climaxed in the 18th year of his reign with the discovery of the Book of the Law.

2. A captive who returned to Jerusalem from Babylon in Zechariah's day (Zech. 6:10), also called Hen (Zech. 6:14).

JOSIAS [jo-si'-as] — a form of JOSIAH.

JOT — the English rendering of the Greek word *iota* (Matt. 5:18), the smallest letter of the Greek alphabet. The word is used figuratively to express a matter that seems to be of small importance.

JOY — a positive attitude or pleasant emotion; delight. Many kinds of joy are reported in the Bible. Even the wicked are said to experience joy in their triumphs over the righteous (1 Cor. 13:6; Rev. 11:10). Many levels of joy are also described, including gladness, contentment, and cheerfulness.

JUBILEE [ju-ba-lee'] — the 50th year after seven cycles of seven years, when specific instructions about property and slavery took effect (Lev. 25:8–55).

The word "jubilee" comes from a Hebrew word that means to be "jubilant" and to "exult." The word is related to the Hebrew word for ram's horn or trumpet. The Jubilee year was launched with a blast from a ram's horn on the Day of Atonement, signifying a call to joy, liberation, and the beginning of a year for doing justice and loving mercy.

JUDAH [ju'-dah] *(praise)* — the name of seven men and a place in the Old Testament, most notably the fourth son of Jacob and Leah and the founder of the family out of which the messianic line came (Gen. 29:35; Num. 26:19–21; Matt. 1:2).

JUDAS [ju'-das] *(praise)* — the name of five men in the New Testament:

1. One of the four brothers of Jesus (Matt. 13:55; Mark 6:3; Juda, KJV). Some scholars believe he was the author of the Epistle of Jude.

2. One of the twelve apostles of Jesus. John is careful to distinguish him from Judas ISCARIOT (John 14:22).

3. Judas of Galilee (Acts 5:37). In the days of the census (Luke 2:2), he led a revolt against Rome. He was killed, and his followers were scattered. According to the Jewish historian Josephus, Judas founded a sect whose main belief was that their only ruler and lord was God.

4. A man with whom the apostle Paul stayed in Damascus after his conversion (Acts 9:11).

5. A disciple surnamed Barsabas who belonged to the church in Jerusalem. The apostles and elders of that church chose Judas and Silas to accompany Paul and Barnabas to Antioch; together they conveyed to the church in that city the decree of the Jerusalem Council about circumcision.

JUDE [jood] *(praise)* — the author of the Epistle of Jude, in which he is described as "a servant of Jesus Christ, and brother of James" (Jude 1). Jude is an English form of the name Judas. Many scholars believe that the James mentioned in this passage is James the brother of Jesus.

JUDE, EPISTLE OF — the last of the general letters of the New Testament and the next to the last book of the Bible. Jude is a brief but hard-hitting epistle written by a man who believed in not allowing negative influences to destroy the church. Jude unmasks false teaching with pointed language and vivid images, while

---

JUDE:
A Study and
Teaching Outline

I. Purpose of Jude 1–4
II. Description of False Teachers 5–16
    A. Past Judgment of False Teachers 5–7
    B. Present Characteristics of False Teachers 8–13
    C. Future Judgment of False Teachers 14–16
III. Defense against False Teachers 17–23
IV. Doxology of Jude 24–25

appealing to the faithful to remember the teachings of the apostles.

Jude writes as a defender of the faith who is "contending earnestly for the faith which was once for all delivered to the saints" (v. 3). The "ungodly" are not the heathen outside the church; they are the false teachers inside (v. 12). Their association with the faith, however, does not mean they live in the faith: the ungodly have not the Spirit (v. 19), whereas the faithful do (v. 20); the ungodly remain in eternal darkness (v. 13), but the saints have eternal life (v. 21). Condemning his opponents in sharp imagery, Jude calls them "raging waves of the sea, foaming up their own shame; wandering stars for whom is reserved the blackness of darkness forever" (v. 13). The saints, on the other hand, must set their anchor in the teaching of the apostles (v. 17), and in the love of God (v. 21). They must work to retrieve from certain destruction those who have been deceived (vv. 22–23).

JUDEA [ju-de′-ah] — the Greco-Roman name for the land of Judah. Judea is first mentioned in Ezra 5:8 (Judaea, KJV; Judah, NIV), where it is used to designate a province of the Persian Empire. The word Judea comes from the adjective "Jewish," a term that was used of the Babylonian captives who returned to the Promised Land, most of whom were from the tribe of Judah.

JUDGE — as a noun, a public official who helps interpret the laws (Ezra 7:25; Matt. 5:25); as a verb, to discern or criticize (Gen. 15:14; Matt. 7:1).

JUDGES, BOOK OF — a historical book of the Old Testament that covers the chaotic time

The Period of the Judges

Events and Judges	Years
Israel serves Cushan-Rishathaim (3:7, 8)	8
Peace following Othniel's deliverance (3:7–11)	40
Israel serves Moab (3:12)	18
Peace follows Ehud's deliverance (3:12–30)	80
Shamgar delivers Israel from Philistines (3:31)	1
Israel serves Canaan (4:1–3)	20
Peace following deliverance by Deborah and Barak (4:1—5:31)	40
Israel serves Midian (6:1–6)	7
Peace following Gideon's deliverance (6:1—8:35)	40
Abimelech, king of Israel (9:1–57)	3
Tola's career (10:1, 2)	23
Jair's career (10:3–5)	22
Israel serves Ammon and Philistia (10:6–10)	18
Jephthah's career (10:6—12:7)	6
Ibzan's career (12:8–10)	7
Elon's career (12:11, 12)	10
Abdon's career (12:13–15)	8
Israel serves Philistia (13:1)	40
Samson's career (12:1—16:31)	20

JUDGES:
A Study and
Teaching Outline

Part One: The Deterioration of Israel and Failure to Complete the Conquest of Canaan (1:1—3:6)

I. The Failure of Israel to Complete the Conquest 1:1–36
II. The Judgment of God for Not Completing the Conquest .... 2:1—3:6

Part Two: The Deliverance of Israel (3:7—16:31)

I. The Southern Campaign. 3:7–31
  A. The Judge Othniel 3:7–11
  B. The Judge Ehud 3:12–30
  C. The Judge Shamgar 3:31
II. The Northern Campaign: The Judges Deborah and Barak .... 4:1—5:31
  A. Deborah and Barak Are Called 4:1–10
  B. Canaanites Are Defeated. 4:11–24
  C. Song of Deborah and Barak 5:1–31
III. The Central Campaign. .... 6:1—10:5
  A. The Judge Gideon .... 6:1—8:32
    1. Israel Sins 6:1–10
    2. Gideon Called. 6:11–40
    3. Midianites Defeated. .... 7:1—8:21
    4. Gideon Judges 8:22–32
  B. Abimelech .... 8:33—9:57
  C. The Judge Tola 10:1–2
  D. The Judge Jair 10:3–5
IV. The Eastern Campaign: The Judge Jephthah .... 10:6—12:7
  A. Israel Sins 10:6–18
  B. Salvation: Jephthah. .... 11:1—12:7
V. The Second Northern Campaign 12:8–15
  A. The Judge Ibzan. 12:8–10
  B. The Judge Elon. 12:11–12
  C. The Judge Abdon 12:13–15
VI. The Western Campaign: The Judge Samson .... 13:1—16:31
  A. Miraculous Birth of Samson. 13:1–25
  B. Sinful Marriage of Samson. 14:1–20
  C. Judgeship of Samson 15:1–20
  D. Failure of Samson 16:1–31

Part Three: The Depravity of Israel (17:1—21:25)

I. The Failure of Israel through Idolatry. . . . 17:1—18:31
  A. Example of Personal Idolatry 17:1–13
  B. Example of Tribal Idolatry 18:1–31
II. The Failure of Israel through Immorality 19:1–30
  A. Example of Personal Immorality 19:1–10
  B. Example of Tribal Immorality. 19:11–30
III. The Failure of Israel through the War between the Tribes. .... 20:1—21:25
  A. War between Israel and Benjamin 20:1–48
  B. Failure of Israel after the War 21:1–25

between Joshua's death and the beginning of a centralized government under King Saul, a period of over 300 years. The "judges" for whom the book is named were actually military leaders whom God raised up to deliver His people from their enemies. Twelve of these heroic deliverers are mentioned in the book.

The Book of Judges points out the problems of the nation of Israel when the people had a succession of "judges" or military leaders to deliver them from their enemies. This is a subtle way of emphasizing the nation's need for a king or a strong, centralized form of government. But even the establishment of kingship failed to lead to a state of perfection. Only after the right king, David, was placed on the throne did the nation break free of its tragic cycle of despair and decline. David, of course, as God's chosen servant, points to the great King to come, the Lord Jesus.

Judges also speaks of our need for an eternal deliverer or a savior. The deliverance of the human judges was always temporary, partial, and imperfect. Some of the judges themselves were flawed and misdirected. The book points forward to Jesus Christ, the great Judge (Ps. 110:6), who is King and Savior of His people.

JUDGMENT — discernment or separation between good and evil. God judges among people and their actions according to the standards of His LAW. Judgment can refer either to this process of discernment or to the punishment meted out to those who fall under His wrath and condemnation (John 5:24).

JUST — right, fair (Gen. 6:9; Rom. 1:17).

JUSTICE — the practice of what is right and just. Justice (or "judgment," KJV) specifies what is right, not only as measured by a code of law, but also by what makes for right relationships as well as harmony and peace.

JUSTIFICATION — the process by which sinful human beings are made acceptable to a holy God.

JUSTIFIED — to be made right (Gal. 2:16).

KADESH, KADESH BARNEA [ka'-desh bar-ne'-ah] *(consecrated)* — a wilderness region between Egypt and the land of Canaan where the Hebrew people camped after the Exodus. Kadesh Barnea (the modern oasis of Ain el-Qudeirat) was situated on the edge of Edom (Num. 20:16) about 114 kilometers (70 miles) from Hebron and 61 kilometers (50 miles) from Beersheba in the Wilderness of Zin. Kadesh Barnea is also said to be in the Wilderness of Paran (Num. 13:26). Paran was probably the general name for the larger wilderness area, while Zin may have been the specific name for a smaller portion of the wilderness territory.

KERYGMA [ke-rig'-ma] — the proclamation, or preaching, of the message of the gospel in the New Testament church. The word is a transliteration of a Greek word that means "proclamation," "preaching," or "message preached" (1 Cor. 1:21).

KIDRON [kid'-ron] *(gloomy)* — a valley on the eastern slope of Jerusalem through which a seasonal brook of the same name runs. The meaning of the name is fitting, in view of the great strife that has surrounded the Kidron throughout Bible times. A torrent in the winter rains, it contains little water in the summer months.

KINDNESS, LOVINGKINDNESS — God's loyal love and favor toward His people. In the Old Testament, the word translated as "kindness" or "lovingkindness" refers to God's long-suffering love—His determination to keep His promises to His chosen people in spite of their sin and rebellion (Deut. 7:12; Hos. 2:14–23). This attribute of

The Kidron Valley, just outside the eastern wall of Jerusalem. Jesus and His disciples crossed this valley and its brook on their way to the Garden of Gethsemane (John 18:1).

An exhausted traveler rests in the shade of a broom bush in the wilderness of Kadesh (Num. 20:16).

God was shown through His divine mercy and forgiveness toward sinners when payment of sins through the sacrificial system was no longer effective (Deut. 22:22; Ps. 51:1).

In the New Testament, the Greek word translated as "grace" best represents the idea of God's kindness or lovingkindness. Because God has been gracious toward believers, they should treat all people with kindness or grace (Luke 6:35). All people are created in God's image and should be treated accordingly, no matter how badly they have twisted and deformed that image (James 3:9). Kindness is not an apathetic response to sin, but a deliberate act to bring the sinner back to God (Hos. 2:14–23; Rom. 2:4).

KIN, KINSMAN, KINDRED — blood kin or relatives. Family was important among the Hebrew people because the clan or tribe was the basic social unit, at least until the time of the

The gold mask buried with Pharaoh Tutankhamun of Egypt about 1350 B.C., illustrating the wealth of his kingdom.

Photo by Howard Vos

United Kingdom under David and Solomon. The family had the responsibility for protecting and preserving its members from injustices at the hand of others (Gen. 34:1–31) or from slavery or loss of land due to poverty.

KINDLE — cause to burn (Acts 28:2).

KINE — cows (Amos 4:1). (see Ox, Oxen).

KING, KINGDOM — ruler of a nation or territory, especially one who inherits his position and rules for life; a state or nation with a form of government in which a king or queen serves as supreme ruler (Matt. 6:10).

KINGDOM OF GOD, KINGDOM OF HEAVEN — God's rule of grace in the world, a future period foretold by the prophets of the Old Testament and identified by Jesus as beginning with His public ministry. The kingdom of God is the experience of blessedness, like that of the Garden of Eden, where evil is fully overcome and where those who live in the kingdom know only happiness, peace, and joy. This was the main expectation of the Old Testament prophets about the future (Matt. 6:10).

KINGS, BOOKS OF — two Old Testament books that recount the history of God's chosen people during four turbulent centuries, from 970 to 586 B.C. The narratives in these books of history are organized around the various kings who reigned during these centuries, thus explaining the titles by which the books are known.

These books cover, in chronological fashion, about 400 years of Judah and Israel's history. The last event mentioned in this chronology is the captivity of Judah's citizens by the Babylonians. This means the book had to be compiled in its final form some time after the Babylonians overran Jerusalem in 586 B.C.

The four centuries covered by 1 and 2 Kings were times of change and political upheaval in the ancient world as the balance of power shifted from one nation to another. Surrounding nations that posed a threat to Israel and Judah at various

FIRST KINGS:
A Study and Teaching Outline

Part One: The United Kingdom (1:1—11:43)

I. The Establishment of Solomon as King . . . . 1:1—2:46
II. The Rise of Solomon as King . . . . 3:1—8:66
III. The Decline of Solomon as King . . . . 9:1—11:43

Part Two: The Divided Kingdom (12:1—22:53)

I. The Division of the Kingdom. . . . . 12:1—14:31
II. The Reigns of Two Kings in Judah 15:1–24
III. The Reigns of Five Kings in Israel . . . . . 15:25—16:28
IV. The Reign of Ahab in Israel . . . . 16:29—22:40
V. The Reign of Jehoshaphat in Judah 22:41–50
VI. The Reign of Ahaziah in Israel 22:51–53

SECOND KINGS:
A Study and Teaching Outline

Part One: The Divided Kingdom (1:1—17:41)

I. The Reign of Ahaziah in Israel 1:1–18
II. The Reign of Jehoram in Israel . . . . 2:1—8:15
III. The Reign of Jehoram in Judah 8:16–24
IV. The Reign of Ahaziah in Judah . . . . 8:25—9:29
V. The Reign of Jehu in Israel . . . . 9:30—10:36
VI. The Reign of Queen Athaliah in Judah 11:1–16
VII. The Reign of Joash in Judah . . . . 11:17—12:21
VIII. The Reign of Jehoahaz in Israel. 13:1–9
IX. The Reign of Jehoash in Israel 13:10–25
X. The Reign of Amaziah in Judah 14:1–22
XI. The Reign of Jeroboam II in Israel 14:23–29
XII. The Reign of Azariah in Judah 15:1–7
XIII. The Reign of Zechariah in Israel 15:8–12
XIV. The Reign of Shallum in Israel. 15:13–15
XV. The Reign of Menahem in Israel 15:16–22
XVI. The Reign of Pekahiah in Israel 15:23–26
XVII. The Reign of Pekah in Israel 15:27–31
XVIII. The Reign of Jotham in Judah 15:32–38
XIX. The Reign of Ahaz in Judah 16:1–20
XX. The Reign of Hoshea in Israel 17:1–41

Part Two: The Surviving Kingdom of Judah (18:1—25:30)

I. The Reign of Hezekiah in Judah. . . . . . 18:1—20:21
II. The Reign of Manasseh in Judah 21:1–18
III. The Reign of Amon in Judah 21:19–26
IV. The Reign of Josiah in Judah . . . . 22:1—23:30
V. The Reign of Jehoahaz in Judah 23:31–34
VI. The Reign of Jehoiakim in Judah . . . . . 23:35—24:7
VII. The Reign of Jehoiachin in Judah. 24:8–16
VIII. The Reign of Zedekiah in Judah . . . . . 24:17—25:21
IX. The Governorship of Gedaliah 25:22–26
X. The Release of Jehoiachin in Babylonia 25:27–30

These tourists are overshadowed by a gigantic urn at Petra, a city built by the Nebateans in southern Palestine. They inhabited the land of the ancient Edomites, a people mentioned often in the Books of 1 and 2 Kings. *Photo by Denis Baly*

times during this period included Syria, Assyria, and Babylonia.

KINSMAN — a male relative; a man sharing the same racial, cultural, or national background as another. In the Old Testament the word "kinsman" is often used as a translation of a Hebrew word that means, "one who has the right to redeem."

KISH — the name of four men in the Old Testament:

1. The father of King Saul (1 Chr. 12:1).

2. A Levite who lived in David's time (1 Chr. 23:21–22; 24:29). He was a son of Mahli and a grandson of Merari.

3. A Levite who helped cleanse the temple during the reign of King Hezekiah of Judah (2 Chr. 29:12).

4. A Benjamite ancestor of MORDECAI (Esth. 2:5).

KISHON [ki'-shon] — a river in Palestine, which flows from sources on Mount Tabor and Mount Gilboa westward through the Plain of Esdraelon and the Valley of Jezreel, then empties into the Mediterranean Sea near the northern base of Mount Carmel. Because the Kishon falls slightly as it crosses the level plain, it often becomes swollen and floods much of the valley during the season of heavy rains.

KISS — a symbolic act done to various parts of the body, especially cheeks, feet, forehead, and lips (Prov. 24:26). Ideally, a kiss shows a close relationship to another person, although the relationship and purpose may vary greatly.

Romantic kisses are mentioned infrequently in the Bible, whether genuinely loving (Song 1:2; 8:1) or seductive (Prov. 7:13). The most common type of kiss, however, was that between relatives (Gen. 29:11–13). A kiss could serve either as a greeting (Ex. 4:27) or a farewell (Ruth 1:9, 14; Acts 20:37). It could even express one's anticipation of departure by death (Gen. 48:10). The family kiss was extended in the New Testament to apply to the Christian family (1 Cor. 16:20; 1 Pet. 5:14).

Friends might kiss in greeting (1 Sam. 20:41; 2 Sam. 19:39), although occasionally such a kiss could be given insincerely (Prov. 27:6). Kissing also has figurative meaning when righteousness and peace are pictured as harmonious friends kissing each other (Ps. 85:10). A kiss can also mean betrayal. Judas' treachery is eternally symbolized by a kiss (Luke 22:47–48).

KNEEL — lower to one's knees; bow (Ps. 95:60; Acts 9:40).

KNEELING — falling to one's knees as a gesture of reverence, obedience, or respect. In the dedication of the temple in Jerusalem, Solomon knelt before God (1 Kin. 8:54). Daniel knelt in prayer three times a day (Dan. 6:10).

KNOW — understand intimately; biblical term for sexual intercourse (Gen. 4:1, 25; Luke 1:34).

KNOWLEDGE — the truth or facts of life that a person acquires either through experience or thought. The greatest truth that a person can possess with the mind or learn through experience is truth about God (Ps. 46:10; John 8:31–32). This cannot be gained by unaided human reason (Job 11:7; Rom. 11:33). It is acquired only as God shows Himself to people—in nature and conscience (Ps. 19; Rom. 1:19–20); in history or providence (Deut. 6:20–25; Dan. 2:21); and especially in the Bible (Ps. 119; Rev. 1:1–3).

Mental knowledge by itself, as good as it may be, is inadequate; it is capable only of producing pride (1 Cor. 8:1; 13:2). Moral knowledge affects a person's will (Prov. 1:7; Phil. 3:11–12; 1 John 4:6). It is knowledge of the heart, not the mind alone.

The Book of Proverbs deals primarily with this kind of knowledge. Experiential knowledge is that gained through one's experience (Gen. 4:1; 2 Cor. 5:21; 1 John 4:7–8).

The apostle Paul's wish for the church at Colosse was that they might increase in the "knowledge of God" (Col. 1:10).

KORAH — the name of four men in the Old Testament, most notably the Levite who, along with Dathan, Abiram, and On of the tribe of Reuben, led a revolt against the leadership of Moses and Aaron (Num. 16:1–49). Korah was the son of Izhar and a first cousin of Moses and Aaron (Ex. 6:21). He was equal in rank with Aaron within the tribe of Levi.

LABAN [la'-ban] *(white)* — father-in-law of Jacob. Laban lived in the city of Nahor in Padan Aram where Abraham sent his servant to find a wife for Isaac. Laban, brother of Rebekah, is introduced when he heard of the servant's presence, saw the golden jewelry given Rebekah, and eagerly invited Abraham's emissary into their home (Gen. 24:29–60). Laban played an important role in the marriage arrangements. His stubbornness and greed characterized his later dealings with Rebekah's son, Jacob.

LABOR — work (1 Cor. 3:8).

LAD — child (John 6:9).

LAMB — a young sheep used as a sacrificial offering (Ex. 29:38).

LAMB OF GOD — a phrase used by John the Baptist to describe Jesus (John 1:29, 36). John publicly identified Jesus as "the Lamb of God who takes away the sin of the world!" Elsewhere in the New Testament Jesus is called a lamb (Acts 8:32; 1 Pet. 1:19; Rev. 5:6). The Book of Revelation speaks of Jesus as a lamb 28 times.

LAME, LAMENESS — a disability in one or more limbs, especially in a foot or leg, so that a person experiences difficulty in walking or moving freely. Lameness is one of the physical imperfections that excluded a priest from entering the holy place or offering sacrifices (Lev. 21:17–21). Jesus healed many lame people (Matt. 11:5; Luke 7:22). Peter and John also healed a man who had been lame from birth (Acts 3:1–11).

LAMECH [la'-mek] — the name of two men in the Old Testament:

LAMENTATIONS:
A Study and Teaching Outline

I. **The Destruction of Jerusalem** 1:1–22
  A. The Lament of the Prophet Jeremiah 1:1–11
  B. The Lament of the City of Jerusalem. 1:12–22
II. **The Anger of God** 2:1–22
  A. The Anger of God 2:1–9
  B. The Agony of Jerusalem 2:10–17
  C. The Appeal of Jerusalem 2:18–22
III. **The Prayer for Mercy** 3:1–66
  A. Jeremiah's Cry of Despair 3:1–18
  B. Jeremiah's Confession of Faith 3:19–39
  C. Jeremiah's Condition of Need 3:40–54
  D. Jeremiah's Confidence in God 3:55–66
IV. **The Siege of Jerusalem** 4:1–22
  A. The Conditions During the Siege 4:1–10
  B. The Cause of the Siege 4:11–20
  C. The Consequences of the Siege 4:21–22
V. **The Prayer for Restoration** 5:1–22
  A. The Review of the Need for Restoration . . . 5:1–15
  B. The Repentance from Sin 5:16–18
  C. The Request for Restoration 5:19–22

Ruins of the city gate in the wall of ancient Laodicea. The church of Laodicea was rebuked by John because of its lukewarm spirit (Rev. 3:14–22). *Photo by Gustav Jeeninga*

1. A son of Methushael and a descendant of Cain (Gen. 4:18–24). Lamech is the first man mentioned in the Bible as having two wives (Gen. 4:19). By Adah he had two sons, Jabal and Jubal; and by Zillah he had a son, Tubal-Cain, and a daughter, Naamah.

2. The first son of Methuselah, and the father of Noah (Gen. 5:25–26, 28–31). Lamech lived to be 777 years old (Gen. 5:31). He is mentioned in the genealogy of Jesus (Luke 3:36).

LAMENTATIONS, BOOK OF — a short Old Testament book, written in poetic form, that expresses deep grief over the destruction of the city of Jerusalem and the temple. Its English title comes from a Greek verb meaning "to cry aloud," which accurately describes the contents of the book.

LANGUISH — weaken, fade (Hos. 4:3).

LAODICEA [la′-od-i-se′-ah] — a city in the Lycus Valley of the province of PHRYGIA where one of the seven churches of Asia Minor was situated (Rev. 3:14). About 65 kilometers (40 miles) east of Ephesus and about 16 kilometers (10 miles) west of Colossae, Laodicea was built on the banks of the river Lycus, a tributary of the Maeander River.

LASCIVIOUSNESS — KJV word for LICEN-TIOUSNESS.

LAST SUPPER — (see LORD'S SUPPER).

LATIN — Roman language (John 19:20).

LAVER — a basin in which the priests washed their hands for purification purposes while officiating at the altar of the TABERNACLE or the TEMPLE. Moses was commanded to make a laver, or

This laver on a stand with wheels dates to about the 12th century B.C. It was discovered in the excavation of a tomb on the island of Cyprus.

basin, so Aaron and the Levitical priests could wash their hands and feet before offering sacrifices (Ex. 30:18–21). The laver and its base were made from the bronze mirrors of the serving women (Ex. 38:8). It stood between the Tent of Meeting and the altar.

LAW — an orderly system of rules and regulations by which a society is governed. In the Bible, particularly the Old Testament, a unique law code was established by direct revelation from God to direct His people in their worship, in their relationship to Him, and in their social relationships with one another.

LAWFUL — allowed, permitted (Matt. 12:2).

LAYING ON OF HANDS — act of dedication and consecration (Acts 6:6).

LAZARUS [laz'-a-rus] *(God has helped)* — the name of two men in the New Testament:

1. The beggar in Jesus' story about a rich man and a poor man (Luke 16:19–25).

2. The brother of Martha and Mary of Bethany (John 11:1). One long account in the Gospel of John tells about his death and resurrection at the command of Jesus (John 11). A second account in the same Gospel describes him as sitting with Jesus in the family home after the resurrection miracle (John 12:1–2). Because of the publicity surrounding this event, the chief priest plotted to kill Lazarus (John 12:9–11).

LEAH [le'-ah] — the older daughter of Laban, who deceitfully gave her in marriage to Jacob instead of her younger sister Rachel (Gen. 29:16–30). Although Rachel was the more beautiful of the two daughters of Laban and obviously was Jacob's favorite wife, the Lord blessed Leah and Jacob with six sons—Reuben, Simeon, Levi, Judah (Gen. 29:31–35), Issachar, and Zebulun (Gen. 30:17–20)—and a daughter, Dinah (Gen. 30:21). Leah's maid, Zilpah, added two more sons: Gad and Asher (Gen. 30:9–13).

LEARN — grow in knowledge and understanding (Deut. 5:1; Matt. 11:29).

LEAVEN — a substance used to produce fermentation in dough (Ex. 12:15, 19–20; yeast, NIV). In Bible times leaven was usually a piece of fermented dough retained from a previous baking that was placed in the new dough to cause it to rise.

LEBANON [leb'-a-non] *(white)* — a nation of the Middle East that includes much of what was ancient PHOENICIA in Bible times. This territory has been an important trade center linking Europe and Asia for more than 4,000 years.

LEES — the sediments or settlings of wine during fermentation and aging; the dregs remaining in a skin of wine. In Bible times, the sediment or lees was often left in the wine to improve its fla-

Traditional tomb of Lazarus, who was raised from the dead by Jesus (John 11:1–44).
Photo by Howard Vos

Cedars of Lebanon on the mountainsides of Lebanon. Reckless cutting of these magnificent trees across the centuries has almost eliminated them from the landscape. *Photo by Gustav Jeeninga*

vor. "A feast of wines on the lees ... of well-refined wines on the lees" (Is. 25:6) is a symbol of the happiness and enjoyment of the righteous in the age to come. But to drink the dregs, or lees, of the cup of God's wrath (Ps. 75:8) means to drain the cup, to endure the judgment and punishment that falls upon the wicked.

LEFT — the side of the body where the heart is located. In the Bible the word "left" is often used with the word "hand." Among the Hebrews the left hand indicated the north (Gen. 14:15; Ezek. 16:46, KJV). The left side is position of honor next to a king (Matt. 20:21–27).

LEGACY — an INHERITANCE (Prov. 3:35).

LEGION — the principal unit of the Roman army, consisting of 3,000 to 6,000 infantry troops and 100 to 200 cavalrymen. The New Testament does not use the word "legion" in its strict military sense, but in a general sense to express a large number. When Jesus healed a man possessed by unclean spirits or demons, He asked the man his name. He replied, "My name is Le-gion; for we are many" (Mark 5:9). The man was inhabited by many demons.

LENTIL — pea-like seed used for food, especially in soups and stews (2 Sam. 17:28).

LEPER, LEPROSY — a slowly progressing and incurable skin disease. In the Bible the word "leprosy" refers to a variety of symptoms (Matt. 8:3). Modern medicine now recognizes that some of these symptoms belonged to diseases other than leprosy.

LEST — in fear of (Matt. 7:6).

LET — allow (Matt. 8:22).

LETTERS — written messages between persons separated by distance, also EPISTLE (Acts 15:30). In the Old Testament David wrote a letter to Joab, sending Uriah the Hittite into the heat of battle and insuring his death. In Bible times, letters were written on sheets of PARCHMENT, or animal skins; fragments of pottery; papyrus; and clay tablets.

LEVI [le′-vi] *(joined)* — the name of four men and one tribe in the Bible:

1. The third son of Jacob and Leah (Gen. 29:34).

2. A tribe descended from Levi (Ex. 6:19).

3. Another name for MATTHEW, one of the twelve apostles (Mark 2:14). Levi was formerly a tax collector.

4. An ancestor of Jesus Christ (Luke 3:24). Levi was a son of Melchi and the father of Matthat.

5. Another ancestor of Jesus Christ (Luke 3:29). This Levi was a son of Simeon and the father of Matthat.

LEVIATHAN [le-vi′-a-than] — a large sea creature (Job 41) that sometimes represented a cruel enemy defeated by God (Job 3:8).

LEVITES [le′-vites] — descendants of Levi who served as assistants to the PRIESTS in the worship system of the nation of Israel. As Levites, AARON and his sons and their descendants were charged with the responsibility of the priesthood—offering burnt offerings and leading the people in worship and confession. But all the other Levites who were not descended directly from Aaron were to serve as priestly assistants, taking care of the tabernacle and the temple and performing other menial duties (Num. 8:6).

The choice of the Levites as a people who would perform special service for God goes back to the days of the Exodus when the children of Israel were camped at Mount Sinai.

LEVITICUS, BOOK OF — an Old Testament book filled with worship instructions for God's chosen people, Israel. The Levites, members of the tribe of Levi, were the priestly family of the nation; the title of the book seems to indicate that its instructions were given specifically for them. Because of its emphasis on holiness, sacrifice, and atonement, the book has an important message for modern believers.

The Book of Leviticus is important because of its clear teachings on three vital spiritual truths: ATONEMENT; SACRIFICE, and holiness. Without the background of these concepts in Leviticus, we could not understand their later fulfillment in the life and ministry of Jesus.

LEVY — forced labor or taxation. The word is found only once in the NKJV (Num. 31:28). It means "to impose a tax or fine." But the same Hebrew word translated "levy" in this passage is also used to describe the taskmasters set over Israel in Egypt (Ex. 1:11); conquered foreigners subjected to forced labor (Deut. 20:11); and the labor force of Israelites drafted by Solomon to build the temple (1 Kin. 5:13–14).

The mound of Gibeon (left), a city assigned to the Levites and priests at the time of Joshua's conquest of Canaan (Josh. 21:17). The modern village of el-Jib is on the right. *Photo by Howard Vos*

LEVITICUS:
A Study and Teaching Outline

Part One: The Laws of an Acceptable Approach to God: *Sacrifice* **(1:1—17:16)**

I. The Laws of Sacrifice . . . . 1:1—7:38
II. The Laws of the Priests . . . . 8:1—10:20
III. The Laws Regarding Purity. . . . . 11:1—15:33
IV. The Laws of National Atonement . . . . 16:1—17:16

Part Two: The Laws of an Acceptable Walk with God: *Sanctification* **(18:1—27:34)**

I. The Laws of Sanctification for the People . . . . 18:1—20:27
II. The Laws of Sanctification for the Priesthood . . . . 21:1—22:33
III. The Laws of Sanctification in Worship . . . 23:1—24:23
IV. The Laws of Sanctification in the Land of Canaan . . . . 25:1—26:46
V. The Laws of Sanctification through Vows 27:1–34

LEWD, LEWDNESS — preoccupation with sex and sexual desire; lust (Judg. 20:6; Hos. 2:10; 6:9; Rom. 13:13). The Hebrew word translated as "lewdness" means an evil plan, purpose, or scheme; a wicked thought, especially with reference to sexual unchastity; ideas and practices that are indecent and disgraceful.

LIBERAL, LIBERALITY — generosity and open-handedness, as opposed to stinginess. The apostle Paul taught that Christians should be liberal and generous in their financial giving (Rom. 12:8; 2 Cor. 8:2).

LIBYA [lib´-e-ah] — a country of northern Africa west of Egypt (Ezek. 27:10), also called Phut (Ezek. 27:10, KJV) or Put (NIV, NRSV). Some people who lived in "the parts of Libya adjoining Cyrene" (Acts 2:10) were in Jerusalem on the Day of PENTECOST. Simon, the man who carried Jesus' cross, was from Cyrene, the New Testament name for Libya (Matt. 27:32).

LICENTIOUSNESS — undisciplined and unrestrained behavior, especially a flagrant disregard of sexual restraints (Mark 7:22; 2 Cor. 12:21; lasciviousness, KJV). The Greek word translated as licentiousness means "outrageous conduct," showing that licentious behavior goes beyond sin to include a disregard for what is right.

LIE — any statement or act designed to deceive another person. The motivation for most lying is a desire either to hurt the one against whom the lie is directed (Gen. 3:1–13; Rom. 3:13) or to protect oneself, usually out of fear or pride (Matt. 26:69–75; Acts 5:1–11).

LIFE, BOOK OF — (see BOOK OF LIFE).

LIGHT — illumination; the opposite of darkness (Gen. 1:3–4). The Bible also speaks of light as the symbol of God's presence and righteous activity.

LIKENESS — in the image of (Gen. 1:26).

LOATHE, LOATHESOME — as a verb, despise (Job 7:16); as an adjective, rejected (Prov. 13:5).

LOCUST — flying, swarming insect with strong appetite (Joel 2:25).

LODGE — to spend the night. The common thread that unites most of the words translated "lodge" in the Bible is the idea of a temporary resting place. The two Israelite spies lodged in

The Levitical Offerings

Name	Scripture References	Purpose	Consisted of	God's Portion	Priests' Portion	Offerer's Portion	Prophetic Significance
(1) Burnt Offering (olah, Heb.). a. Sweet aroma. b. Voluntary.	Lev. 1:3–17; 6:8–13.	(1) To propitiate for sin in general (1:4). (2) To signify complete dedication and consecration to God; hence it is called the "whole burnt offering."	According to wealth: (1) Bull without blemish (1:3–9); (2) Male sheep or goat without blemish (1:10–13); (3) Turtledoves or young pigeons (1:14–17).	Entirety burned on the altar of burnt offering (1:9), except the skin (7:8).	Skin only (7:8).	None.	Signifies complete dedication of life to God: (1) On the part of Christ (Matt. 26:39–44; Mark 14:36; Luke 22:42; Phil. 2:5–11). (2) On the part of the believer (Rom. 12:1, 2; Heb. 13:15).
(2) Grain Offering (minhah, Heb.). a. Sweet aroma. b. Voluntary.	Lev. 2:1–16; 6:14–18; 7:12, 13.	The grain offering accompanied all the burnt offerings; it signified one's homage and thanksgiving to God.	Three types: (1) Fine flour mixed with oil and frankincense (2:1–3); (2) Cakes made of fine flour mixed with oil and baked in an oven (2:4), in a pan (2:5), or in a covered pan (2:7); (3) Green heads of roasted grain mixed with oil and frankincense (2:14, 15).	Memorial portion burned on the altar of burnt offering (2:2, 9, 16).	Remainder to be eaten in the court of the tabernacle (2:3, 10; 6:16–18; 7:14, 15).	None.	Signifies the perfect humanity of Christ: (1) The absence of leaven typifies the sinlessness of Christ (Heb. 4:15; 1 John 3:5). (2) The presence of oil is emblematic of the Holy Spirit (Luke 4:18; 1 John 2:20, 27).
(3) Peace Offering (shelem, Heb.). a. Sweet aroma. b. Voluntary.	Lev. 3:1–17; 7:11–21, 28–34.	The peace offering generally expressed peace and fellowship between the offerer and God; hence it culminated in a communal meal. There were three types: (1) Thank Offering: to express gratitude for an unexpected blessing or deliverance. (2) Votive Offering: to express gratitude for a blessing or deliverance granted when a vow had accompanied the petition. (3) Freewill Offering: to express gratitude to God without regard to any specific blessing or deliverance.	According to wealth: (1) From the herd, a male or female without blemish (3:1–5); (2) From the flock, a male or female without blemish (3:6–11); (3) From the goats (3:12–17). Note: Minor imperfections were permitted when the peace offering was a freewill offering of a bull or a lamb (22:23).	Fatty portions burned on the altar of burnt offering (3:3–5).	Breast (wave offering) and right thigh (heave offering; 7:30–34).	Remainder to be eaten in the court by the offerer and his family: a. Thank offering—to be eaten the same day (7:15). b. Votive and freewill offerings—to be eaten the first and second day (7:16–18). Note: this is the only offering in which the offerer shared.	Foreshadows the peace which the believer has with God through Jesus Christ (Rom. 5:1; Col. 1:20).

Name	Scripture References	Purpose	Consisted of	God's Portion	Priests' Portion	Offerer's Portion	Prophetic Significance
(4) Sin Offering (*hattat*, Heb.): a. Non-sweet aroma; b. Compulsory.	Lev. 4:1 — 5:13; 6:24–30.	To atone for sins committed unknowingly, especially where no restitution was possible. Note Num. 15:30, 31: The sin offering was of no avail in cases of defiant rebellion against God	(1) For the high priest, a bull without blemish (4:3–12). (2) For the congregation, a bull without blemish (4:13–21). (3) For a ruler, a male goat without blemish (4:22–26). (4) For a commoner, a female goat or female lamb without blemish (4:27–35). (5) In cases of poverty, two turtledoves or two young pigeons (one for a sin offering, the other for a burnt offering) could be substituted (5:7–10). (6) In cases of extreme poverty, fine flour could be substituted (5:11–13; cf. Heb. 9:22).	(1) Fatty portions to be burned on the altar of burnt offering (4:8–10, 19, 26, 31, 35). (2) When the sin offering was for the high priest or congregation, the remainder of the bull was to be burned outside the camp (4:11, 12, 20, 21).	When the sin offering was for a ruler or commoner, the remainder of the goat or lamb was to be eaten in the tabernacle court (6:26).	None.	Prefigures the fact that in His death: (1) Christ was made sin for us (2 Cor. 5:21); (2) Christ suffered outside the gates of Jerusalem (Heb. 13:11–13).
(5) Trespass Offering (*'asham*, Heb.): a. Non-sweet aroma; b. Compulsory.	Lev. 5:14 — 6:7, 7:1–7.	To atone for sins committed unknowingly, especially where restitution was possible.	(1) If the offense were against the Lord (tithes, offerings, etc.), a ram without blemish was to be brought; restitution was reckoned according to the priest's estimate of the value of the trespass, plus one-fifth (5:15, 16). (2) If the offense were against man, a ram without blemish was to be brought; restitution was reckoned according to the value plus one-fifth (6:4–6).	Fatty portions to be burned on the altar of burnt offering (7:3–5).	Remainder to be eaten in a holy place (7:6, 7).	None.	Foreshadows the fact that Christ is also our trespass offering (Col. 2:13).

the house of Rahab (Josh. 2:1); the Israelites lodged by the Jordan River before passing over into the Promised Land; and Peter lodged with Simon the tanner (Acts 10:18). The word "lodge" also refers to the temporary hut built by a watchman in a cucumber field (Is. 1:8).

LOFTY — high (Is. 57:7); proud (Is. 2:12).

LOINS — the lower abdomen, including the reproductive organs. A man's loins are described as the source of his offspring (Gen. 35:11, KJV; body, NIV). When a man was ready to work, he put a belt around his waist; then he tucked up his robe so his legs would not be hindered. This is the meaning of "girded up his loins" (1 Kin. 18:46). To "gird up the loins of your mind" (1 Pet. 1:13) means to prepare for strenuous mental activity.

LOINCLOTH — piece of clothing worn by men (Job 12:18, NIV).

LONGING — desire (Ps. 119:20).

LORD (see GOD, NAMES OF).

LORD'S PRAYER — the model prayer that Jesus taught His disciples (Matt. 6:5–15; Luke 11:1–4). In the Gospel of Matthew the Lord's Prayer occurs in the Sermon on the Mount. He emphasized that prayer should not be an attempt to get God's attention by repeating words. Instead, it should be a quiet, confident expression of needs to our heavenly Father. Our attitude in prayer is important; in the Sermon on the Mount Jesus shows His disciples how to pray.

LORD'S SUPPER — the ritualistic practice, usually during a worship service, in which Christians partake of bread and wine (or grape juice) with the purpose of remembering Christ, receiving strength from Him, and rededicating themselves to His cause. It is one of two sacraments or ordinances instituted by Christ to be observed by His church until He returns (BAPTISM is the other).

The term "Lord's Supper" is used only in 1 Corinthians 11:20. The practice is also known as Communion (from 1 Cor. 10:16), the Lord's Table (from 1 Cor. 10:21), and the Eucharist (from the Greek word for "giving thanks"; Luke 22:17, 19; 1 Cor. 11:24). The expression "breaking of bread" (Acts 2:42, 46; 20:7, 11) probably refers to receiving the Lord's Supper with a common meal known as the Love Feast (2 Pet. 2:13; Jude 12).

The institution of the Lord's Supper (Matt. 26:17–30; Mark 14:12–26; Luke 22:1–23; 1 Cor. 11:23–25) took place on the night before Jesus died, at a meal commonly known as the Last Supper. Although there is considerable debate over the issue, the Last Supper probably was the Jewish PASSOVER meal, first instituted by God in the days of Moses (Ex. 12:1–14; Num. 9:1–5).

LOT [laht] — Abraham's nephew. Lot accompanied Abraham from Mesopotamia to Canaan and to and from Egypt (Gen. 11:27–31; 12:4–5; 13:1). Both Lot and Abraham had large herds of cattle, and their herdsmen quarreled over their pasturelands. At Abraham's suggestion, the two decided to separate.

Abraham gave Lot his choice of land; and Lot chose the more fertile, well-watered site—the Jordan River valley—as opposed to the rocky hill country. Failing to take into account the character of the inhabitants, Lot "pitched his tent toward Sodom" (Gen. 13:12, KJV).

LOTS, CASTING OF — a way of making decisions in Bible times, similar to drawing straws or casting a pair of dice to determine what course or direction to follow. The word "lots" occurs 70 times in the Old Testament and seven in the New Testament. Most of the occurrences were in the early period when little of the Bible was available and when God approved of this means for determining His will (Prov. 16:33).

LOVE — the high esteem that God has for His human children and the high regard which they, in turn, should have for Him and other people. Because of the hundreds of references to love in the Bible, it is certainly the most remarkable book of love in the world. It records the greatest love story ever written—God's unconditional love for us that sent His Son to die on the Cross (John 3:16; 1 John 4:10).

LOVINGKINDNESS — God's merciful and steady love (Ps. 17:7). (See KINDNESS.)

LOW, LOWLY — humble (Is. 2:12; Luke 1:52).

LUCIFER [lu'-sif-er] *(morning star)* — the Latin name for the planet Venus. The word Lucifer appears only once in the Bible: "How you are fallen from heaven, O Lucifer, son of the morning! How you are cut down to the ground, you who weakened the nations!" (Is. 14:12). Literally, the passage describes the overthrow of a tyrant, the king of Babylon. But many Bible scholars see in this passage a description of SATAN, who rebelled against the throne of God and was "brought down to Sheol, to the lowest depths of the Pit" (Is. 14:15). The same kind of interpretation is often given to Ezekiel 28:11–19. The description of the king of Tyre thus is believed to reach beyond that of an earthly ruler to the archangel who was cast out of heaven for leading a revolt against God.

LUKE — a "fellow laborer" of the apostle Paul (Philem. 24) and the author of the Gospel of Luke and the Acts of the Apostles. By profession he was a physician (Col. 4:14). During one of Paul's imprisonments, probably in Rome, Luke's faithfulness was recorded by Paul when he declared, "Only Luke is with me" (2 Tim. 4:11). These three references are our only direct knowledge of Luke in the New Testament.

LUKE, GOSPEL OF — the third Gospel, in which the great truths of Jesus are communicated primarily through vivid stories. Luke is the first of a two-part work. In this work, the history of the Gospel is traced from its beginnings in the life of Jesus (the Gospel of Luke) to the founding of the early church (the Acts of the Apostles).

The author of the Gospel of Luke is more interested in persons, especially those in trouble, than in ideas. He also is a skilled writer, and the literary quality of the Gospel of Luke is the highest of all four Gospels. Luke often is the most

LUKE:
A Study and Teaching Outline

Part One: The Introduction of the Son of Man (1:1—4:13)

I. The Purpose and Method of Luke's Gospel. 1:1–4
II. The Events Preceding Christ's Birth. 1:5–56
III. The Events Accompanying Christ's Birth . . 1:57—2:38
IV. The Events During Christ's Childhood. 2:39–52
V. The Events Preceding Christ's
　Presentation . . . . 3:1—4:13

Part Two: The Ministry of the Son of Man (4:14—9:50)

I. The Presentation of Christ 4:14–30
II. The Demonstration of Christ's Powers . . . . 4:31—5:28
III. The Explanation of Christ's Program . . . . . 5:29—6:49
IV. The Expansion of Christ's Program . . . . 7:1—9:50

Part Three: The Rejection of the Son of Man (9:51—19:27)

I. The Increasing Opposition to Christ. . . . . 9:51—11:54
II. The Instruction in View of Christ's
　Rejection . . . . 12:1—19:27

Part Four: The Crucifixion and Resurrection of the Son of Man (19:28—24:53)

I. The Last Week of Christ. . . . . 19:28—23:56
II. The Victory of Christ 24:1–53

interesting Gospel to read. But he is also a serious historian who places Jesus within the context of world history. He presents Jesus and the church as the fulfillment of the history of salvation.

Luke has the most universal outlook of all the Gospels; he portrays Jesus as a man with compassion for all peoples. Whereas Matthew traces Jesus' genealogy back to Abraham, the father of the Hebrew people (1:2), Luke traces it back to Adam, the father of the human race (3:38). In Matthew Jesus sends His disciples "to the lost sheep of the house of Israel" (10:6) only, but Luke omits this limitation.

LUST — desire for what is forbidden; an obsessive sexual craving. Although there are legitimate desires for which God makes provision (Deut. 12:15, 20–21), lust refers to the desire for things that are contrary to the will of God. The "lust after evil things" (1 Cor. 10:6) of the Israelites in the wilderness serves as an example of the lusts that should be avoided by Christians.

Christians are able to resist lust through the power of the Holy Spirit. The flesh, with its passions and lusts, is to be crucified (Gal. 5:24; Titus 2:12).

LUZ [luhz] *(almond tree)* — the name of two cities in the Old Testament:

1. A city of the Canaanites renamed BETHEL by Jacob (Gen. 28:19). Assigned to the tribe of Benjamin, Luz was near the border of Ephraim, about 18 kilometers (11 miles) north of Jerusalem.

2. A city of the Hittites (Judg. 1:26). The site is unknown, but some scholars suggest Luweiziyeh, about 7 kilometers (4.5 miles) northwest of Mount Hermon.

LYDIA [lid′-e-ah] — the name of a woman and a geographical region:

1. A prosperous businesswoman from the city of THYATIRA who became a convert to Christianity after hearing the apostle Paul speak (Acts 16:12–15, 40).

2. A large territory in western Asia Minor

The Chapel of Lydia by the riverside at Phillippi. Lydia was converted to Christianity through the ministry of the apostle Paul (Acts 16:13–15). *Photo by Howard Vos*

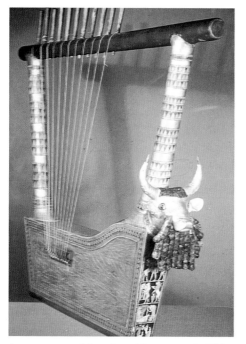

A reconstructed lyre from Mesopotamia. This was a popular musical instrument about 2500 B.C., several centuries before Abraham's time.
Photo by Howard Vos

(modern Turkey) rich in natural resources. Its fertile land produced figs, grain, grapes, and olives. The Lydians are mentioned by the prophet Ezekiel as "men of war," or mercenaries, who fought to defend Tyre (Ezek. 27:10) and who made an alliance with Egypt (Ezek. 30:5; Lud, NRSV).

LYRE — a small harp.

LYSTRA [lis′-trah] — a city of Lycaonia, in central Anatolia in modern Turkey, where Paul preached after being driven from Iconium. Lystra was built on a small hill about 46 meters (150 feet) above the plain that stretched northeastward to Iconium and southeastward to Derbe.

The mound of ancient Lystra, a city in the province of Lycaonia where Paul was stoned by a mob (Acts 14:8–20). *Photo by Howard Vos*

M

MACEDONIA [mas-e-do′-nee-ah] — a mountainous country north of Greece (Achaia) in the Balkan Peninsula. This area was visited twice, and perhaps three times, by the apostle Paul.

MACEDONIANS [mas-e-do′-nee-ans] — natives or residents of MACEDONIA, a region of northern Greece (Acts 19:29; 2 Cor. 9:2).

MADNESS — a state of mental instability (1 Sam. 21:13; Eccl. 1:17; John 10:20).

MAGDALA [mag′-da-lah] *(tower)* — a place on the Sea of Galilee, perhaps on the west shore, about five kilometers (three miles) northwest of Tiberias. Jesus and His disciples withdrew to this place after the feeding of the 4,000 (Matt. 15:39; Magadan, NIV, NASB, REB, NRSV). The parallel passage (Mark 8:10) has Dalmanutha. Magdala was either the birthplace or the home of Mary Magdalene.

MAGDALENE [mag′-da-leen] *(from Magdala)* — the designation given to a woman named Mary, one of Jesus' most prominent Galilean female disciples, to distinguish her from the other Marys. The first appearance of Mary Magdalene in the Gospels is in Luke 8:2, which mentions her among those who were ministering to Jesus. Mary Magdalene has sometimes mistakenly been described as a woman of bad character and loose morals, simply because Mark 16:9 states that Jesus had cast seven demons out of her. Nor is there any reason to conclude that she was the same person as the sinful woman whom Simon the Pharisee treated with such disdain and contempt (Luke 7:36–50).

MAGISTRATE — judge (Ezra 7:25).

MALACHI:
A Study and
Teaching Outline

I. The Privilege of the Nation 1:1–5
II. The Pollution of the Nation . . . . 1:6—3:15
  A. The Sin of the Priests of Israel . . . . 1:6—2:9
    1. The Priests Despise the Name of
      the Lord 1:6–14
    2. The Lord Curses the Priests 2:2:1–9
  B. The Sin of the People of Israel . . . . 2:10—3:15
    1. The People Commit Idolatry 2:10–12
    2. The People Practice Divorce 2:13–16
    3. The Lord Will Judge at His Coming . . 2:17—3:7
    4. The People Rob God 3:8–12
    5. The People Doubt the Character
      of God 3:13–15
III. The Promises to the Nation . . . . 3:16—4:6
  A. The Rewards of the Book of
    Remembrance 3:16–18
  B. The Rewards of the Coming of Christ 4:1–3
  C. The Prophecy of the Coming of Elijah 4:4–6

MAGNIFY — exalt (Luke 1:46).

MAGOG [ma′-gog] *(land of Gog)* — the name of a man and a people in the Bible:

1. The second son of Japheth and a grandson of Noah (Gen. 10:2).

2. The descendants of Magog (Ezek. 38:2), possibly a people who lived in northern Asia and Europe.

MAHANAIM [ma-ha′na-im] *(two armies)* — an ancient town in Gilead, east of the Jordan River in the vicinity of the River Jabbok. Located on the border between the tribes of Manasseh and Gad (Josh. 13:26, 30), Mahanaim was later assigned to the Merarite Levites (Josh. 21:38).

MAIMED — missing a limb or having a damaged limb (Mark 10:43; Luke 14:13–14).

MAKER — creator (Hab. 2:18); often used as a reference to God (Job 35:10).

MALACHI [mal′-a-ki] *(my messenger)* — Old Testament prophet and author of the prophetic book that bears his name. Nothing is known about Malachi's life except the few facts that may be inferred from his prophecies. He apparently prophesied after the CAPTIVITY, during the time when NEHEMIAH was leading the people to rebuild Jerusalem's wall and recommit themselves to following God's Law. The people's negligence in paying tithes to God was condemned by both Nehemiah and Malachi (Neh. 13:10–14; Mal. 3:8–10).

MALACHI, BOOK OF — a short prophetic book of the Old Testament written to rebuke the people of Israel for their shallow worship practices. The name comes from the Hebrew word *malachi* (1:1), meaning "my messenger" or "messenger of the LORD."

The prophecy of Malachi is noted for its vivid portrayal of the love of God as well as His might and power. Israel needed to be reminded of these truths at a time when widespread doubt had dashed its expectations of the Messiah.

Malachi leaves us with the feeling that the story is not yet finished, that God still has promises to fulfill on behalf of His people. After Malachi came 400 long years of silence. But when the time was right, heaven would burst forth in song at the arrival of the Messiah.

MALCHUS [mal′-kus] *(ruler)* — a servant of the high priest who was present at the arrest of Jesus in the Garden of Gethsemane. Simon Peter struck Malchus with a sword and cut off his ear (John 18:10).

MALEFACTOR — KJV translation of two Greek words meaning "evildoer" (John 18:30) and "evil worker" (Luke 23:32–33, 39). The two thieves crucified with Jesus were malefactors. (Luke 23:32–33, 39; criminals, NKJV, NIV).

MALICE, MALICIOUSNESS — a vicious intention, or a desire of one person to hurt another (Titus 3:3). Malice is often irrational, usually based on the false belief that the person against whom it is directed has the same intention. It is contrary to love (1 Cor. 13:4–7). Christians are instructed to rid their lives of malice (Eph. 4:31–32).

MALTA [mal′-ta] — a small island in the Mediterranean Sea between Sicily and Africa, about 145 kilometers (90 miles) southwest of

St. Paul's Bay at Malta. The beach on which Paul's ship ran aground (Acts 27:39—28:10) has eroded across the centuries, leaving this rocky shore. *Photo by Howard Vos*

Syracuse. The apostle Paul was shipwrecked on Malta (Acts 28:1).

MAMMON [mam'-mon] *(riches)* — a word that speaks of wealth (Matt. 6:24; Luke 16:9, 11, 13), especially wealth that is used in opposition to God. Mammon is a transliteration of an Aramaic word that means "wealth, riches," or "earthly goods."

MAMRE [mam'-re] — the name of a man and a place in the Old Testament:

1. An Amorite chief who formed an alliance with Abraham against Chedorlaomer (Gen. 14:13, 24).

2. A place in the district of Hebron, west of Machpelah, where Abraham lived. It was noted for its "terebinth trees" (Gen. 13:18; 18:1), or "oaks" (NRSV). Near Mamre was the cave of Machpelah, in which Abraham, Isaac, and Jacob—and their wives, Sarah, Rebekah, and Leah—were buried (Gen. 49:13). The site of ancient Mamre has been identified as Ramet el-Khalil, about three kilometers (two miles) north of Hebron.

MAN, MANKIND — God's highest creation, made in God's own image.

MANASSEH [ma-na'-seh] *(causing to forget)* — the name of five men in the Old Testament:

1. Joseph's firstborn son who was born in Egypt to Asenath the daughter of Poti-Pherah, priest of On (Gen. 41:50–51).

2. The grandfather of the Jonathan who was one of the priests of the graven image erected by the tribe of Dan (Judg. 18:30).

3. The 14th king of Judah, the son of HEZEKIAH born to Hephzibah (2 Kin. 21:1–18). Manasseh reigned longer (55 years) than any other Israelite king and had the dubious distinction of being Judah's most wicked king. He came to the throne at the age of 12, although he probably co-reigned with Hezekiah for ten years. His father's godly influence appears to have affected Manasseh only negatively, and he reverted to the ways of his evil grandfather, Ahaz.

4. A descendant, or resident, of Pahath-Moab (Ezra 10:30).

5. An Israelite of the family of Hashum (Ezra 10:33).

MANASSEH, TRIBE OF [ma-na'-seh] — the tribe that traced its origin to MANASSEH no. 1. The tribe of Manasseh descended through Manasseh's son, Machir; Machir's son, Gilead; and Gilead's six sons (Num. 26:28–34). During their first 430 years in Egypt, the tribe of Manasseh increased to 32,200 men of war (Num. 1:34–35). By the second census, 39 years later, it numbered 52,700 (Num. 26:34).

MANDRAKE — wild plant (Gen. 30:14–16).

MANGER — a feedingtrough, crib, or open box in a stable designed to hold fodder for livestock (Luke 2:7, 12; 13:15). In Bible times, mangers were made of clay mixed with straw or from stones cemented with mud. In structures built by King Ahab at Megiddo, a manger cut from a limestone block was discovered. Mangers were also carved in natural outcroppings of rock, such as livestock being stabled in a cave; some were constructed of masonry.

MANIFEST — to show, to make visible or apparent (John 1:31).

MANIFOLD — abundant (Eph. 3:10).

MANNA — the food that God provided miraculously for the Israelites in the wilderness during their Exodus (Ex. 16:15, 31, 33; Num. 11:6–9).

MANTLE — a covering such as a robe (2 Kin. 2:8).

MARK, GOSPEL OF — the second book of the New Testament and the earliest of the four Gospels, according to most New Testament scholars. The Gospel of Mark portrays the person of Jesus more by what He does than by what He says. It is characterized by a vivid, direct style that leaves the impression of familiarity with the original events.

MARK:
A Study and Teaching Outline

Part One: The Presentation of the Servant (1:1—2:12)

I. The Forerunner of the Servant 1:1–8
II. The Baptism of the Servant 1:9–11
III. The Temptation of the Servant 1:12–13
IV. The Mission of the Servant . . . . 1:14—2:12

Part Two: The Opposition to the Servant (2:13—8:26)

I. The Initial Opposition to the Servant . . . . . 2:13—3:35
II. The Parables of the Servant. 4:1–34
III. The Miracles of the Servant . . . . 4:35—5:43
IV. The Growing Opposition to the Servant . . . . . 6:1—8:26

Part Three: The Instruction by the Servant (8:27—10:52)

I. Peter's Confession of Christ. 8:27–33
II. The Cost of Discipleship . . . . 8:34—9:1
III. The Transfiguration 9:2–13
IV. A Demon-possessed Son Is Delivered 9:14–29
V. Jesus Foretells His Death. 9:30–32
VI. Jesus Teaches to Prepare the Disciples . . 9:33—10:45
VII. Blind Bartimaeus Is Healed 10:46–52

Part Four: The Rejection of the Servant (11:1—15:47)

I. The Formal Presentation of the Servant. 11:1–19
II. The Instruction on Prayer. 11:20–26
III. The Opposition by the Leaders . . . . 11:27—12:44
IV. The Instruction on the Future. 13:1–37
V. The Passion of the Servant . . . . 14:1—15:47

Part Five: The Resurrection of the Servant (16:1–20)

I. The Resurrection of Jesus 16:1–8
II. The Appearances of Jesus 16:9–18
III. The Ascension of Jesus 16:19–20

MARK, JOHN — an occasional associate of Peter and Paul, and the probable author of the second Gospel. Mark's lasting impact on the Christian church comes from his writing rather than his life. He was the first to develop the literary form known as the "gospel" and is rightly regarded as a creative literary artist.

John Mark appears in the New Testament only in association with more prominent personalities and events. His mother, Mary, was an influential woman of Jerusalem who possessed a large house with servants. The early church gathered in this house during Peter's imprisonment under Herod Agrippa I (Acts 12:12). Barnabas and Saul (Paul) took John Mark with them when they returned from Jerusalem to Antioch after their famine-relief visit (Acts 12:25). Shortly thereafter, Mark accompanied Paul and Barnabas on their first missionary journey as far as Perga. He served in the capacity of "assistant" (Acts 13:5), which probably involved making arrangements for travel, food, and lodging; he may have done some teaching, too.

MARRIAGE — the union of a man and a woman as husband and wife (Gen. 2:24–25), which becomes the foundation for a home and family.

MARTHA [mar'-tha] *(lady, mistress)* — the sister of Mary and Lazarus of Bethany (Luke 10:38–41; John 11:1–44; 12:1–3). All three were sincere followers of Jesus, but Mary and Martha expressed their love for Him in different ways. The account of the two women given by Luke reveals a clash of temperaments between Mary and Martha. Martha "was distracted with much serving" (Luke 10:40); she was an activist busy with household chores. Her sister Mary "sat at Jesus' feet and heard His word" (Luke 10:39); her instinct was to sit still, meditate, and receive spiritual instruction.

MARY [ma'-ry] — the name of six women in the New Testament:

1. Mary, the mother of Jesus (Luke 1—2). We know nothing of Mary's background other than that she was a peasant and a resident of Nazareth, a city of Galilee.

2. Mary Magdalene, the woman from whom Jesus cast out seven demons. The name Magdalene indicates that she came from Magdala, a city on the southwest coast of the Sea of Galilee. After Jesus cast seven demons from her, she became one of His followers (Luke 8:1–2).

3. Mary of Bethany, sister of Martha and Lazarus (Luke 10:38–42).

4. Mary, the mother of the disciple James and Joses (Matt. 27:55–61).

5. Mary, the mother of John Mark (Acts 12:12).

6. Mary of Rome (Rom. 16:6). All we know about this Christian woman of Rome is found in Paul's salutation: "Greet Mary, who labored much for us."

MASTER — a person having authority, power, and control over the actions of other people (Gen. 24:12; Matt. 8:19).

MATTHEW [math'-ew] *(gift of the Lord)* — a tax collector who became one of the twelve apostles of Jesus (Matt. 9:9).

MATTHEW, GOSPEL OF — the opening book of the New Testament. Matthew has had perhaps a greater influence on Christian worship and literature than any other New Testament writing. For 17 centuries the church took its readings for Sundays and Holy Days from Matthew, drawing from the other Gospels only where it felt Matthew was insufficient.

Matthew offers the most systematic arrangement of Jesus' teaching in the New Testament, and the early church used it heavily for its instruction of converts. Because of its emphasis on the fulfillment of Old Testament prophecy, Matthew is well suited as the opening book of the New Testament. In it the promises of God are recalled and their fulfillment in Jesus Christ is announced.

MATTHIAS [mat'-thias] *(gift of the Lord)* — a disciple chosen to succeed Judas Iscariot as an apostle (Acts 1:23, 26).

MEASURE — as a noun, a reference to dry, liquid or area amounts; as a verb, the act of determining such amounts.

MEAT — the edible flesh of animals, often referring to the flesh of mammals, as distinguished from fish and poultry (Num. 11:4; Deut. 12:15, 20).

Meat was often sacrificed on pagan altars and dedicated to pagan gods in Paul's day. Later this meat was offered for sale in the public meat markets. Some Christians wondered if it were morally right for Christians to eat such meat that had previously been sacrificed to pagan gods. Paul explained that they should not eat such meat if it would cause weaker Christians to sin (1 Cor. 8:13).

MEAT OFFERING — an offering presented to God (Leviticus 2).

MEDE — an inhabitant of Media (Is. 13:17).

MEDIATOR — one who goes between two groups or persons to help them work out their differences and reach an agreement. A mediator usually is a neutral party, a go-between, intermediary, or arbitrator (Job 9:33; daysman, KJV) who brings about reconciliation in a hostile situation when divided persons are not able to work out their differences themselves.

MEDITATION — the practice of reflection or contemplation. The word "meditation" or its verb form, "to meditate," is found mainly in the

MATTHEW:
A Study and Teaching Outline

Part One: The Presentation of the King (1:1—4:11)

I. The Advent of the King . . . . 1:1—2:23
II. The Announcer of the King 3:1–12
III. The Approval of the King . . . . 3:13—4:11

Part Two: The Proclamation of the King (4:12—7:29)

I. The Background for the Sermon 4:12–25
II. The Sermon on the Mount. . . . . 5:1—7:29

Part Three: The Power of the King (8:1—11:1)

I. The Demonstration of the King's Power . . . . 8:1—9:34
II. The Delegation of the King's Power . . . . . . 9:35—11:1

Part Four: The Progressive Rejection of the King (11:2—16:12)

I. The Beginning of the Rejection 11:2–30
II. The Rejection by the Pharisees. 12:1–50
III. The Consequences of the Rejection 13:1–53
IV. The Continuing Rejection . . . . 13:54—16:12

Part Five: The Preparation of the Disciples of the King (16:13—20:28)

I. The Revelation of Great Truths . . . . 16:13—17:13
II. The Instruction in View of Rejection. . . . 17:14—20:28

Part Six: The Presentation and Rejection of the King (20:29—27:66)

I. The Blind Men Recognize the King 20:29–34
II. The Public Presentation of the King 21:1–17
III. The Nation Respects the King. . . . . 21:18—22:46
IV. The King Rejects the Nation 23:1–39
V. The Predictions of the King's Second Coming . . . . 24:1—25:46
VI. The Passion of the King . . . . 26:1—27:66

Part Seven: The Proof of the King (28:1–20)

I. The Empty Tomb 28:1–8
II. The Appearance of Jesus to the Women 28:9–10
III. The Bribery of the Soldiers 28:11–15
IV. The Appearance of Jesus to the Disciples . . . 28:16–17
V. The Great Commission. 28:18–20

Old Testament. The Hebrew words behind this concept mean "to murmur," "a murmuring," "sighing," or "moaning." This concept is reflected in Psalm 1:2, where the "blessed man" meditates on God's law day and night. The psalmist also prayed that the meditation of his heart would be acceptable in God's sight (Ps. 19:14). Joshua was instructed to meditate on the Book of the Law for the purpose of obeying all that was written in it (Josh. 1:8).

MEEK, MEEKNESS — an attitude of humility toward God and gentleness toward people, springing from a recognition that God is in control. Although weakness and meekness may look similar, they are not the same. Weakness is due to negative circumstances, such as lack of strength or lack of courage. But meekness is due to a person's conscious choice. It is strength and courage under control, coupled with kindness.

MEET — various meanings including right (Ex. 8:26), necessary (Luke 15:32), sufficient (Col. 1:12).

MEGIDDO [me-ghid'-do] — a walled city east of the Carmel Mountain range where many important battles were fought in Old Testament times. Megiddo was situated on the main road that linked Egypt and Syria. Overlooking the Valley of Jezreel (Plain of Esdraelon), Megiddo was one of the most strategic cities in Palestine. All major traffic through northern Palestine traveled past Megiddo, making it a strategic military stronghold (2 Kin. 9:27; 23:29).

MELCHISEDEC [mel-kis'-e-dek] — a form of MELCHIZEDEK.

MELCHIZEDEK [mel-kiz'-e-dek] *(king of righteousness)* — a king of Salem (Jerusalem) and priest of the Most High God (Gen. 14:18–20; Ps. 110:4; Heb. 5:6–11; 6:20—7:28). Melchizedek's appearance and disappearance in the Book of Genesis are somewhat mysterious. Melchizedek and Abraham first met after Abraham's defeat of Chedorlaomer and his three allies. Melchizedek presented bread and wine to Abraham and his weary men, demonstrating friendship and religious kinship. He bestowed a blessing on Abraham in the name of El Elyon ("God Most High"), and praised God for giving Abraham a victory in battle (Gen. 14:18–20).

MEMORIAL — a monument, statue, holiday, or ritual that serves as a remembrance or reminder of a person or an event. The Feast of the PASSOVER was a memorial of God's sparing the firstborn of the Israelites in Egypt and of Israel's deliverance from Egyptian bondage (Ex. 12:14).

MENE, MENE, TEKEL, UPHARSIN [me'-ne, me'-ne, tek'-el, u-far'-sin] *(numbered, numbered, weighed, and divided)* — a puzzling inscription that appeared on the wall of the palace of Belshazzar, king of Babylon, during a drunken feast (Dan. 5:1–29).

The words of the inscription refer to three Babylonian weights of decreasing size and their equivalent monetary values. In his interpretation of this inscription, Daniel used a play on words to give the message God had for Belshazzar and Babylon.

"Mene: God has numbered your kingdom, and finished it." God had counted the days allotted to Belshazzar's rule and his time had run out. "Tekel: You have been weighed in the balances and found wanting." Belshazzar's character, his moral values and spiritual worth, had been evaluated and he was found to be deficient. "Peres: Your kingdom has been divided, and given to the Medes and Persians." Belshazzar's empire had been broken into bits and pieces, dissolved and destroyed.

MEPHIBOSHETH [me-fib'-o-sheth] *(from the mouth of* [the] *shame* [ful god Baal]) — the name of two men in the Old Testament:

1. A son of Jonathan and grandson of Saul. Mephibosheth was also called Merib-Baal (1 Chr. 8:34; 9:40), probably his original name, meaning "a striver against Baal." His name was changed because the word "Baal" was associated with idol worship.

2. A son of King Saul and Rizpah (2 Sam. 21:8).

MERCY — the aspect of God's love that causes Him to help the miserable, just as grace is the aspect of His love that moves Him to forgive the guilty. Those who are miserable may be so either because of breaking God's Law or because of circumstances beyond their control.

MERCY SEAT — the golden lid or covering on the ARK OF THE COVENANT, regarded as the resting place of God (Ex. 25:17–22; 1 Chr. 28:11; Heb. 9:5; atonement cover, NIV).

MESHACH [me'-shak] — the Chaldean name given to Mishael, one of Daniel's companions (Dan. 1:7). Along with SHADRACH and ABED-NEGO, Meshach would not bow down and worship the pagan image of gold set up by Nebuchadnezzar. They were cast into "the burning fiery furnace," but were preserved from harm by the power of God.

MESOPOTAMIA [mes-o-po-ta′-me-ah] *(land between the rivers)* — a region situated between the Tigris and Euphrates Rivers; the general area inhabited by the ancient Assyrians and Babylonians. In the New Testament the word Mesopotamia refers to the areas between and around the Tigris and Euphrates Rivers, including ancient Syria, Accad, Babylonia, and Sumer. But in the Old Testament, Mesopotamia usually translates a phrase that means "Aram of the two rivers" and is restricted to northwest Mesopotamia.

MESSAGE, MESSENGER — word, one who brings the word (Judg. 3:20; 1 John 1:5).

MESSIAH [mes-si′-ah] *(anointed one)* — the one anointed by God and empowered by God's spirit to deliver His people and establish His kingdom. In Jewish thought, the Messiah would be the king of the Jews, a political leader who would defeat their enemies and bring in a golden era of peace and prosperity. In Christian thought, the term Messiah refers to Jesus' role as a spiritual deliverer, setting His people free from sin and death.

METHUSELAH [me-thu′-se-lah] — a son of Enoch and the grandfather of Noah. At the age of 187, Methuselah became the father of Lamech.

After the birth of Lamech, Methuselah lived 782 years and died at the age of 969. He lived longer than any other human. He was an ancestor of Jesus (Luke 3:37; Mathusala, KJV).

MICAH [mi′-cah] *(Who is like the Lord)* — the name of six men in the Old Testament, most notably an Old Testament prophet and author of the Book of Micah. A younger contemporary of the great prophet Isaiah, Micah was from Moresheth Gath (Mic. 1:1, 14), a town in southern Judah. His prophecy reveals his country origins; he uses many images from country life (Mic. 7:1).

MICAH, BOOK OF — a brief prophetic book of the Old Testament, known for its condemnation of the rich because of their exploitation of the poor. Micah also contains a clear prediction of the Messiah's birth in Bethlehem, centuries before Jesus was actually born in this humble little village. The book takes its title from its author, the prophet Micah, whose name means, "Who is like the Lord?"

The mixture of judgment and promise in the Book of Micah is a striking characteristic of the Old Testament prophets. These contrasting passages give real insight into the character of God. In His wrath He remembers mercy; He cannot maintain His anger forever. Judgment with love is the ironic, but essential, work of the Lord. In the darkest days of impending judgment on Israel

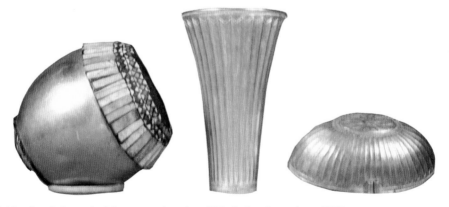

Golden bowls from the Mesopotamian city of Ur, dating from about 2500 B.C. *Photo by Howard Vos*

MICAH:
A Study and Teaching Outline

I. **The Prediction of Judgment** . . . . 1:1—3:12
  A. Introduction to the Book of Micah 1:1
  B. The Judgment on the People. . . . . 1:2—2:13
    1. Judgment on Samaria 1:2–7
    2. Judgment on Judah 1:8–16
    3. Cause of Judgment. 2:1–11
    4. Promise of Future Restoration. 2:12–13
  C. The Judgment on the Leadership. 3:1–12
    1. Judgment on Princes 3:1–4
    2. Judgment on Prophets. 3:5–8
    3. Promise of Future Judgment 3:9–12
II. **The Prediction of Restoration.** . . . . 4:1—5:15
  A. The Promise of the Coming Kingdom 4:1–5
  B. The Promise of the Coming Captivities. . . 4:6—5:1
  C. The Promise of the Coming King. 5:2–15
    1. Birth of the Messiah 5:2
    2. Rejection of the Messiah 5:3
    3. Work of the Messiah. 5:4–15
III. **The Plea for Repentance** . . . . 6:1—7:20
  A. The First Plea of God 6:1–8
    1. God Pleads 6:1–5
    2. Micah Replies. 6:6–8
  B. The Second Plea of God. . . . . 6:9—7:6
    1. God Pleads 6:9–16
    2. Micah Replies. 7:1–6
  C. The Promise of Final Salvation 7:7–20

and Judah, there always was the possibility that a remnant would be spared. God was determined to maintain His holiness, and so He acted in judgment on those who had broken His covenant. But He was just as determined to fulfill the promises He had made to Abraham centuries earlier. This compelled Him to point to the fulfillment of the covenant in the kingdom to come.

Perhaps the greatest contribution of the Book of Micah is its clear prediction of a coming Savior. The future Messiah is referred to indirectly in some of the prophetic books of the Old Testament. But He is mentioned directly in the Book of Micah.

MICAIAH [mi-ka-i'-ah] *(who is like the Lord?)* — the prophet who predicted the death of King Ahab of Israel in the battle against the Syrians at Ramoth Gilead (1 Kin. 22:8–28; 2 Chr. 18:7–27).

MICHAEL [mi'-ka-el] *(who is like God?)* — the name of ten men and an archangel in the Bible but usually in reference to an archangel, or an angel of high rank, who served as prince or guardian over the destinies of the nation of Israel (Dan. 10:21; 12:1).

MICHAL [mi'-kal] *(who is like God?)* — the younger daughter of King Saul who became David's wife. After David had become a hero by slaying GOLIATH, Saul offered to give Michal to David as his wife. But instead of a dowry, Saul requested of David "one hundred foreskins of the Philistines" (1 Sam. 18:25), hoping that David would be killed by the Philistines.

Instead, David won an impressive victory. He and his warriors killed 200 Philistines and brought their foreskins to the king. Then Saul presented Michal to David to become his wife (1 Sam. 18:27–28).

MIDIAN [mid'-e-an] — the name of a man and a territory in the Old Testament:

1. A son of Abraham by his concubine Keturah (Gen. 25:1–6). Midian had four sons (1 Chr. 1:33).

2. The land inhabited by the descendants of Midian. Situated east of the Jordan River and the

Bedouin tents in the land of Midian, where Moses fled after killing an Egyptian (Ex. 2:11–15).

Dead Sea, the land stretched southward through the Arabian desert as far as the southern and eastern parts of the peninsula of Sinai.

MIDIANITES [mid'-e-an-ites] — a nomadic people who were enemies of the Israelites in Old Testament times. The Midianites were distantly related to the Israelites, since they sprang from MIDIAN, one of the sons of Abraham. But they usually were foes rather than friends of the Hebrew people.

MIDRASH [mid'-rash] *(inquiry)* — any of a group of Jewish commentaries on the Hebrew Scriptures written between A.D. 400 and A.D. 1200. The word Midrash is based on a Hebrew word that means "to search out." The implication is that of discovering a thought or truth not seen on the surface—therefore a study, commentary, or homiletical exposition.

MIDWIFE — a person who helps deliver a baby (Gen. 35:17).

MILLENNIUM, THE — the thousand-year period mentioned in connection with the de-scription of Christ's coming to reign with His saints over the earth (Rev. 20:1–9). Many Old Testament passages are reputed to refer to the Millennium (Is. 11:4; Jer. 3:17; Zech. 14:9).

MILLSTONE — heavy stones used to grind grain (Matt. 18:6).

MINISTER, MINISTRY — a distinctive biblical idea that means "to serve" or "service." In the Old Testament the word "servant" was used primarily for court servants (1 Kin. 10:5; Esth. 1:10). During the period between the Old and New Testaments, it came to be used in connection with ministering to the poor. This use of the word is close to the work of the seven in waiting on tables in the New Testament (Acts 6:1–7).

MIRACLES — historical events or natural phenomena that appear to violate natural laws but that reveal God to the eye of faith at the same time. A valuable way of understanding the meaning of miracles is to examine the various terms for miracles used in the Bible.

MIRIAM [mir'-e-am] — the name of two women in the Old Testament:

The Miracles of Jesus Christ

Miracle	Matthew	Mark	Luke	John
1. Cleansing a Leper	8:2	1:40	5:12	
2. Healing a Centurion's Servant (of paralysis)	8:5		7:1	
3. Healing Peter's Mother-in-Law	8:14	1:30	4:38	
4. Healing the Sick at Evening	8:16	1:32	4:40	
5. Stilling the Storm	8:23	4:35	8:22	
6. Demons Entering a Herd of Swine	8:28	5:1	8:26	
7. Healing a Paralytic	9:2	2:3	5:18	
8. Raising the Ruler's Daughter	9:18, 23	5:22, 35	8:40, 49	
9. Healing the Hemorrhaging Woman	9:20	5:25	8:43	
10. Healing Two Blind Men	9:27			
11. Curing a Demon-Possessed, Mute Man	9:32			
12. Healing a Man's Withered Hand	12:9	3:1	6:6	
13. Curing a Demon-Possessed, Blind and Mute Man	12:22		11:14	
14. Feeding the Five Thousand	14:13	6:30	9:10	6:1
15. Walking on the Sea	14:25	6:48		6:19
16. Healing the Gentile Woman's Daughter	15:21	7:24		
17. Feeding the Four Thousand	15:32	8:1		
18. Healing the Epileptic Boy	17:14	9:17	9:38	
19. Temple Tax in the Fish's Mouth	17:24			
20. Healing Two Blind Men	20:30	10:46	18:35	
21. Withering the Fig Tree	21:18	11:12		
22. Casting Out an Unclean Spirit		1:23	4:33	
23. Healing a Deaf-Mute		7:31		
24. Healing a Blind Man at Bethsaida		8:22		
25. Escape from the Hostile Multitude			4:30	
26. Catch of Fish			5:1	
27. Raising of a Widow's Son at Nain			7:11	
28. Healing the Infirm, Bent Woman			13:11	
29. Healing the Man with Dropsy			14:1	
30. Cleansing the Ten Lepers			17:11	
31. Restoring a Servant's Ear			22:51	
32. Turning Water into Wine				2:1
33. Healing the Nobleman's Son (of fever)				4:46
34. Healing an Infirm Man at Bethesda				5:1
35. Healing the Man Born Blind				9:1
36. Raising of Lazarus				11:43
37. Second Catch of Fish				21:1

1. A sister of Aaron and Moses (Num. 26:59; 1 Chr. 6:3). Called "Miriam the prophetess" (Ex. 15:20), she is described as one of the leaders sent by the Lord to guide Israel (Mic. 6:4). Although the Bible does not specifically say so, Miriam was probably the sister who watched over the infant Moses in the ark of bulrushes (Ex. 2:4–8). Miriam's song of victory after the Israelites' successful crossing of the Red Sea (Ex. 15:20–21) is one of the earliest poems.

2. A daughter of Ezrah of the tribe of Judah (1 Chr. 4:17).

MIRTH — joy, gladness (Is. 24:8).

MISHAEL [mish′-a-el] *(who is what God is?)* — the name of three men in the Old Testament:

1. A son of Uzziel and grandson of Kohath, of the tribe of Levi (Lev. 10:4).

2. An Israelite who helped Ezra read the Book of the Law to the people (Neh. 8:4).

3. One of the three friends of Daniel who were cast into the fiery furnace. "Now from among those of the sons of Judah were Daniel, Hananiah, Mishael, and Azariah." The Babylonians changed his name to MESHACH (Dan. 1:6–7).

MIZPAH [miz′-pah] *(watchtower)* — the name of six sites in the Old Testament (Gen. 31:49; Josh. 11:3, 8; Josh. 15:38; 1 Kin. 15:22; Judg. 11:29, 34; 1 Sam. 22:3).

MOAB [mo′-ab] *(of my father)* — the name of a man and a nation in the Old Testament:

1. A son of Lot by an incestuous union with his older daughter (Gen. 19:37). Moab became an ancestor of the MOABITES.

2. A neighboring nation whose history was closely linked to the fortunes of the Hebrew people.

MOABITES [mo′-ab-ites] — natives or inhabitants of the land of MOAB (Num. 22:4).

MOCK — insult (Gal. 6:7).

MODERATION — self-control, not given to sudden impulses or excesses (1 Tim. 2:9). Although the term rarely occurs in the Bible, the concept of moderation is common. The Pharisees were not moderate. Jesus described them as those "who strain out a gnat to swallow a camel" (Matt. 23:24). They emphasized the minor aspects of the Law, neglecting the weightier matters. By contrast, Christian believers ought to be moderate in all things (1 Cor. 9:25; temperate, NKJV).

MOLECH [mo′-lek] — an Ammonite god (Lev. 18:21).

MOLTEN — melted (Ezek. 24:11).

MONEY OF THE BIBLE. As soon as ancient people stopped living the lives of wandering

The denarius coin was considered a day's wages for a laborer in the time of Jesus (Matt. 20:1–16). This particular denarius featured the image of the Roman Emperor Tiberius.

Photo by Gleason Archer

A fifth century B.C. coin from Athens, Greece, showing the sacred owl on the reverse side.

Photo by Howard Vos

This silver shekel was issued by the Jewish people during their first revolt against Roman rule (A.D. 66–70). It portrayed the blossom of an almond tree on one side and a silver chalice on the other. *Photo by Gleason Archer*

hunters and began an agricultural system, a medium of exchange became necessary. A system of barter, or trading of property, preceded the creation of any formal currency that can be called money.

MONEYCHANGERS — bankers who exchanged one nation's currency, or one size of coin, for another. These people provided a convenience, charging a fee (often exorbitant) for their services.

MONOGAMY — faithful marriage to one mate.

MONTH — one of the 12 divisions of a year, measured by the completed cycle in the changing of the Moon. Solomon had 12 governors over all Israel, who provided food for the king and his household; each made provision for one month of the year (1 Kin. 4:7). The military divisions of Israel were also 12 in number, one for each month of the year, each division consisting of 14,000 men (1 Chr. 27:1–15).

MORDECAI [mor'-de-cay] *(related to Marduk)* — the name of two men in the Old Testament:

Monies			
Unit	Monetary Value	Equivalents	Translations
Jewish Weights			
Talent	gold—$5,760,000 [1] silver—$384,000	3,000 shekels; 6,000 bekas	talent, one hundred pounds
Shekel	gold—$1,920 silver—$128	4 days' wages; 2 bekas: 20 gerahs	shekel
Beka	gold—$960 silver—$64	½ shekel; 10 gerahs	beka
Gerah	gold—$96 silver—$6.40	1/20 shekel	gerahs
Persian Coins			
Daric	gold—$1,280 [2] silver—$64	2 days' wages; ½ Jewish silver shekel	daric, drachma
Greek Coins			
Tetradrachma	$128	4 drachmas	stater
Didrachma	$64	2 drachmas	two-drachma tax
Drachma	$32	1 day's wage	coin, silver coins
Lepton	$.25	½ of a Roman kodrantes	cents, small copper coin
Roman Coins			
Aureus	$800	25 denarii	gold
Denarius	$32	1 day's wage	denarii
Assarius	$2	1/16 of a denarius	cent
Kodrantes	$.50	¼ of an assarius	cent

[1] Value of gold is fifteen times the value of silver
[2] Value of gold is twenty times the value of silver

1. One of the Jewish captives who returned with Zerubbabel from Babylon (Ezra 2:2; Neh. 7:7).

2. The hero of the Book of Esther. Mordecai was probably born in Babylonia during the years of the CAPTIVITY of the Jewish people by this pagan nation. He was a resident of Susa (Shushan), the Persian capital during the reign of Ahasuerus (Xerxes I), the king of Persia (ruled 486—465 B.C.).

MORNING STAR — (see LUCIFER).

MORTAL — a biblical term that describes the weak, fleeting nature of human life, emphasizing human weakness and limitation (Job 4:17; 10:5; Is. 13:12). The word carries the meaning of "one certain to die." In contrast, according to the apostle Paul, "Our Savior Jesus Christ has abolished death and brought life and immortality to light through the gospel" (2 Tim. 1:10).

MOSES [mo′-zez] — the Hebrew prophet who delivered the Israelites from Egyptian slavery and who was their leader and lawgiver during their years of wandering in the wilderness. He was from the family line of Amram and Jochebed (Ex. 6:18, 20; Num. 26:58–59), Kohath and Levi. He was also the brother of Aaron and Miriam.

Moses was a leader so inspired by God that he was able to build a united nation from a race of oppressed and weary slaves. In the covenant ceremony at Mount Sinai, where the TEN COMMANDMENTS were given, he founded the religious community known as Israel. As the interpreter of these covenant laws, he was the organizer of the community's religious and civil traditions. His story is told in the Old Testament—in the books of Exodus, Leviticus, Numbers, and Deuteronomy.

MOST HIGH — a name for God that appears frequently in the Old Testament, particularly in the Psalms and the Books of Isaiah and Daniel (Ps. 92:1; Is. 14:14; Dan. 4:17). The name emphasizes the might and power of God.

MOST HOLY PLACE — the innermost part of the temple (Ex. 26:34).

MOUNT, MOUNTAIN — elevations higher than hills, although the Hebrew words for hill and mountain are often used interchangeably. The mountains of Palestine consist of two main ridges.

The ridge west of the Jordan Rift (the Arabah) is the rugged hill country of Galilee, Samaria, and Judah.

The second ridge, east of the Jordan, includes the loftiest of the area's mountains—Mount Hermon (about 2,800 meters, 9,166 feet)—and runs through Gilead, Ammon, Moab, and Edom.

MOUNT OF OLIVES — a north-to-south ridge of hills east of Jerusalem where Jesus was betrayed on the night before His Crucifixion. This prominent feature of Jerusalem's landscape is a gently rounded hill, rising to a height of

Michelangelo's statue of Moses, great lawgiver and leader of the Hebrew people.

Photo by Ben Chapman

about 830 meters (2,676 feet) and overlooking the TEMPLE.

MULTITUDE — large crowd (Matt. 4:25).

MURMUR — to grumble (Ex. 15:24).

MUSTARD SEED — the very tiny seed of a mustard plant (Matt. 13:31–32).

MUSTER — to gather (2 Kin. 25:19).

MUTE, MUTENESS — silent, unable to speak (Mark 7:37, NIV).

MUZZLE — a leather or wire covering for the mouth of an animal that prevented it from eating or biting. The command in the Book of Deuter-onomy, "You shall not muzzle an ox while it treads out the grain" (Deut. 25:4), implies that an animal helping with threshing must be allowed to eat some of the grain. The apostle Paul applied this verse symbolically to Christian workers (1 Cor. 9:9–10).

MYRRH — fragrant gum extracted from a shrub. It had many uses (Gen. 37:25; Matt. 2:11).

MYRTLE — a shrub often used during the Feast of the TABERNACLES (Lev. 23:40; Neh. 8:15).

MYSTERY — the hidden, eternal plan of God that is being revealed to God's people in accordance with His plan.

NAAMAN [na'-a-man] *(pleasant)* — the name of three or four men in the Old Testament:

1. A son of Benjamin (Gen. 46:21).

2. A son of Bela and the founder of a family, the Naamites (Num. 26:40). He may be the same person as No. 1.

3. A commander of the Syrian army who was cured of leprosy by the Lord through the prophet Elisha.

4. A son of Ehud, of the tribe of Benjamin (1 Chr. 8:7).

NABAL [na'-bal] — a wealthy sheepmaster of Maon and a member of the house of Caleb (1 Sam. 25:2–39). Nabal pastured his sheep near the Judahite town of CARMEL on the edge of the wilderness. Nabal was "harsh and evil in his doings" and was "such a scoundrel" that no one could reason with him (1 Sam. 25:3, 17).

While David was hiding from Saul, he sent ten men to Nabal to ask for food for himself and his followers. Nabal refused. David, who had protected people in the area from bands of marauding Bedouin, was so angered by Nabal's refusal that he determined to kill Nabal and every male in his household (1 Sam. 25:4–22).

Nabal's wife Abigail was "a woman of good understanding and beautiful appearance" (v. 3). She realized the danger threatening her family because of her husband's stupidity. "Then Abigail made haste and took two hundred loaves of bread, two skins of wine, five sheep already dressed, five seahs of roasted grain, one hundred clusters of raisins, and two hundred cakes of figs, and loaded them on donkeys" (1 Sam. 25:18). She took these gifts of food to David, fell to the ground, and apologized for her husband's behavior. Her quick action soothed David's anger.

When Abigail returned home, she found a great feast in progress. Oblivious to his narrow brush with death, "Nabal's heart was merry within him, for he was very drunk" (1 Sam. 25:36). Abigail waited until the next morning to tell him of the destruction and death that he almost brought upon his household. Immediately, Nabal's "heart died within him, and he became like a stone" (1 Sam. 25:37). He died about ten days later.

NABOTH [na'-both] — an Israelite of Jezreel who owned a vineyard next to the summer palace of Ahab, king of Samaria (1 Kin. 21:1). Ahab coveted this property. He wanted to turn it into a vegetable garden to furnish delicacies for his table. He offered Naboth its worth in money or a better vineyard. But Naboth refused to part with his property, explaining that it was a family inheritance to be passed on to his descendants.

Jezebel obtained the property for Ahab by bribing two men to bear false witness against Naboth and testify that he blasphemed God and the king. Because of their lies, Naboth was found guilty; and both he and his sons (2 Kin. 9:26) were stoned to death. Elijah the prophet pronounced doom upon Ahab and his house for this disgusting act of false witness (1 Kin. 21:1–29; 2 Kin. 9:21–26).

NADAB [na'-dab] *(liberal or willing)* — the name of four men in the Old Testament:

1. A son of Aaron and Elisheba (Ex. 6:23). Along with his father and brothers—Abihu, Eleazar, and Ithamar—he was consecrated a priest to minister at the tabernacle (Ex. 28:1).

Later, Nadab and Abihu were guilty of offering "profane fire before the Lord" in the Wilderness of Sinai; and both died when "fire went out from the Lord and devoured them" (Lev. 10:1–2).

2. A king of Israel (about 910—909 B.C.). Nadab was the son and successor of Jeroboam I (1 Kin. 14:20; 15:25). About the only noteworthy event that happened during Nadab's reign was the siege of Gibbethon by the Israelites. During the siege, Nadab was assassinated by his successor, Baasha (1 Kin. 15:27–28).

3. A son of Shammai, of the family of Jerahmeel.

4. A Benjamite, son of Jeiel and Maacah (1 Chr. 8:30).

NAHUM [na′-hum] *(compassionate)* — the name of two men in the Bible:

1. An Old Testament prophet and author of the Book of Nahum whose prophecy pronounced God's judgment against the mighty nation of Assyria.

2. An ancestor of Jesus (Luke 3:25).

NAHUM, BOOK OF — a short prophetic book of the Old Testament that foretells the destruction of the nation of Assyria and its capital city, Nineveh.

This book teaches the sure judgment of God against those who oppose His will and abuse His people. Acts of inhumanity are acts against God, and He will serve as the ultimate and final Judge. God sometimes uses a pagan nation as an instrument of His judgment, just as He used the Assyrians against the nation of Israel. But this does not excuse the pagan nation from God's Laws and requirements. It will be judged by the same standards of righteousness and holiness that God applies to all the other people of the world.

NAOMI [na′-o-mee] *(my joy)* — the mother-in-law of Ruth. After her husband and two sons died, Naomi returned to her home in Bethlehem, accompanied by Ruth. Naomi advised Ruth to work for a near KINSMAN, BOAZ (Ruth 2:1), and to seek his favor. When Boaz and Ruth eventually married, they had a son, whom they named Obed. This child became the father of Jesse, the grandfather of David, and an ancestor of Jesus (Ruth 4:21–22; Matt. 1:5).

NAPHTALI [naf′-ta-li] *(my wrestling)* — the sixth son of Jacob (Gen. 35:25). Because Jacob's wife Rachel was barren and her sister Leah had borne four sons to Jacob, Rachel was distraught. She gave her maidservant Bilhah to Jacob. Any offspring of this union were regarded as Rachel's. When Bilhah gave birth to Dan and Naphtali, Rachel was joyous. "With great wrestlings I have wrestled with my sister," she said, "and indeed I

NAHUM:
A Study and Teaching Outline

I. **The Destruction of Nineveh Is Decreed** 1:1–15
  A. The General Principles of Divine Judgment . . 1:1–8
    1. God's Vengeance in Judgment 1:1–2
    2. God's Power in Judgment 1:3–8
  B. The Destruction of Nineveh and
    Deliverance of Judah 1:9–15
II. **The Destruction of Nineveh Is Described** 2:1–13
  A. The Call to Battle 2:1–2
  B. The Destruction of Nineveh 2:3–13
III. **The Destruction of Nineveh Is Deserved.** 3:1–19
  A. The Reasons for the Destruction of
    Nineveh 3:1–11
    1. Nineveh's Great Ungodliness 3:1–7
    2. Comparison of Nineveh to No Amon 3:8–11
  B. The Destruction of Nineveh Is Inevitable . . 3:12–19
    1. Nineveh's Strongholds Are Weak 3:12–15
    2. Nineveh's Leaders Are Weak. 3:16–19

have prevailed" (Gen. 30:8). So she called his name Naphtali, which means "my wrestling."

NATHAN [na'-than] *(he gave)* — the name of several men in the Old Testament but most notably, a prophet during the reign of David and Solomon who told David that he would not be the one to build the temple (1 Chr. 17:1–15). Also a son of David and Bathsheba and an older brother of Solomon.

NATHANAEL [na-than'-a-el] *(God has given)* — a native of Cana in Galilee (John 21:2) who became a disciple of Jesus (John 1:45–49). Nathanael was introduced to Jesus by his friend Philip, who claimed Jesus was the MESSIAH. This claim troubled Nathanael. He knew that Nazareth, the town where Jesus grew up, was not mentioned in the Old Testament prophecies. He considered Nazareth an insignificant town, hardly the place where one would look to find the Redeemer of Israel. "Can anything good come out of Nazareth?" he asked. Philip did not argue with him, but simply said, "Come and see." After Nathanael met Jesus, he acknowledged Him to be the Messiah, calling Him "the Son of God" and "the King of Israel" (John 1:46, 49).

Nathanael was one of those privileged to speak face to face with Jesus after His Resurrection (John 21:1–14). Some scholars see Nathanael as a type, or symbol, of a true Israelite—"an Israelite indeed" (John 1:47)—who accepts Jesus as Lord and Savior by faith.

Many scholars believe Nathanael is the same person as BARTHOLOMEW (Matt. 10:3), one of the twelve apostles of Christ.

NAVE — wheel hub (1 Kin. 7:33).

NAZARENE [naz-a-reen'] — an inhabitant or native of NAZARETH. The word "Nazarene" is used many times to identify Christ.

NAZARETH [naz'-a-reth] *(watchtower)* — a town of lower Galilee where Jesus spent His boyhood years (Matt. 2:23).

NAZIRITE [naz'-a-rite] *(separated, consecrated)* — a person who took a vow to separate from certain worldly things and to consecrate himself to God (Num. 6:1–8). Among the Hebrew people anyone could take this vow; there were no

Modern Nazareth, successor to the village in lower Galilee where Jesus grew up (Luke 2:39; 4:16, 31–34). *Photo by Howard Vos*

tribal restrictions as in the case of the priest. Rich or poor, man or woman, master or slave— all were free to become Nazirites.

Samson, Samuel, and John the Baptist were the only "Nazirites for life" recorded in the Bible. Before they were born, their vows were taken for them by their parents.

NEBO [ne′-bo] — the name of a mountain of the Abarim range in Moab opposite Jericho (Num. 33:47). From Nebo Moses was permitted to view the Promised Land. He was buried in a nearby valley (Deut. 32:49, 50; 34:6).

Also the name of two towns (Num. 32:3, 38; Ezra 2:29), a man (Ezra 10:43), and a Babylonian god.

NEBUCHADNEZZAR [neb-u-kad-nez′-ar] *(O god Nabu, protect my son)* — the king of the Neo-Babylonian Empire (ruled 605—562 B.C.) who captured Jerusalem, destroyed the temple, and carried the people of Judah into captivity in Babylonia. He plays a prominent role in the

Books of Jeremiah (21—52) and Daniel (1:1— 5:18) and also appears in 2 Kings (24:1—25:22), Ezra (1:7—6:5), and Ezekiel (26:7—30:10).

NECROMANCER — one who attempts to communicate with the dead (Deut. 18:10–12).

NEEDLE, EYE OF — expression Jesus used while teaching to explain the difficulty a rich person would have entering the kingdom of heaven (Matt. 19:24).

NEHEMIAH [ne-he-mi′-ah] *(the Lord is consolation)* — the name of three men:

1. A clan leader who returned with Zerubbabel from the Captivity (Ezra 2:2; Neh. 7:7).

2. The governor of Jerusalem who helped rebuild the wall of the city (Neh. 1:1; 8:9; 10:1; 12:26, 47). Nehemiah was a descendant of the Jewish population that had been taken captive to Babylon in 586 B.C. In 539 B.C. Cyrus the Persian gained control over all of Mesopotamia. He permitted the Jewish exiles to return to the city of Jerusalem. Nearly a century later, in Nehemiah's

Excavated section of the wall built by Nehemiah in Jerusalem after the Jewish people returned from the Captivity in Babylonia. *Photo: Levant Photo Service*

time, the Persian ruler was Artaxerxes I Longimanus (ruled 465—424 B.C.). Nehemiah was his personal cupbearer (Neh. 1:11).

3. A son of Azbuk and leader of half the district of Beth Zur (Neh. 3:16). After his return from the Captivity, Nehemiah helped with the repair work on the wall of Jerusalem.

NEHEMIAH, BOOK OF — a historical book of the Old Testament that describes the rebuilding of the city walls around Jerusalem. The book is named for its major personality, a Jewish servant of a Persian king and effective leader, who organized and guided the building project.

Nehemiah is an excellent case study in courageous, resourceful leadership. Against overwhelming odds, he encouraged the people to "rise up and build" (2:18). Their rapid completion of the wall has been an inspiration to countless Christians across the centuries who have faced the challenge of completing some major task to the glory of God.

Nehemiah also teaches that prayer is an important part of the faith of every follower of God. At several crucial points in his book, he prayed for God's direction (1:5–11; 2:1–20; 4:1–14; 6:9–14).

If this courageous leader needed to claim God's strength and guidance through prayer, how much more fervently should we pray for God's will to be done through us as we face the important decisions of life! Nehemiah is an excellent object lesson on the power of prayer for all believers.

NEPHILIM [nef'-il-im] *(fallen ones)* — the offspring of marriages between the "sons of God" and the "daughters of men" (Gen. 6:4). The word "Nephilim" is translated as "giants" by the KJV and NKJV (Gen. 6:4; Num. 13:33; Nephilim, NIV, REB, NASB, NRSV). Some scholars believe the Nephilim were descended from famous rulers, outstanding leaders, and mighty warriors who lived before the Flood. These men, so the theory goes, gathered great harems and were guilty of the sin of polygamy. The Nephilim were the product of these marriages.

NETHER — under (Lev. 19:17).

NETTLE — thorn (Job 30:7).

NETWORK — a word with two distinct meanings in the Old Testament:

NEHEMIAH: A Study and Teaching Outline

Part One: The Reconstruction of the Wall (1:1—7:73)

I. **Preparation to Reconstruct the Wall** . . . . . . 1:1—2:20
  A. Discovery of the Broken Wall 1:1–3
  B. Intercession of Nehemiah . . . . 1:4—2:8
  C. Arrival of Nehemiah in Jerusalem 2:9–11
  D. Preparation to Reconstruct the Wall 2:12–20
II. **Reconstruction of the Wall** . . . . 3:1—7:73
  A. Record of the Builders 3:1–32
  B. Opposition to the Reconstruction . . . . . . 4:1—6:14
  C. Completion of the Reconstruction 6:15–19
  D. Organization of Jerusalem 7:1–4
  E. Registration of Jerusalem 7:5–73

Part Two: The Restoration of the People (8:1—13:31)

I. **Renewal of the Covenant** . . . . 8:1—10:39
  A. Interpretation of the Law 8:1–18
  B. Reaffirmation of the Covenant . . . . 9:1—10:39
II. **Obedience to the Covenant** . . . . 11:1—13:31
  A. Resettlement of the People 11:1–36
  B. Register of the Priests and the
    Levites 12:1–26
  C. Dedication of the Jerusalem Wall 12:27–47
  D. Restoration of the People 13:1–31

1. The grate of bronze inside the altar of burnt offering before the tabernacle (Ex. 27:4; 38:4).

2. The ornamental network of bronze on the capitals of Jachin and BOAZ, the two great bronze pillars in Solomon's temple (1 Kin. 7:18; 2 Chr. 4:12; Jer. 52:22–23). The latticework was built for Solomon by Hiram, a craftsman from Tyre who specialized in producing skillful works of bronze.

NEW JERUSALEM — (see JERUSALEM, NEW).

NEW TESTAMENT — the second major division of the Bible. It tells of the life and ministry of Jesus and the growth of the early church. The word "testament" is best translated as "covenant." The New Testament embodies the New Covenant of which Jesus was MEDIATOR (Jer. 31:31–34; Heb. 9:15). This New Covenant was sealed with the atoning death of Jesus Christ.

The 27 books of the New Testament were formally adopted as the New Testament canon by the Synod of Carthage in A.D. 397, thus confirming three centuries of usage by spiritually sensitive members of various Christian communities.

NICODEMUS [nic-o-de'-mus] *(conqueror of the people)* — a PHARISEE and a member of the SANHEDRIN who probably became a disciple of Jesus (John 3:1, 4, 9; 7:50). He was described by Jesus as "the teacher of Israel," implying he was well trained in Old Testament law and tradition.

NIGER [ni'-jur] *(black)* — the Latin surname of Simeon, one of the Christian prophets and teachers in the church of Syrian Antioch when Barnabas and Paul were called to missionary service (Acts 13:1–3). Some scholars believe he is the same person as Simon of Cyrene, who carried the cross of Christ (Matt. 27:32); but there is no evidence for this theory.

NIGH — near (Ps. 145:18).

NILE [nile] — the great river of Egypt that flows more than 5,700 kilometers (3,500 miles) from central Africa north through the desert to a rich delta area on the Mediterranean Sea. The source of the Nile is derived from two rivers: the Blue Nile from Ethiopia and the White Nile from Lake Victoria in central Africa.

NIMROD [nim'-rod] — a son of Cush and grandson of Ham, the youngest son of Noah (Gen. 10:8–12; 1 Chr. 1:10). Nimrod was a "mighty one on the earth"—a skilled hunter–warrior who became a powerful king. He is the first mighty hero mentioned in the Bible.

NINEVEH [nin'-e-veh] — ancient capital city of the Assyrian Empire, a place associated with

The mound of Kuyunjik, one of the major mounds of the magnificent city of Nineveh in ancient Assyria. *Photo by Howard Vos*

NUMBERS:

A Study and
Teaching Outline

**Part One: The Preparation
of the Old Generation to
Inherit the Promised Land
(1:1—10:10)**

**Part Two: The Failure of
the Old Generation to
Inherit the Promised Land
(10:11—25:18)**

**Part Three: The Preparation
of the New Generation
(26:1—36:13)**

I. **The Organization of Israel** . . . . 1:1—4:49
   A. Organization of the People . . . . 1:1—2:34
   B. Organization of the Priests . . . . 3:1—4:49
II. **The Sanctification of Israel** . . . . 5:1—10:10
   A. Sanctification through Separation 5:1–31
   B. Sanctification through the Nazirite Vow 6:1–27
   C. Sanctification through Worship . . . . 7:1—9:14
   D. Sanctification through Divine
      Guidance . . . . 9:15—10:10

I. **The Failure of Israel En Route to
   Kadesh** . . . . 10:11—12:16
   A. Israel Departs from Mount Sinai 10:11–36
   B. Failure of the People 11:1–9
   C. Failure of Moses 11:10–15
   D. God Provides for Moses 11:16–30
   E. God Provides for the People 11:31–35
   F. Failure of Miriam and Aaron 12:1–16
II. **The Climactic Failure of Israel
    at Kadesh** . . . . 13:1—14:45
   A. Investigation of the Promised Land 13:1–33
   B. Israel Rebels against God 14:1–10
   C. Moses Intercedes 14:11–19
   D. God Judges Israel 14:20–38
   E. Israel Rebels against the Judgment of
      God 14:39–45
III. **The Failure of Israel in the Wilderness** . . 15:1—19:22
   A. Review of the Offerings 15:1–41
   B. Rebellion of Korah 16:1–40
   C. Rebellion of Israel against Moses and
      Aaron 16:41–50
   D. Role of the Priesthood . . . . 17:1—19:22
IV. **The Failure of Israel En Route to Moab** . . 20:1—25:18
   A. Miriam Dies 20:1
   B. Moses and Aaron Fail 20:2–13
   C. Edom Refuses Passage 20:14–21
   D. Aaron Dies 20:22–29
   E. Israel's Victory over the Canaanites 21:1–3
   F. The Failure of Israel 21:4–9
   G. Journey to Moab 21:10–20
   H. Israel's Victory over Sihon 21:21–32
   I. Israel's Victory over Bashan 21:33–35
   J. Failure with the Moabites . . . . 22:1—25:18

I. **The Reorganization of Israel** . . . . 26:1—27:23
   A. The Second Census 26:1–51
   B. Method for Dividing the Land 26:52–56
   C. Exceptions for Dividing the Land . . . . 26:57—27:11
   D. Appointment for Israel's New Leader 27:12–23
II. **The Regulations of Sacrifices and
    Vows** . . . . 28:1—30:16
   A. The Regulations of Sacrifices . . . . 28:1—29:40
   B. The Regulations of Vows 30:1–16
III. **The Conquest and Division of Israel** . . . . . 31:1—36:13
   A. Victory over Midian 31:1–54
   B. Division of the Land East of Jordan 32:1–42
   C. The Summary of Israel's Journeys 33:1–49
   D. Division of the Land West of Jordan . 33:50—34:29
   E. Special Cities in Canaan 35:1–34
   F. Special Problems of Inheritance in Canaan . 36:1–13

the ministry of the prophet Jonah. The residents of this pagan city repented and turned to God after Jonah's preaching of a clear message of God's judgment (Jon. 3:5–10).

NISAN [ni'-san] — the name given after the Captivity to Abib, the first month of the Jewish sacred year (Esth. 3:7). (see CALENDAR).

NOAH [no'-ah] *(rest, relief)* — the name of a man and a woman in the Bible:

1. A son of Lamech and the father of Shem, Ham, and Japheth. He was a hero of faith who obeyed God by building an ark (a giant boat), thus becoming God's instrument in saving mankind from total destruction by the Flood (Gen. 5:28—9:29).

NORTHERN KINGDOM — the northern ten tribes of Israel (1 Kin. 14:19–30).

NUMBER, NUMBERS — figures, characters, or symbols used for counting and enumerating in the special discipline known as mathematics. The people of the Bible used numbers in a practical way rather than as a mathematical theory. They applied numbers to common problems of everyday life.

NUMBERS, BOOK OF — an Old Testament book that traces the Israelites through their long period of wandering in the wilderness as they prepared to enter the Promised Land. Numbers takes its name from the two censuses or "numberings" of the people recorded in the book (chs. 1 and 26). But Numbers contains a great deal more than a listing of names and figures.

The Book of Numbers presents the concept of God's correcting wrath upon His own disobedient people. Through their rebellion, the Hebrews had broken the covenant. Even Moses was not exempt from God's wrath when he disobeyed God.

But even in His wrath, God did not give up on His people. While He might punish them in the present, He was still determined to bless them and bring them ultimately into a land of their own. Even the false prophet Balaam recognized this truth about God's sovereign purpose. Balaam declared: "God is not a man, that He should lie, nor a son of man, that He should repent. Has He said, and will He not do it? Or has He spoken, and will He not make it good?" (23:19).

NUN *(fish)* — the father of Joshua (pronounced *none*) and an Ephraimite (Ex. 33:11; Num. 27:18) as well as the 14th letter of the Hebrew alphabet (pronounced *noon*), used as a heading over Psalm 119:105–112. In the original Hebrew language, each of these eight verses began with the letter nun.

OATH — a solemn statement or claim used to validate a promise. In Bible times, oaths were sometimes accompanied by protective curses to make sure the oaths were kept (1 Sam. 14:24; Gen. 24:41). Such curses were also used to protect property rights from thieves (Judg. 17:2) or from those who found a stolen object or knew of a theft (Lev. 5:1).

OBADIAH [o-ba-di-ah] *(servant of the Lord)* — the name of thirteen men in the Old Testament but most notably the governor of Ahab's palace (1 Kin. 18:3–7, 16), and a prophet of Judah (Obadiah 1). The fourth of the "minor" prophets, Obadiah's message was directed against Edom.

OBADIAH, BOOK OF — a brief prophetic book of the Old Testament that pronounces God's judgment against the EDOMITES, ancient enemies of Israel. The book is the shortest in the Old Testament, containing one chapter of only 21 verses.

The Book of Obadiah makes it clear that God takes His promises to His covenant people seriously. He declared in the Book of Genesis that He would bless the rest of the world through Abraham and his descendants. He also promised to protect His special people against any who would try to do them harm (Gen. 12:1–3). This promise is affirmed in the Book of Obadiah. God is determined to keep faith with His people, in spite of their unworthiness and disobedience.

OBED [o′-bed] *(worshiper)* —a son of Boaz and Ruth (Ruth 4:17–22; 1 Chr. 2:12) and an ancestor of Jesus (Matt. 1:5). Also the name of four other men in the Old Testament (1 Chr. 2:37–38; 1 Chr. 11:47; 1 Chr. 26:7; 2 Chr. 23:1).

OBEDIENCE — carrying out the word and will of another person, especially the will of God. In both the Old and New Testaments the word "obey" is related to the idea of hearing. Obedience is a positive, active response to what a person hears. God summons people to active obedience to His revelation. People's failure to obey God results in judgment.

OBEISANCE — the KJV translation of a Hebrew verb that means "to bow down." The NKJV translates as "bowed down to" (Gen. 37:7, Ex. 18:7), "prostrated" (2 Sam. 1:2), and "did homage" (1 Kin. 1:16).

OBLATION — an offering (Jer. 14:12).

OBSERVE — to watch, to keep or practice as in *observe the Sabbath* (Deut. 5:32).

ODIOUS — repulsive (1 Chr. 19:6).

ODOR, ODOUR — fragrance, aroma (Gen. 8:21).

OBADIAH:
A Study and
Teaching Outline

I. The Predictions of Judgment on Edom 1–9
II. The Reasons for Judgment of Edom 10–14
III. The Results of Judgment on Edom 15–16
IV. The Possession of Edom by Israel 17–21

179

OFFENCE, OFFEND — a stumbling block; to cause one to stumble (Matt. 16:23).

OG [ahg] — a king of the Amorites of the land of Bashan, a territory east of the Jordan River and north of the River Jabbok (Num. 21:33; 32:33). Og was king over 60 fortified cities, including Ashtaroth and Edrei. He was defeated by Moses and the Israelites (Deut. 3:6). Then his kingdom was given to the tribes of Reuben, Gad, and the half-tribe of Manasseh.

Og was the last survivor of the race of giants (Deut. 3:11). His huge iron bedstead was kept on display in Rabbah long after his death (Deut. 3:11).

OIL — typically from olive trees; had multiple uses such as food, health and beauty, and energy (Matt. 25:3). (see OINTMENT).

OINTMENT — a perfumed oil, sometimes used in Bible times to anoint people as well as bodies for burial.

The term "ointment" frequently means oil, particularly olive oil mixed with aromatic ingredients such as spices, myrrh, and extracts of the nard plant. Many of these ingredients were expensive, leading the prophet Amos to associate those who used "the best ointment" with a life of self-indulgence (Amos 6:6). The use of ointment originated with the Egyptians, and it eventually spread to neighboring nations, including Israel. Ointment was often imported from Phoenicia in small alabaster boxes that best preserved its aroma. Some of the better ointments were known to keep their distinctive scents for centuries.

OLD TESTAMENT — the first of the two major sections into which the Bible is divided, the other being the New Testament. The title "Old Testament" apparently came from the writings of the apostle Paul, who declared, "For until this day the same veil remains unlifted in the reading of the Old Testament, because the veil is taken away in Christ" (2 Cor. 3:14).

The word testament is best-translated "covenant." God called a people, the nation of Israel, to live in covenant with Him. The Old Testament begins with God's creation of the universe and continues by describing the mighty acts of God in and through His people. It closes about 400 years before the coming of Jesus Christ, who established a New Covenant as prophesied by the prophet Jeremiah (Jer. 31:31–34).

OLIVE — fruit of the olive tree (Deut. 6:11; Rom. 11:17), the branch of the olive tree is also symbolic of peace.

OLIVET DISCOURSE — Jesus' discussion on the Mount of Olives about the destruction of Jerusalem and the end of the world (Matt. 24:1—25:46; Mark 13:1–37; Luke 21:5–36).

OMEGA [o-may'-gah] — the last letter of the Greek alphabet, used figuratively in the phrase "the Alpha and the Omega" to describe the Lord Jesus Christ as the beginning and ending (Rev. 1:8, 11).

OMEN — a sign used by magicians and fortune tellers to predict future events. God commanded the Israelites not to allow one who interprets omens (Deut. 18:10; an augur, NRSV) to live among them.

OMER — a unit of dry measure (Eph. 16:16). (see WEIGHTS AND MEASURES OF THE BIBLE).

OMNIPOTENCE [om-nip'-o-tence] — a theological term that refers to the all-encompassing power of God. The almighty God expects human beings to obey Him, and He holds them responsible for their thoughts and actions. Nevertheless, He is the all-powerful Lord who has created all things and sustains them by the Word of His power (Gen. 1:1–3; Heb. 1:3).

God reveals in the Bible that He is all-powerful and in the final sense is the ruler of nature and history. Before Him "the nations are as a drop in a bucket, and are counted as the small dust on the balance" (Is. 40:15). Yet He has so fashioned humankind that He graciously appeals to every person to return to Him.

OMNIPRESENCE [om-ne-pres'-ence] — a theological term that refers to the unlimited nature of God or His ability to be everywhere at all times. God is not like the manufactured idols of ancient cultures that were limited to one altar or temple area. God reveals Himself in the Bible as the Lord who is everywhere. God was present as Lord in all creation (Ps. 139:7–12), and there is no escaping Him. He is present in our innermost thoughts. Even as we are formed in the womb, He knows all the days of our future.

OMNISCIENCE [om-nish'-ence] — a theological term that refers to God's power to know all things. God is the Lord who knows our thoughts from afar and is acquainted with all our ways, knowing our words even before they are on our tongues (Ps. 139:1–6, 13–16). He needs to consult no one for knowledge or understanding (Is. 40:13–14). He is the all-knowing Lord who prophesies the events of the future, including the death and Resurrection of His Son (Isaiah 53) and the return of Christ at the end of this age when death will be finally overcome (Rom. 8:18–39; 1 Cor. 15:51–57).

OMRI [om'-ri] — the name of four men in the Old Testament:

1. The sixth king of the northern kingdom of Israel (885—874 B.C.).

2. A member of the tribe of Benjamin and a son of Becher (1 Chr. 7:8).

3. A member of the tribe of Judah and a son of Imri (1 Chr. 9:4).

4. The son of Michael and a prince of the tribe of Issachar during the time of David (1 Chr. 27:18).

ONESIMUS [o-nes'-i-mus] *(useful)* — a slave of Philemon and an inhabitant of Colossae (Col. 4:9; Philem. 10). When Onesimus fled from his master to Rome, he met the apostle Paul. Paul witnessed to him, and Onesimus became a Christian. In his letter to Philemon, Paul spoke of Onesimus as "my own heart" (Philem. 12), indicating that Onesimus had become like a son to him.

ONYX — a gemstone (Ex. 25:7).

ORACLE [or'-i-cal] — a prophetic speech, utterance, or declaration. In Greek religion, an oracle was a response given by a pagan god to a human question. Oracles were uttered by persons entranced, by those who interpreted dreams, and by those who saw or heard patterns in nature. The most famous oracle, in this sense, was the Oracle at Delphi. Delphi was the shrine of Apollo—the Greek god of the sun, prophecy, music, medicine, and poetry.

The temple of Apollo at Delphi. The oracle of Delphi was revered throughout the ancient world because people believed it had the power to foretell the future. *Photo by Gustav Jeeninga*

ORDAIN, ORDINATION — the process of commissioning or consecrating a priest for sanctuary service (Exodus 29) or a pastor or other officer of the church. This process is seldom mentioned in the New Testament. Some scholars doubt whether the solemn service we know today as ordination was practiced in the time of Christ. However, while the technical sense of the term does not occur in the New Testament, several references do indicate an official commissioning ceremony.

ORDER — proper arrangement (1 Cor. 14:40).

ORDINANCE — a law (Ex. 12:24).

OTHNIEL [oth'-ne-el] — the name of two men in the Old Testament:

1. The first judge of Israel (Judg. 1:13; 3:9, 11). Othniel was a son of Kenaz and probably was a nephew of Caleb. When the Israelites forgot the Lord and served the pagan gods of Canaan, the king of Mesopotamia oppressed them for eight years. When the Israelites repented of their evil and cried out to the Lord for deliverance, Othniel was raised up by the Lord to deliver His people. Othniel was one of four judges (the other three were Gideon, Jephthah, and Samson) of whom the Scripture says, "The Spirit of the LORD came upon him" (Judg. 3:10).

2. An ancestor of Heldai (1 Chr. 27:15).

OUTCASTS — a word used in the Old Testament to refer to refugees or exiles from the land of Israel (Ps. 147:2; Is. 11:12; 56:8). The modern idea of outcasts refers to those who are rejected by society. In the Bible, however, the word corresponds to our refugees—those forced from their homes by terror of war (Is. 16:3–4; Jer. 40:12; 49:5, 36). It is used also of those who were taken into captivity for breaking God's covenant (Is. 11:12; 56:8). Thus, "the outcasts" is a technical term for the DISPERSION.

OVERCOME — to prevail, defeat (Num. 13:30).

OVERLAID — covered (Ex. 26:32; Heb. 9:4).

OVERSEER — administrator (Acts 20:28).

OVERWHELM — greatly come upon (Ps. 55:5).

OX, OXEN — what we think of as cattle, the Bible calls oxen. A wild ox—a massive, untameable beast—is also mentioned (Job 39:9–10). The KJV calls it a unicorn.

Oxen were hollow-horned, divided-hoof, cud-chewing animals considered "clean" by the Jews. They needed considerable food and space because of their large size, so a person who kept many cattle was rich indeed. The pastures and grain country of Bashan, located east of the Jordan River and south of Damascus, were ideal places to raise oxen.

Scripture speaks of oxen as a measure of wealth (Job 42:12), beasts of burden (1 Chr. 12:40), draft animals (Deut. 22:10), meat (Gen. 18:7), and sacrificial offerings (2 Sam. 6:13).

PALACE — the residence of the king (2 Chr. 9:11).

PALESTINE [pal'-es-tine] — the land promised by God to Abraham and his descendants and eventually the region where the Hebrew people lived.

Palestine (or Palestina) is a tiny land bridge between the continents of Asia, Africa, and Europe. The word itself originally identified the region as "the land of the Philistines," but the older name, the term most frequently used in the Old Testament for Palestine, was CANAAN. After the Israelites took the land from the Canaanites, the entire country became known as the "land of Israel" (1 Sam. 13:19; Matt. 2:20) and the "land of promise" (Heb. 11:9).

PALM TREE — a tree that grows in the Jordan Valley (1 Kin. 6:29). Palm branches were considered a symbol of victory (John 17:13; Rev. 7:9).

PALSY — paralysis (Luke 5:18).

PAMPHYLIA [pam-fil'-e-ah] *(a region of every tribe)* — a Roman province on the southern coast of central Asia Minor (modern Turkey). The province consisted mainly of a plain about 130 kilometers (80 miles) long and up to about 32 kilometers (20 miles) wide. The capital city of Pamphylia, its largest city, was Perga (Acts 13:13–14).

PANGS — pain, especially that of childbirth (Is. 26:17).

The Hasbani Brook in northern Palestine— one of the tributaries of the Jordan River— with Mount Hermon in the background.

Photo by Gustav Jeeninga

Palm trees in southern Palestine. The leaves of palm trees were used as tokens of peace and victory (John 12:12–13; Rev. 7:9).

Photo by Ben Chapman

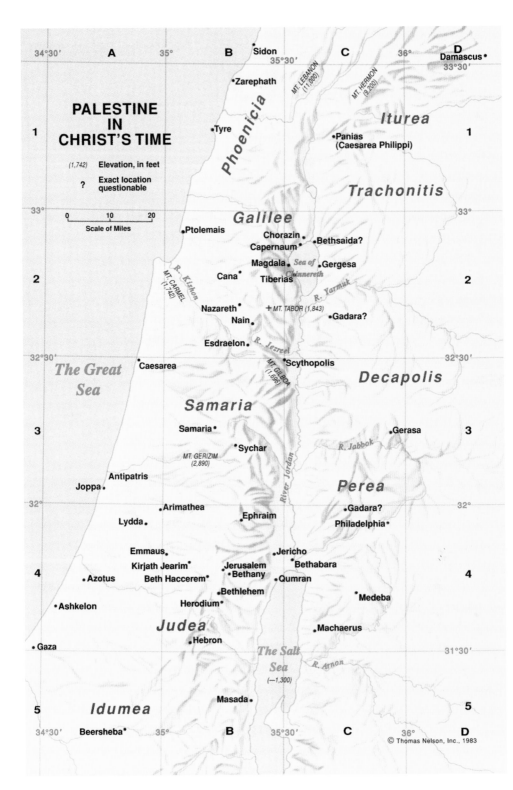

PALESTINE IN CHRIST'S TIME

(1,742)   Elevation, in feet

?   Exact location questionable

0   10   20
Scale of Miles

Sidon
34°30'   A   35°   B   35°30'   C   36°   D   Damascus
33°30'

Zarephath

Phoenicia

MT. LEBANON (11,000)   MT. HERMON (9,200)

Iturea

Tyre   1   Panias (Caesarea Philippi)   1

Trachonitis

33°   Galilee   33°

Ptolemais   Chorazin   Bethsaida?
Capernaum
Magdala   Sea of Chinnereth   Gergesa
Cana   Tiberias
R. Kishon   R. Yarmuk
MT. CARMEL (1,742)
2   2
Nazareth   +MT. TABOR (1,843)
Nain   Gadara?
R. Jezreel
Esdraelon
32°30'   MT. GILBOA (1,696)   32°30'
The Great   Caesarea   Scythopolis   Decapolis
Sea
Samaria

Samaria   Gerasa   3
3   Sychar   R. Jabbok
MT. GERIZIM (2,890)
Antipatris   Perea
Joppa   Gadara?
32°   Arimathea   Ephraim   Philadelphia   32°
Lydda
Emmaus   Jericho
Kirjath Jearim   Jerusalem   Bethabara
4   Azotus   Beth Haccerem   Bethany   Qumran   4
Bethlehem   Medeba
Ashkelon   Herodium
Judea   Machaerus
Gaza   Hebron
The Salt   31°30'
Sea   R. Arnon
(−1,300)
Masada
5   Idumea   5
34°30'   Beersheba   35°   B   35°30'   C   36°   D

© Thomas Nelson, Inc., 1983

PAPHOS [pa′-fos] — a city on the southwestern extremity of the island of Cyprus. Paul, Barnabas, and John Mark visited Paphos during Paul's first missionary journey, about A.D. 47 or 48 (Acts 13:6–13).

PAPYRUS [pa-py′-rus] —a tall aquatic plant of southern Europe and northern Africa, especially of the Nile River valley. This plant is now unknown in its wild state in Egypt, but it still grows plentifully in the Sudan. Extensive growths of papyrus may also be found in the marshes at the northern end of Lake Huleh in Palestine. Also a form of paper made from the stems of the papyrus plant.

PARABLE — a short, simple story designed to communicate a spiritual truth, religious principle, or moral lesson; a figure of speech in which truth is illustrated by a comparison or example drawn from everyday experiences (Luke 15).

Several stalks of papyrus, reed-like plants used for making a primitive type of paper in Bible times. *Photo by Willem A. VanGemeren*

PARACLETE [par′-a-clete] — a transliteration of the Greek word *parakletos,* which means "one who speaks in favor of," as an intercessor, advocate, or legal assistant. The word, translated as "Comforter" or "Counselor," appears only in the Gospel of John. Jesus applied the term to the HOLY SPIRIT, who would be an advocate on behalf of Jesus' followers after His Ascension; the Spirit would plead their cause before God (John 14:16, 26; 15:26; 16:7).

PARADISE *(park, garden)* — a place of exceptional blessedness, happiness, and delight; a descriptive name for heaven. Originally "paradise" was a Persian word meaning "a wooded park," "an enclosed or walled orchard," or "a garden with fruit trees." Traditional Hebrew theology held that the dead descended to SHEOL. After the emergence of belief in the resurrection, however, this view was drastically modified. In the period between the Old and New Testaments, the Jews believed that, after the resurrection, the righteous would go to Paradise, a place much like the Garden of Eden before the Fall.

PARAMOUR — an adulterous lover, either male or female; a mistress. In Ezekiel 23:20 the word "paramours" in the NKJV refers to male lovers (male prostitutes, REB). In all other occurrences in the NKJV, however, the Hebrew word for paramours is translated as CONCUBINES.

PARAN [pa′-ran] — a wilderness region in the central part of the Sinai Peninsula. Although the boundaries of this desert region are somewhat obscure, it probably bordered the Arabah and the Gulf of Aqaba on the east. The modern Wadi Feiran in central Sinai preserves the ancient name.

PARCHED — burnt, roasted (Jer. 17:6; Ruth 2:14).

PARCHMENT — writing material made from animal skins (2 Tim. 4:13).

PARDON — to forgive; to release a person from punishment. The Bible portrays God as "ready to pardon" (Mic. 7:18).

The Parables of Jesus Christ

Parable	Matthew	Mark	Luke
1. Lamp Under a Basket	5:14–16	4:21, 22	8:16, 17 11:33–36
2. A Wise Man Builds on Rock and a Foolish Man Builds on Sand	7:24–27		6:47–49
3. Unshrunk (New) Cloth on an Old Garment	9:16	2:21	5:36
4. New Wine in Old Wineskins	9:17	2:22	5:37, 38
5. The Sower	13:3–23	4:2–20	8:4–15
6. The Tares (Weeds)	13:24–30		
7. The Mustard Seed	13:31, 32	4:30–32	13:18, 19
8. The Leaven	13:33		13:20, 21
9. The Hidden Treasure	13:44		
10. The Pearl of Great Price	13:45, 46		
11. The Dragnet	13:47–50		
12. The Lost Sheep	18:12–14		15:3–7
13. The Unforgiving Servant	18:23–35		
14. The Laborers in the Vineyard	20:1–16		
15. The Two Sons	21:28–32		
16. The Wicked Vinedressers	21:33–45	12:1–12	20:9–19
17. The Wedding Feast	22:2–14		
18. The Fig Tree	24:32–44	13:28–32	21:29–33
19. The Wise and Foolish Virgins	25:1–13		
20. The Talents	25:14–30		
21. The Growing Seed		4:26–29	
22. The Absent Householder		13:33–37	
23. The Creditor and Two Debtors			7:41–43
24. The Good Samaritan			10:30–37
25. A Friend in Need			11:5–13
26. The Rich Fool			12:16–21
27. The Watchful Servants			12:35–40
28. The Faithful Servant and the Evil Servant			12:42–48
29. The Barren Fig Tree			13:6–9
30. The Great Supper			14:16–24
31. Building a Tower and a King Making War			14:25–35
32. The Lost Coin			15:8–10
33. The Lost Son			15:11–32
34. The Unjust Steward			16:1–13
35. The Rich Man and Lazarus			16:19–31
36. Unprofitable Servants			17:7–10
37. The Persistent Widow			18:1–8
38. The Pharisee and the Tax Collector			18:9–14
39. The Minas			19:11–27

PARTAKE — to join in (Heb. 3:1).

PARTIALITY — favoring one person or party more than another and thus acting in a prejudiced or biased manner. In the Old Testament, the Hebrew people were reminded that just as God shows no partiality, so should they show no favoritism to the rich or poor, great or small (Lev. 19:15; Deut. 16:19; 2 Chr. 19:7). The New Testament declares that salvation is freely given to all who believe in Jesus Christ, whether Jew or Gentile, male or female, bondslave or free (Gal. 3:28).

PASCHAL [pas'-kal] — relating to PASSOVER (1 Cor. 5:7, RSV).

PASSAGE — a word used by the NKJV in two ways:

1. A right of way; the right to travel through an area. The Edomites refused to give the Israelites passage through their territory (Num. 20:21).

2. A ford or river crossing (Jer. 51:32).

PASSION OF CHRIST — KJV words referring to the suffering and death of Jesus Christ by crucifixion (Acts 1:3). The NKJV refers to Jesus' ordeal on the Cross by using the word "suffering" in its translation of the verse.

PASSOVER, FEAST OF — the first of the three great FEASTS of the Israelite people. It referred to the sacrifice of a lamb in Egypt when the people of Israel were slaves. They smeared the blood of the lamb on their doorposts as a signal to God to "pass over" their houses when He destroyed all the firstborn of Egypt (Ex. 12:13).

Passover was observed on the fourteenth day of the first month, with the service beginning in the evening (Lev. 23:6). It was on the evening of this day that Israel left Egypt. Passover commemorated this departure from Egypt in haste. Unleavend bread was used in the celebration, because the people had no time to leaven their bread as they ate their final meal in Egypt.

PASTOR — the feeder, protector, and guide, or shepherd, of a flock of God's people in New Testament times. In speaking of spiritual gifts, the apostle Paul wrote that Christ "gave some to be apostles, some prophets, some evangelists, and some pastors and teachers" (Eph. 4:11). The term "pastor" by this time in church history had not yet become an official title. The term implied the nourishing of and caring for God's people.

PASTORAL EPISTLES — the name given to three letters of the apostle PAUL: 1 TIMOTHY, 2 TIMOTHY, and TITUS. They are called the Pastoral Epistles because they clearly show Paul's love and concern as pastor and administrator of several local churches.

PATIENCE — forebearance under suffering and endurance in the face of adversity (Rom. 5:3).

PATMOS [pat'-mos] — a small rocky island to which the apostle John was banished and where he wrote the Book of Revelation (Rev. 1:9).

PATRIARCH [pa'-tre-ark] *(head of a father's house)* — the founder or ruler of a tribe, family, or clan; the forefathers of the Israelite nation. The phrase "the patriarchs" usually refers to the tribal leaders of Israel who lived before the time of Moses. Specifically, it is used of Abraham, Isaac, Jacob, and the twelve sons of Jacob. Therefore, the patriarchs were the ancestors of the Israelites from Abraham to Joseph (Acts 7:8–9; Heb. 7:4).

PAUL, THE APOSTLE — the earliest and most influential interpreter of Christ's message and teaching; an early Christian missionary; correspondent with several early Christian churches.

PAVILION — any kind of temporary shelter, such as a tent, tabernacle, or booth (2 Kin. 16:18; Ps. 27:5; 31:20; Jer. 43:10). Psalm 31:20 refers to the pavilion of God in which the righteous are sheltered. But usually the Hebrew word *sukkah* refers to a tent or similar kind of shelter. Leviticus 23:42 mentions booths, or dwellings made of branches, in which the Jews lived during the Feast of TABERNACLES.

PEACE — a word with several different meanings in the Old and New Testaments.

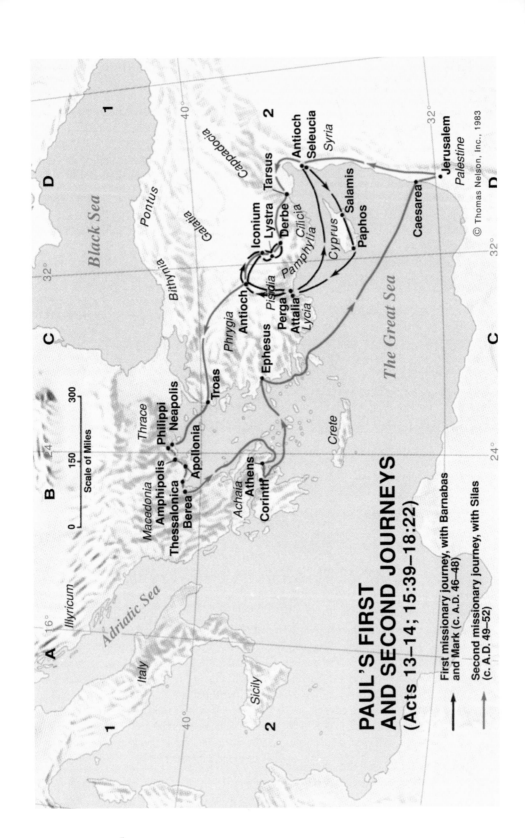

PAUL'S FIRST AND SECOND JOURNEYS
(Acts 13–14; 15:39–18:22)

First missionary journey, with Barnabas and Mark (c. A.D. 46–48)

Second missionary journey, with Silas (c. A.D. 49–52)

© Thomas Nelson, Inc., 1983

Scale of Miles
0   150   300

Black Sea

Pontus

Bithynia

Galatia

Cappadocia

Phrygia

Antioch

Pisidia

Iconium

Lystra

Derbe

Tarsus

Cilicia

Antioch

Seleucia

Syria

Salamis

Paphos

Cyprus

Pamphylia

Perga

Attalia

Lycia

Ephesus

Troas

Caesarea

Jerusalem

Palestine

The Great Sea

Crete

Achaia

Athens

Corinth

Berea

Apollonia

Thessalonica

Amphipolis

Macedonia

Philippi

Neapolis

Thrace

Adriatic Sea

Illyricum

Italy

Sicily

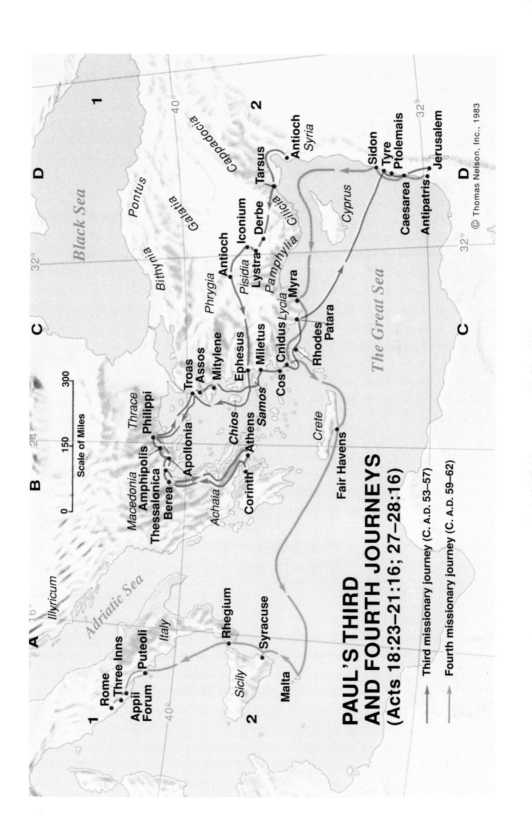

PAUL'S THIRD AND FOURTH JOURNEYS
(Acts 18:23–21:16; 27–28:16)

Third missionary journey (C. A.D. 53–57) →
Fourth missionary journey (C. A.D. 59–62) →

Scale of Miles
0   150   300

© Thomas Nelson, Inc., 1983

The Old Testament meaning of peace was completeness, soundness, and well-being of the total person (Ps. 119:165; Ps. 4:8; Is. 26:3; Ps. 122:6–7; 1 Sam. 7:14). The traditional Jewish greeting, *shalom,* means "peace" and was a wish for peace.

In the New Testament, peace often refers to the inner tranquility and poise of the Christian whose trust is in God through Christ The peace that Jesus Christ spoke of was a combination of hope, trust, and quiet in the mind and soul, brought about by a reconciliation with God (Luke 2:14; Matt. 5:9; John 14:27).

PEACE OFFERING — animal sacrifice (Ex. 20:24).

PEARL — used for jewelry and décor (1 Tim. 2:9) and also symbolized spiritual truth (Matt. 13:46).

PENTATEUCH [pen'-ta-tyook] — a Greek term meaning "five–volumed" which refers to the first five books of the Old Testament. The Jews traditionally refer to this collection as "the Book of the Law," or simply "the Law." Another word for this collection, "Torah," means "instruction, teaching, or doctrine." It describes such basic sections of the Pentateuch as parts of Exodus, Leviticus, and Deuteronomy.

PENTECOST, FEAST OF — Another name for the FEAST OF WEEKS, a yearly Jewish celebration of harvest (Deut. 16:9–10). The early Christian believers, who were gathered in Jerusalem for observance of this feast, experienced the outpouring of God's Holy Spirit in a miraculous way (Acts 2:1–4).

PERCEIVE — to know (John 4:19).

PERDITION — destruction, ruin, or waste, especially through the eternal destruction brought upon the wicked by God (Heb. 10:39; 2 Pet. 3:7).

PEREZ [pe'-res] *(breakthrough)* — the name of a man and a tribal family in the Old Testament:

1. The firstborn of the twin sons of Judah by Tamar (Gen. 38:29; Pharez, KJV). Perez was an ancestor of David and Jesus (Ruth 4:12, 18; Matt. 1:3; Luke 3:33).

2. A tribal family that took its name from Perez (1 Chr. 27:3). After the Captivity, 468 valiant "sons of Perez" lived in Jerusalem (Neh. 11:4, 6).

PERFECT, PERFECTION — without flaw or error; a state of completion or fulfillment. God's perfection means that He is complete in Himself.

The Pentateuch

Book	Key Idea	The Nation	The People	God's Character	God's Role	God's Command
Genesis	Beginnings	Chosen	Prepared	Powerful Sovereign	Creator	"Let there be!"
Exodus	Redemption	Delivered	Redeemed	Merciful	Deliverer	"Let my people go!"
Leviticus	Worship	Set Apart	Taught	Holy	Sanctifier	"Be holy!"
Numbers	Wandering	Directed	Tested	Just	Sustainer	"Go in!"
Deuteronomy	Renewed Covenant	Made Ready	Retaught	Loving Lord	Rewarder	"Obey!"

Chronology of Israel in the Pentateuch

Date	Event	Reference
Fifteenth day, first month, first year	Exodus	Exodus 12
Fifteenth day, second month, first year	Arrival in Wilderness of Sin	Exodus 16:1
Third month, first year	Arrival in Wilderness of Sinai	Exodus 19:1
First day, first month, second year	Erection of Tabernacle	Exodus 40:1, 17
	Dedication of Altar	Numbers 7:1
	Consecration of Levites	Numbers 8:1–26
Fourteenth day, first month, second year	Passover	Numbers 9:5
First day, second month, second year	Census	Numbers 1:1, 18
Fourteenth day, second month, second year	Supplemental Passover	Numbers 9:11
Twentieth day, second month, second year	Departure from Sinai	Numbers 10:11
First month, fortieth year	In Wilderness of Zin	Numbers 20:1, 22–29; 33:38
First day, fifth month, fortieth year	Death of Aaron	Numbers 20:22–29; 33:38
First day, eleventh month, fortieth year	Moses' Address	Deuteronomy 1:3

He lacks nothing; He has no flaws. He is perfect in all the characteristics of His nature. He is the basis for and standard by which all other perfection is to be measured (Job 36:4; Ps. 18:30; 19:7; Matt. 5:48).

PERFORM — to do, complete, or confirm (Rom. 15:28; Deut. 9:5).

PERGA [pur′-gah] — the capital city of Pamphylia, a province on the southern coast of Asia Minor, twice visited by the apostle Paul. During Paul's first missionary journey, he sailed to Perga from Paphos, on the island of Cyprus (Acts 13:13–14). Some time later, Paul and Barnabas stopped a second time at Perga (Acts 14:25).

Ruins of the walls and city gate at Perga, a city visited by Paul and Barnabas on their first missionary journey (Acts 13:13, 14).

Photo by Howard Vos

The modern city of Pergamum, or Pergamos, with the ruins of the Basilica of St. John in the center. *Photo by Howard Vos*

PERGAMOS [pur'-ga-mos] — the chief city of Mysia, near the Caicus River in northwest Asia Minor (modern Turkey) and the site of one of the seven churches of Asia (Rev. 1:11; 2:12–17; Pergamum, NRSV, NIV, REB, NASB). The city, situated opposite the island of Lesbos, was about 24 kilometers (15 miles) from the Aegean Sea.

PERISH — be lost, destroyed (Ps. 1:6; John 3:15).

PERIZZITES [per'-iz-ites] *(villagers)* — inhabitants of the "forest country" (Josh. 17:15) in the territory of the tribes of Ephraim, Manasseh, and Judah (Judg. 1:4–5).

PERPLEXED — confused (Esth. 3:15).

PERSECUTE, PERSECUTION — the hatred and affliction that follows the witness and holy life of God's people in a hostile world (Matt. 5:10).

PERSEVERANCE — the steadfast effort to follow God's commands and to do His work. The New Testament makes it clear that faith alone can save. But it makes it equally clear that perseverance in doing good works is the greatest indica-

tion that an individual's faith is genuine (James 2:14–26).

PERSIA [per'-she-ah] — an ancient world empire that flourished from 539—331 B.C. The Babylonian Empire fell to the Persians, setting the stage for the return of the Jews to Jerusalem in 538 B.C., following their long period of captivity by the Babylonians.

PERVERSE — improper, wrong, evil (Prov. 14:2; Matt. 17:17).

PERVERT — to change; usally has a negative connotation (Ex. 23:8; Acts 1:10).

PESTILENCE — plague (Ex. 5:3).

PETER, EPISTLES OF — two New Testament epistles bearing the name of "Peter, an apostle of Jesus Christ" (1 Pet. 1:1) and "Simon Peter, a servant and apostle of Jesus Christ" (2 Pet. 1:1), though otherwise having little in common.

First Peter, the longer of the two epistles, is written in fine Greek and refers frequently to the Old Testament. It is an epistle for the downhearted, written to give encouragement in times of trial and disappointment. First Peter anchors

FIRST PETER:
A Study and Teaching Outline

Part One: The Salvation of the Believer (1:1—2:12)

I. Salutation 1:1–2
II. Salvation of the Believer 1:3–12
  A. Hope for the Future 1:3–4
  B. Trials for the Present 1:5–9
  C. Anticipation in the Past 1:10–12
III. Sanctification of the Believer . . . . 1:13—2:12
  A. "Be Holy" 1:13–21
  B. "Love One Another" 1:22–25
  C. "Desire the Pure Milk of the Word" 2:1–3
  D. "Offer Up Spiritual Sacrifices" 2:4–10
  E. "Abstain from Fleshly Lusts" 2:11–12

Part Two: The Submission of the Believer (2:13—3:12)

I. Submission to the Government 2:13–17
II. Submission in Business 2:18–25
III. Submission in Marriage 3:1–8
IV. Submission in All of Life 3:9–12

Part Three: The Suffering of the Believer (3:13—5:14)

I. Conduct in Suffering 3:13–17
II. Christ's Example of Suffering . . . . 3:18—4:6
III. Commands in Suffering 4:7–19
IV. Ministry in Suffering 5:1–9
  A. Elders, Shepherd the Flock 5:1–4
  B. Saints, Humble Yourselves 5:5–9
V. Benediction 5:10–14

SECOND PETER:
A Study and Teaching Outline

I. Cultivation of Christian Character 1:1–21
  A. Salutation 1:1–2
  B. Growth in Christ 1:3–14
  C. Grounds of Belief 1:15–21
    1. Experience of the Transfiguration 1:15–18
    2. Certainty of the Scriptures 1:19–21
II. Condemnation of False Teachers 2:1–22
  A. Danger of False Teachers 2:1–3
  B. Destruction of False Teachers 2:4–9
  C. Description of False Teachers 2:10–22
III. Confidence in Christ's Return 3:1–18
  A. Mockery in the Last Days 3:1–7
  B. Manifestation of the Day of the Lord 3:8–10
  C. Maturity in View of the Day of the Lord . . 3:11–18

the Christian's hope not on logic or persuasion, but on the matchless sacrifice of Jesus Christ, who "suffered for us, leaving us an example, that you should follow His steps" (2:21).

In contrast to 1 Peter, 2 Peter is briefer and written in a forced style. It rails against false teachers, while reminding believers of their election by God and assuring them of Christ's return.

PETER, SIMON — the most prominent of Jesus' twelve apostles. The New Testament gives a more complete picture of Peter than of any other disciple, with the exception of Paul. Peter is often considered to be a big, blundering fisherman. But this is a shallow portrayal. The picture of his personality portrayed in the New Testament is rich and many-sided. A more fitting appraisal of Peter

Jaffa, the biblical Joppa, where Peter received the heavenly vision about God's acceptance of the Gentiles (Acts 10:1–23).

Photo by Willem A. VanGemeren

is that he was a pioneer among the twelve apostles and the early church, breaking ground that the church would later follow.

PHARAOH [fa′-ra-o] — the title of the kings of Egypt until 323 B.C. (Gen. 12:15). In the Egyptian language the word pharaoh means "great house." This word was originally used to describe the palace of the king. Around 1500 B.C. this term was applied to the Egyptian kings. It meant something like "his honor, his majesty."

PHARISEES [far′-i-sees] *(separated ones)* — a religious and political party in Palestine in New Testament times (Matthew 23). The Pharisees were known for insisting that the Law of God be observed as the scribes interpreted it and for their special commitment to keeping the laws of tithing and ritual purity.

PHILADELPHIA [fil-a-del′-fe-ah] *(brotherly love)* — a city of the province of Lydia in western Asia Minor (modern Turkey) and the site of one of the seven churches of Asia to which John wrote in the Book of Revelation (Rev. 1:11).

Entrance to the tomb of Pharaoh Tutankhamun of Egypt in the foreground with the tomb of Ramses VI just behind it. *Photo by Howard Vos*

The modern Turkish city of Alashehir, the biblical Philadelphia, on the Hermus River. John commended the Christians at Philadelphia for their faithfulness (Rev. 1:11; 3:7–13).

Photo by Gustav Jeeninga

PHILEMON [fi-le′-mon] — a wealthy Christian of Colossae who hosted a house church. Philemon was converted under the apostle Paul (Philem. 19), perhaps when Paul ministered in Ephesus (Acts 19:10). He is remembered because of his runaway slave, Onesimus, who, after damaging or stealing his master's property (Philem. 11, 18), made his way to Rome, where he was converted under Paul's ministry (Philem. 10).

Accompanied by Tychicus (Col. 4:7), Onesimus later returned to his master, Philemon. He carried with him the Epistle to the Colossians, plus the shorter Epistle to Philemon. In the latter, Paul asked Philemon to receive Onesimus, not as a slave but as a "beloved brother" (Philem. 16).

PHILEMON, EPISTLE TO — the shortest and most personal of Paul's epistles. Philemon tells the story of the conversion of a runaway slave, ONESIMUS, and the appeal to his owner, PHILEMON, to accept him back. The letter is warm and masterful, reminding us that the presence of Christ drastically changes every relationship in life.

The Epistle to Philemon is a lesson in the art of Christian relationships. No finer example of "speaking the truth in love" (Eph. 4:15) exists than this beautiful letter. While it was Philemon's legal right in the ancient world to punish or even kill a runaway slave, Paul hoped—indeed expected (v. 19)—that Philemon would receive Onesimus back as a brother in the Lord, not as a slave (v. 16). From beginning to end Paul addresses Philemon as a trusted friend rather than as an adversary (v. 22); he appeals to the best in his character (vv. 4–7, 13–14, 17, 21). In spite of Paul's subtle pressures for Philemon to restore Onesimus, he is careful not to force Philemon to do what is right; he helps him choose it for himself (vv. 8–9, 14).

PHILEMON:
A Study and Teaching Outline

I. The Prayer of Thanksgiving for Philemon 1–7
II. The Petition of Paul for Onesimus 8–16
III. The Promise of Paul to Philemon 17–25

PHILIP [fil'-ip] *(lover of horses)* — the name of four men in the New Testament:

1. One of the twelve apostles of Christ (Matt. 10:3; Mark 3:18; Luke 6:14) and a native of Bethsaida in Galilee (John 1:44; 12:21).

2. A son of Herod the Great and Mariamne; first husband of Herodias (Matt. 14:3; Luke 3:19). He was either the brother or half-brother of Herod Antipas.

3. Philip the tetrarch, a son of Herod the Great by Cleopatra of Jerusalem.

4. Philip the evangelist, one of the seven men chosen to serve the early church because they were reported to be "full of faith and the Holy Spirit" (Acts 6:5).

PHILIPPI [fil'-ip-pi] *(city of Philip)* — a city in eastern Macedonia (modern Greece) visited by the apostle Paul. Situated on a plain surrounded by mountains, Philippi lay about 16 kilometers (10 miles) inland from the Aegean Sea. The Egnatian Way, the main overland route between Asia and the West, ran through the city. Philippi was named for Philip II of Macedonia, the father of Alexander the Great. In 356 B.C. Philip enlarged and renamed the city, which was formerly known as Krenides. Philip resettled people from the countryside in Philippi and built a wall around the city and an acropolis atop the surrounding mountain. Although they date from later periods, other points of interest in Philippi

Ruins of the agora, or marketplace, of Philippi, with the ruins of a pagan temple in the foreground. *Photo by Howard Vos*

include a forum the size of a football field, an open-air theater, two large temples, public buildings, a library, and Roman baths.

PHILIPPIANS [fi-lip'-pe-ans] — natives or inhabitants of PHILIPPI (Phil. 4:15), a city of Macedonia situated about 113 kilometers (70 miles) northeast of Thessalonica (Acts 16:12; Phil. 1:1).

PHILIPPIANS, EPISTLE TO THE — one of four shorter epistles written by the apostle Paul while he was in prison. The others are Ephesians, Colossians, and Philemon. Paul founded the church at Philippi (Acts 16:12–40). Throughout his life the Philippians held a special place in his heart. Paul writes to them with affection, and the epistle breathes a note of joy throughout. When Paul first came to Philippi, he was thrown in jail. In the deep of the night, bound and beaten, he sang a hymn to God (Acts 16:25). A decade later Paul was again in prison, and he still was celebrating the Christian's joy in the midst of suffering, "Rejoice in the Lord always. Again I will say, rejoice!" (Phil. 4:4).

PHILISTIA [fil-is'-te-ah] — the land of the PHILISTINES as used in the poetry of the Book of Psalms (60:8; 108:9). This land lay between Joppa and Gaza on the coastal plain of Palestine.

PHILISTINES [fil-is'-tinz] — an aggressive nation that occupied part of southwest Palestine from about 1200 to 600 B.C. The name Philistine was used first among the Egyptians to describe the sea people defeated by Rameses III in a naval battle about 1188 B.C. Among the Assyrians the group was known as Pilisti or Palastu. The Hebrew word *pelishti* is the basis of the name Palestine, a later name for Canaan, the country occupied by God's covenant people.

PHILOSOPHY — the love of wisdom (from *phileo,* "to love," and *sophia,* "wisdom"). At the sporting events of ancient Greece, the philosopher Pythagoras said, there were three types of people: lovers of money (selling refreshments), lovers of fame (sports heroes), and lovers of wisdom (seekers of wisdom in sports and life in general).

PHINEHAS [fin'-e-has] *(the Nubian)* — the name of three men in the Old Testament:

PHILIPPIANS:
A Study and Teaching Outline

I. **Paul's Account of His Present Circumstance. . .** 1:1–30
   A. Paul's Prayer of Thanksgiving 1:1–11
   B. Paul's Afflictions Promote the Gospel. 1:12–18
   C. Paul's Afflictions Exalt the Lord 1:19–26
   D. Paul's Exhortation to the Afflicted 1:27–30
II. **Paul's Appeal to Have the Mind of Christ** 2:1–30
   A. Paul's Exhortation to Humility 2:1–4
   B. Christ's Example of Humility. 2:5–16
   C. Paul's Example of Humility 2:17–18
   D. Timothy's Example of Humility 2:19–24
   E. Epaphroditus' Example of Humility. 2:25–30
III. **Paul's Appeal to Have the Knowledge
   of Christ.** 3:1–21
   A. Warning against Confidence in the Flesh. . . . 3:1–9
   B. Exhortation to Know Christ. 3:10–16
   C. Warning against Living for the Flesh 3:17–21
IV. **Paul's Appeal to Have the Peace of Christ** 4:1–23
   A. Peace with the Brethren. 4:1–3
   B. Peace with the Lord 4:4–9
   C. Peace in All Circumstances 4:10–19
   D. Conclusion 4:20–23

1. A son of Eleazar and grandson of Aaron (Ex. 6:25).

2. The younger of the two sons of Eli the priest (1 Sam. 1:3). Phinehas and his brother, Hophni, were priests also; but they disgraced their priestly office by greed, irreverence, and immorality (1 Sam. 2:12–17, 22–25).

3. The father of Eleazar (Ezra 8:33).

PHOEBE [fee'-bee] — deaconess recommended by Paul (Rom. 16:1–2).

PHOENICIA [fo-nee'-she-ah] — the land north of Palestine on the eastern shore of the Mediterranean Sea between the Litani and Arvad Rivers. Phoenicia is a Greek word that means "land of purple." The area was famous from early times for its purple dyes, produced from shellfish. In the KJV, Phoenicia is spelled Phenicia.

The low hills and plain are very fertile. Phoenicia was famous in biblical times for its lush plant life, which included fruit, flowers, and trees (Hos. 14:5–7). "They shall be revived like grain, and grow like the vine. Their scent shall be like the wine of Lebanon" (v. 7).

The cedars of Phoenicia were cut and shipped as far away as Egypt and eastern Mesopotamia, because most other nations in this part of the world had very few trees suitable for timber.

PHRYGIA [frij'-e-ah] — a large province of the mountainous region of Asia Minor (modern Turkey); visited by the apostle Paul (Acts 2:10; 16:6; 18:23). Because of its size, Phrygia was made a part of other provinces. In Roman times the region was split between two provinces. The cities of Colossae, Laodicea, and Hierapolis belonged to Asia, while Iconium and Antioch belonged to Galatia.

PHYLACTERIES [fi-lack'-ter-ies] — small square leather boxes or cases, each containing four strips of parchment inscribed with quotations from the Pentateuch, the first five books of the Old Testament (Ex. 13:1–10; 13:11–16; Deut. 6:4–9; 11:13–21). Phylacteries were worn by every male Israelite above 13 years of age during morning prayer, except on the Sabbath and holidays.

PIETY — a word usually defined as religious devotion and reverence to God. In its only occurrence in the NKJV, however, it means faithfulness in performing one's responsibilities to the family, especially to parents (1 Tim. 5:4).

PILATE, PONTIUS [pi'-lut, pon'-shius] — the fifth Roman prefect of Judea (ruled A.D. 26—36), who issued the official order sentencing Jesus to death by crucifixion (Matthew 27; Mark 15; Luke 23; John 18—19).

PILLAR — can refer to an architectural element that supports a roof, or upright standing stones with religious significance. The Bible also contains many figurative references to pillars. For instance, the physical demonstration of God's presence during the Exodus was described as a "pillar of fire" and a "pillar of cloud" (Ex. 13:21).

This inscription from a theater in Caesarea mentions Pontius Pilate, prefect of Judea, who pronounced the death sentence against Jesus (**Mark 15**). *Photo by Gustav Jeeninga*

PINE — as an adjective, a type of tree (Is. 41:19); as a verb, be weary or sick of heart (Ezek. 24:23).

PINNACLE — a part of the temple mentioned in the temptation of Jesus (Matt. 4:5; Luke 4:9). The pinnacle was an elevated part of the temple now unknown. It probably was either the battlement or the roof of Solomon's porch. Whatever its exact location, the pinnacle offered a vast view of Jerusalem.

PIPE — a musical instrument that may have been similar to a flute or bagpipes (1 Sam. 10:5).

PISGAH [piz'-gah] — a word that refers to the rugged ridge that crowns a mountain. As a proper noun, the word "Pisgah" was sometimes identified with Mount Nebo. But the word more likely refers to the entire ridge of the Abarim Mountains, which extends from the Moabite plateau toward the Dead Sea.

PISIDIA [pi-sid'-e-ah] — a mountainous province in central Asia Minor (modern Turkey), twice visited by the apostle Paul (Acts 13:14; 14:24). Pisidia was a wild, mountainous country infested with bandits. When Paul wrote that he had been "in perils of robbers" (2 Cor. 11:26), he may have been referring to his dangerous journey through the mountains of Pisidia.

PIT — a deep hole in the ground, either natural (Gen. 14:10) or man-made (Gen. 37:20).

PITCH — as a verb, set up as in a tent (Heb. 8:2); as a noun, a tar-like substance (Ex. 2:3).

PITY — a sense of sympathetic sorrow for the unfortunate (Matt. 18:33). In this respect, pity is the emotional side of mercy, the desire to help people in this state.

PLAGUE — an affliction sent by God as punishment for sin and disobedience. In most cases in the Bible the affliction is an epidemic or disease. The Hebrew word for "plague" literally means a blow or a lash, implying punishment or chastisement (Ex. 7:14—12:30).

The Ten Plagues on Egypt

The Plague	The Effect
1. Blood (7:20)	Pharaoh hardened (7:22)
2. Frogs (8:6)	Pharaoh begs relief, promises freedom (8:8), but is hardened (8:15)
3. Lice (8:17)	Pharaoh hardened (8:19)
4. Flies (8:24)	Pharaoh bargains (8:28), but is hardened (8:32)
5. Livestock diseased (9:6)	Pharaoh hardened (9:7)
6. Boils (9:10)	Pharaoh hardened (9:12)
7. Hail (9:23)	Pharaoh begs relief (9:27), promises freedom (9:28), but is hardened (9:35)
8. Locusts (10:13)	Pharaoh bargains (10:11), begs relief (10:17), but is hardened (10:20)
9. Darkness (10:22)	Pharaoh bargains (10:24), but is hardened (10:27)
10. Death of firstborn (12:29)	Pharaoh and Egyptians beg Israel to leave Egypt (12:31–33)

God multiplied His signs and wonders in the land of Egypt that the Egyptians might know that He is the Lord.

Statue of Rameses II of Egypt. Many scholars believe he was the ruling pharaoh at the time of the Exodus.

PLASTER — clay wall covering (Deut. 27:2).

PLEDGE — something held as security to guarantee fulfillment of an obligation. As proof of his intention to send Tamar a young goat from his flock, Judah left his signet, cord, and staff with her as a pledge (Gen. 38:17–18, 20).

PLEIADES [ple′-ya-dez] — a brilliant cluster of stars seen in the shoulder of Taurus (the Bull). The name Pleiades comes from the seven daughters of Atlas and Pleione in Greek mythology.

PLOWSHARE — the blade of a plow used for tilling the soil. In early times plows were constructed of wood; but with the development of metallurgy, metal tips were placed over the wood. The prophets Micah and Isaiah spoke of making plowshares from weapons as a sign of the peace to be accomplished in the coming reign of God (Is. 2:4; Mic. 4:3).

PLUCK — to remove (John 10:28).

PLUMBLINE, PLUMMET — A small heavy weight on the end of a long cord, used to make sure a wall is standing vertically (2 Kin. 21:13; level, Is. 28:17, NASB). In a vision, the prophet Amos saw the Lord measuring the nation of Israel with a plumbline. The people were not considered true and straight in their devotion to God because they had fallen into worship of false gods (Amos 7:7–8).

POLLUTE — to make ceremonially unclean or morally impure; to defile, profane, or corrupt. Allowing a murderer to go unpunished polluted the land of Israel (Num. 35:33).

POLYGAMY — the practice of having several spouses, especially wives, at one time. Polygamy includes polygyny (marriage to more than one woman) and polyandry (marriage to more than one man). The term polygamy is more often used, however, as a synonym for polygyny, which was common throughout the ancient world.

POLYTHEISM — belief in many gods.

POMEGRANATE — A round, sweet fruit about ten centimeters (four inches) across with a hard rind. It is green when young and turns red when ripe. There are numerous edible seeds inside the pomegranate.

The hem of Aaron's robe was decorated with blue, purple, and red pomegranates (Ex. 28:33–34; 39:24–26). It was listed among the pleasant fruits of Egypt (Num. 20:5). Solomon decorated the temple with the likeness of the pomegranate (1 Kin. 7:18, 20). A spiced wine was made from the juice (Song 8:2).

A flowering pomegranate. In biblical times pomegranates were widely cultivated in Palestine (Num. 13:23; Deut. 8:7–8). The juice of the fruit made a pleasant drink (Song 8:2).

Photo by Gustav Jeeninga

POMP — much show (Acts 25:23).

POSSESSED — acquired, owned; also under control of (Matt. 4:24).

POSTERITY — descendants (Dan. 11:4).

POTIPHAR [pot'-i-far] *(dedicated to Ra)* — the Egyptian to whom the Ishmaelites (Gen. 39:1) sold Joseph when he was brought to Egypt as a slave. Potiphar was a high officer of Pharaoh and a wealthy man (Gen. 37:36). In time, he put Joseph in charge of his household.

POTSHERD — a fragment of broken pottery; a shard found in an archaeological excavation. Job used a potsherd to scrape the sores of his body (Job 2:8).

POTTAGE — a soup or stew (Gen. 25:29).

POTTER'S FIELD — the field bought with the 30 pieces of silver paid to Judas for his betrayal of Jesus (Matt. 27:7, 10). Since the field was purchased with blood money, it was considered good for nothing but a cemetery in which foreigners were buried. According to tradition, the potter's field was at the eastern end of the Valley of Hinnom.

POUND — a weight, an amount of money (John 12:3; Ezra 2:69; Luke 19:13). (see MONEY OF THE BIBLE, WEIGHTS AND MEASURES OF THE BIBLE).

POWER — the ability or strength to perform an activity or deed (Ps. 111:6). Power is sometimes used with the word authority. If power suggests physical strength, authority suggests a moral right or privilege.

PRAETORIUM, PRAETORIAN GUARD
— a special group of Roman soldiers in New Testament times, established to guard the emperor of the Roman Empire (Mark 15:16). Originally, they were restricted to the city of Rome, but later they were sent to the Roman provinces as well. This guard was an elite corps of soldiers whose salaries, privileges, and terms of service were better than the other soldiers of the Roman Empire.

PRAISE — an act of worship or acknowledgment by which the virtues or deeds of another are recognized and extolled. The praise of one human being toward another, although often beneficial (1 Cor. 11:2; 1 Pet. 2:14), can be a snare (Prov. 27:21; Matt. 6:1–5). But the praise of God toward people is the highest commendation they can receive. Such an act of praise reflects a true servant's heart (Matt. 25:21; 1 Cor. 4:5; Eph. 1:3–14).

PRAYER — communication with God. Because God is personal, all people can offer prayers. However, sinners who have not trusted Jesus Christ for their salvation remain alienated from God. So while unbelievers may pray, they do not have the basis for a rewarding fellowship with God. They have not met the conditions laid down in the Bible for effectiveness in prayer.

PRECEPT — lesson, principle (Ps. 119:4).

PREDESTINATION — the biblical teaching that declares the sovereignty of God over human beings in such a way that the freedom of the human will is also preserved (Rom. 8:29–30).

PREEMINENCE — top honor, first place (Col. 1:18).

PREPARATION DAY — the day immediately before the Sabbath and other Jewish festivals. Preparation Day always fell on Friday among the Jewish people, because all religious festivals began on the Sabbath, or Saturday (Matt. 27:62; John 19:14, 31).

PRESCRIBE — write (Is. 10:1).

PRESENCE OF GOD — God's ways of making Himself known to an individual (Ex. 3:2–5; Ex. 40:34–38; John 1:14).

PRESS — as a noun, a tool used to collect juice or oil from foods (Prov. 3:10); as a verb, strain (Phil. 3:14).

PRESUMPTUOUS — overly bold, filled with pride (Ex 21:14; 2 Pet. 2:10).

PREVAIL — to conquer (Matt. 16:18).

An ancient oilpress in Capernaum, used for crushing olives in Bible times (Is. 5:2). *Photo by Gustav Jeeninga*

PREVENT — anticipate (Ps. 119:147) or precede (Matt. 17:25; 1 Thess. 4:15). In the King James version of the Bible, prevent does not mean to stop from happening.

PREY — victim (Num. 14:3).

PRIDE — arrogance, inordinate or unjustified self-esteem (Prov. 29:23).

PRIEST, HIGH — a chief priest of the Hebrew people, especially of the ancient Levitical priesthood traditionally traced from AARON. "Head priest," "the great one from his brothers," and "ruler of the house of God" are literal translations of references to this officer (Lev. 21:10; 2 Chr. 19:11). The high priest was the supreme religious head of his people. Aaron held this position above his sons that was to continue in the firstborn of successive holders of the office. The high priest was distinguished from his fellow priests by the clothes he wore, the duties he performed, and the particular requirements placed upon him.

PRIESTS — official ministers or worship leaders in the nation of Israel who represented the people before God and conducted various rituals to atone for their sins. This function was carried out by the father of a family (Job 1:5) or the head of a tribe in the days before Moses and his brother Aaron. But with the appointment of Aaron by God as the first high priest, the priesthood was formally established. Aaron's descendants were established as the priestly line in Israel. They carried out their important duties from generation to generation as a special class devoted to God's service.

PRINCIPALITY — a powerful ruler, or the rule of someone in authority. The word (often found in the plural) may refer to human rulers (Titus 3:1, KJV), demonic spirits (Rom. 8:38; Eph. 6:12; Col. 2:15), angels and demons in general (Eph. 3:10; Col. 1:16), or (especially when used in the singular) any type of rule other than God Himself (Eph. 1:21; Col. 2:10). While Christians must often wrestle against evil principalities (Eph. 6:12), they can be victorious because Christ defeated all wicked spirits (Col. 2:15).

PRISCILLA [pris'-sil-lah] — the wife of AQUILA and a zealous advocate of the Christian cause (Rom. 16:3; 1 Cor. 16:19). Her name is also given as Prisca (2 Tim. 4:19). Aquila and Priscilla left their home in Rome for Corinth when the emperor Claudius commanded all Jews to depart from the city (Acts 18:2). Thus, they were fellow passengers of the apostle Paul from Corinth to Ephesus (Acts 18:18), where they met Apollos and instructed him further in the Christian faith (Acts 18:26).

PRISON, PRISONER — a place of forcible restraint or confinement. Most prisons of the ancient world were crude and dehumanizing. Persons guilty of violating the laws of a community were detained in several different types of prisons.

PRIZE — an award (1 Cor. 9:24; Phil. 3:14).

PROCLAIM — to tell, announce (Ex. 33:19; Luke 12:3).

PROCLAMATION — an official public announcement (Dan. 5:29).

PROCONSUL [pro-con'-sul] — a title given to the governor of a senatorial province in the Roman Empire. Under the Roman system of government, the Empire was divided into senatorial provinces and imperial provinces. Imperial provinces were administered by representatives of the emperor. The senatorial provinces were presided over by proconsuls appointed by the Roman senate. Two proconsuls are mentioned in the New Testament: Sergius Paulus (Acts 13:7–8, 12) and Gallio (Acts 18:12; deputy, KJV; governor, REB).

PROFANE — to treat anything holy with disrespect. In the Bible, many things could be profaned by disregarding God's Laws about their correct use: the Sabbath (Is. 56:6), the temple (Acts 24:6), the covenant (Mal. 2:10), and God's name (Ex. 19:22). The term "profane" is often applied to foolish or irresponsible people. Esau, who sold his birthright, was a "profane" person (Heb. 12:16).

PROMISE — a solemn pledge to perform or grant a specified thing. God did not have to promise anything to sinful people. But the fact that almost all biblical promises are those made by God to human beings indicates that His nature is characterized chiefly by grace and faithfulness.

PRONOUNCE — say, speak (Jer. 11:17).

PROPHECY, PROPHESY — predictions about the future and the end–time; special messages from God, often uttered through human spokesmen, which indicate the divine will for mankind on earth and in heaven (Mark 7:6).

PROPHET — a person who spoke for God and who communicated God's message courageously to God's chosen people—the nation of Israel (Mic. 1:1; Judg. 4:4; Acts 21:9).

PROPHETESS — a female prophet.

PROPITIATION [pro-pish'-e-a-shun] — the atoning death of Jesus on the Cross, through which He paid the penalty demanded by God because of people's sin, thus setting them free from sin and death. The word means "appeasement." Thus, propitiation expresses the idea that Jesus died on the Cross to pay the price for sin that a holy God demanded (1 John 2:2; 4:10).

PROSELYTE — a convert from one religious belief or party to another. In the New Testament (Matt. 23:15; Acts 2:10), the term is used in a specific sense to designate Gentile converts who had committed themselves to the teachings of the Jewish faith or who were attracted to the teachings of Judaism.

PROSTITUTE, PROSTITUTION — the act or practice of promiscuous sexual relations, especially for money. Several words are used for a woman

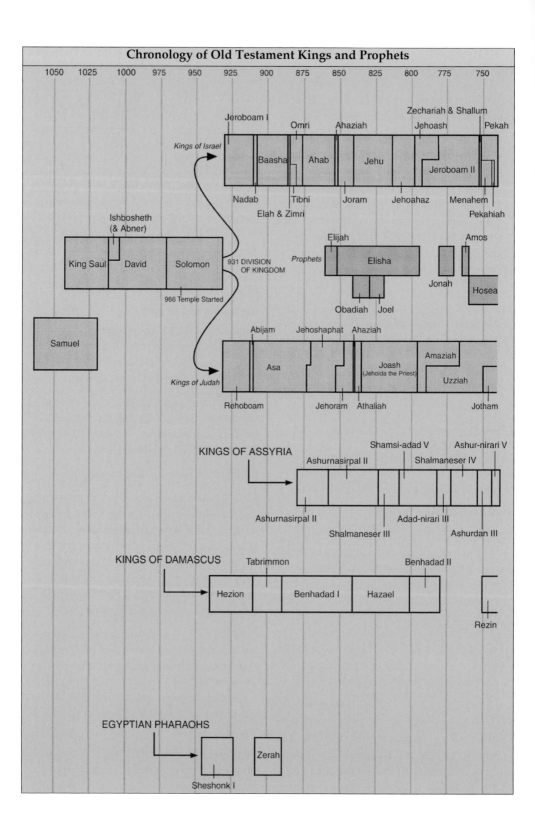

Chronology of Old Testament Kings and Prophets

1050 | 1025 | 1000 | 975 | 950 | 925 | 900 | 875 | 850 | 825 | 800 | 775 | 750

Kings of Israel
Jeroboam I
Nadab
Baasha
Elah & Zimri
Tibni
Omri
Ahab
Joram
Ahaziah
Jehu
Jehoahaz
Zechariah & Shallum
Jehoash
Jeroboam II
Menahem
Pekah
Pekahiah

King Saul
Ishbosheth (& Abner)
David
Solomon
931 DIVISION OF KINGDOM
966 Temple Started

Samuel

Prophets
Elijah
Elisha
Obadiah   Joel
Amos
Jonah
Hosea

Kings of Judah
Rehoboam
Abijam
Asa
Jehoshaphat
Jehoram
Ahaziah
Athaliah
Joash (Jehoida the Priest)
Amaziah
Uzziah
Jotham

KINGS OF ASSYRIA
Ashurnasirpal II
Ashurnasirpal II
Shalmaneser III
Shamsi-adad V
Adad-nirari III
Shalmaneser IV
Ashurdan III
Ashur-nirari V

KINGS OF DAMASCUS
Hezion
Tabrimmon
Benhadad I
Hazael
Benhadad II
Rezin

EGYPTIAN PHARAOHS
Sheshonk I
Zerah

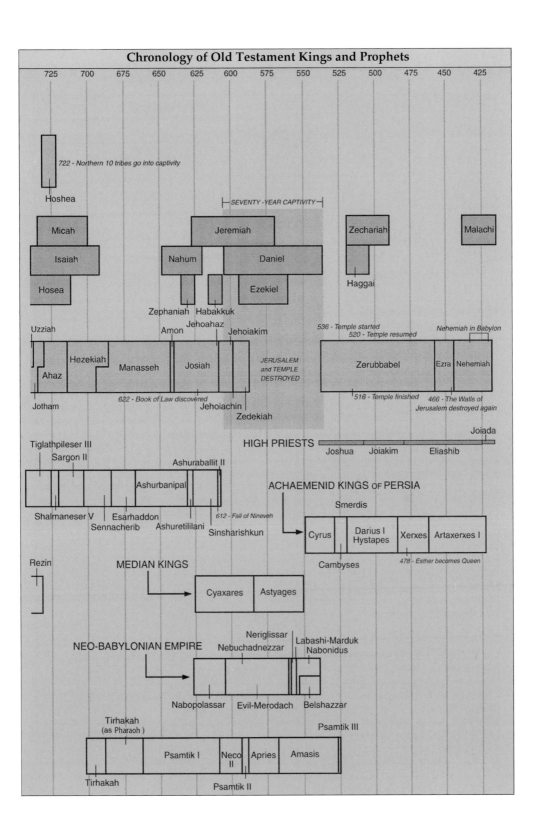

Chronology of Old Testament Kings and Prophets

Fulfilled Prophecies from Isaiah

The Prophecy	The Fulfillment
The Messiah . . .	**Jesus Christ . . .**
will be born of a virgin (Is. 7:14).	was born of a virgin named Mary (Luke 1:26–31).
will have a Galilean ministry (Is. 9:1, 2).	ministered in Galilee of the Gentiles (Matt. 4:13–16).
will be an heir to the throne of David (Is. 9:7).	was given the throne of His father David (Luke 1:32, 33).
will have His way prepared (Is. 40:3–5).	was announced by John the Baptist (John 1:19–28).
will be spat on and struck (Is. 50:6).	was spat on and beaten (Matt. 26:67).
will be exalted (Is. 52:13).	was highly exalted by God and the people (Phil. 2:9, 10).
will be disfigured by suffering (Is. 52:14; 53:2).	was scourged by the soldiers who gave Him a crown of thorns (Mark 15:15–19).
will make a blood atonement (Is. 53:5).	shed His blood to atone for our sins (1 Pet. 1:2).
will be widely rejected (Is. 53:1, 3).	was not accepted by many (John 12:37, 38).
will bear our sins and sorrows (Is. 53:4, 5).	died because of our sins (Rom. 4:25; 1 Pet. 2:24, 25).
will be our substitute (Is. 53:6, 8).	died in our place (Rom. 5:6, 8; 2 Cor. 5:21).
will voluntarily accept our guilt and punishment (Is. 53:7, 8).	was silent about our sin (Mark 15:4, 5; John 10:11; 19:30).
will be buried in a rich man's tomb (Is. 53:9).	was buried in the tomb of Joseph, a rich man from Arimathea (Matt. 27:57–60; John 19:38–42).
will save us who believe in Him (Is. 53:10, 11).	provided salvation for all who believe (John 3:16; Acts 16:31).
will die with transgressors (Is. 53:12).	was numbered with the transgressors (Mark 15:27, 28; Luke 22:37).
will heal the brokenhearted (Is. 61:1, 2).	healed the brokenhearted (Luke 4:18, 19).

who engages in illicit sexual activity for pay, including HARLOT, whore, and prostitute (Hosea 1).

PROVE — to try or test (Ps. 17:3; Luke 14:9).

PROVENDER — grass-based animal food (Judg. 19:21).

PROVERB — a short, pithy statement about human nature and life. In the Bible Solomon is singled out for his use of proverbs (1 Kin. 4:32). His wisdom was shown by his ability to make clear, true commentaries upon the nature of things. The Hebrew word most frequently translated as proverb means literally "a similitude," or loosely, "a representation." So in the declaration that Israel would be "a proverb ... among all peoples" (1 Kin. 9:7), God indicated that the name Israel would come to symbolize disobedience. Proverbs are designed to make God's truth accessible to all people, so they might direct their lives in accordance with His will.

PROVERBS, BOOK OF — one of the "wisdom books" of the Old Testament, containing

PROVERBS:
A Study and Teaching Outline

I. The Purpose of Proverbs 1:1–7
II. Proverbs to Youth . . . . 1:8—9:18
   A. Obey Parents 1:8–9
   B. Avoid Bad Company 1:10–19
   C. Seek Wisdom . . . . 1:20—2:22
   D. Benefits of Wisdom 3:1–26
   E. Be Kind to Others 3:27–35
   F. Security in Wisdom 4:1–13
   G. Avoid the Wicked 4:14–22
   H. Keep Your Heart 4:23–27
   I. Do Not Commit Adultery 5:1–14
   J. Be Faithful to Your Spouse 5:15–23
   K. Avoid Surety 6:1–5
   L. Do Not Be Lazy 6:6–19
   M. Do Not Commit Adultery . . . . 6:20—7:27
   N. Praise of Wisdom . . . . 8:1—9:12
   O. Avoid Folly 9:13–18
III. Proverbs of Solomon . . . . 10:1—22:16
   A. Proverbs Contrasting the Godly
      and the Wicked . . . . 10:1—15:33
   B. Proverbs Encouraging Godly
      Lives . . . . 16:1—22:16
IV. Proverbs Concerning Various
     Situations . . . . 22:17—24:34
V. Proverbs of Solomon Copied by
     Hezekiah's Men . . . . 25:1—29:27
   A. Proverbs Regulating Relation-
      ships with Others . . . . 25:1—26:28
      1. Relationships with Kings 25:1–7
      2. Relationships with Neighbors 25:8–20
      3. Relationships with Enemies 25:21–24
      4. Relationships with Yourself 25:25–28
      5. Relationships with Fools 26:1–12
      6. Relationships with Sluggards 26:13–16
      7. Relationships with Gossips 26:17–28
   B. Proverbs Regulating Various
      Activities . . . . 27:1—29:27
VI. The Words of Agur 30:1–33
VII. The Words of King Lemuel 31:1–9
VIII. The Poem About the Wise Woman 31:10–31

instructions on many of the practical matters of daily life. The PROVERB was a familiar literary form in all ancient cultures; it was a very suitable device for collecting and summarizing the wisdom of the centuries. But the Book of Proverbs has one important difference: it points the believer to God with instructions on how to live a holy, upright life.

PROVIDENCE — the continuous activity of God in His creation by which He preserves and governs (Acts 24:2). The doctrine of providence affirms God's absolute lordship over His creation and confirms the dependence of all creation on the Creator. It is the denial of the idea that the universe is governed by chance or fate.

PROVINCE — an administrative district of the government or civil ruling authority. The word "province" is used only four times of rulers in Israel. All these occurrences come from the time of King Ahab (1 Kin. 20:14–15, 17, 19).

The other occurrences of the word refer to the administrative districts during the Babylonian and Persian rules (Ezra 2:1; 4:15; Neh. 1:3). The term occurs only twice in the New Testament (Acts 23:34; 25:1).

PROVOCATION — anything that provokes, excites, incites, or stimulates. The reference in Hebrews 3:8, 15 to "the provocation" (KJV), or "the rebellion" (NKJV, NIV), is a quotation from Psalm 95:7–11. This passage points back to a specific time when the Israelites provoked God by their rebellion against Moses during the Exodus (Ex. 17:1–7). The name of that place was called Massah (testing, temptation) and Meribah (strife, contention).

PRUDENT — smart, wise (Prov. 18:15; Matt. 11:25).

PRUNING HOOKS — small knives with curved blades used for pruning grapevines. The prophets Isaiah, Joel, and Micah contrasted pruning hooks with spears in a way that allowed these knives to become symbols of peace, not war (Is. 2:4; Joel 3:10; Mic. 4:3)

PSALM — a song (Col. 3:16).

PSALMS, BOOK OF — a collection of prayers, poems, and hymns that focus the worshiper's thoughts on God in praise and adoration. Parts of this book were used as a hymnal in the worship services of ancient Israel.

The musical heritage of the Psalms is demonstrated by its title. It comes from a Greek word that means "a song sung to the accompaniment of a musical instrument."

PSEUDEPIGRAPHA [su-de-pig'-graph-ah] — a collection of Jewish books containing various forms of literature, using names of famous people in Israel's history for the titles of the books. The real authors are unknown. Such names as Ezra, Baruch, Enoch, Solomon, Moses, and Adam are used to add authority to the writing.

PUBLICAN — KJV word for Tax Collector (Matt. 9:10).

PUBLISH — to proclaim (Mark 1:45).

PUFFED UP —full of false pride (1 Cor. 4:6).

PULPIT — KJV word for a raised platform reached by steps, or a desk used for preaching and teaching in a service of worship (Neh. 8:4; platform, NKJV). Such a platform is mentioned in connection with the gathering of the people of Israel to hear the reading of the Law of God and its interpretation.

PURE — (see CHASTE).

PURGE — to cast out whatever is impure or undesirable; to refine or free from impurities (Dan. 11:35; 1 Cor. 5:7; Heb. 9:14).

PURIFICATION — the act of making clean and pure before God and people. The Mosaic Law provided instructions for both physical and spiri-

PSALMS:
A Study and
Teaching Outline

I. Praise Hymns and Liturgies

Psalm 8—The Lord's Glory Is in All the Earth

Psalms 14, 53—To the Shame of the Godless, the Lord Restores His People

Psalm 15—Only the Godly May Dwell with the Lord

Psalm 19—The Lord Reveals Himself in His World and in His Word

Psalm 24—The Lord Is the King of Glory

Psalm 29—The Voice of the Lord Is Powerful and Majestic

Psalm 33—The Lord Is Sovereign in Creation and History

Psalm 46—God Is the Mighty Fortress of His People

Psalm 47—God Is the Great King over All the Earth

Psalm 48—God Is the Great King in Zion

Psalm 50—God Is the Righteous Judge of His People

Psalm 65—God Saves and Sustains His People

Psalm 67—Let All the Peoples Praise God

Psalm 68—God Is the Strength and Power of His People

Psalm 75—Sing Praise to God for His Righteous Judgment

Psalm 76—God Is Majestic When He Judges

Psalm 78—God Guides His People Even When They Stray

Psalm 81—God Wants His People to Praise and Obey Him

Psalm 82—God Will Inherit All the Nations

Psalm 84—Those Who Dwell in God's House Are Blessed

Psalm 85—God's Salvation Is Near to Those Who Fear Him

Psalm 87—The City of God Is Glorious

Psalm 93—The Lord Our King Is Clothed with Majesty

Psalm 95—The Lord Is the Great King above All Gods

Psalm 96—The Lord Our King Is Great and Greatly to Be Praised

Psalm 97—The Lord Our King Is Exalted Far above All Gods

Psalm 98—The Lord Our King Saves and Judges

Psalm 99—The Lord Our King Is Holy

Psalm 100—Be Thankful to the Lord and Praise His Name

Psalm 101—Walk Before the Lord with a Perfect Heart

Psalm 103—Praise the Lord for All His Benefits

Psalm 104—The Lord Provides His Creatures with Everything They Need

Psalm 105—The Lord Is Always Faithful to His People

Psalm 106—The Lord Saved His People Again and Again

Psalm 111—The Lord Is Always Faithful to His Covenant

Psalm 113—Praise the Name of the Lord

Psalm 114—God Brought Israel out of Egypt by His Miraculous Power

Psalm 115—Idols Are Nothing but the Lord Is Everything

Psalm 117—Let All Peoples Praise the Lord
Psalm 118—Praise the Lord for His Wonderful
   Salvation
Psalm 119—Praise the Lord for His Wonderful Word
Psalm 121—Our Help Comes Only from the Lord
Psalm 122—Be Glad When You Go to the House of
   the Lord
Psalm 123—Look to the Lord for Mercy
Psalm 124—The Lord Is on the Side of His People
Psalm 125—The Lord Surrounds His People with His
   Protection
Psalm 126—The Lord Brings His People Back from
   Captivity
Psalm 129—The Lord Is Victorious over His People's
   Enemies
Psalm 134—Let All the Servants of the Lord Praise
   Him
Psalm 135—Whatever the Lord Pleases He Does
Psalm 136—The Mercy of the Lord Endures Forever
Psalm 145—Praise the Name of the Lord Forever and
   Ever
Psalm 147—Praise the Lord for His Sustaining Word
Psalm 148—Praise the Lord from the Heavens and
   from the Earth
Psalm 149—Let the Lord's People Sing Praise to Him
Psalm 150—Let Everything That Has Breath Praise
   the Lord

II. Individual and Communal Laments
   Psalm 3—Lord, Arise and Save Me
   Psalm 4—God, Have Mercy on Me and Hear My Prayer
   Psalm 5—Give Heed to the Voice of My Cry, O Lord
   Psalm 6—O Lord, Heal Me
   Psalm 7—O Lord, Save Me from All Those Who
      Persecute Me
   Psalm 9—Arise, O Lord, Do Not Let Man Prevail
   Psalm 10—Why Do You Stand Afar Off, O Lord?
   Psalm 11—The Lord Tests the Righteous
   Psalm 12—May the Lord Cut Off the Tongue That
      Speaks Proud Things
   Psalm 13—O Lord, How Long Will You Hide Your
      Face from Me?
   Psalm 17—O Lord, Deliver My Life from the Wicked
   Psalm 22—My God, My God, Why Have You Forsaken
      Me?
   Psalm 25—O My God, Let Not My Enemies Triumph
      Over Me
   Psalm 26—Vindicate Me, O Lord
   Psalm 27—Do Not Leave Me or Forsake Me, O God of
      My Salvation
   Psalm 28—O Lord My Rock, Do Not Be Silent to Me
   Psalm 31—O Lord, Let Me Never Be Ashamed
   Psalm 35—O Lord, Fight Against Those Who Fight
      Against Me
   Psalm 36—There Is No Fear of God Before the Eyes of
      the Wicked
   Psalm 38—O Lord, Do Not Rebuke Me in Your Wrath

Psalm 39—O Lord, Do Not Be Silent at My Tears
Psalm 41—O Lord, Be Merciful to Me and Raise Me Up
Psalm 42—Why Are You Cast Down, O My Soul?
Psalm 43—O God, Plead My Cause Against an
Ungodly Nation
Psalm 44—O God, Redeem Us for Your Mercies' Sake
Psalm 51—O God, Blot Out My Transgressions
Psalm 52—Why Do You Boast in Evil, O Mighty Man?
Psalm 54—Save Me, O God, by Your Name
Psalm 55—O God, Do Not Hide Yourself from My
Supplication
Psalm 56—In Anger Cast Down the Peoples, O God
Psalm 57—Be Merciful to Me, O God, Be Merciful to
Me
Psalm 58—The Poison of the Wicked Is Like the Poison
of a Serpent
Psalm 59—Deliver Me from My Enemies, O My God
Psalm 60—O God, You Have Cast Us Off
Psalm 62—My Soul, Wait Silently for God Alone
Psalm 64—O God, Early Will I Seek You
Psalm 69—Save Me, O God, For the Waters Have Come
Up to My Neck
Psalm 70—Make Haste, O God, to Deliver Me
Psalm 71—O Lord, Let Me Never Be Put to Shame
Psalm 74—O God, Why Have You Cast Us Off Forever?
Psalm 77—Has God Forgotten to Be Gracious?
Psalm 79—O God, the Nations Have Laid Jerusalem
in Heaps
Psalm 80—Restore Us, O Lord God of Hosts
Psalm 83—Do Not Hold Your Peace, O God
Psalm 86—Bow Down Your Ear, O Lord, For I Am Poor
and Needy
Psalm 88—O Lord, I Have Cried Out Day and Night
Before You
Psalm 90—Lord, We Have Been Consumed by Your
Anger
Psalm 94—Lord, How Long Will the Wicked Triumph?
Psalm 102—O Lord, Answer Me Speedily
Psalm 108—Is It Not You, O God, Who Cast Us Off?
Psalm 109—Do Not Keep Silent, O God of My Praise
Psalm 120—In My Distress I Cried to the Lord
Psalm 130—Out of the Depths I Have Cried to You,
O Lord
Psalm 137—By the Rivers of Babylon, We Wept When
We Remembered Zion
Psalm 140—Deliver Me, O Lord, from Evil Men
Psalm 141—Set a Guard, O Lord, over My Mouth
Psalm 142—I Cry Out to the Lord with My Voice
Psalm 143—Revive Me, O Lord, for Your Name's Sake

III. Songs of Individual Thanksgiving
Psalm 23—The Lord Is My Shepherd
Psalm 30—I Will Extol You, O Lord, For You Have Lifted
Me Up
Psalm 32—Blessed Is He Whose Transgression Is
Forgiven
Psalm 34—I Will Bless the Lord at All Times

Psalm 40—The Lord Has Put a New Song in My Mouth
Psalm 66—Make a Joyful Shout to God, All the Earth
Psalm 92—It Is Good to Give Thanks to the Lord
Psalm 107—Let the Redeemed of the Lord Say So
Psalm 116—I Love the Lord Because He Has Heard My Voice
Psalm 138—I Will Praise You with My Whole Heart
Psalm 139—Search Me, O God, and Know My Heart
Psalm 146—I Will Sing Praises to My God While I Have My Being

IV. Royal Psalms
Psalm 2—The Lord Has Said to Me, "You Are My Son"
Psalm 18—The Lord Gives Great Deliverance to His King
Psalm 20—Now I Know that the Lord Saves His Anointed
Psalm 21—The King Shall Have Joy in Your Strength, O Lord
Psalm 45—Your Throne, O God, Is Forever and Ever
Psalm 61—O God, You Will Prolong the King's Life
Psalm 63—The King Shall Rejoice in God
Psalm 72—Give the King Your Judgments, O God
Psalm 89—Our King Belongs to the Holy One of Israel
Psalm 110—The Lord Said to My Lord, "Sit at My Right Hand"
Psalm 132—Lord, Remember David and All His Afflictions
Psalm 144—Blessed Be the Lord My Rock, Who Trains My Hands for War

V. Psalms of Trust and Wisdom
Psalm 1—The Delight of the Righteous Is in the Law of the Lord
Psalm 16—I Will Bless the Lord Who Has Given Me Counsel
Psalm 37—Trust in the Lord and Do Good
Psalm 49—My Mouth Shall Speak Wisdom
Psalm 73—I Have Put My Trust in the Lord God
Psalm 91—The Lord Is My Refuge and My Fortress
Psalm 112—Blessed Is the Man Who Fears the Lord
Psalm 127—Children Are a Heritage from the Lord
Psalm 128—Blessed Is Everyone Who Walks in His Ways
Psalm 131—O Israel, Hope in the Lord
Psalm 133—How Good It Is for Brethren to Dwell Together in Unity

tual purification. These laws and regulations were much more than sanitary instructions. The act of purification also involved religious and spiritual cleansing.

The Mosaic Law recognized and detailed purification rituals for three distinct categories of uncleanness. These were skin diseases (Lev. 13—14), sexual discharges (Leviticus 15), and contact with a dead body (Num. 19:11–19).

PURIM [pur′-im] *(lots)* — a Jewish holiday observed on the 14th and 15th of the month of Adar, a month before PASSOVER, in commemoration of the deliverance of the Jews, by ESTHER and MORDECAI, from a massacre plotted by HAMAN (Esth. 3:7; 9:24–32).

PURPLE — a color that represents royalty (Acts 16:14).

Q — the letter Q (from the German word *Quelle,* meaning "source") refers to a hypothetical document that contained material from which Matthew and Luke drew as they wrote certain sections of their Gospels. This document supposedly consisted mostly of sayings of Jesus in narrative form. Not all scholars accept the existence of Q as a background document to these Gospels.

QUAIL — a small bird. The Hebrew people probably ate dried, salted quail while they were enslaved by the Egyptians. When they longed for meat in the Sinai desert, God promised He would provide enough meat for a month. Then He directed thousands of quail to their camp, where the birds dropped in exhaustion (Num. 11:31–34; Ex. 16:13; Ps. 105:40).

QUARRY — an open excavation from which stone is cut, usually for building purposes. Archaeologists have discovered quarries throughout Palestine. The most notable quarries built during the Old Testament period are those near Megiddo, Samaria, Jerusalem, and Ramat Rahel. These four quarries date to about 850 B.C.

QUEEN — a female member of the royal house, either the wife of a king, or a woman who reigns by her own power. The term may refer to an actual ruler of state, such as the queen of

This massive cut stone was never removed from an ancient quarry at the Phoenician city of Baalbek, perhaps because of its weight and size. *Photo by Howard Vos*

Sheba (1 Kings 10) or Candace the queen of the Ethiopians (Acts 8:27). Bathsheba and Jezebel are not called queens, but certainly they ruled with their husbands (1 Kin. 1:21). On the other hand, a queen might be simply the king's favorite mate or wife—as probably was the case with both Vashti and Esther (Esther 1—2).

QUICK, QUICKEN — KJV translation of several Hebrew and Greek words translated by the NKJV as "alive" (Ps. 55:15), "living" (Acts 10:42), "revive" (Ps. 119:25), and "gives life to" (John 5:21).

QUIRINIUS [kwy-ren′-e-us] — Roman governor of Syria at the time of Jesus' birth (Luke 2:1–5; Cyrenius, KJV). Quirinius is mentioned in connection with a census taken for tax purposes. The census was not a local affair; the Roman emperor Augustus (ruled 31 B.C.—A.D. 14) had decreed that all the world, or the Roman Empire, should be taxed. For this purpose, Joseph and

Mary made their pilgrimage to Bethlehem. While they were there, Jesus was born.

QUIVER — as a verb, tremble (Hab. 3:16); as a noun, pouch for carrying arrows (Lam. 3:13).

QUMRAN, KHIRBET [kir′-bet koom′-rahn] — an ancient ruin on the northwestern shore of the Dead Sea. In 1947 a wandering goatherder looking for his goats in the caves above the dry riverbed of Qumran found several large jars. These jars contained the ancient scrolls that have since become known as the Dead Sea Scrolls. Following the discovery, the area was opened for extensive archaeological research.

From 1951 to 1956 excavation of the area revealed more scrolls, as well as dated coins, pottery, and fragments from scrolls. These items made it possible to connect the Dead Sea Scrolls discovered in nearby caves to the Qumran community, which lived in Khirbet Qumran from 130 B.C. to A.D. 135.

Cave Four at Qumran, where hundreds of Dead Sea Scrolls were discovered, is visible at upper right. The Dead Sea looms in the background. *Photo by Gustav Jeeninga*

R

RABBI [rab'-bi], **RABBONI** [rab-bo'-ni] *(my teacher)* — a title of honor and respect given by the Jews to a doctor (teacher) of the Law (John 1:38; 20:16). In our day rabbi means a Jew trained for professional religious leadership. In Jesus' day, however, the term had not yet become a formal title. Instead, it was a term of dignity given by the Jews to their distinguished teachers.

RABSHAKEH, THE [rab'-sha-keh] *(chief cup-bearer)* — the title of an Assyrian military official under Sennacherib, king of Assyria (2 Kin. 18:17–37; Is. 36:2–22).

RACA [ra'-cah] *(stupid)* — an expression of contempt (Matt. 5:22). The word appears often in the writings of the Jewish rabbis with the meaning of "ignorant, senseless, empty-headed." To say "Raca" to a person was like saying, "You idiot!"

RACHEL [ra'-chel] *(lamb)* — the younger daughter of Laban; the second wife of Jacob; and the mother of Joseph and Benjamin.

RAHAB [ra'-hab] — a harlot of Jericho who hid two Hebrew spies, helping them to escape, and who became an ancestor of David and Jesus (Josh. 2:1–21; 6:17–25; Matt. 1:5).

RAHAB THE DRAGON [ra'-hab] — a mythological sea monster or dragon representing the evil forces of chaos that God subdued by His creative power. The name Rahab as it occurs in Job 9:13(NIV), Job 26:12(NIV), Psalm 87:4 and 89:10, Isaiah 30:7(NIV), and Isaiah 51:9 has no connection with the personal name of Rahab, the harlot of Jericho, in Joshua 2:1–21. The references to Rahab in the Books of Job, Psalms, and Isaiah speak of an evil power overcome by God.

Ancient tomb near Bethlehem, traditionally identified as the burial place of Rachel (Gen. 48:2, 7). *Photo by Howard Vos*

216

RAIL — KJV translation of Hebrew and Greek words rendered by the NKJV as revile (2 Chr. 32:17; 1 Sam. 25:14), blasphemed (Mark 15:29; Luke 23:39), reviling (1 Tim. 6:4; 1 Pet. 3:9; 2 Pet. 2:11; Jude 9), and reviler (1 Cor. 5:11).

RAIMENT — clothing (Gen. 24:53; Matt. 3:4).

RAINBOW — an arch of colors in the sky, caused by light passing through moisture in the air. The most important reference to the rainbow in the Bible occurs in Genesis 9:13–17, where the rainbow serves as a sign of God's covenant with Noah.

RAM [ramm] *(high, exalted)* — a male goat used in sacrifices (Gen. 15:9), also a weapon, and the name of three men in the Bible.

RAMA [ra'-mah], **RAMAH** [ra'-mah] *(height)* — the name of six cities in the Old Testament. Two of importance being:

1. Ramah of Benjamin, one of the cities allotted to the tribe of Benjamin (Josh. 18:25) in the vicinity of Bethel (Judg. 4:5) and Gibeah (Judg. 19:13). According to Judges 4:5, Deborah lived between Ramah and Bethel.

2. Ramah of Ephraim, the birthplace, home, and burial place of the prophet Samuel (1 Sam. 7:17; 19:18–23; 28:3). It is elsewhere referred to as Ramathaim Zophim (1 Sam. 1:1). The exact location of this Ramah is unknown.

RAMESES, RAAMSES [ram'-ah-seez, ram'-seez] *(the god Ra has fathered a son)* — the royal city of the Egyptian kings of the 19th and 20th dynasties (about 1300—1100 B.C.) situated in the northeastern section of the Nile Delta. While the people of Israel were slaves in Egypt, they were forced to work on at least two of Pharaoh's vast construction projects—building the supply cities of Pithom and Raamses (Ex. 1:11, KJV, NASB, NKJV; Rameses, NIV, NRSV, REB).

RAMPART — a fortification consisting of an elevation or embankment often provided with a wall to protect soldiers. A rampart was used as a protective barrier against an attacking army. The Hebrew word translated as rampart (Lam. 2:8; Nah. 3:8) means encirclement; it is variously translated by the KJV as army, bulwark, host, rampart, trench, and wall.

RAPTURE — reference to the concept of Christians joining Christ upon His return (Mark

The modern village of Ramah, successor to the Old Testament city where the prophet Samuel was born and buried. *Photo by Howard Vos*

13:26–27; 1 Thess. 4:16–17). This word does not appear in the KJV.

RASH — impulsive (Eccl. 5:2).

REAP, REAPING — the practice of harvesting grain.

REAR — to raise, as with a child (Ex. 26:30).

REBECCA [re-bek′-kah]**, REBEKAH** [re-bek′-kah] — the wife of Isaac and the mother of Esau and Jacob. The story of Rebekah (Genesis 24) begins when Abraham, advanced in age, instructs his chief servant to go to Mesopotamia and seek a bride for Isaac. Abraham insisted that Isaac marry a young woman from his own country and kindred, not a Canaanite.

REBUKE — strong disapproval (Is. 25:8).

RECHAB [re′-kab] *(charioteer)* — the name of three men in the Old Testament:

1. A son of Rimmon, a Benjamite from Beeroth (2 Sam. 4:2, 5, 9; Recab, NIV).

2. The father of Jehonadab (2 Kin. 10:15, 23). Jehonadab assisted Jehu in his violent purge of the house of Ahab and zealous war against Baal worshipers. Jehonadab was the ancestor of the Rechabites (Jer. 35:1–19).

3. The father of Malchijah (Neh. 3:14). Malchijah may have been the head of the Rechabites

A rocky shore along the Red Sea, at a point north of where the Israelites crossed during the Exodus (Exodus 14). *Photo by Howard Vos*

after the Captivity. Malchijah helped Nehemiah rebuild the wall of Jerusalem.

RECKON — consider, count (Rom. 4:4).

RECOMPENSE — pay back, reward (Ruth 2:12; Luke 14:14).

RECONCILE, RECONCILIATION — the process by which God and people are brought together again. The Bible teaches that they are alienated from one another because of God's holiness and human sinfulness. Although God loves the sinner (Rom. 5:8), it is impossible for Him not to judge sin (Heb. 10:27).

RECORD — witness (John 1:19).

RECOUNT — call, summon (Nah. 2:5).

RED HEIFER — a young cow "without blemish" that was slaughtered outside the camp of the Israelites and then burned in the fire. Its ashes were used as a sin offering to bring about PURIFICATION from uncleanness. The need for purification from uncleanness would arise when a person touched a corpse, a human bone, or a grave (Num. 19:2–17).

RED SEA — a narrow body of water that stretches in a southeasterly direction from Suez to the Gulf of Aden for about 2,100 kilometers (1,300 miles). It is an important section of a large volcanic split in the earth that goes southward into east Africa and continues north along the Jordan Valley to the Lebanon mountain range.

REDEEM — to buy back or pay for (Gal. 3:13).

REDEMPTION — deliverance by payment of a price. In the New Testament, redemption refers to salvation from sin, death, and the wrath of God by Christ's sacrifice. In the Old Testament, the word redemption refers to redemption by a KINSMAN (Lev. 25:24, 51–52; Ruth 4:6; Jer. 32:7–8), rescue or deliverance (Num. 3:49), and ransom (Ps. 111:9; 130:7).

REED — a plant used to make baskets and paper (Matt. 27:30).

REEL — wobble like a drunk person (Is. 24:20).

REFINE — to separate pure metal from the impurities in the ore in the smelting process. This procedure is spoken of in the Old Testament as a symbol of God's purification of the nation of Israel when he sent hardship and affliction upon them in punishment for their sins (Jer. 9:7; Zech. 13:9).

REFRAIN — keep from doing (Acts 5:38).

REFUGE — safe place (Ps. 46:1).

REGENERATION — the spiritual change brought about in a person's life by an act of God. In regeneration a person's sinful nature is changed, and that person is enabled to respond to God in faith.

REGISTER — written record (Ezra 2:62).

REHOBOAM [re-ho-bo'-am] *(the people is enlarged)* — the son and successor of Solomon and the last king of the united monarchy and first king of the southern kingdom, Judah (reigned about 931—913 B.C.). His mother was Naamah, a woman of Ammon (1 Kin. 14:31).

REIGN — to rule (Matt. 2:22).

RELIEF — aid (Acts 11:29).

RELIGION, RELIGIOUS — belief in and reverence for God or some supernatural power that is recognized as the creator and ruler of the universe; an organized system of doctrine with an approved pattern of behavior and a proper form of worship. The classic New Testament passage on religion is James 2:17. Faith divorced from deeds, says James, is as lifeless as a corpse.

REMISSION — release from sin (Acts 2:38; Heb. 9:22).

REMNANT — the part of a community or nation that remains after a dreadful judgment or devastating calamity, especially those who have escaped and remain to form the nucleus of a new community (Is. 10:20–23). The survival of a righteous remnant rests solely on God's

The Preservation of the Remnant

In the eighth century B.C., Amos prophesied Israel's doom (8:1, 2), but he also declared the possibility of deliverance for the "remnant of Joseph" (5:15). Throughout history God has always preserved a remnant of His people, as the following chart shows.

People or Group	Reference
Noah and family in the Flood	Gen. 7:1
Joseph in Egypt during the famine	Gen. 45:7
Israel to their homeland	Deut. 4:27–31
7,000 who had not worshiped Baal	1 Kin. 19:18
Portion of Judah after captivity	Is. 10:20–23
Remnant to Zion	Mic. 2:12, 13
The church—both Jews and Gentiles	Rom. 9:22–27

providential care for His chosen people and His faithfulness to keep His COVENANT promises.

REND, RENT — to tear or pull apart. In the ancient world, rending one's garments was a sign of grief, despair, or sorrow. To "rend your heart" (Joel 2:13) signified inward, spiritual repentance and sorrow for sin. God's primary requirement from sinners is "a broken and a contrite heart" (Ps. 51:17).

RENDER — pay, return (Matt. 22:21).

RENOWN — fame (Ezek. 16:14).

REPENTANCE — a turning away from sin, disobedience, or rebellion and a turning back to God (Matt. 9:13; Luke 5:32). In a more general sense, repentance means a change of mind (Gen. 6:6–7) or a feeling of remorse or regret for past conduct (Matt. 27:3). True repentance is a "godly sorrow" for sin, an act of turning around and going in the opposite direction. This type of repentance leads to a fundamental change in a person's relationship to God.

REPHIDIM [ref'-i-dim] — an Israelite encampment in the wilderness (Ex. 17:1–7). The Amalekites attacked the Israelites at Rephidim (Ex. 17:8–16). During the battle Moses stood on a hill and held the rod of God aloft. Aaron and Hur supported his arms until sundown, and the Israelites won the battle. Rephidim is probably the modern Wadi Feiran in south central Sinai.

REPORT — testimony (Acts 6:3; 22:12).

REPROACH — scorn, rebuke, or shame (1 Tim. 3:7). On the Cross Christ bore the shame of our sin. Followers of Jesus are called to bear the reproach of Christ and to suffer for His name (2 Cor. 12:10; 1 Pet. 4:14)..

REPROBATE — one who fails to pass a test and is rejected. While the word "reprobate" only appears in the KJV, it speaks graphically of those whom God has rejected and left to their own cor-

ruption (Rom. 1:28). The prophet Jeremiah speaks of "reprobate silver" (Jer. 6:30, KJV).

REPROVE — convict (John 16:8).

REQUITE — repay (1 Tim. 5:4).

RESIDUE — that which remains; left over (Acts 15:17).

RESOLVED — figured out (Luke 16:4).

RESPECT OF PERSONS — showing favoritism or partiality toward some people as opposed to others (Acts 10:34; James 2:1).

RESPITE — relief, rest (Ex. 8:15).

RESTITUTION — the act of restoring to the rightful owner something that has been taken away, stolen, lost, or surrendered. Leviticus 6:1–7 gives the Mosaic Law of restitution; this law establishes the procedure to be followed in restoring stolen property.

RESURRECTION — being raised from the dead. Resurrection refers to individuals who have been brought back to life (resuscitated) in this present world (Matt. 22:23).

RESURRECTION OF JESUS CHRIST — a central doctrine of Christianity that affirms that God raised Jesus from the dead on the third day. Without the Resurrection, the apostle Paul declared, Christian preaching and belief are meaningless (1 Cor. 15:14). The Resurrection is the point at which God's intention for Jesus becomes clear (Rom. 1:4) and believers are assured that Jesus is the Christ.

REUBEN [ru'-ben] *(behold a son)* — the firstborn son of Jacob, born to Leah in Padan Aram (Gen. 29:31–32; 35:23). Leah named her first son Reuben because the Lord had looked upon her sorrow at being unloved by her husband. By presenting a son to Jacob, she hoped he would respond to her in love.

REVELATION — God's communication to people concerning Himself, His moral standards, and His plan of salvation (Rom. 16:25).

REVELATION:
A Study and Teaching Outline

Part One: *"The Things Which You Have Seen"* (1:1–20)

I. Introduction 1:1–8
II. Revelation of Christ. 1:9–20

Part Two: *"The Things Which Are"* (2:1—3:22)

I. Message to Ephesus 2:1–7
II. Message to Smyrna. 2:8–11
III. Message to Pergamos 2:12–17
IV. Message to Thyatria 2:18–29
V. Message to Sardis 3:1–6
VI. Message to Philadelphia 3:7–13
VII. Message to Laodicea. 3:14–22

Part Three: *"The Things Which Will Take Place after This"* (4:1—22:21)

I. Person of the Judge . . . . 4:1—5:14
   A. The Throne of God 4:1–11
   B. The Sealed Book. 5:1–14
II. Prophecies of Tribulation . . . . 6:1—19:6
   A. Seven Seals of Judgment. . . . . 6:1—8:5
   B. Seven Trumpets of Judgment . . . . 8:6—11:19
   C. Explanatory Prophecies . . . . 12:1—14:20
   D. Seven Bowls of Judgment . . . . 15:1—19:6
III. Prophecies of the Second Coming. 19:7–21
   A. Marriage Supper of the Lamb. 19:7–10
   B. Second Coming of Christ 19:11–21
IV. Prophecies of the Millennium. 20:1–15
   A. Satan Is Bound 1000 Years. 20:1–3
   B. Saints Reign 1000 Years. 20:4–6
   C. Satan Is Released and Leads Rebellion 20:7–9
   D. Satan Is Tormented Forever. 20:10
   E. Great White Throne Judgment. 20:11–15
V. Prophecies of the Eternal State . . . . 21:1—22:5
   A. New Heaven and Earth Are Created 21:1
   B. New Jerusalem Descends 21:2–8
   C. New Jerusalem Is Described . . . . 21:9—22:5
VI. Conclusion. 22:6–21

REVELATION OF JOHN — the last book of the Bible, and the only book of Apocalyptic Literature in the New Testament. *Apocalypsis*, the title of this book in the original Greek, means "unveiling" or "disclosure" of hidden things known only to God. Other examples of apocalyptic literature can be found in the Old Testament in Daniel (chs. 7–12), Isaiah (chs. 24–27), Ezekiel (chs. 37–41), and Zechariah (chs. 9–12).

The grand theme of the Book of Revelation is that of two warring powers, God and Satan, and of God's ultimate victory. It would be a mistake to consider the two powers as equal in might. God is stronger than Satan, and Satan continues his scheming plots only because God permits him to do so. Thus, at the final battle Satan and his followers are utterly destroyed—without a contest—by fire from heaven (20:7–10).

The Seven Churches of Revelation

	Commendation	Criticism	Instruction	Promise
Ephesus (2:1–7)	Rejects evil, perseveres, has patience	Love for Christ no longer fervent	Do the works you did at first	The tree of life
Smyrna (2:8–11)	Gracefully bears suffering	None	Be faithful until death	The crown of life
Pergamos (2:12–17)	Keeps the faith of Christ	Tolerates immo- rality, idolatry, and heresies	Repent	Hidden manna and a stone with a new name
Thyatira (2:18–29)	Love, service, faith, patience is greater than at first	Tolerates cult of idolatry and immorality	Judgment coming; keep the faith	Rule over nations and receive morning star
Sardis (3:1–6)	Some have kept the faith	A dead church	Repent; strengthen what remains	Faithful honored and clothed in white
Philadelphia (3:7–13)	Perseveres in the faith	None	Keep the faith	A place in God's presence, a new name, and the New Jerusalem
Laodicea (3:14–22)	None	Indifferent	Be zealous and repent	Share Christ's throne

REVERENCE — a feeling of profound awe and respect. Because of His majesty and holiness, God arouses a feeling of reverence in those who worship and serve Him (Heb. 12:28–29).

REVILE — to insult, despise (John 9:28).

REVIVE — bring back to life (Neh. 4:2; Rom. 14:9).

REVOLT — rebel against (2 Kin. 8:20).

REWARD — something offered in return for some service or benefit received. In the Bible, a reward can refer to something given for either a good or bad act. The psalmist, for example, speaks of "a reward for the righteous" (Ps. 58:11) and of "the reward of the wicked" (Ps. 91:8). When the Son of Man returns in glory, "He will reward each according to his works" (Matt. 16:27).

REZIN [re′-zin] — the name of two men in the Old Testament:

1. The last king of Syria. Rezin was killed by Tiglath–Pileser III, king of Assyria, in 732 B.C.

2. The founder of a family of Nethinim, or temple servants, whose descendants returned from the Captivity with Zerubbabel (Ezra 2:48).

RHODA [ro′-dah] *(rose)* — a servant girl in the home of Mary, the mother of John Mark (Acts 12:13). According to tradition, this house in Jerusalem was the site of the Last Supper; it may also have been the headquarters of the early church in Jerusalem. Following his miraculous release from prison, the apostle Peter went to Mary's house. Rhoda answered his knock and was filled with such surprise and joy that she forgot to let him in and ran back to tell the others. Peter had to continue knocking until someone let him in (Acts 12:16).

RHODES [rodes] *(a rose)* — a large island in the Aegean Sea off the southwest coast of Asia Minor visited by the apostle Paul (Acts 21:1). The island is about 68 kilometers (42 miles) long and about 24 kilometers (15 miles) wide; it lies about 19 kilometers (12 miles) off the coast of the province of Caria.

On the northeast corner of the island was the city of Rhodes, an important commercial, cultural, and tourist center for the Greeks as well as the Romans. At the entrance to the harbor of Rhodes stood the famous Colossus of Rhodes, a huge bronze statue of the sun-god Apollo built by the Greek sculptor Chares between 292 and 280 B.C. This towering statue was one of the seven wonders of the ancient world.

RIGHTEOUS — right with God (Mal. 3:18).

RIGHTEOUSNESS — holy and upright living, in accordance with God's standard. The word "righteousness" comes from a root word that means "straightness." It refers to a state that conforms to an authoritative standard. Righteousness is a moral concept. God's character is the definition and source of all righteousness (Gen. 18:25; Deut. 32:4; Rom. 9:14). Therefore, the righteousness of human beings is defined in terms of God's.

RIMMON [rim'-mon] *(pomegranate)* —a town in southern Judah allotted to the tribe of Simeon (Josh. 19:7; Remmon, KJV). Also a town on the border of Zebulun assigned to the Levites (Josh. 19:13; Rimmon-methoar, KJV; 1 Chr. 6:77), a rock near Gibeah, in the territory of Benjamin, where 600 Benjamites took refuge for four months (Judg. 20:45, 47), man from Beeroth in the territory of Benjamin whose two sons, Baanah and RECHAB, murdered Saul's son Ishbosheth, beheaded him, and took his head to David—an act for which they were executed (2 Sam. 4:1–12) and a Syrian god whose temple was at Damascus. NAAMAN the Syrian and his lord, the king of

St. Paul's Harbor at Rhodes where Paul's ship landed on its way back to Palestine after his third missionary journey (Acts 21:1). *Photo by Howard Vos*

Syria, worshiped Rimmon (2 Kin. 5:18). Rimmon was the god of rain and storm, lightning and thunder.

RIZPAH [riz'-pah] — a daughter of Aiah who became a concubine of King Saul (2 Sam. 3:7; 21:8, 10–11). She bore two sons, Armoni and Mephibosheth. After Saul's death, Abner had sexual relations with Rizpah (2 Sam. 3:7)—an act that amounted to claiming the throne of Israel.

ROBE — a cloak (John 19:2).

ROD — a staff, pole, or stick with many uses: a staff upon which a person may lean (Gen. 32:10; staff, KJV; Ex. 4:2); a club-like weapon (Ex. 21:20; 1 Sam. 14:27; Ps. 23:4); an instrument of punishment (2 Sam. 7:14; 1 Cor. 4:21); a shepherd's crook (Ezek. 20:37); a mark of authority, a scepter—such as Moses' rod (Ex. 4:20) and Aaron's rod (Num. 17:2–10); a measuring stick (Ezek. 40:3; Rev. 11:1); and a tool used to thresh grain (Is. 28:27).

ROE, ROEBUCK — a small deer (Deut. 12:15).

ROMANS, EPISTLE TO THE — the most formal and systematic of Paul's epistles. The main theme of Romans is that righteousness comes as a free gift of God and is receivable by faith alone. Romans stands at the head of the Pauline epistles because it is the longest of his letters, but it is also Paul's most important epistle.

The great theme of Romans is God's power to save. The Romans understood power; when Paul wrote this epistle to the capital of the ancient world, Rome ruled supreme. The gospel, however, is nothing to be ashamed of in comparison; for it, too, is power—indeed the "power of God to salvation for everyone" (1:16). In the gospel both Jews and Gentiles find access to God, not on the basis of human achievement, but because of God's free grace bestowed on those who accept it in faith.

ROME, CITY OF — capital city of the ancient Roman Empire and present capital of modern Italy.

Founded in 753 B.C., Rome was situated 24 kilometers (15 miles) from where the Tiber River flows into the Mediterranean Sea. From its initial

Ruins of the Forum in the city of Rome. The Forum was the meetingplace, marketplace, and religious and political center of the Roman Empire's capital city. *Photo by Gustav Jeeninga*

ROMANS:
A Study and
Teaching Outline

Part One: The Revelation of the Righteousness of God (1:1—8:39)

I.   Introduction 1:1–17
II. Condemnation: The Need for
     God's Righteousness . . . . 1:18—3:20
     A. Guilt of the Gentile 1:18–32
     B. Guilt of the Jew . . . . 2:1—3:8
     C. Conclusion: All Are Guilty before
         God 3:9–20
III. Justification: God's Righteousness . . . . . . 3:21—5:21
     A. Description of Righteousness 3:21–31
     B. Illustration of Righteousness 4:1–25
     C. Benefits of Righteousness 5:1–11
     D. Contrast of Righteousness and
         Condemnation 5:12–21
IV. Sanctification: The Demonstration of God's
     Righteousness . . . . 6:1—8:39
     A. Sanctification and Sin 6:1–23
     B. Sanctification and the Law 7:1–25
     C. Sanctification and the Spirit 8:1–39

Part Two: The Vindication of the Righteousness of God (9:1—11:36)

I.   Israel's Past: The Election of God 9:1–29
     A. A. Paul's Sorrow 9:1–5
     B. God's Sovereignty 9:6–29
II. Israel's Present: The Rejection of God . . . 9:30—10:21
     A. Israel Seeks Righteousness by
         Works 9:30–33
     B. Israel Rejects Christ 10:1–15
     C. Israel Rejects the Prophets 10:16–21
III. Israel's Future: The Restoration by God 11:1–36
     A. Israel's Rejection Is Not Total 11:1–10
     B. Israel's Rejection Is Not Final 11:11–32
     C. Israel's Restoration: The Occasion for
         Glorifying God 11:33–36

Part Three: The Application of the Righteousness of God (12:1—16:27)

I.   Righteousness of God Demonstrated in
     Christian Duties . . . . 12:1—13:14
     A. Responsibilities Toward God 12:1–2
     B. Responsibilities Toward Society 12:3–21
     C. Responsibilities Toward Government 13:1–7
     D. Responsibilities Toward Neighbors 13:8–14
II. Righteousness of God Demonstrated in
     Christian Liberties . . . . 14:1—15:13
     A. Principles of Christian Liberty 14:1–23
     B. Practices of Christian Liberty 15:1–13
III. Conclusion . . . . 15:14—16:27
     A. Paul's Purposes for Writing 15:14–21
     B. Paul's Plans for Traveling 15:22–33
     C. Paul's Praise and Greetings 16:1–27

settlement on the Palatine Hill near the river, the city gradually grew and embraced the surrounding area. Ultimately, the city was situated on seven hills: Capital, Palatine, Aventine, Caelian, Esquiline, Viminal, and Quirinal.

ROOT — the part of a plant that provides stability and nourishment for the plant. Most of the references to roots in the Bible are symbolic, based on this important relationship of the root to the plant. As a metaphor, to be rooted means

RUTH:
A Study and Teaching Outline

Part One: Ruth's Love Is Demonstrated (1:1—2:23)

Part Two: Ruth's Love Rewarded (3:1—4:22)

I. **Ruth's Decision to Remain with Naomi** 1:1–18
   A. Ruth's Need to Remain with Naomi 1:1–5
   B. Ruth's Opportunity to Leave Naomi 1:6–15
   C. Ruth's Choice to Remain with Naomi 1:16–18
II. **Ruth's Devotion to Care for Naomi.** . . . . . . 1:19—2:23
   A. Ruth and Naomi Return to Bethlehem. . . . 1:19–22
   B. Ruth Gleans for Food 2:1–23
      1. Boaz Meets Ruth 2:1–7
      2. Boaz Protects Ruth 2:8–16
      3. Boaz Provides for Ruth 2:17–23

I. **Ruth's Request for Redemption by Boaz** 3:1–18
   A. Naomi Seeks Redemption for Ruth 3:1–5
   B. Ruth Obeys Naomi 3:6–9
   C. Boaz Desires to Redeem Ruth 3:10–18
II. **Ruth's Reward of Redemption by Boaz.** 4:1–22
   A. Boaz Marries Ruth 4:1–12
   B. Ruth Bears a Son, Obed 4:13–15
   C. Naomi Receives a New Family 4:16
   D. Ruth Is the Great-grandmother
      David 4:17–22

to be established; to be uprooted means to be dispossessed.

RUDDY — a healthy, reddish color. In two places in the Bible the word refers to the rosy complexion of vigorous health (Song 5:10; Lam. 4:7). As a boy, David was also described as ruddy (1 Sam. 16:12; 17:42). Some scholars believe the word in this case may mean that David had red hair.

RUSH — a plant (Is. 9:14). (see BULRUSH).

RUTH [rooth] *(friendship)* — the mother of Obed and great-grandmother of David. A woman of the country of Moab, Ruth married Mahlon, one of the two sons of Elimelech and Naomi. With his wife and sons, Elimelech had migrated to Moab to escape a famine in the land of Israel. When Elimelech and both of his sons died, they left three widows: Naomi, Ruth, and Orpah (Ruth's sister-in-law). When Naomi decided to return home to Bethlehem, Ruth chose to accom-

pany her, saying, "Wherever you go, I will go" (Ruth 1:16).

RUTH, BOOK OF — a short Old Testament book about a devoted Gentile woman, Ruth of Moab, who became an ancestor of King David of Israel.

Ruth's life gives us a beautiful example of the providence of God. He brought Ruth to precisely the right field where she could meet Boaz. God is also portrayed in the book as the model of loyal and abiding love (2:20).

The name Ruth means "friendship," and this book contains one of the most touching examples of friendship in the Bible. Ruth's words to her mother-in-law are quoted often as a pledge of love and devotion. "Entreat me not to leave you, or to turn back from following after you; for wherever you go, I will go; wherever you lodge, I will lodge; your people shall be my people, and your God, my God" (1:16).

S

SABBATH [sab'-bath] — the practice of observing one day in seven as a time for rest and worship. This practice apparently originated in creation, because God created the universe in six days and rested on the seventh (Genesis 1). By this act, God ordained a pattern for living—that people should work six days each week at subduing and ruling the creation and should rest one day a week. This is the understanding of the creation set forth by Moses in Exodus 20:3–11, when he wrote the Ten Commandments at God's direction.

SACKCLOTH — a rough, coarse cloth, or a baglike garment made of this cloth and worn as a symbol of mourning or repentance. In the Bible sackcloth was often used to symbolize certain actions. In the case of mourning, either over a death (Gen. 37:34; Joel 1:8) or another calamity (Esth. 4:1–4; Job 16:15), the Israelites showed their grief by wearing sackcloth and ashes. This was done also in instances of confession and grief over sin (1 Kin. 21:27).

SACRIFICE — the ritual through which the Hebrew people offered the blood or the flesh of an animal to God as a substitute payment for their sin. Sacrifice and sacrificing originated in the Garden of Eden soon after the FALL of mankind.

SADDUCEES [sad'-du-sees] — members of a Jewish faction that opposed Jesus during His

Sacrificial altar for wine and fruit at the Nabatean city of Petra in southern Canaan. *Photo by Gustav Jeeninga*

227

ministry. Known for their denial of the bodily resurrection, the Sadducees came from the leading families of the nation—the priests, merchants, and aristocrats. The high priests and the most powerful members of the priesthood were mainly Sadducees (Acts 5:17).

SAINTS — people who have been separated from the world and consecrated to the worship and service of God. Followers of the Lord are referred to by this phrase throughout the Bible, although its meaning is developed more fully in the New Testament. Consecration (setting apart) and purity are the basic meanings of the term. Believers are called "saints" (Rom. 1:7) and "saints in Christ Jesus" (Phil. 1:1) because they belong to the One who provided their sanctification.

SALVATION — deliverance from the power of sin; redemption.

In the Old Testament, the word "salvation" sometimes refers to deliverance from danger (Jer. 15:20), deliverance of the weak from an oppressor (Ps. 35:9–10), the healing of sickness (Is. 38:20), and deliverance from blood guilt and its consequences (Ps. 51:14). It may also refer to national deliverance from military threat (Ex. 14:13) or release from captivity (Ps. 14:7). But salvation finds its deepest meaning in the spiritual realm of life. Our universal need for salvation is one of the clearest teachings of the Bible.

SAMARIA, CITY OF [sa-ma′-re-ah] *(look-out)* — the capital city of the northern kingdom of Israel.

Built about 880 B.C. by Omri, the sixth king of Israel (1 Kin. 16:24), Samaria occupied a 91-meter (300-foot) high hill about 68 kilometers (42 miles) north of Jerusalem and 40 kilometers (25 miles) east of the Mediterranean Sea. This hill was situated on the major north-south road through Palestine. It also commanded the east-west route to the Plain of Sharon and the Mediterranean Sea. Because of its hilltop location, Samaria could be defended easily. Its only

weakness was that the nearest spring was a mile distant, but this difficulty was overcome by the use of cisterns.

SAMARITANS [sa-mar′-i-tans] — natives or inhabitants of Samaria, a distinct territory or region in central Canaan.

SAMUEL [sam′-u-el] *(name of God)* — the earliest of the great Hebrew prophets (after Moses) and the last judge of Israel. Samuel led his people against their Philistine oppressors. When he was an old man, Samuel anointed Saul as the first king of Israel and later anointed David as Saul's successor. Samuel is recognized as one of the greatest leaders of Israel (Jer. 15:1; Heb. 11:32).

SAMUEL, BOOKS OF — two historical books of the Old Testament that cover the nation of Israel's transition from a loose tribal form of government to a united kingship under Saul and David. The books are named for the prophet Samuel, who anointed these two leaders.

The major theological contribution of 1 and 2 Samuel is the negative and positive views of the kingship that they present. On the negative side, the books make it clear that in calling for a king the people were rejecting God's rule. Because Israel was unable to live under God's rule through the judges, God gave in to their demands and granted them a king. But He also warned them about the dangers of the kingship (1 Sam. 8:9–21).

On the positive side, 1 and 2 Samuel portray the kingship as established through David as a clear picture of God's purpose for His people. The COVENANT that God established with David demonstrated God's purpose through David's family line; David's ancestors would be adopted as the sons of God in a special sense (2 Samuel 7). David's line would continue through the centuries, and his throne would be established forever (2 Sam. 7:13). In the person of Jesus Christ the Messiah, this great covenant came to its fulfillment.

FIRST SAMUEL:
A Study and Teaching Outline

Part One: Samuel, the Last Judge (1:1—7:17)

I. **The First Transition of National Leadership: Eli-Samuel**............................1:1—3:21
  A. The Birth of the New Leader..........1:1—2:11
  B. The Need of the New Leader.........2:12—2:36
  C. The Transition from Eli to Samuel.......3:1—18
  D. Samuel Is Recognized as the New Leader of Israel................................3:19—21
II. **The Judgeship of Samuel** ....4:1—7:17
  A. The Need for Samuel's Leadership .....4:1—6:21
  B. The Victories under Samuel's Leadership . . 7:1—17

Part Two: Saul, the First King (8:1—31:13)

I. **The Second Transition of National Leadership: Samuel-Saul** ....8:1—12:25
  A. The Causes of the Transition.............8:1—9
  B. The Transition from Samuel to Saul . . 8:10—12:25
II. **The Reign of King Saul** ....13:1—16:13
  A. The Early Success of King Saul..........13:1—4
  B. The Failures of King Saul ....13:5—16:13
III. **The Third Transition of National Leadership: Saul-David**........................16:14—31:13
  A. The Transition of Kingship from Saul to David.........................16:14—18:9
  B. The Attempts of Saul to Slay David . . 18:10—20:42
  C. The Rise of David in Exile...........21:1—28:2
  D. The Final Decline of Saul ....28:3—31:13

SECOND SAMUEL:
A Study and Teaching Outline

Part One: The Triumphs of David (1:1—10:19)

I. **The Political Triumphs of David** ....1:1—5:25
  A. The Reign of David in Hebron over Judah ....1:1—4:12
  B. The Reign of David in Jerusalem over All Israel ....5:1—25
II. **The Spiritual Triumphs of David** ....6:1—7:29
  A. The Transportation of the Ark ....6:1—23
  B. The Institution of the Davidic Covenant . . . 7:1—29
III. **The Military Triumphs of David** ....8:1—10:19
  A. The Triumphs of David over His Enemies . . 8:1—12
  B. The Righteous Rule of David.........8:13—9:13
  C. The Triumphs of David over Ammon and Syria...........................10:1—19

Part Two: The Transgressions of David (11:1—27)

I. **The Sin of Adultery** ....11:1—5
II. **The Sin of Murder** ....11:6—27
  A. Uriah Does Not Sleep with Bathsheba .... 11:6—13
  B. David Commands Uriah's Murder ......11:14—25
  C. David and Bathsheba Marry...........11:26—27

Part Three: The Troubles of David (12:1—24:25)

I. **The Troubles in David's House** ....12:1—13:36
  A. Prophecy by Nathan..................12:1—14
  B. David's Son Dies....................12:15—25
  C. Joab's Loyalty to David...............12:26—31
  D. Incest in David's House ....13:1—20
  E. Amnon Is Murdered.................13:21—36
II. **The Troubles in David's Kingdom**.......13:37—24:25
  A. Rebellion of Absalom..............13:37—17:29
  B. Absalom Is Murdered..................18:1—33
  C. David Is Restored as King ....19:1—20:26
  D. The Commentary on the Reign of David........................21:1—24:25

A fragment of 1 Samuel 23:9–16 discovered at Qumran. It dates from the third century B.C.

Photo by Howard Vos

SANCTIFICATION — the process of God's grace by which the believer is separated from sin and becomes dedicated to God's righteousness. Accomplished by the Word of God (John 17:7) and the Holy Spirit (Rom. 8:3–4), sanctification results in holiness, or purification from the guilt and power of sin.

SANCTIFY — to set apart (Gen. 2:3), dedicate for God's use (Ex. 13:2).

SANHEDRIN [san'-he-drin] — the highest ruling body and court of justice among the Jewish people in the time of Jesus. Headed by the high priest of Israel, the Sanhedrin was granted limited authority over certain religious, civil, and criminal matters by the foreign nationas that dominated Israel at various times in its history.

SAPPHIRA [saf-fi'-rah] — a dishonest woman who, along with her husband Ananias, held back goods from the early Christian community after they had agreed to share everything. Because of their hypocrisy and deceit, they were struck dead by God (Acts 5:1–11). This may seem like a severe punishment for such an offense. But it points out the need for absolute honesty in all our dealings with God.

SARAH, SARAI [sa'-rah, sa'-rahee] *(noble lady)* — the name of two women in the Bible:

1. The wife of ABRAHAM, and the mother of ISAAC. Sarah's name was originally Sarai, but it was changed to Sarah by God, much as her husband's name was changed from Abram to Abraham. Ten years younger than Abraham, Sarah was his half-sister; they had the same father but different mothers (Gen. 20:12).

2. A daughter of Asher (Num. 26:46, KJV; Serah, NKJV, NIV).

SATAN [sa'-tun] *(adversary)* — the great opposer, or Adversary, of God and humankind; the personal name of the devil.

SAUL [sawl] *(asked* [of God]*)* — the name of three men in the Bible:

1. The sixth of the ancient kings of Edom (Gen. 36:36–38; 1 Chr. 1:48–49).

2. The first king of Israel (1 Sam. 9:2–31:12; 1 Chr. 5:10—26:28).

3. The original name of PAUL, a persecutor of the church, who became an apostle of Christ and a missionary of the early church (Acts 7:58—9:26; 11:25—13:9).

SAVIOR — a person who rescues others from evil, danger, or destruction. The Old Testament viewed God Himself as the Savior: "There is no other God besides Me, a just God and a Savior" (Is. 45:21). Because God is the source of salvation, He sent human deliverers to rescue His people, Israel (Ps. 106:21; Is. 43:3, 11). This word was also used to describe the judges of Israel, those "saviors" or "deliverers" who rescued God's people from oppression by their enemies (Judg. 3:9, 15).

Names of Satan		
1. Accuser	Opposes believers before God	Rev. 12:10
2. Adversary	Against God	1 Pet. 5:8
3. Beelzebub	Lord of the fly	Matt. 12:24
4. Belial	Worthless	2 Cor. 6:15
5. Devil	Slanderer	Matt. 4:1
6. Dragon	Destructive	Rev. 12:3, 7, 9
7. Enemy	Opponent	Matt. 13:28
8. Evil one	Intrinsically evil	John 17:15
9. God of this age	Influences thinking of world	2 Cor. 4:4
10. Liar	Perverts the truth	John 8:44
11. Murderer	Leads people to eternal death	John 8:44
12. Prince of the power of the air	Control of unbelievers	Eph. 2:2
13. Roaring lion	One who destroys	1 Pet. 5:8
14. Ruler of demons	Leader of fallen angels	Mark 3:22
15. Ruler of this world	Rules in world system	John 12:31
16. Satan	Adversary	1 Tim. 5:15
17. Serpent of old	Deceiver in garden	Rev. 12:9; 20:2
18. Tempter	Solicits people to sin	1 Thess. 3:5

In the New Testament the word for "savior" describes both God the Father (1 Tim. 1:1; Jude 25) and Jesus Christ the Son (Acts 5:31; Phil. 3:20). The apostles rejoiced that in Christ, God had become the "Savior of all men" (1 Tim. 4:10). He was the Savior of Gentiles as well as Jews. As Christians, we are exhorted to "grow in the grace and knowledge of our Lord and Savior Jesus Christ" (2 Pet. 3:18).

SCAPEGOAT — a live goat over whose head AARON confessed all the sins of the people of Israel. The goat was then sent into the wilderness on the Day of Atonement, symbolically taking away their sins (Lev. 16:8, 10, 26; Azazel, NRSV).

SCROLL — a roll of papyrus, leather, or parchment on which an ancient document—particularly a text of the Bible—was written (Ezra 6:2). Rolled up on a stick, a scroll was usually about 11 meters (35 feet) long—the size required, for instance, for the Book of Luke or the Book of Acts. Longer books of the Bible required two or more scrolls.

SECURITY OF THE BELIEVER — the "once saved, always saved" concept taught from the Bible (Rom. 8:38–39; Phil. 1:6) Denominations have differing opinions on this topic.

SELAH [se'-lah] — This word occurs 71 times in the Book of Psalms. Scholars agree that the

These copper scrolls were discovered among the Dead Sea Scrolls at Qumran. Most scrolls in ancient times were written on papyrus, parchment, or leather. *Photo by Howard Vos*

term is a musical direction of some sort, but they are not agreed on what the direction is. It may mean: (1) an interlude—a pause in the singing while the orchestra continues; (2) the equivalent of today's "Amen"; as such it would separate psalms or sections of psalms which have different liturgical purposes; and (3) an acrostic that means "a change of voices" or "repeat."

SEMITES — descendants of Shem, Noah's son, including the people of Assyria (Gen. 5:32; Luke 3:36).

SEPTUAGINT — The oldest Bible translation in the world was made in Alexandria, Egypt, where the Old Testament was translated from Hebrew into Greek for the benefit of the Greek-speaking Jews of that city. A Jewish community had existed in Alexandria almost from its foundation by the Great in 331 B.C. In two or three generations this community had forgotten its native Palestinian language. These Jews realized they needed the Hebrew Scriptures rendered into the only language they knew—Greek.

This version is commonly called the Septuagint, from the Latin word for seventy. This name was selected because of a tradition that the Pentateuch was translated into Greek by about seventy elders of Israel who were brought to Alexandria especially for this purpose.

SEPULCHER, SEPULCHRE — tomb (Matt. 27:61).

SERAPHIM [ser'-a-fim] *(fiery, burning ones)* — angelic or heavenly beings associated with Isaiah's vision of God in the temple when he was called to his ministry (Is. 6:1–7). This is the only place in the Bible that mentions these mysterious creatures. Each seraph had six wings. They used two to fly, two to cover their feet, and two to cover their faces (Is. 6:2). The seraphim flew about the throne on which God was seated, singing His praises as they called special attention to His glory and majesty.

SERPENT — a crawling reptile, or snake, often associated in the Bible with temptation, sin, and evil. A serpent is the Bible's first—and final—animal villan (Gen. 3; Rev. 20:2).

SERVANT — slave (Rom. 1:1).

SETH [seth] *(appoint, compensate)* — the third son of Adam and Eve, born after Cain murdered Abel (Gen. 4:25–26; 5:3–8; Sheth, KJV). The father of Enosh (or Enos) and an ancestor of Jesus Christ (Luke 3:38), Seth died at the age of 912.

SHADRACH [sha'-drak] *(command of* [the god] *Aku)* — the name that Ashpenaz, the chief of Nebuchadnezzar's eunuchs, gave to Hananiah, one of the Jewish princes who were carried away to Babylon in 605 B.C. (Dan. 1:7; 3:12–30).

Shadrach was one of the three faithful Jews who refused to worship the golden image that King Nebuchadnezzar of Babylon set up (Dan. 3:1). Along with his two companions, MESHACH and ABED-NEGO, Shadrach was "cast into the midst of a burning fiery furnace" (Dan. 3:11, 21). But they were protected by a fourth "man" in the fire (Dan. 3:25), and they emerged without even the smell of fire upon them (Dan. 3:27).

SHEKEL — a unit measure (Ex. 30:23–24). (see WEIGHTS AND MEASURES OF THE BIBLE).

SHEKINAH [she-ki'-nah] *(dwelling)* — a visible manifestation of the presence of God (also spelled Shechinah and Shekhinah). Although the word is not found in the Bible, it occurs frequently in later Jewish writings.

SHEMA, THE [she-mah'] *(hear thou)* — the Jewish confession of faith that begins, "Hear, O Israel: The Lord our God, the LORD is one!" (Deut. 6:4). The complete Shema is found in three passages from the Old Testament: Numbers 15:37–41, Deuteronomy 6:4–9 and 11:13–21.

SHEOL [she'-ol] — in Old Testament thought, the abode of the dead. Sheol is the Hebrew equivalent of the Greek *Hades*, which means "the unseen world."

SHOWBREAD — holy or consecrated bread placed in the sanctuary of the tabernacle or temple every Sabbath to symbolize God's presence and provision for the people. The ritual always involved twelve loaves of bread, representing the twelve tribes of the nation of Israel. It was called showbread (shewbread, KJV; bread of the Presence, NIV) because it was kept continually before God's presence in the tabernacle.

SIN — lawlessness (1 John 3:4) or transgression of God's will, either by omitting to do what God's Law requires or by doing what it forbids. The transgression can occur in thought (1 John 3:15), word (Matt. 5:22), or deed (Rom. 1:32).

SIN OFFERING — offering given out of repentance (Lev. 4:2–35).

SINAI [si′-nai] — the name of a peninsula, a wilderness, and a mountain in the Bible.

SOLEMN ASSEMBLY — a day set aside to devote one's self to God and be humble (Lev. 23:36); different from the Sabbath.

SOLOMON [sol′-o-mon] *(peaceful)* — the builder of the temple in Jerusalem and the first king of Israel to trade commercial goods profitably to other nations; author of much of the Book of Proverbs and perhaps also the author of the Song of Solomon and Ecclesiastes.

SONG OF SOLOMON, THE — an Old Testament book written in the form of a lyrical love song. Some interpreters believe this song speaks symbolically of the love of God for the nation of Israel. But others insist it should be interpreted literally—as a healthy expression of romantic love between a man and a woman. No matter how the book is interpreted, it is certainly one of the most unusual in the Bible. Its title, "the song of songs" (1:1), implies it was the loveliest and best-known of all the songs of Solomon.

The great message of the Song of Solomon is the beauty of love between a man and a woman as experienced in the relationship of marriage. In its frank but beautiful language, the song praises the mutual love that husband and wife feel toward each other in this highest of all human relationships.

The sexual and physical side of marriage is a natural and proper part of God's plan, reflecting His purpose and desire for the human race. This is the same truth so evident at the beginning of time in the Creation itself. God created man and woman and brought them together to serve as

---

SONG OF SOLOMON:
A Study and Teaching Outline

I. **The Beginning of Love** . . . . 1:1—5:1
  A. Falling in Love . . . . 1:1—3:5
    1. Bride's Longing for Affection 1:1–8
    2. Expressions of Mutual Love . . . . 1:9—2:7
    3. Visit of the King to the Bride's Home . . . 2:8–17
    4. Bride's Dream of Separation 3:1–5
  B. United in Love . . . . 3:6—5:1
    1. Wedding Procession 3:6–11
    2. Bride's Beauty Is Praised 4:1–15
    3. Marriage Is Consummated . . . . 4:16—5:1
II. **The Broadening of Love** . . . . 5:2—8:14
  A. Struggling in Love . . . . 5:2—7:9
    1. Bride's Second Dream of Separation 5:2–8
    2. Bridegroom's Handsomeness
       Is Praised . . . . 5:9—6:3
    3. Bride's Beauty Is Praised . . . . 6:4—7:9
  B. Growing in Love . . . . 7:10—8:14
    1. Bride's Desire to Visit Her Home . . . . 7:10—8:4
    2. Journey and Homecoming 8:5–14

Solomon's Empire

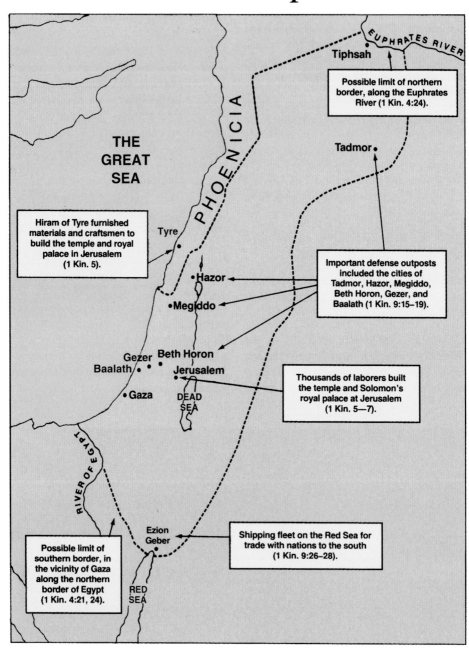

THE
GREAT
SEA

PHOENICIA

EUPHRATES RIVER

Tiphsah

Possible limit of northern
border, along the Euphrates
River (1 Kin. 4:24).

Tadmor

Hiram of Tyre furnished
materials and craftsmen to
build the temple and royal
palace in Jerusalem
(1 Kin. 5).

Tyre

•Hazor

•Megiddo

Important defense outposts
included the cities of
Tadmor, Hazor, Megiddo,
Beth Horon, Gezer, and
Baalath (1 Kin. 9:15–19).

Gezer Beth Horon
Baalath/• •
Jerusalem

• Gaza   DEAD
            SEA

Thousands of laborers built
the temple and Solomon's
royal palace at Jerusalem
(1 Kin. 5—7).

RIVER OF EGYPT

Ezion
Geber
•

Shipping fleet on the Red Sea for
trade with nations to the south
(1 Kin. 9:26–28).

Possible limit of
southern border, in
the vicinity of Gaza
along the northern
border of Egypt
(1 Kin. 4:21, 24).

RED
SEA

Solomon's Twelve Districts

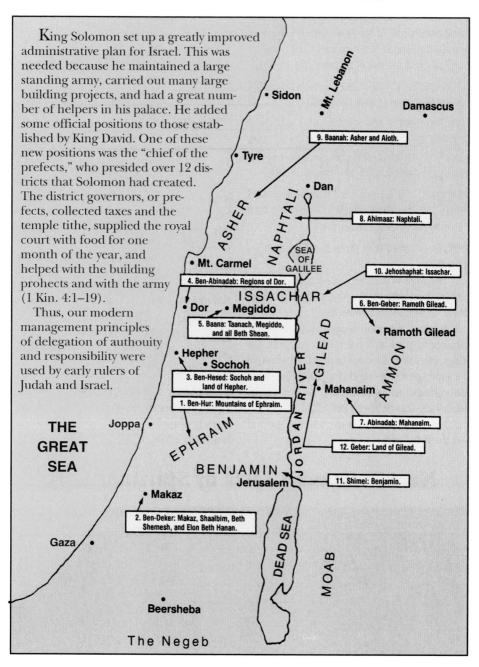

King Solomon set up a greatly improved administrative plan for Israel. This was needed because he maintained a large standing army, carried out many large building projects, and had a great number of helpers in his palace. He added some official positions to those established by King David. One of these new positions was the "chief of the prefects," who presided over 12 districts that Solomon had created. The district governors, or prefects, collected taxes and the temple tithe, supplied the royal court with food for one month of the year, and helped with the building prohects and with the army (1 Kin. 4:1–19).

Thus, our modern management principles of delegation of authouity and responsibility were used by early rulers of Judah and Israel.

• Sidon

Mt. Lebanon

Damascus

9. Baanah: Asher and Aloth.

• Tyre

• Dan

ASHER

NAPHTALI

8. Ahimaaz: Naphtali.

SEA OF GALILEE

• Mt. Carmel

10. Jehoshaphat: Issachar.

4. Ben-Abinadab: Regions of Dor.

ISSACHAR

• Dor   • Megiddo

6. Ben-Geber: Ramoth Gilead.

5. Baana: Taanach, Megiddo, and all Beth Shean.

GILEAD

• Ramoth Gilead

AMMON

• Hepher
  • Sochoh

3. Ben-Hesed: Sochoh and land of Hepher.

JORDAN RIVER

• Mahanaim

1. Ben-Hur: Mountains of Ephraim.

7. Abinadab: Mahanaim.

THE GREAT SEA

Joppa •

EPHRAIM

12. Geber: Land of Gilead.

BENJAMIN

Jerusalem

11. Shimei: Benjamin.

• Makaz

2. Ben-Deker: Makaz, Shaalbim, Beth Shemesh, and Elon Beth Hanan.

DEAD SEA

MOAB

Gaza •

• Beersheba

The Negeb

companions and to share their lives with one another: "Therefore a man shall leave his father and mother and be joined to his wife, and they shall become one flesh" (Gen. 2:24). Like the Book of Genesis, the Song of Solomon says a bold "yes" to the beauty and sanctity of married love.

SOUTHERN KINGDOM — the tribes of Judah and Benjamin (1 Kin. 14:19–30).

SOVEREIGNTY OF GOD — a theological term that refers to the unlimited power of God, who has sovereign control over the affairs of nature and history (Is. 45:9–19; Rom. 8:18–39).

SPAN — the distance between the extended thumb and the little finger (Ex. 28:16). (see WEIGHTS AND MEASURES OF THE BIBLE).

SPIRIT — a word with three distinct meanings in the Bible:

1. The word is used as a general reference in the New Testament to the spirit of human beings (Matt. 5:3; Rom. 8:16; Heb. 4:12).

2. A second common usage of the word is in reference to good and evil spirits, meaning the beings other than God and humans. An example of a good spirit is an angel (Ps. 104:4). The Bible also contains many references to evil spirits (Mark 9:25; Acts 19:12–17; Rev. 18:2).

3. The word "spirit" also refers to the Spirit of God, the Holy Spirit.

SPIRITUAL — of the spirit or nonmaterial. The word spiritual refers to nonmaterial things, including a spiritual body (1 Cor. 15:44–46) and spiritual things as distinct from earthly goods (Rom. 15:27; 1 Cor. 9:11). But the most important use of the word is in reference to the Holy Spirit. The Spirit gave the law (Rom. 7:14) and supplied Israel with water and food (1 Cor. 10:3–4).

SPIRITUAL GIFTS — special gifts bestowed by the Holy Spirit upon Christians for the purpose of building up the church. The list of spiritual gifts in 1 Corinthians 12:8–10 includes wisdom, knowledge, faith, healing, miracles, prophecy, discerning of spirits, speaking in tongues, and interpretation of tongues. Similar lists appear in Ephesians 4:7–13 and Romans 12:3–8.

STATUTE — a decree or law issued by a ruler or governing body, or especially by God as the supreme ruler (Gen. 26:5; Ps. 18:22; Ezek. 5:6).

STEPHEN [ste'-ven] — one of the first seven deacons of the early church and the first Christian martyr. The story of Stephen is found in Acts 6:7—7:60.

STEWARD, STEWARDSHIP — one who manages money or property for another; the management of another person's property, finances, or household affairs. As far as Christians are con-

New Testament Lists of Spiritual Gifts

Romans 12:6–8	1 Cor. 12:8–10	1 Cor. 12:28–30	Eph. 4:11	1 Peter 4:9–11
Prophecy	Word of Wisdom	Apostleship	Apostleship	Speaking
Serving	Word of Knowledge	Prophecy	Prophecy	Serving
Teaching	Faith	Teaching	Evangelism	
Exhortation	Healings	Miracles	Pastor/Teacher	
Giving	Miracles	Healing		
Leading	Prophecy	Helping		
Showing Mercy	Discerning of Spirits	Administrating		
	Tongues	Tongues		
	Interpretation of Tongues	Interpretation of Tongues		

cerned, stewardship involves the responsibility of managing God's work through the church. God has appointed all Christians to be His stewards on earth. Stewardship is not an option, as Paul points out about his own call. Being a steward is a necessary part of believing the gospel, even if it involves sacrificing personal rewards (1 Cor. 9:17).

SUBJECT — obedient to (Luke 2:51); under control of (Heb. 2:15).

SUBMISSION, SUBMIT — yield; can be by force or voluntary (Eph. 5:21; Jas. 4:7).

SUFFER, SUFFERING — agony, affliction, or distress; intense pain or sorrow. Suffering has been part of the human experience since people fell into sin (Genesis 3).

SUPPLICATION — request humbly and earnestly, usually in the form of prayer (Job 8:5).

SWADDLE — to wrap in swaddling cloths. These were long, narrow strips of cloth wrapped around a newborn infant to restrict movement (Job 38:9; Luke 2:7, 12).

SWADDLING BAND — a long, narrow strip of cloth used to wrap a newborn baby. To swaddle a child was to wrap an infant in strips of cloth, much like narrow bandages. This was believed to ensure the correct early development of the limbs. Thus, swaddling was a mark of parental love and care, while the need for swaddling symbolized the humble, dependent position of the newborn child (Ezek. 16:4).

SYCAMORE — large tree good for climbing (Luke 19:4); not the same as a modern day sycamore tree.

SYNAGOGUE [syn'-a-gog] — a congregation of Jews for worship or religious study. The word synagogue comes from the Greek *synagoge* (literally, "a leading or bringing together"), which refers to any assembly or gathering of people for secular or religious purposes. Eventually the term came to refer exclusively to an assembly of Jewish people.

The synagogue was a place where local groups of Jews in cities and villages anywhere could gather for the reading and explanation of the Jewish sacred Scriptures and for prayer. The original emphasis was not on preaching but instruction in the Law of Moses.

SYRIA [sihr'-e-ah] — a major nation northeast of Palestine that served as a political threat to the nations of Judah and Israel during much of their history.

A synagogue at Masada. The synagogue was a place of worship, instruction, teaching of Scripture, and prayer for the Jewish people (Acts 13:13–15). *Photo by Gustav Jeeninga*

Remains of a synagogue at Capernaum. It was probably built during the third or fourth century A.D. *Photo by Gustav Jeeninga*

TABERNACLE [tab'-er-nack-el] — the tent that served as a place of worship for the nation of Israel during their early history.

TABERNACLES, FEAST OF — Festival observed on the fifteenth day of the seventh month to celebrate the completion of the autumn harvest. Features of the celebration included a holy convocation on the first and eighth days, and the offering of animal sacrifices. The Israelites were also commanded to live in booths made of palm and willow trees during the festival to commemorate their period of wilderness wandering when they lived in temporary shelters. (Ex. 23:16; Lev. 23:34–36; Num 29:12–32; Deut. 16:13–16).

TABITHA [tab'-ith-ah] — a follower of Jesus (Acts 9:36–42). Another name for DORCAS.

TABLE — an article of furniture used for ritual, eating, and money changing. The tabernacle had a table of acacia wood overlaid with gold on which the showbread was placed (Ex. 25:23; Num. 3:31; Heb. 9:2). A table of gold was in the temple (1 Kin. 7:48). Tables for the burnt offering were furnishings of Ezekiel's temple (Ezek. 40:39–43). There was also a table before the sanctuary (Ezek. 41:22; 44:16). The prophet Malachi spoke of the altar as the Lord's table (Mal. 1:7, 12).

TABLET — a word with several different meanings in the Bible:

1. The tablets of stone on which God wrote the law given to Moses at Mount Sinai (Ex. 24:12; Deut. 10:1–5).

2. Ordinary writing tablets made of clay or wood (Ezek. 4:1; Luke 1:63).

3. The Bible also uses the word "tablet" to speak of God's Law written on the heart (Prov. 3:3; Jer. 17:1; 2 Cor. 3:3).

TALENT — used as a unit of weight and also as money (Ex. 25:39; Rev. 16:21). (see WEIGHTS AND MEASURES OF THE BIBLE, MONEY OF THE BIBLE).

TAMAR [ta'-mar] *(palm)* — the name of three women and a city in the Bible, most notably the lovely daughter of David by Maacah, and sister of Absalom (2 Sam. 13:1–22, 32; 1 Chr. 3:9). Tamar was raped by her half-brother Amnon. She fled to Absalom, who plotted revenge. Two years later Absalom got his revenge for Tamar by arranging Amnon's murder.

TANNER — a person who makes leather from animal skins (Acts 9:43).

TARRY — wait or delay (Heb. 10:37).

TARSHISH [tar'-shish] *(jasper)* — the name of a type of ship, a city or territory, a man, and a precious stone in the Old Testament:

1. The Hebrew name for a type of cargo ship fitted for long sea voyages (1 Kin. 10:22; Tharshish, KJV).

2. A city or territory in the western portion of the Mediterranean Sea with which the Phoenicians traded (2 Chr. 9:21; Ps. 72:10).

3. A high official at Shushan (Susa). He was one of seven princes of Persia and Media "who had access to the king's presence" (Esth. 1:14).

4. The Hebrew name of a precious stone (Ex. 28:20; Ezek. 28:13). Its brilliant color is associated with the glorious appearance of God Himself (Ezek. 1:16; Dan. 10:6).

The Plan of the Tabernacle

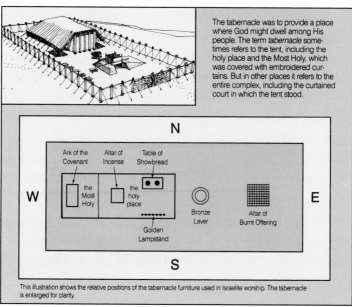

The tabernacle was to provide a place where God might dwell among His people. The term *tabernacle* sometimes refers to the tent, including the holy place and the Most Holy, which was covered with embroidered curtains. But in other places it refers to the entire complex, including the curtained court in which the tent stood.

This illustration shows the relative positions of the tabernacle furniture used in Israelite worship. The tabernacle is enlarged for clarity.

The Furniture of the Tabernacle

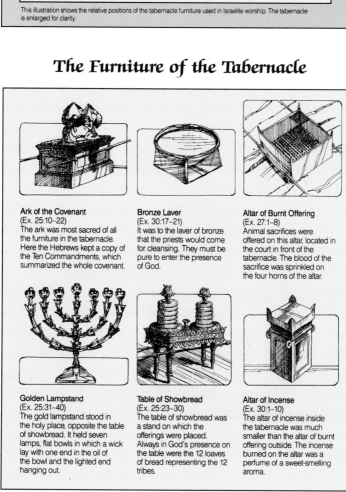

Ark of the Covenant
(Ex. 25:10–22)
The ark was most sacred of all the furniture in the tabernacle. Here the Hebrews kept a copy of the Ten Commandments, which summarized the whole covenant.

Bronze Laver
(Ex. 30:17–21)
It was to the laver of bronze that the priests would come for cleansing. They must be pure to enter the presence of God.

Altar of Burnt Offering
(Ex. 27:1–8)
Animal sacrifices were offered on this altar, located in the court in front of the tabernacle. The blood of the sacrifice was sprinkled on the four horns of the altar.

Golden Lampstand
(Ex. 25:31–40)
The gold lampstand stood in the holy place, opposite the table of showbread. It held seven lamps, flat bowls in which a wick lay with one end in the oil of the bowl and the lighted end hanging out.

Table of Showbread
(Ex. 25:23–30)
The table of showbread was a stand on which the offerings were placed. Always in God's presence on the table were the 12 loaves of bread representing the 12 tribes.

Altar of Incense
(Ex. 30:1–10)
The altar of incense inside the tabernacle was much smaller than the altar of burnt offering outside. The incense burned on the altar was a perfume of a sweet-smelling aroma.

TARSUS [tar'-sus] — the birthplace of the apostle Paul (Acts 21:39; 22:3), formerly known as Saul of Tarsus (Acts 9:11). Tarsus was the chief city of Cilicia, a province of southeast Asia Minor (modern Turkey). This important city was situated on the banks of the Cydnus River about 16 kilometers (10 miles) north of the shore of the Mediterranean Sea.

TASKMASTER — a harsh supervisor (Ex. 1:11).

TASSEL — a decorative ornament around the hems of the clothes of the Hebrew people, worn to remind them of God's commandments in the Law (Deut. 22:12) and to encourage them to do His will.

TAX, TAXES — a compulsory fee or financial contribution for the maintenance of government. Taxes may have originated with the custom of giving presents for protection from harm (Gen. 32:13–21; 33:10; 43:11). When Joseph revealed to the Pharaoh in Egypt that there would be seven years of famine after seven years of abundance, Pharaoh put him in charge of raising revenues. During the time of famine as well as plenty, he collected a 20 percent tax to store up food and then to buy land for Pharaoh (Gen. 47:20–26).

TEACH, TEACHING — cause one to understand (John 3:2); the act of instructing students or imparting knowledge and information. As used in the New Testament, the concept of teaching usually means instruction in the faith. Thus, teaching is to be distinguished from preaching, or the proclamation of the gospel to the non–Christian world. Teaching in the Christian faith was validated by Jesus, who was called "Teacher" more than anything else.

TEKOA [te-ko'-ah] **TEKOAH** *(trumpet blast)* — the birthplace of the prophet Amos. Situated in Judah (1 Chr. 2:24; 4:5), Tekoa is identified today with Khirbet Taqu'a, about 10 kilometers (6 miles) southeast of Bethlehem and about 16 kilometers (10 miles) south of Jerusalem. It was built on a hill in the wilderness of Tekoa toward En Gedi (2 Chr. 11:6; 20:20).

St. Paul's Gate at Tarsus. The chief city of Cilicia in eastern Asia Minor, Tarsus was the birthplace of the apostle Paul (Acts 21:39). *Photo by Gustav Jeeninga*

The mound of Tekoa south of Jerusalem—home of the prophet Amos (Amos 1:1).

Photo: Levant Photo Service

TEMPERANCE — control over sensual desires. The meaning of the word "temperate" in English translations of the Bible should not be restricted to the kind of self-control a person exerts by abstaining from alcoholic beverages. The temperance of which the Bible speaks is far more inclusive. It indicates a self-control that masters all kinds of sensual desires, such as sexual desire or the desire for material comfort. Through temperance Christians can discipline body and spirit, so that they are more capable of striving for their spiritual reward (1 Cor. 9:24–27).

TEMPEST — violent storm (Matt. 8:24).

TEMPLE — a building in which a god (or gods) is worshiped. The Old Testament describes

The temple of Hephaestus (Vulcan) in Athens is one of the best-preserved Greek temples from ancient times. *Photo by Howard Vos*

The Temples of the Bible

The Temple	Date	Description	Reference
The Tabernacle (Mobile Temple)	about 1444 B.C.	Detailed plan received by Moses from the Lord Constructed by divinely appointed artisans Desecrated by Nadab and Abihu	Ex. 25—30; Ex. 35:30—40:38; Lev. 10:1-7
Solomon's Temple	966–586 B.C.	Planned by David Constructed by Solomon Destroyed by Nebuchadnezzar	2 Sam. 7:1-29; 1 Kin. 8:1-66; Jer. 32:28-44
Zerubbabel's Temple	516–169 B.C.	Envisioned by Zerubbabel Constructed by Zerubbabel and the elders of the Jews Desecrated by Antiochus Epiphanes	Ezra 6:1-22; Ezra 3:1-8; 4:1-14; Matt. 24:15
Herod's Temple	19 B.C.–A.D. 70.	Zerubbabel's temple restored by Herod the Great Destroyed by the Romans	Mark 13:2, 14-23; Luke 1:11-20; 2:22-38; 2:42-51; 4:21-24; Acts 21:27-33
The Present Temple	Present Age.	Found in the heart of the believer The body of the believer is the Lord's only temple until the Messiah returns	1 Cor. 6:19, 20; 2 Cor. 6:16-18
The Temple of Revelation 11	Tribulation Period.	To be constructed during the Tribulation by the Antichrist To be desecrated and destroyed	Dan. 9:2; Matt. 24:15; 2 Thess. 2:4; Rev. 17:18
Ezekiel's (Millennial) Temple	Millennium.	Envisioned by the prophet Ezekiel To be built by the Messiah during His millennial reign	Ezek. 40:1—42:20; Zech. 6:12, 13
The Eternal Temple of His Presence	The Eternal Kingdom.	The greatest temple of all ("The Lord God Almighty and the Lamb are its temple") A spiritual temple	Rev. 21:22; Rev. 22:1-21

The temple (Gk. *hieron*) is a place of worship, a sacred or holy space built primarily for the national worship of God.

243

3 THADDAEUS**

temples as some of the oldest buildings ever constructed. The Tower of Babel (Gen. 11:4) is the first recorded example of a structure that implies the existence of a temple, although this tower was not a temple itself. A temple was thought of as the building where the god manifested his presence, so the place the temple occupied was holy, or sacred. Because the god was thought to dwell in the temple, the Old Testament had no specific word for temple. It refers instead to the "house" of a deity.

TEMPTATION — an enticement or invitation to sin, with the implied promise of greater good to be derived from following the way of disobedience. In this sense, God does not tempt people, nor can He Himself as the holy God be tempted (James 1:13). God cannot be induced to deny Himself (2 Tim. 2:13). The supreme tempter is Satan (Matt. 4:3; 1 Cor. 7:5; 1 Thess. 3:5), who is able to play upon the weakness of corrupted human nature (James 1:14) and so to lead people to destruction.

TEMPTATION OF CHRIST — the 40-day period in the wilderness when Jesus was tempted by the devil (Matt. 4:1–13; Mark 1:12–13). Jesus' first temptation (to turn stones to bread) was to use His divine power to satisfy His own physical needs. The second (to jump off the temple) was to perform a spectacular feat so the people would follow Him. The third was to gain possession of the world by worshiping Satan.

One motive lay behind all these temptations: Satan wanted to destroy Jesus' mission. Because Jesus' death would destroy Satan's power, Satan wanted Jesus to pollute His life and ministry. The ultimate issue behind these temptations was idolatry. The real purpose of Satan's temptation was that he might be worshiped instead of God.

TEN COMMANDMENTS — rules for living given to the Israelites by God through Moses (Ex. 20:1–17).

TENDER EYED — timid, eye weakness (Gen. 29:17).

TERAH [te'-rah] — the name of a man and a place in the Bible:

1. The father of Abraham and an ancestor of Christ (Gen. 11:26–27; Luke 3:34; Thara, KJV).

2. An encampment of the Israelites in the wilderness (Num. 33:27–28; Tarah, KJV).

TERAPHIM [ter'-ra-fim] — figurines or images in human form used in the ancient world as household gods.

TERRESTRIAL — of the earth (1 Cor. 15:40).

TERRIBLE — horrible, scary (Heb. 12:21).

TESTAMENT — a written document that provides for the disposition of one's personal property after death; a bequest. The word "testament" occurs only two times in the NKJV (2 Cor. 3:14; Heb. 9:16–17). In the KJV the word appears in several additional places (Matt. 26:28; 2 Cor. 3:6; Rev. 11:19)—translated in all these cases as "covenant" by the NKJV.

The word "testament" also refers to either of the two main divisions of the Bible: the Old Testament and the New Testament, or, more accurately, the Old Covenant and the New Covenant (2 Cor. 3:14).

TESTIFY — tell as a witness (Acts 2:40).

TESTIMONY — witness (John 3:32); the Law (Ex. 2:21).

TETRARCH [tet'-rark] *(ruler of a fourth part)* — the ruler or governor of the fourth part of a country, which was divided into these parts for efficient government, especially under the Roman Empire. (Luke 3:1).

THADDAEUS [that-de'-us] — one of the twelve apostles of Jesus (Matt. 10:3; Mark 3:18; Thaddeus, KJV), also called Lebbaeus (Matt. 10:3) and Judas the son of James (Luke 6:16; Acts 1:13). He is carefully distinguished from Judas Iscariot (John 14:22). Nothing else is known about this most obscure of the apostles, but some scholars attribute the Epistle of Jude to him.

THANK OFFERING — a sacrificial offering given in response to an unsolicited divine blessing. This was a bloody offering presented to God. Part of the offering was eaten by the priest, and part was eaten by worshipers and their guests. Thus, God hosted the meal, communing with the worshiper and other participants (2 Chr. 29:31; 33:16).

THANKSGIVING — the aspect of praise that gives thanks to God for what He does for us. Ideally, thanksgiving should spring from a grateful heart; but it is required of all believers, regardless of their initial attitude (1 Thess. 5:18). We should be grateful to God for all things (Eph. 5:20; Col. 3:17; 1 Thess. 5:18), but especially for His work of salvation and sanctification (Rom. 7:25; Col. 1:3–5; 1 Thess. 1:2–7; 2:13). We ought also to thank God in anticipation of His answering our prayers (Phil. 4:6), knowing that His answers will always be in accord with His perfect will for our lives (Rom. 8:28–29).

THENCE — from there (Gen. 11:8).

THEOPHILUS [the-off'-i-lus] *(lover of God)* — a Christian to whom Luke dedicated the Gospel of Luke and the Book of Acts (Luke 1:3; Acts 1:1). The fact that Luke spoke of Theophilus as "most excellent" indicates that he was a prominent man of high rank and possibly a Roman. He may have chosen the name when he was converted to Christianity. According to tradition, both Luke and Theophilus were natives of Antioch in Syria. Much speculation surrounds Theophilus, but little is known for certain about him.

THESSALONIANS, EPISTLES TO THE — two letters written by the apostle Paul, which are among the earliest of Paul and of the New Testament. The major theological theme of 1 and 2 Thessalonians is the return of Christ to earth. Important as this theme is, however, the Thessalonian letters leave the reader wide awake to the responsibilities of the present, not gazing into the future. Both epistles aim to establish and strengthen a young church in a stormy setting (1 Thess. 3:2, 13; 2 Thess. 2:17; 3:3). In neither epistle does Paul fight any grave errors in the church. In both epistles the reader feels the heartbeat of Paul the pastor as he identifies with a young congregation taking its first steps in faith.

Three themes appear in the Thessalonian correspondence: thanksgiving for their faith and example in the past; encouragement for those undergoing persecution in the present; and exhortation to further work and growth in the future.

FIRST THESSALONIANS:
A Study and Teaching Outline

I. **Paul's Personal Reflections on the Thessalonians** .... 1:1—3:13
  A. Paul's Praise of Their Growth 1:1–10
  B. Paul's Founding of the Church 2:1–16
  C. Timothy's Strengthening of the Church .... 2:17—3:13
    1. Satan Hinders Paul................. 2:17–20
    2. Timothy's Visit 3:1–5
    3. Timothy's Encouraging Report....... 3:6–10
    4. Paul's Desire to Visit Them.......... 3:11–13
II. **Paul's Instructions to the Thessalonians** ... 4:1—5:28
  A. Directions for Growth 4:1–12
  B. Revelation Concerning the Dead in Christ.......................... 4:13–18
  C. Description of the Day of the Lord....... 5:1–11
  D. Instruction for Holy Living 5:12–22
  E. Conclusion......................... 5:23–28

SECOND THESSALONIANS:
A Study and Teaching Outline

I. **Paul's Encouragement in Persecution** 1:1–12
A. Thanksgiving for Their Growth 1:1–4
B. Encouragement in Their Persecution 1:5–10
C. Prayer for God's Blessing 1:11–12
II. **Paul's Explanation of the Day of the Lord** 2:1–17
A. The Events Preceding the Day
   of the Lord 2:1–12
   1. First a Falling Away 2:1–3
   2. The Man of Sin Is Revealed 2:4–5
   3. The Restrainer Is Taken Out of the Way . . 2:6–7
   4. The Second Coming of Christ 2:8–12
B. The Comfort of the Believer on the Day of
   the Lord 2:13–17
III. **Paul's Exhortation to the Church** 3:1–18
A. Wait Patiently for Christ 3:1–5
B. Withdraw from the Disorderly 3:6–15
C. Conclusion 3:16–18

THESSALONICA [thes-sa-lo-ni´-cah] — a city in Macedonia visited by the apostle Paul (Acts 17:1, 11, 13; 27:2; Phil. 4:16). Situated on the Thermaic Gulf, Thessalonica was the chief seaport of Macedonia. The city was founded in about 315 B.C. by Cassander, who resettled the site with inhabitants from 26 villages that he had destroyed. He named the city after his wife, the sister of Alexander the Great and daughter of Philip II of Macedonia. The Egnatian Way, the main overland route from Rome to the East, ran directly through the city and can still be traced today.

The ancient walls of Thessalonica, a city in Macedonia where Paul founded a church (Acts 17:1–4; 1 Thess. 1:1). *Photo by Howard Vos*

THISTLES, THORNS — a stickery plant; also symbolizes trouble (Matt. 7:16; 2 Kin. 14:9).

THITHER — there (1 Sam. 10:22).

THOMAS [tom´-us] *(twin)* — one of the twelve apostles of Jesus; also called *Didymus,* the Greek word for "twin" (Matt. 10:3; Mark 3:18; Luke 6:15). Thomas is probably best known for his inability to believe that Jesus had indeed risen from the dead. For that inability to believe, he forever earned the name "doubting Thomas."

THONGS — straps (Acts 22:25).

THORN IN THE FLESH — a reference to some extreme difficulty "in the flesh" that the apostle Paul encountered in his ministry (2 Cor. 12:7).

THRESH, THRESHING — removing the kernel of grain from its stalk. Different methods were used to accomplish this. The most basic method, beating the grain, was used by farmers

A threshing floor in Samaria. The oxen are dragging a weighted sled over the harvest to separate the grain from the stalks. *Photo by Gustav Jeeninga*

with a small amount of grain to thresh. These farmers sometimes would walk their animals over the grain to thresh it.

THRESHING FLOOR — a flat surface prepared for the threshing of grain. The threshing floor was usually located at the edge of a village, frequently on a large flat rock outcropping. When no flat rock was available, the threshing floor would be prepared by leveling the ground and pounding the earth to create a hard surface.

THRONG — crowd (Mark 5:31).

THYATIRA [thi-a-ti′-rah] — a city of the province of LYDIA in western Asia Minor (modern Turkey) situated on the road from Pergamos to Sardis. The city was on the southern bank of the Lycus River, a branch of the Hermus River.

Although never a large city, Thyatira was a thriving manufacturing and commercial center during New Testament times. Archaeologists have uncovered evidence of many trade guilds and unions here. Membership in these trade guilds, necessary for financial and social success, often involved pagan customs and practices such as superstitious worship, union feasts using food sacrificed to pagan gods, and loose sexual morality.

The apostle Paul's first convert in Europe was "a certain woman named LYDIA ... a seller of

purple from the city of Thyatira" (Acts 16:14). The modern name of Thyatira is Akhisar, which means "white castle."

TIBERIAS, SEA OF — a body of water also known as Chinnereth and the Sea of Galilee (Num. 34:11; John 6:1).

TIDINGS — news, information (Luke 2:10; Rom. 10:15).

TIGLATH-PILESER [tig′-lath-pi-le′-zur] *(the firstborn of* [the god] *Esharra is my confidence)* — a king of Assyria (ruled 745—727 B.C.) and,

A stone carving of Tiglath-Pileser III of Assyria, from his excavated palace at Nimrud. *Photo by Howard Vos*

under the name Pul (2 Kin. 15:19), king of Babylonia (729—727 B.C.). He is also called Tilgath-Pilneser (1 Chr. 5:6, 26; 2 Chr. 28:20).

TIGRIS [ti′-gris] — a major river of southwest Asia. Flowing about 1,850 kilometers (1,150 miles) from the Taurus Mountains of eastern Turkey, the Tigris joins the Euphrates River north of Basra. The Tigris and Euphrates flow roughly parallel to each other for hundreds of miles in the "Land of the Two Rivers," or Mesopotamia. The Tigris is identical with Hiddekel (Gen. 2:14, KJV, NKJV), one of the four branches of the river that flowed from the Garden of Eden.

TILL — plow (Gen. 2:5).

TIMBREL — a musical instrument similar to a tambourine (Ps. 81:2).

TIME — a measurable period during which an action or condition exists or continues. Among the Hebrew people, units of time were measured in hours, days, weeks, months, and years. The more abstract concept of time is also mentioned in the Bible.

TIMOTHY [tim′-o-thy] *(honored by God)* — Paul's friend and chief associate, who is mentioned as joint sender in six of Paul's epistles (2 Cor. 1:1; Phil. 1:1; Col. 1:1; 1 Thess. 1:1; 2 Thess. 1:1; Philem. 1).

TIMOTHY, EPISTLES TO — two letters of the apostle Paul, which, along with the Epistle to Titus, form a trilogy called the Pastoral Epistles. These letters are called Pastoral Epistles because they deal with matters affecting pastors and congregations. In these letters to Timothy, Paul's primary concern is to instruct his young associate to guard the spiritual heritage that he has received (1 Tim. 6:20; 2 Tim. 1:12–14; 2:2) by establishing sound doctrine in the church.

FIRST TIMOTHY:
A Study and Teaching Outline

I. **Paul's Charge Concerning Doctrine** 1:1–20
  A. Paul's Past Charge to Timothy. 1:1–11
  B. Christ's Past Charge to Paul 1:12–17
  C. First Charge: "Wage the Good Warfare". . . 1:18–20
II. **Paul's Charge Concerning Public Worship** . . 2:1—3:16
  A. Prayer in Public Worship. 2:1–8
  B. Women in Public Worship. 2:9–15
  C. Qualifications of Bishops. 3:1–7
  D. Qualifications of Deacons 3:8–13
  E. Second Charge: "Conduct Yourself in the House of God" 3:14–16
III. **Paul's Charge Concerning False Teachers** 4:1–16
  A. Description of False Teachers 4:1–5
  B. Instruction for the True Teacher 4:6–10
  C. Third Charge: "Do Not Neglect the Gift" . . 4:11–16
IV. **Paul's Charge Concerning Church Discipline** . . 5:1–25
  A. How to Treat All People. 5:1–2
  B. How to Treat Widows. 5:3–16
  C. How to Treat Elders. 5:17–20
  D. Fourth Charge: "Observe These Things without Prejudice". 5:21–25
V. **Paul's Charge Concerning Pastoral Motives** . . . 6:1–21
  A. Exhortation to Servants. 6:1–2
  B. Exhortation to Godliness with Contentment 6:3–16
  C. Exhortation to the Rich. 6:17–19
  D. Fifth Charge: "Guard What Was Committed". 6:20–21

SECOND TIMOTHY: A Study and Teaching Outline

I. **Persevere in Present Testings** . . . . 1:1—2:26
   A. Thanksgiving for Timothy's Faith 1:1–5
   B. Reminder of Timothy's Responsibility 1:6–18
   C. Characteristics of a Faithful Minister. 2:1–26
      1. Discipling Teacher 2:1–2
      2. Single-minded Soldier 2:3–5
      3. Enduring Farmer 2:6–13
      4. Diligent Workman 2:14–19
      5. Sanctified Vessel. 2:20–23
      6. Gentle Servant 2:24–26
II. **Endure in Future Testings.** . . . . 3:1—4:22
   A. Approaching Day of Denial 3:1–17
      1. Coming of Denial 3:1–9
      2. Confronting Denial. 3:10–17
   B. Charge to Preach the Word 4:1–5
   C. Approaching Death of Paul 4:6–22
      1. Paul's Hope in Death 4:6–8
      2. Paul's Situation in Prison. 4:9–18
      3. Paul's Closing Greetings. 4:19–22

The message of 1 and 2 Timothy can be summed up by words like remember (2 Tim. 2:8), guard (1 Tim. 6:20), be strong (2 Tim. 2:1), and commit (1 Tim. 1:18; 2:2). For Paul, the best medicine for false teaching and apostasy is "sound doctrine" (1 Tim. 1:10; 4:3). The gospel is a spiritual inheritance to be received from faithful witnesses and passed on to such (2 Tim. 2:2). It brings about wholeness or health (which is the meaning of "sound" in Greek), not only in belief, but also in good deeds. So vital is sound doctrine to the health of the church that it is something to be pursued (1 Tim. 6:11), fought for (1 Tim. 6:12), and even suffered for (2 Tim. 1:8; 2:3, 11–13).

TISHBITE [tish'-bite] — a name applied to Elijah the prophet (1 Kin. 17:1; 21:17; 2 Kin. 9:36). Some scholars believe Elijah was from a town named Tishbe, in Galilee (Naphtali). Most scholars, however, believe Elijah was from Transjordan, an area east of the Jordan River, specifically in the land of Gilead.

TITHE — the practice of giving a tenth of one's income or property as an offering to God. The custom of paying a tithe was an ancient practice found among many nations of the ancient world.

TITTLE — an ornamental stroke decorating the letters of the Hebrew alphabet (Matt. 5:18; Luke 16:17; stroke, NRSV; the smallest stroke, NASB; the least stroke of a pen, NIV). The word "tittle" comes from a Greek word that means "little horn." Jesus meant that even the smallest detail of the Law of Moses would never fail or pass away.

TITUS [ti'-tus] — a "partner and fellow worker" (2 Cor. 8:23) of the apostle Paul. Although Titus is not mentioned in the Book of Acts, Paul's letters reveal that he was the man of the hour at a number of key points in Paul's life.

TITUS, EPISTLE TO — one of three PASTORAL EPISTLES among Paul's writings, the others being 1 and 2 TIMOTHY. The Pastoral Epistles are so named because they deal with matters concerning pastors and congregations. They are the only letters of Paul addressed to individuals (Philemon is addressed "to the church in your house," 1:2). The purpose of the Epistle to Titus was to warn against false teaching and to provide guidance for one of Paul's younger associates on sound doctrine and good works.

Titus emphasizes sound doctrine (1:9; 2:8, 10) and challenges believers to good works (1:16; 2:14; 3:14). Paul summons Titus "to affirm constantly that those who have believed in God

TITUS:
A Study and
Teaching Outline

I. **Appoint Elders** 1:1–16
    A. Introduction 1:1–4
    B. Ordain Qualified Elders 1:5–9
    C. Rebuke False Teachers 1:10–16
II. **Set Things in Order** . . . . 2:1—3:15
    A. Speak Sound Doctrine 2:1–15
    B. Maintain Good Works 3:1–11
    C. Conclusion 3:12–15

should be careful to maintain good works" (3:8). This letter will allow no separation between belief and action. We often hear it said that it makes no difference what we believe, as long as we do what is right. The truth, however, is that we become what we think, and all action is shaped by belief.

Two passages (2:11–14; 3:4–7) remind us of this truth. In a world such as ours, we cannot be reminded too often to hold fast to the truth of the gospel of our salvation.

TOIL — strenuous labor, hard work (Gen. 5:29; Matt. 6:28).

TOKEN — a sign or symbol. Rahab the harlot begged the two spies to give her a "true token" that her family would be spared when Joshua attacked Jericho (Josh. 2:12).

TOLERABLE, TOLERATE — able to bear (Matt. 10:15).

TOLL — tax (Ezra 4:13).

TOMB — an elaborate burial place for the dead. In Palestine ordinary people were buried in shallow graves covered by stones or a stone slab. People of importance and wealth were placed in tombs.

TONGUES, GIFT OF — the Spirit-given ability to speak in languages not known to the speaker or in an ecstatic language that could not normally be understood by the speaker or the hearers (Is. 28:11; Mark 16:17; Acts 2:4; 1 Cor. 12 and 14).

TORAH [tor-rah'] — guidance or direction from God to His people. In earlier times, the term Torah referred directly to the five books of Moses, or the PENTATEUCH.

TORMENT — to inflict physical pain or mental agony. Job cried out against his three friends who had come to comfort him, "How long will you torment my soul?" (Job 19:2). The rich man in Jesus' account of the rich man and Lazarus also described hell as a "place of torment" (Luke 16:28).

TOW — KJV word for the refuse of flax produced in the manufacture of linen (Judg. 16:9; yarn, NKJV; Is. 1:31, KJV; tinder, NKJV, NIV).

TOWER — a tall building erected for defense. Some landowners used towers to protect their crops (Is. 5:2; Matt. 21:33; Mark 12:1). In the wilderness, towers were used to watch for

This massive stone tower was part of the defense system of the ancient city of Jericho. It dates back to about 6000 B.C., long before Joshua and his army destroyed the city.

approaching marauders (2 Kin. 17:9; 2 Chr. 26:10). In cities towers were part of the walls built for defensive purposes (2 Chr. 14:7; Neh. 3:1). They were erected at the corners of the wall, beside the city gates, and at intervals along the walls (2 Chr. 26:9). Watchmen secured the towers (2 Kin. 9:17), and military machines that threw arrows and stones could be mounted on the massive structures (2 Chr. 26:15).

TRADITION — customs and practices from the past that are passed on as accepted standards of behavior for the present. Jesus criticized the Pharisees for slavishly following their traditions and making them more authoritative than the Scripture (Matt. 15:2; Mark 7:3).

TRAIN — the lowest and back hem of the outer garment (Is. 6:1). The outermost garment worn by the Hebrew people was a long, loosely fitting robe. Usually sleeveless, its rear skirt was drawn up through the legs and attached around the waist by a belt or girdle when the person was working. This long skirt is called a train when it is not girded. To have a robe or cloak with a long train was a sign of favor and wealth (Ex. 28:33).

TRANSFIGURATION — a display of God's glory in the person of His Son, Jesus Christ (Matt. 17:1–8; Mark 9:2–8; Luke 9:28–36). Peter cites the Transfiguration as historical proof of the true gospel of Christ (2 Pet. 1:16–18).

TRANSFIGURED — changed (Mark 9:2).

TRANSFORM, TRANSFORMED — to change radically in inner character, condition, or nature. In Romans 12:2 the apostle Paul exhorted Christians, "Do not be conformed to this world, but be transformed by the renewing of your mind." Followers of Christ should not be conformed, either inwardly or in appearance, to the values, ideals, and behavior of a fallen world. Believers should continually renew their minds through prayer and the study of God's Word, by the power of the Holy Spirit, and so be transformed and made like Christ (2 Cor. 3:18).

TRANSGRESS, TRANSGRESSION — the violation of a law, command, or duty. The Hebrew word most often translated as "transgression" in the Old Testament means "revolt" or "rebellion." The psalmist wrote, "Blessed is he whose transgression is forgiven, whose sin is covered" (Ps. 32:1). In the New Testament every occurrence of the word "transgression" (NKJV) is a translation of a Greek word that means "a deliberate breach of the law" (Rom. 4:15; 1 Tim. 2:14; Heb. 2:2).

TRANSLATE, TRANSLATION — to remove a person or thing from one condition, place, or state to another. In the Bible, the word "translation" or the concept of translation is used in three senses: (1) the physical translation of Enoch (Gen. 5:24; Heb. 11:5) and Elijah (2 Kin. 2:11) to heaven without the intervening experience of death; (2) the spiritual translation of Christians in their present experience from "the power of darkness" into "the kingdom of the Son of His love" (Col. 1:13); and (3) the future, physical translation and transformation of Christians at the Second Coming of Christ (1 Cor. 15:51–57; Phil. 3:21; 1 Thess. 4:13–18).

Translation is a special act of God. It is permanent in its results; it occurs in response to faith; and it has heaven as its reward.

TRAVAIL — physical or mental pain or anguish. Rachel travailed in childbirth, dying as she gave birth to Benjamin (Gen. 35:16–19). The prophet Isaiah spoke of the Suffering Servant: "He [God] shall see the labor of His soul, and be satisfied" (Is. 53:11). Our salvation has been secured through the pain and suffering of God's Son.

TREACHEROUS — tricky, deceitful (Hos. 6:7).

TREAD — trample (Lam. 1:15).

TREASON — conspiracy (1 Kin. 16:20).

TREASURE, TREASURY — something of value; a place for storing valuables. In the Old Testament a treasure was described as something "laid aside," "possessed," or "hidden," and thus valuable (Gen. 43:23; Deut. 32:34). A treasury is a place to keep such valuables (Esth. 3:9; 4:7). A place where royal records are stored might, therefore, be called a "treasure house" (Ezra 5:17).

TREE OF KNOWLEDGE — one of two special trees planted by God in the Garden of Eden. The other was the tree of life (Gen. 2:9). Since "the tree of the knowledge of good and evil" symbolized all moral knowledge, knowledge that only God could have, its fruit was forbidden to Adam and Eve (Gen. 2:17). But the tempter suggested to them that, by adding to their knowledge, the tree's fruit would make them "like God" (Gen. 3:5). So they chose to disobey God. This act of rebellion marked the entrance of sin into the world.

The result was quite different than Adam and Eve expected. Instead of gaining superior knowledge that made them equal with God, they gained awareness or knowledge of their guilt, shame, and condemnation.

TREE OF LIFE — the tree in the Garden of Eden that bestowed continuing life (Gen. 2:9, 17; 3:1–24). Before Adam and Eve sinned, they had free access to the Tree of Life; after their act of rebellion, two CHERUBIM guarded the way to its fruit.

TRESPASS — the violation of a law. The Hebrew word translated as "trespass" means "a stepping aside from the (correct) path" (Gen. 31:36; Ex. 22:9). In the New Testament "trespass" is often a translation of a Greek word that means "a falling aside" (Mark 11:25–26; Eph. 2:1, 5). The apostle Paul wrote: "God was in Christ reconciling the world to Himself, not imputing their trespasses to them" (2 Cor. 5:19).

TRIAL — a temptation or an adversity, the enduring of which proves the merit of an individual's faith. For Christians, to encounter adversity is to undergo a trial in which their faith is proved either true or false before God, the highest Judge. Since many positive things come about through such trials, Christians are urged to rejoice at their occurrence (James 1:2; 1 Pet. 4:13). Christ Himself set the example in how trials should be endured when He defeated Satan's temptations by appealing to the word and will of God (Luke 4:1–13).

TRIBE — a social group composed of many clans and families, together with their dependents, outside the ties of blood kinship, who had become associated with the group through covenant, marriage, adoption, or slavery. The nation of ancient Israel, especially at the time of the events recorded in the Book of Judges, was a tribal society (Numbers 1; 2; 26; Joshua 13—21; Judges 19—21). Several neighboring nations also were organized along tribal lines (Gen. 25:13–16).

Israel was an association of twelve tribes, designated by the names of the ancestors from whom they were descended (Deut. 27:12–13; Ezek. 48:1–35). The historical origins of the tribal units may be traced to the Book of Genesis. Jacob, whose name was later changed to Israel (Gen. 32:28), was the father of twelve sons (Gen. 29:31—30:24; 35:18, 22–26). The sons of Jacob, excluding Levi and Joseph but including Joseph's sons, Manasseh and Ephraim, were the ancestors of the later tribal units in the nation's history. The development of the tribes begins with the events described in the Book of Exodus.

TRIBULATION — great adversity and anguish; intense oppression or persecution. Tribulation is linked to God's process for making the world right again. His Son underwent great suffering, just as His people undergo a great deal of tribulation from the world (Rom. 5:3; Acts 14:22). This tribulation has its source in the conflict between God and the devil (Gen. 3:15), which will end with the devil being cast into the lake of fire to suffer eternal tribulation (Rev. 20:10).

TRIBULATION, THE GREAT — a short but intense period of distress and suffering at the end of time. The exact phrase, "the great tribula-tion," is found only once in the Bible (Rev. 7:14). The Great Tribulation is to be distinguished from the general tribulation a believer faces in the world (Matt. 13:21; John 16:33; Acts 14:22). It is also to be distinguished from God's specific wrath upon the unbelieving world at the end of the age (Mark 13:24; Rom. 2:5–10; 2 Thess. 1:6).

The Great Tribulation fulfills Daniel's prophe-cies (Daniel 7—12). It will be a time of evil from false christs and false prophets (Mark 13:22) when natural disasters will occur throughout the world.

TRIBUTE — a compulsory fee or financial con-tribution levied on an inferior by a superior ruler or nation; also a tax (Ezra 4:20).

TRINITY — the coexistence of the Father, the Son, and the Holy Spirit in the unity of the God-head (divine nature or essence). The doctrine of the Trinity means that within the being and ac-tivity of the one God there are three distinct per-sons: Father, Son, and Holy Spirit. Although the word "trinity" does not appear in the Bible, the "trinitarian formula" is mentioned in the Great

Commission (Matt. 28:19) and in the benedic-tion of the apostle Paul's Second Epistle to the Corinthians (2 Cor. 13:14).

TRIUMPH — the joy or exultation of victory (Ps. 47:1).

TRIUMPHAL ENTRY — Jesus' entrance into Jerusalem on the Sunday (Palm Sunday) before His Crucifixion (Matt. 21:1–9; Mark 11:1–10; Luke 19:29–38; John 12:12–16).

TROAS [tro′-as] — an important city on the coast of Mysia, in northwest Asia Minor (modern Turkey), visited at least three times by the apostle Paul (Acts 16:8, 11; 20:5–6; 2 Cor. 2:12; 2 Tim. 4:13). Troas was situated about 16 kilometers (ten miles) southwest of Hissarlik, the ruins of ancient Troy.

At Troas, on his second missionary journey, the apostle Paul saw a vision of a "man of Mace-donia" inviting him to preach the gospel of Christ in Europe (Acts 16:8–9). After ministering in Greece (Acts 20:2), Paul returned to Troas. Here he restored to life a young man named Eutychus,

Ruins of Roman baths at Troas—the city where Paul received a vision to evangelize Macedonia (Acts 16:6–10). *Photo by Howard Vos*

who had fallen from a third-story window while Paul preached late into the night (Acts 20:5–12).

TROPHIMUS [trof'-ih-mus] — a Gentile Christian who lived in Ephesus and who accompanied Paul to Jerusalem at the end of Paul's third missionary journey (Acts 20:4).

TROUGH — a place for animal food or water (Ex. 2:16).

TRUE, TRUTH — conformity to fact or actuality; faithfulness to an original or to a standard.

In the Old and New Testaments, truth is a fundamental moral and personal quality of God. God proclaimed that He is "merciful and gracious, longsuffering, and abounding in goodness and truth" (Ex. 34:6).

TRUMPETS, FEAST OF — a Hebrew festival that celebrated the new civil year (Num. 29:1).

TUMULT — riot (Matt. 27:24).

TUNIC — loose-fitting garment (Mark 6:9, NIV).

TURBAN — a long piece of linen cloth wound around the head and fastened in the back to form a type of headdress worn by men in Bible times (Job 29:14). Such a turban was a distinctive form of headdress worn by the priests of the nation of Israel (Ex. 28:39). The Hebrew word for turban is rendered as tire, bonnet, and mitre by some English translations of the Bible.

TURTLEDOVE another name for dove, a bird poor people used for their sacrifices (Lev. 12:6–8).

TWELVE, THE — a term for the band of Jesus' closest disciples (Mark 4:10). Early in His ministry Jesus selected twelve of His followers and named them "apostles" (Luke 6:12–16). They are also referred to as the "twelve disciples" (Matt. 10:1). Jesus appointed them to travel with Him, preach, heal, and cast out demons (Mark 3:14–15).

TWO-EDGED — sharp on both sides (Heb. 4:12).

TYCHICUS [tik'-ik-us] — a Christian of the province of Asia (Acts 20:4). Tychicus was a faithful friend, fellow worker, and messenger of the apostle Paul (Eph. 6:21–22; Col. 4:7–8). Along with other disciples, Tychicus traveled ahead of Paul from Macedonia to Troas, where he waited for the apostle's arrival (Acts 20:4).

TYRE [tire] *(rock)* — an ancient seaport city of the Phoenicians situated north of Israel. Tyre was the principal seaport of the Phoenician coast, about 40 kilometers (25 miles) south of Sidon and 56 kilometers (35 miles) north of Carmel. It consisted of two cities: a rocky coastal city on the mainland and a small island city. The

Roman ruins at the ancient city of Tyre, with buildings of the modern city in the background. *Photo by Bernice Johnson*

island city was just off the shore. The mainland city was on a coastal plain, a strip only 24 kilometers (15 miles) long and 3 kilometers (2 miles) wide.

Behind the plain of Tyre stood the rocky mountains of Lebanon. Tyre was easily defended because it had the sea on the west, the mountains on the east, and several other rocky cliffs (one the famous "Ladder of Tyre") around it, making it difficult to invade.

UNBELIEF — lack of belief or faith in God. While unbelief does not hinder God's faithfulness (Rom. 3:3), it does affect the individual's capacity to receive the benefits of that faithfulness. The unbelief of many Israelites, for example, kept them from seeing the Promised Land (Heb. 3:19). The unbelief of the Nazarenes prevented them from witnessing Christ's miracles (Matt. 13:58). Doubting skeptics are limited in what they might see or know, while "all things are possible to him who believes" (Mark 9:23).

UNCIRCUMCISED — a word with several different meanings in the Bible:

1. Not circumcised; a man who has not gone through the Jewish rite of CIRCUMCISION.

2. Not Jewish, Gentile (Ex. 12:48).

3. Spiritually impure; a heathen; one who has closed his ears and heart to God's call (Acts 7:51).

The issue is not whether a man has been circumcised but whether he has faith in Christ (1 Cor. 7:18–19).

UNCLEAN, UNCLEANNESS — defiled, foul, unfit. To be unclean refers to foods that are unfit, to defilement of a moral or religious character, and to spiritual impurity. The Old Testament distinguishes between what is clean and helpful and what is unclean and unacceptable (Lev. 10:10; 11:47). The priest was to teach the people the difference (Ezek. 44:23).

UNDEFILED — unstained, unsoiled, not tainted with evil, clean, pure, faultless. The word undefiled is used of the sinless Christ (Heb. 7:26), of sex in marriage (Heb. 13:4), of a pure and faultless religion (James 1:27), and of

our incorruptible inheritance in heaven (1 Pet. 1:4).

UNFAITHFUL — deceitful (Prov. 25:19).

UNGODLY — wicked, lost (Rom. 5:6).

UNHOLY — wicked, evil (2 Tim. 3:2).

UNITY — oneness, harmony, agreement. Unity was apparent on the day of PENTECOST when the believers "were all with one accord in one place" (Acts 2:1). The church is a unity in diversity, a fellowship of faith, hope, and love that binds believers together (Eph. 4:3, 13).

UNLEAVENED BREAD — bread baked from unfermented dough, or dough without yeast or "leaven" (Gen. 19:3; Josh. 5:11; 1 Sam. 28:24). Unleavened bread was the flat bread used in the PASSOVER celebration and the priestly rituals (Lev. 23:4–8). The tradition of eating unleavened bread goes back to the time of the Exodus, when the Hebrews left Egypt in such haste that they had no time to bake their bread (Ex. 12:8, 15–20, 34, 39; 13:6–7). Leaven was produced by the souring of bread dough. Its exclusion from ceremonial breads probably symbolized purity.

UNLEAVENED BREAD, FEAST OF — also called Passover, a reminder of the Israelites deliverance (Exodus 12).

UNPARDONABLE SIN — blasphemy against the Holy Spirit (Matt. 12:31–32; Mark 3:29).

UNRIGHTEOUS — unacceptable to God (Is. 55:7).

UNSEARCHABLE — beyond understanding (Job 5:9).

UNWITTINGLY — unknowingly (Lev. 22:14), by accident (Josh. 20:3).

UPPER ROOM — place where Jesus met with His disciples prior to the Crucifixion (Matt. 14:15). (see Lord's Supper).

UR — Abraham's native city in southern Mesopotamia; an important metropolis of the ancient world situated on the Euphrates River. Strategically situated about halfway between the head of the Persian Gulf and Baghdad, in present-day Iraq, Ur was the capital of Sumer for two centuries until the Elamites captured the city. The city came to be known as "Ur of the Chaldeans" after the Chaldeans entered southern Babylonia after 1000 B.C. References to "Ur of the Chaldeans" in connection with Abraham are thus examples of later editorial updating.

Abraham lived in the city of Ur (Gen. 11:28, 31) at the height of its splendor. The city was a prosperous center of religion and industry. Thousands of recovered clay documents attest to thriving business activity. Excavations of the royal cemetery, which dates from about 2900 to 2500 B.C., have revealed a surprisingly advanced culture. Uncovered were beautiful jewelry and art treasures, including headwear, personal jewelry, and exquisite dishes and cups.

Ruins of ancient Ur on the Euphrates River in Mesopotamia—the city from which Abraham migrated (Gen. 11:31).

URIAH [u-ri′-ah] *(the Lord is my light)* — the name of three men in the Old Testament:

1. A Hittite married to Bathsheba. Uriah was one of David's mighty men (2 Sam. 11:3–26; 12:9–10, 15; 1 Kin. 15:5; Matt. 1:6; Urias, KJV).

Judging from the usual interpretation of his name and good conduct, Uriah was a worshiper of God. David's adultery with Uriah's wife, Bathsheba, occurred while Uriah was engaged in war at Rabbah, the Ammonite capital. Uriah was immediately recalled to Jerusalem to hide what had happened, but his sense of duty and loyalty only frustrated the king. Failing to use Uriah as a shield to cover his sin with Bathsheba, David ordered this valiant soldier to the front line of battle, where he was killed.

2. A priest, the son of Koz and father of Meremoth. Uriah helped rebuild the wall of Jerusalem under Nehemiah. He stood with Ezra the scribe as Ezra read the law and addressed the people (Ezra 8:33). The NKJV spells his name Urijah in Nehemiah 3:4, 21; 8:4.

3. A priest, one of two faithful witnesses to a scroll written by the prophet Isaiah (Is. 8:2).

URIM AND THUMMIM [u′-rim, thum′-mem] — gems or stones carried by the high priest and used by him to determine God's will in certain matters. Many scholars believe these gems were lots that were cast, much as dice are thrown, to aid the high priest in making important decisions.

The Urim and Thummim were either on, by, or in the high priest's breastplate. For this reason the breastplate is often called the breastplate of judgment, or decision. In the instructions for making the breastplate, the linen was to be doubled to form a square (Ex. 28:16). If the top edge was not stitched together, the breastplate would be an envelope or pouch. Many scholars believe the Urim and Thummim were kept in this pouch and were stones or gems with engraved symbols that signified yes-no or true-false. By these the high priest reached a decision, according to this theory.

USURY — interest paid on borrowed money. In the Bible the word usury does not necessarily have the negative connotations of our modern meaning of lending money at an excessive interest rate. Instead, it usually means the charging of interest on money that has been loaned (Matt. 25:27).

UTTER — as a verb, speak (Matt. 13:35); as an adjective, complete (1 Kin. 20:42).

UTTERANCE — spoken words (Acts 2:4).

UZZA, UZZAH [uz'-zah] *(strength)* — the name of five men in the Old Testament:

1. A man who was struck dead by God because he touched the ARK OF THE COVENANT (2 Sam. 6:3–8; 1 Chr. 13:7–11).

2. A person in whose garden Manasseh, king of Judah, and Amon (Manasseh's son), also king of Judah, were buried (2 Kin. 21:18, 26).

3. A Levite of the family of Merari (1 Chr. 6:29).

4. A descendant of Ehud mentioned in the family tree of King Saul (1 Chr. 8:7).

5. An ancestor of a family of Nethinim (temple servants) who returned with Zerubbabel from the Captivity (Ezra 2:49; Neh. 7:51).

UZZIAH [uz-zi'-ah] *(the Lord is my strength)* — the name of five men in the Old Testament but most notably, the son of Amaziah and Jecholiah; ninth king of Judah and father of Jotham (2 Kin. 15:1–7; 2 Chronicles 26). Uzziah is also called Azariah (2 Kin. 14:21; 15:1–7).

Uzziah ascended the throne at age 16 and reigned longer than any previous king of Judah or Israel—52 years. He probably co-reigned with his father and had his son Jotham as his co-regent during his final years as a leper. A wise, pious, and powerful king, he extended Judah's territory and brought the nation to a time of great prosperity. In the south he maintained control over Edom and rebuilt port facilities at Elath on the Gulf of Aqaba. To the west he warred against the Philistines, seizing several cities. He also apparently defeated and subdued the Ammonites.

VAGABOND — one who moves from place to place without a permanent home; an aimless wanderer (Ps. 109:10).

VAIN — empty, useless (Ps. 73:13; 1 Cor. 15:14).

VALIANT — brave (Jer. 46:15).

VANITY — emptiness, worthlessness, or futility. The word occurs about 37 times in the Old Testament (NKJV), most frequently in Ecclesiastes. The word "vanity" as used in the Bible does not mean conceit or a "superiority complex," like the modern meaning of the term. When applied to persons, it means emptiness or futility of natural human life (Job 7:3; Eccl. 1:2; 2:1; 4:4; 1:10).

When applied to things, vanity is especially used to describe idols, because there is no spiritual reality to them (Is. 41:29). Believers are urged to stay away from vain things and to live their lives in the reality of their relationship to Christ. Anything short of God Himself that people trust to meet their deepest needs is vanity (Eph. 4:17–24).

VARIANCE — separate (Matt. 10:35), turmoil (Gal. 5:20).

VASHTI [vash′-ti] — the beautiful queen of King Ahasuerus (Xerxes I, reigned 486—465 B.C.) who was banished from court for refusing the king's command to exhibit herself during a period of drunken feasting (Esth. 1:11). Her departure allowed Esther to become Ahasuerus' new queen and to be used as God's instrument in saving the Jewish people from destruction.

VASSAL — a slave or a person in a subservient position. Hoshea, king of Israel, became the vassal of Shalmaneser, king of Assyria, and paid him tribute money (2 Kin. 17:3). Jehoiakim, king of Judah, became the vassal of Nebuchadnezzar, king of Babylon, for three years (2 Kin. 24:1).

VEIL — 1. a woman's head covering (Gen. 24:65; 38:14; Is. 3:23); 2. a curtain in the tabernacle or temple that separated the Holy Place from the Holy of Holies (or Most Holy Place).

VENGEANCE — punishment in retaliation for an injury or offense; repayment for a wrong suffered. The Levitical law prescribed, "You shall not take vengeance" (Lev. 19:18). Only God was qualified to take vengeance, because His acts were based on His holiness, righteousness, and justice, which punishes sin and vindicates the oppressed and the poor in spirit (Deut. 32:35; Rom. 12:19).

VESSEL — any kind of container or receptacle. The vessels of the Hebrew people were usually earthenware. But vessels of glass, metal, leather, wicker, and stone were not uncommon. They were used to hold everything from documents (Jer. 32:14) to wine, fruits, and oil (Jer. 40:10).

In a broader sense, ships are sometimes referred to as vessels (Is. 18:2) since they are the receptacles of people. In an even broader sense, vessel refers to people who carry within them the knowledge of God (2 Cor. 4:6–7). Just as any clay vessel reflects the craftsmanship of its potter, so people reflect the craftsmanship of God. We are in God's hands and are formed in accordance with His plan (Rom. 9:21–23).

VESTMENT, VESTURE — clothing (2 Kin. 10:22), garment (Matt. 27:35).

VEXATION — wrong (Eccl. 1:14), trouble (2 Chr. 15:15), sadness (Is. 65:14).

VILE — disgusting, despised (Ps. 12:8).

VINE, VINEYARD — a wandering plant that produces fruit usually referencing grapes and grapevines (Matt. 26:29).

VINEGAR — a drink made from wine that had been soured or overfermented. In accordance with their vow, the NAZIRITES separated themselves from any product of the grapevine, including vinegar (Num. 6:3).

VINTAGE — harvest (Lev. 26:5).

VIOLATE — commit violence against (Ezek. 22:26).

VIOLENCE — the use of physical force, usually with an intent to violate or destroy. Violence is a violation of God's perfect order. Thus the Greek word translated as "violent force" applies to the disorderly mob of Acts 21:35. But if godly people are subject to the human instability that causes violence, they also have the hope of seeking refuge in God's stability (2 Sam. 22:3). Faith in

Him can lead to a quenching of the violence of fire (Heb. 11:34).

VIPER — poisonous snake (Acts 28:3), also symbolic reference to evil leaders (Matt. 3:7; 12:34).

VIRGIN — a person who has not had sexual intercourse. Leviticus 21:7, 14 specified that a priest must not marry a widow, a divorced woman, or a prostitute, but only a virgin. The term was sometimes used to describe the nation of Israel (Is. 37:22; Jer. 31:4) to emphasize its purity and holiness as the CHOSEN PEOPLE of God.

VIRGIN BIRTH — the theological doctrine that Jesus was miraculously begotten by God and born of Mary, who was a virgin. The term "virgin birth" explains the way in which the Son of God entered human existence; it means that Mary had not had sexual relations with any man when she conceived Jesus (Matt. 1:18–25).

VIRTUE — moral excellence or goodness (Phil. 4:8). Virtue is considered a necessary ingredient in the exercise of faith (2 Pet. 1:3, 5). Sometimes

A modern vineyard at the foot of the mound of ancient Lachish. As in biblical times, winemaking is still an important industry in Israel. *Photo by Willem A. VanGemeren*

the Greek word for virtue is used to express the idea of power or strength (Luke 6:19).

VISIONS — experiences similar to dreams through which supernatural insight or awareness is given by revelation. But the difference between a dream and a vision is that dreams occur only during sleep, while visions can happen while a person is awake (Dan. 10:7).

VISAGE — face (Is. 52:14), representation (Dan. 3:19).

VISION — revelation from God (Acts 9:10).

VOCATION — a call or an invitation to a profession or way of life. But in theological discussions, the word "vocation" is not used in reference to the professional trade one pursues. Vocation refers to the invitation God has given to all people to become His children through Christ's work. This vocation, or calling, does not come to people because they deserve it; it comes strictly as a result of God's GRACE (2 Tim. 1:9). However, it is up to people themselves to decide whether they will accept and act upon the vocation.

VOID — an emptiness; a great desolation. When the earth was first created, it was void and formless (Gen. 1:2). This means it was a desolate place, not yet filled with the plants and creatures that God later created. In a similar vein, the prophet Jeremiah envisioned an earth "without form, and void" (Jer. 4:23), indicating that invading armies would turn the nation of Israel into an uninhabited wasteland.

VOW — a solemn promise or pledge that binds a person to perform a specified act or to behave in a certain manner. The first mention of a vow in the Bible is of Jacob at Bethel (Gen. 28:20–22; 31:13).

WAGES — compensation for performing work or service. In Bible times, wages were often paid in the form of property or privileges, not money. Such "in kind" payment for tasks completed especially suited the nomadic peoples of the Old Testament.

The term "wages" also denotes the consequences of a person's acts or deeds, as in Paul's immortal declaration, "The wages of sin is death" (Rom. 6:23).

WAIL — a mournful cry of grief, sorrow, or lamentation. In ancient funeral processions, wailing relatives, often accompanied by professional mourners and musicians, preceded the body to the grave (Jer. 9:17).

WALK — to move at a pace slower than a run; one's conduct of life. The literal sense predominates in the Old Testament, but the figurative meaning of the word does occur (Gen. 5:24; 6:9; Eccl. 11:9). In the New Testament the word usually is used literally in the Gospels, while it is usually used figuratively in Paul and John's letters.

WALL — a thick, high, continuous structure of stones or brick that formed a defensive barricade around an ancient city. Interior walls of houses in Palestine were also made of bricks or stones, but these were usually plastered over to give them a smooth surface (1 Kin. 5:15).

WANTONNESS — characterized as acting without restraint or inhibition (Rom. 13:13; 2 Pet. 2:18).

WARD — prison, hospital, place of confinement (Gen. 42:16–19).

WARE — goods, utensils (Neh. 13:16).

WASTE — trash, garbage, place of desolation (Lev. 26:31).

WATCH — either a group of soldiers or others posted to keep guard (Neh. 4:9; 7:3; 12:25) or one of the units of time into which the night was divided (Ps. 63:6; Lam. 2:19; Luke 12:38).

WATCHMAN — a guard or lookout person (2 Kin. 9:17).

WATCHTOWER — an observation tower upon which a guard or lookout was stationed to keep watch; an elevated structure offering an extensive view (2 Kin. 17:9; 18:8; Is. 21:8).

WAX — a sticky substance secreted by bees to build the honeycomb, also called beeswax. The wicked melt like wax before God's judgment (Ps. 68:2).

WEAN — to make independent of; usually in reference to a child and mother (1 Sam. 1:23).

WEAVING — the skill of making cloth from threads. Egyptian paintings from as early as 2000 B.C. depict weaving as an advanced skill. This skill was widely practiced throughout the ancient world long before this time. About 2500 B.C. the city of Ebla boasted a highly developed textile industry, and weavers of this city traded their goods widely. The Hebrews practiced

A mosaic of the wedding procession of the virgins (Matt. 25:1–13) in an ancient church in Ravenna, Italy. *Photo by Howard Vos*

weaving probably as early as Abraham's time, about 2000 B.C. The great skill required to weave the tabernacle curtains (Exodus 26) and priestly garments (35:35) was probably learned in Egypt.

WEDDING — a marriage ceremony with its accompanying festivities (Luke 12:36; 14:8). Among the Israelites a wedding was a festive occasion in which the whole community participated.

WEEK — any seven consecutive days; the interval between two sabbaths (Lev. 12:5; Jer. 5:24; Luke 18:12). The Hebrew people observed the seventh day of the week, from Friday evening (beginning at sunset) to Saturday evening, as their SABBATH, or day of rest and worship (Ex. 16:23–27).

The early Christians, to commemorate the Resurrection of Christ, worshiped not on the old Jewish Sabbath, but on the Lord's Day (the first day of the week, or Sunday), which became the new Christian "sabbath" (Mark 16:2, 9; Acts 20:7; 1 Cor. 16:2).

WEEKS, FEAST OF — This feast was observed early in the third month on the fiftieth day after the offering of the barley sheaf at the Feast of PASSOVER. It included a holy convocation with the usual restriction on manual labor. Numbers 28:26-31 describes the number and nature of offerings and Deuteronomy 16:9–12 describes those who were to be invited. This feast was also known as the Feast of Harvest as well as PENTECOST (a Greek word meaning "fifty").

WEIGHTS AND MEASURES OF THE BIBLE. — weighing (pounds) and measuring (volume, length, and area) are two distinct functions in the Bible.

Weights

The balance was an early method of determining weight. The balance consisted of a beam supported in the middle with a pan suspended by cords on each end. A known quantity of

Ancient weights were frequently cast in the shapes of animals such as turtles, ducks, and lions to make them easily recognizable and easy to handle. *Photo by Gustav Jeeninga*

weight would be placed in the pan on one side of the balance and the object to be weighed on the other side. By adding or removing known weights until each side was equal, the weight of the object could be determined. These ancient weights were sometimes used as money.

Measures

Measurements recorded in the Bible are of three types: (1) measures of volume, which told the amount of dry commodity (for example, flour) or liquid (for example, oil) that could be contained in a vessel; (2) measures of length, for height, width, and depth of an object or person; and (3) measures of total area, which described the size of a building, field, or city.

Weights			
Unit	**Weight**	**Equivalents**	**Translations**
Jewish Weights			
Talent	ca. 75 pounds for common talent, ca. 150 pounds for royal talent	60 minas; 3000 shekels	talent, one hundred pounds
Mina	1.25 pounds	50 shekels	maneh, mina
Shekel	ca. .4 ounce (11.4 grams) for common shekel ca. .8 ounce for royal shekel	2 bekas; 20 gerahs	shekel
Beka	ca. .2 ounce (5.7 grams)	$^{1}/_{2}$ shekel; 10 gerahs	half-shekel
Gerah	ca. .02 ounce (.57 grams)	$^{1}/_{20}$ shekel	gerah
Roman Weight			
Litra	12 ounces		pound, pint

Measures of Length			
Unit	**Length**	**Equivalents**	**Translations**
Day's journey	ca. 20 miles		day's journey, day's walk
Roman mile	4,854 feet	8 stadia	mile
Sabbath day's journey	3,637 feet	6 stadia	a Sabbath day's journey
Stadion	606 feet	$^{1}/_{8}$ Roman mile	mile, stadion
Rod	9 feet (10.5 feet in Ezekiel)	3 paces; 6 cubits	measuring rod
Fathom	6 feet	4 cubits	fathom
Pace	3 feet	$^{1}/_{3}$ rod; 2 cubits	pace
Cubit	18 inches	$^{1}/_{2}$ pace; 2 spans	cubit, yards
Span	9 inches	$^{1}/_{2}$ cubit; 3 handbreadths	span
Handbreadth	3 inches	$^{1}/_{3}$ span; 4 fingers	handbreadth
Finger	.75 inches	$^{1}/_{4}$ handbreadth	finger

Dry Measures			
Unit	**Measures**	**Equivalents**	**Translations**
Homer	6.52 bushels	10 ephahs	homer
Kor	6.52 bushels	1 homer; 10 ephahs	kor, measure
Lethech	3.26 bushels	$^1/_2$ kor	a homer and a half
Ephah	.65 bushel, 20.8 quarts	$^1/_{10}$ homer	ephah
Modius	7.68 quarts		peck-measure
Seah	7 quarts	$^1/_3$ ephah	measure, pecks
Omer	2.08 quarts	$^1/_{10}$ ephah; $1^4/_5$ kab	omer
Kab	1.16 quarts	4 logs	kab
Choenix	1 quart		quart
Xestes	$1^1/_{16}$ pints		pitcher
Log	.58 pint	$^1/_4$ kab	log

Liquid Measures			
Unit	**Measures**	**Equivalents**	**Translations**
Kor	60 gallons	10 baths	kor
Metretes	10.2 gallons		gallon
Bath	6 gallons	6 hins	measure, bath
Hin	1 gallon	2 kabs	hin
Kab	2 quarts	4 logs	kab
Log	1 pint	$^1/_4$ kab	log

WELFARE — state of being; completeness, prosperity (Neh. 2:10).

WELL — a pit or hole sunk into the earth to provide water. References in English versions of the Bible sometimes confuse wells, natural springs, and cisterns. Many different types of wells are mentioned in the Bible. These include a cistern dug in the ground (Gen. 16:14; 2 Sam. 17:18); a spring (Ps. 84:6); a fountain, also called a living spring (Neh. 2:13); and a pit or hole (John 4:11–12).

WHEAT — grain used to make flour; also symbolized commitment to God (John 12:24; Matt. 3:12; Luke 3:17).

WHELP — a young offspring of various carnivorous mammals, such as a dog, wolf, or lion; a puppy or cub. In the Bible the word "whelp" al-ways refers to a lion cub and is always used figuratively, for instance, of the tribes of Judah (Gen. 49:9) and Dan (Deut. 33:22).

WHENCE — from where (Phil. 3:20).

WHEREAS — since, because (James 4:14).

WHIRLWIND — any violent storm or destructive wind (Is. 66:15). Windstorms are common in Palestine, especially in the northern Jordan River Valley and around the Sea of Galilee, because of the proximity of these bodies of water to the hot desert.

WHITEWASHED — covered with white paint to hide corruption, uncleanness (Matt. 23:27).

WHITHER — where (Gen. 28:15).

WHOLE, WHOLESOME — well, complete, healthy, all, entire (Prov. 15:4).

WHORE, WHOREDOM — prostitute; crime of prostitution; symbolized idolatry (Hos. 1:2).

WICKED — evil, wrong, malicious (Ps. 9:16; 1 Thess. 3:2).

WIDOW — a woman whose husband has died and who has not remarried. If a man died in Bible times, his widow often suffered at the hands of the powerful (Job 24:21). This was especially true if she had no family to provide for her and her children.

WIFE — a man's marriage partner. After creating Adam, God declared, "It is not good that man should live alone" (Gen. 2:18). Then God created woman and united the couple and they became "one flesh" (Gen. 2:24). The wife is to honor her husband (Eph. 5:22), and the husband is to love his wife as Christ loved the church (Eph. 5:25–33).

WILDERNESS — a land not suited for farming. Wilderness land was too dry, rough, or rocky to be cultivated, but it was sufficient for grazing (Gen. 14:6; Ex. 3:18). Occasionally, the word wilderness means "desert."

WILL — a word with two distinct meanings in the Bible:

1. Wishing, desiring, or choosing especially in reference to the will of God. In the Gospels, primarily in John, Jesus is said to be acting not according to His own will, but according to the will of the heavenly Father (John 5:30; 6:38).

2. A legal declaration of how a person's possessions are to be disposed after death.

WIMPLE — KJV word for a cloth covering wound around the head, framing the face, and drawn into folds beneath the chin (Is. 3:22). Other translations are veil (KJV), mantle (NRSV), and shawl (NKJV, NIV).

WIND — the natural movement of air as a part of the weather pattern.

In a figurative sense, war is compared to the east wind (Jer. 18:17). The wind, or breath, is used as a metaphor for the brevity of life. Persons of uncertain faith are said to be tossed about on "every wind of doctrine" (Eph. 4:14).

WINE — the fermented juice of grapes. Wine was a common commodity in Hebrew life and was regularly included in summaries of agricultural products (Gen. 27:28; 2 Kin. 18:32; Jer. 31:12).

Wine was a significant trade item in Palestine, and fines were sometimes paid with wine (Amos 2:8).

Wine was also used in worship (Ex. 29:40; Num. 28:7; Lev. 23:13; Num. 15:4), as a common beverage, and also as medicine. It was said to revive the faint (2 Sam. 16:2) and was suitable as a sedative for people in distress (Prov. 31:6). The Samaritan poured oil and wine on the wounds of the injured traveler (Luke 10:34) and the apostle Paul charged Timothy, "No longer drink only water, but use a little wine for your stomach's sake" (1 Tim. 5:23).

The dangers of drunkenness are abundantly recognized in the Bible (Prov. 20:1; 23:29–35). Wine often enslaved the heart (Hos. 4:11). The prophets accused Israel of being overcome with wine (Is. 28:1), of drinking wine by bowlfuls (Amos 6:6), and of wanting prophets who spoke of wine (Mic. 2:11). Leaders were interested in drinking and were not concerned about the ruin of the country (Is. 5:11–12; 22:13).

While the use of wine continued in New Testament times, Paul admonished his readers to be filled with the Holy Spirit rather than with wine (Eph. 5:18).

WINEBIBBERS — those who drink too much wine. The Bible warns against associating with such persons (Prov. 23:20).

WINEPRESS — a vat in which the juice is pressed from grapes in the process of making wine (Deut. 16:13; Judg. 6:11). A winepress was made by digging a square basin in the rock (Neh. 13:15). At a slightly lower level on the slope was a second basin where the juice could be collected in clay jars or in WINESKINS for storage. Digging a winepress was a fixed part of the preparation of a vineyard (Is. 5:2; Matt. 21:33; Mark 12:1). Winepresses were owned by common people (Num. 18:27, 30; Deut. 15:14), as well as kings (Judg. 7:25; Zech. 14:10).

WINESKIN — a bag for holding and dispensing WINE, made from the skin of a goat or another animal (Job 32:19). In Bible times, wineskins were manufactured from whole animal hides.

Jesus used the analogy of wineskins to show that the Jewish legalism of the Old Testament was inflexible and outdated: "No one puts new wine into old wineskins; or else the new wine bursts the wineskins, the wine is spilled, and the wineskins are ruined" (Matt. 9:17; Mark 2:22; Luke 5:37–38). The "old wineskins" of Judaism could not contain the dynamic new faith of Christianity.

WINNOWING — the process of separating the kernels of threshed grain, such as wheat or barley, from the CHAFF with a current of air. The grain and its mixture of straw and husks were thrown into the air. The kernels of wheat or barley would fall into a pile on the THRESHING FLOOR; and the chaff, or refuse, would be blown away by the wind (Ps. 1:4).

WISDOM — ability to judge correctly and to follow the best course of action, based on knowledge and understanding (1 Kin. 4:29–34).

The biblical concept of wisdom, therefore, is quite different from the classical view of wisdom, which sought through philosophy and human rational thought to determine the mysteries of existence and the universe. The first principle of biblical wisdom is that people should humble themselves before God in reverence and worship, obedient to His commands. This idea is found especially in the Wisdom Literature: the Books of Job, Proverbs, and Ecclesiastes.

WISE — one who understands and makes informed decisions based on knowledge (Prov. 10:5).

WISE MEN — the men from the East who were led by a star to come to Palestine to worship the infant Christ (Matt. 2:1, 7, 16). The Greek word for wise men in this account (*magoi*) is rendered as "astrologers" where it occurs in the SEPTUAGINT, the Greek translation of the Old Testament (Dan. 1:20; 2:2) and as "sorcerer" in its other occurrences in the New Testament (Acts 13:6, 8).

WIT, WIST, WOT — to know (Luke 2:49).

WIT, TO — specifically (Rom. 8:23).

WITHER — deplete; dry up, become ineffective (Ps. 102:4; 1 Pet. 1:24).

WITHSTAND — stand up against (Eph. 6:13).

WITNESS, WITNESSING — a person who gives testimony; testimony given for or against someone, often in a law-court setting, where there is considerable concern for the truth of the testimony. "You shall not bear false witness against your neighbor" (Ex. 20:16; Deut. 17:6; Prov. 25:18). Also used in reference to telling what you know; specifically the gospel.

WIZARD — magician or sorcerer; one who speaks with the dead (Is. 8:19).

WOE — deep sorrow, grief, or affliction. The word "woe" is often used by the Old Testament prophets, as an exclamation expressing dismay or misfortune (Is. 3:9, 11; Jer. 10:19; Amos 5:18). In the New Testament Jesus pronounced woes on the cities of Chorazin and Bethsaida (Matt. 11:21), on the scribes, Pharisees, and lawyers (Luke 11:42–44), and on the one who betrayed Him (Mark 14:21).

WOMAN — an adult female.

When God created mankind, He created both "male and female" (Gen. 1:27; 5:2). Both were created in God's image and both were given the responsibility of exercising authority over God's creation. The man was created before the woman. Because the man needed companionship and a helper, God caused the man to sleep. From

Old Testament Women

Name	Description	Biblical Reference
Bathsheba	Wife of David; mother of Solomon	2 Sam. 11:3, 27
Deborah	Judge who defeated the Canaanites	Judg. 4:4
Delilah	Philistine who tricked Samson	Judg. 16:4, 5
Dinah	Only daughter of Jacob	Gen. 30:21
Eve	First woman	Gen. 3:20
Gomer	Prophet Hosea's unfaithful wife	Hos. 1:2, 3
Hagar	Sarah's maid; mother of Ishmael	Gen. 16:3–16
Hannah	Mother of Samuel	1 Sam. 1
Jezebel	Wicked wife of King Ahab	1 Kin. 16:30, 31
Jochebed	Mother of Moses	Ex. 6:20
Miriam	Sister of Moses; a prophetess	Ex. 15:20
Naomi	Ruth's mother-in-law	Ruth 1:2, 4
Orpah	Ruth's sister-in-law	Ruth 1:4
Rachel	Wife of Jacob	Gen. 29:28
Rahab	Harlot who harbored Israel's spies; ancestor of Jesus	Josh. 2:3–1; Matt. 1:5
Ruth	Wife of Boaz and mother of Obed; ancestor of Jesus	Ruth 4:13, 17; Matt. 1:5
Sarah	Wife of Abraham; mother of Isaac	Gen. 11:29; 21:2, 3
Tamar	A daughter of David	2 Sam. 13:1
Zipporah	Wife of Moses	Ex. 2:21

him He created a woman, "a helper comparable to him" (Gen. 2:18, 20). Man is incomplete without woman. Because she is called a "helper" does not imply that she is inferior to man. The same Hebrew word translated as helper is used of God in His relationship to Israel (Ps. 33:20; 70:5).

WOMB — a woman's uterus (Gen. 25:24).

WONDER — something amazing; a miracle. The feeling of witnessing such an event (Matt. 24:24; Acts 3:10).

WONT — used to; established; habit (Luke 22:39).

WORD, THE — a theological phrase that expresses the absolute, eternal, and ultimate being of Jesus Christ (John 1:1–14; 1 John 1:1; Rev. 19:13).

WORD OF GOD — the means by which God makes Himself known, declares His will, and brings about His purposes. Phrases such as "word of God," and "word of the Lord" are applied to the commanding word of God that brought creation into existence (Genesis 1; 2 Pet. 3:5) and also destroyed that same world through the waters of the Flood (2 Pet. 3:6); to God's announcement of an impending or future act of judgment (Ex. 9:20–21; 1 Kin. 2:27); to the word that declares God's commitment and promises His blessing (Gen. 15:1, 4); and to a particular instruction from God (Josh. 8:27).

WORK — physical or mental activity directed toward the accomplishment of a task; the labor by which people earn their livelihoods.

Man as created was intended to work. One of his primary tasks in the Garden of Eden was to

New Testament Women

Mary, the virgin mother of Jesus, has a place of honor among the women of the New Testament. She is an enduring example of faith, humility, and service (Luke 1:26–56). Other notable women of the New Testament include the following:

Name	Description	Biblical Reference
Anna	Recognized Jesus as the long-awaited Messiah	Luke 2:36–38
Bernice	Sister of Agrippa before whom Paul made his defense	Acts 25:13
Candace	A queen of Ethiopia	Acts 8:27
Chloe	Woman who knew of divisions in the church at Corinth	1 Cor. 1:11
Claudia	Christian of Rome	2 Tim. 4:21
Damaris	Woman of Athens converted under Paul's ministry	Acts 17:34
Dorcas (Tabitha)	Christian in Joppa who was raised from the dead by Peter	Acts 9:36–41
Drusilla	Wife of Felix, governor of Judea	Acts 24:24
Elizabeth	Mother of John the Baptist	Luke 1:5, 13
Eunice	Mother of Timothy	2 Tim. 1:5
Herodias	Queen who demanded the execution of John the Baptist	Matt. 14:3–10
Joanna	Provided for the material needs of Jesus	Luke 8:3
Lois	Grandmother of Timothy	2 Tim. 1:5
Lydia	Converted under Paul's ministry in Philippi	Acts 16:14
Martha and Mary	Sisters of Lazarus; friends of Jesus	Luke 10:38–42
Mary Magdalene	Woman from whom Jesus cast out demons	Matt. 27:56–61; Mark 16:9
Phoebe	A servant, perhaps a deaconess, in the church at Cenchrea	Rom. 16:1, 2
Priscilla	Wife of Aquila; laborer with Paul at Corinth and Ephesus	Acts 18:2, 18, 19
Salome	Mother of Jesus' disciples James and John	Matt. 20:20–24
Sapphira	Held back goods from the early Christian community	Acts 5:1
Susanna	Provided for the material needs of Jesus	Luke 8:3

"till [work] the ground" (Gen. 2:5). Although work was ordained by God as a blessing, it became a curse as a result of the FALL (Gen. 3:17–19). Man would now have to work for his food, and much of his produce would be frustration.

WORLD — the heavens and the earth that form the universe and the place where people and animals live. Among both the Hebrew people and the Greeks the terms "world" and "earth" were used interchangeably to mean the created

universe, the fruitful and habitable earth. The biblical declaration, "The earth is the Lord's, and all its fullness, the world and those who dwell therein" (Ps. 24:1), denotes the whole of created nature.

"World" is also associated with mankind. Christ said of His disciples, "You are the light of the world" (Matt. 5:14). Often world is used to indicate "the men of this world" who are said to lie in wickedness (Eph. 2:2; 1 John 5:19). The men are called "the world," not only because they compose the greater part of the world's population, but mainly because they pursue and cherish the things of this world. The Psalmist describes these men "as having their portion in this life" (Ps. 17:14).

"World" may also denote the fleeting character of life's riches and pleasures and the folly of making them of central importance in life. "Will a person gain anything if he wins the whole world, but loses his life?" (Matt. 16:26).

WORM, WORMS — crawling creature; often used as a symbol of weakness (Job 17:14; Is. 41:14).

WORMWOOD — any of several aromatic plants that yield a bitter, dark green oil (Deut. 29:18; Rev. 8:11).

WORSHIP — reverent devotion and allegiance pledged to God; the rituals or ceremonies by which this reverence is expressed (John 4:23). The English word "worship" comes from the Old English word "worthship," a word that denotes the worthiness of the one receiving the special honor or devotion.

WRATH — the personal manifestation of God's holy, moral character in judgment against sin. Wrath is neither an impersonal process nor irrational and fitful like anger. It is in no way vindictive or malicious. It is holy indignation—God's anger directed against sin (Rom. 1:18).

WREST — change, manipulate (2 Pet. 3:16).

WROTH — angry (Gen. 4:5; Rev. 12:17).

XYZ

XERXES [zurk'-sees] — the Greek name of AHASUERUS, the king mentioned in the Book of Esther (Esth. 1:1; 2:1; 3:1, NIV). Known as Xerxes the Great, he was the king of Persia from 486—465 B.C.

YAHWEH, YAHWEH ELOHIM [yah'-way, el-oh-heem'] — name for God; pronunciation of the Hebrew consonants YHWH, usually translated "the LORD" (Ex. 3:15).

YEA — an obsolete or poetic word meaning "yes, indeed, truly" (Ps. 23:4). The word is also used to introduce a more explicit or emphatic phrase: not only so but (Ps. 19:10; 137:1).

YEAR — the period of time required for the earth to complete a single revolution around the sun. The year of the Hebrew people consisted of 12 months (1 Kin. 4:7; 1 Chr. 27:1–5). These months were based on the changing cycles of the moon. Such a year would contain about 354 days. Periodically a 13th month had to be added to the Hebrew calendar to make up for this discrepancy of time.

YEAR OF JUBILEE — The Jubilee Year took place after seven Sabbatical years, or every 49 years; and the 50th year was thereby set aside as the Year of Jubilee.

The Year of Jubilee was a special year in family renewal. A man who was bound to another as a slave or indentured servant was set free and returned to his own family. If any members of his family were also bound, the entire family was set free. Houses and lands could also be redeemed in the Year of Jubilee (Lev. 25:9–14).

YEARN — feel strongly about (1 Kin. 3:26).

YHWH — the Hebrew name of the God of Israel, probably originally pronounced Yahweh. Eventually the Jews gave up pronouncing it, considering the name too holy for human lips. Instead they said *Adonai* or "Lord." This oral tradition came to be reflected in the written Greek translation of the Old Testament as *kurios* or "Lord," and it is often so quoted in the New Testament (Mark 1:3; Rom. 4:8). English versions of the Old Testament also tend to translate this word as "LORD." There is also a shorter form, YAH (Ps. 68:4; Is. 12:2; 26:4; 38:11). In Exodus 3:14–16 YHWH is linked with the verb *hayah,* "to be," probably referring to the presence of God with His people (Ex. 3:12).

YOKE — a device that harnesses animals together (Deut. 21:3). Also symbolic for slavery or burden (Gal. 5:1).

YONDER — there (Matt. 26:36).

ZACCHAEUS [zak-ke'-us] *(pure)* — a chief tax collector of Jericho who had grown rich by overtaxing the people. When Jesus visited Jericho, Zacchaeus climbed a tree in order to see Jesus (Luke 19:3). Jesus asked him to come down and then went to visit Zacchaeus as a guest. As a result of Jesus' visit, Zacchaeus became a follower of the Lord, repented of his sins, and made restitution for his wrongdoing. He gave half of his goods to the poor and restored fourfold those whom he had cheated. In associating with people like Zacchaeus, Jesus showed that He came to call sinners to repentance.

The mound of New Testament Jericho, the home of Zacchaeus the tax collector who became a disciple of Jesus (Luke 19:1–10). *Photo by Willem A. VenGemeren*

ZACHARIAH [zak-a-ri′-ah] — a form of ZECHARIAH.

ZACHARIAS [zak′-a-ri′-as] *(the Lord has re-membered)* — the name of two men in the New Testament:

1. The prophet whom the Jews "murdered be-tween the temple and the altar" (Matt. 23:35, KJV) because he rebuked them for breaking God's commandments (Luke 11:51, KJV).

2. The father of John the Baptist (Luke 1:13; 3:2). Zacharias was a priest of the division of Abijah. His wife, Elizabeth, was one "of the daughters of Aaron" (Luke 1:5), meaning she also was of priestly descent.

ZADOK [za′-dok] *(just, righteous)* — the name of several men in the Bible but most notably, a high priest in the time of David.

Zadok was a son of Ahitub (2 Sam. 8:17) and a descendant of Aaron through Eleazar (1 Chr. 24:3). During David's reign he served jointly as high priest with Abiathar (2 Sam. 8:17).

ZEAL, ZEALOUS — enthusiastic devotion; eager desire; single-minded allegiance (2 Sam.

21:2; 2 Kin. 10:16; 19:31). The psalmist wrote, "Zeal for Your house has eaten me up" (Ps. 69:9). When Jesus cleansed the temple, His zeal re-minded the disciples of the psalmist's words (John 2:17). Even before he became a Christian, Paul was zealous toward God and the Law of Moses (Acts 22:3; Phil. 3:6).

ZEALOT [zel′-ot] *(devoted supporter)* — a nickname given to Simon, one of Jesus' twelve apostles (Luke 6:15; Acts 1:13), perhaps to distin-guish him from Simon Peter. The Aramaic form of the name means "to be jealous" or "zealous."

A Zealot was a member of a fanatical Jewish sect that militantly opposed the Roman domina-tion of Palestine during the first century A.D.

Like the PHARISEES, the Zealots were devoted to the Jewish law and religion. But unlike most Pharisees, they thought it was treason against God to pay tribute to the Roman emperor, since God alone was Israel's king. They were willing to fight to the death for Jewish independence.

ZEBEDEE [zeb′-e-dee] *(gift* [of the Lord]*)* — the father of James and John, (Matt. 4:21–22;

Mark 1:19–20). He was a fisherman on the Sea of Galilee, perhaps living in Capernaum or Bethsaida. Zebedee was probably wealthy since he had "hired servants" (Mark 1:20).

ZEBULUN [zeb'-u-lun] — the name of a man and a territory in the Old Testament:

1. The tenth of Jacob's 12 sons; the sixth and last son of Leah (Gen. 30:19–20; 35:23; 1 Chr. 2:1). Zebulun had three sons: Sered, Elon, and Jahleel (Gen. 46:14; Num. 26:26–27). These are the only details about Zebulun that appear in the Bible.

2. The territory in which the tribe of Zebulun lived.

ZEBULUN, TRIBE OF — the tribe that sprang from Zebulun, son of Jacob (Num. 1:9; Deut. 27:13; Josh. 19:10, 16; Judg. 1:30). The tribe was divided into three great families headed by Zebulun's three sons (Num. 26:26–27). At the first census taken in the wilderness, the tribe numbered 57,400 fighting men (Num. 1:30–31). The second census included 60,500 members of the tribe of Zebulun (Num. 26:27).

Zebulun played an important role in Israel's history during the period of the JUDGES.

ZECHARIAH [zec-a-ri'-ah] *(the Lord remembers)* — the name of about 30 men in the Bible. A few of these are:

1. The 15th king of Israel (2 Kin. 14:29; 15:8, 11; Zachariah, KJV), the last of the house of Jehu. The son of Jeroboam II, Zechariah became king when his father died. He reigned only six months (about 753/52 B.C.) before being assassinated by Shallum.

2. A son of Meshelemiah (1 Chr. 9:21; 26:2, 14) and a Levite doorkeeper in the days of David.

3. A Levite who helped cleanse the temple during the reign of King Hezekiah of Judah (2 Chr. 29:13).

4. A prophet in the days of Ezra (Ezra 5:1; 6:14; Zech. 1:1, 7; 7:1, 8) and author of the Book of Zechariah. A leader in the restoration of the nation of Israel following the Captivity, Zechariah

A painting of the prophet Zechariah by Michelangelo, in the Sistine Chapel in Rome.
Photo by Howard Vos

was a contemporary of the prophet Haggai, the governor Zerubbabel, and the high priest Joshua. Zechariah himself was an important person during the period of the restoration of the community of Israel in the land of Palestine after the Captivity.

5. A Levite who led a group of musicians at the dedication of the rebuilt wall of Jerusalem (Neh. 12:35–36).

ZECHARIAH, BOOK OF — an Old Testament prophetic book that portrays the coming glory of the MESSIAH. Many scholars describe Zechariah as "the most messianic of all the Old Testament books" because it contains eight specific references to the Messiah in its brief 14 chapters.

The 14 chapters of Zechariah fall naturally into two major sections: chapters 1—8, the prophet's encouragement to the people to finish the work of rebuilding the temple, and chapters 9—14, Zechariah's picture of Israel's glorious future and the coming of the Messiah.

ZECHARIAH:
A Study and Teaching Outline

I. **The Call to Repentance** 1:1–6
II. **The Eight Visions of Zechariah** . . . . 1:7—6:8
   A. The Horses among the Myrtle Trees 1:7–17
   B. The Four Horns and Four Craftsmen 1:18–21
   C. The Man with the Measuring Line 2:1–13
   D. The Cleansing of Joshua, the High Priest . . 3:1–10
   E. The Golden Lampstand and Olive Trees 4:1–14
   F. The Flying Scroll 5:1–4
   G. The Woman in the Basket 5:5–11
   H. The Four Chariots 6:1–8
III. **The Crowning of Joshua** 6:9–15
IV. **The Question of Fasting** 7:1–3
V. **The Four Messages of Zechariah** . . . . 7:4—8:23
   A. Rebuke of Hypocrisy 7:4–7
   B. Repent of Disobedience 7:8–14
   C. Restoration of Israel 8:1–17
   D. Rejoice in Israel's Future 8:18–23
VI. **The Two Burdens of Zechariah** . . . . 9:1—14:21
   A. The First Burden: The Rejection of
      the Messiah . . . . 9:1—11:17
      1. Judgment on Surrounding Nations 9:1–8
      2. Coming of the Messiah . . . . 9:9—10:12
      3. Rejection of the Messiah 11:1–17
   B. The Second Burden: The Reign of
      the Messiah . . . . 12:1—14:21
      1. Deliverance of Israel . . . . 12:1—13:9
      2. Reign of the Messiah 14:1–21

ZEDEKIAH [zed-e-ki'-ah] *(the Lord my righ-teousness)* — the name of five men in the Old Testament two of which are:

1. A false prophet, son of Chenaanah, who advised King Ahab of Israel to attack the Syrian army at Ramoth Gilead (1 Kin. 22:11).

2. The last king of Judah (597—586 B.C.). The son of Josiah, Zedekiah was successor to Jehoiachin as king (2 Kin. 24:17–20; 25:1–7; 2 Chr. 36:10–13). After Jehoiachin had reigned only three months, he was deposed and carried off to Babylonia. Nebuchadnezzar installed Zedekiah on the throne as a puppet king and made him swear an oath that he would remain loyal (2 Chr. 36:13; Ezek. 17:13). Zedekiah's original name was Mattaniah, but Nebuchadnezzar renamed him to demonstrate his authority over him and his ownership of him (2 Kin. 24:17). Although Zedekiah reigned in Jerusalem for 11 years, he was never fully accepted as their king by the people of Judah.

ZEPHANIAH [zef-a-ni'-ah] *(the Lord has hidden)* — the name of four men in the Old Testament:

1. A son of Maaseiah (2 Kin. 25:18; Jer. 21:1; 29:25, 29; 37:3).

2. A Levite of the family of Kohath (1 Chr. 6:36).

3. An Old Testament prophet and the author of the Book of Zephaniah (Zeph. 1:1). As God's spokesman to the southern kingdom of Judah, Zephaniah began his ministry about 627 B.C., the same year as the great prophet JEREMIAH. Zephaniah was a member of the royal house of Judah, since he traced his ancestry back to King Hezekiah. He prophesied during the reign of King Josiah (ruled 640—609 B.C.). One theme of his message was that through His judgment God would preserve a remnant, a small group of people who would continue to serve as His faithful servants in the world (Zeph. 3:8–13). 4. Father of Josiah (Zech. 6:10).

ZEPHANIAH, BOOK OF — a brief prophetic book of the Old Testament that emphasizes the certainty of God's judgment and the preservation of a remnant, a small group of people who will continue to serve as God's faithful servants in the world. The book takes its title from its author, the prophet Zephaniah, whose name means "the Lord has hidden."

Zephaniah contains only three short chapters, but these chapters are filled with some of the most vivid pictures of God's judgment to be found in the Bible. After a brief introduction of himself as God's spokesman, the prophet launches immediately into a description of God's approaching wrath. He portrays this great "day of the Lord" as a time of "trouble and distress," "darkness and gloominess," "trumpet and alarm" (1:14–15).

In spite of its underlying theme of judgment and punishment, the Book of Zephaniah closes on a positive note. After God judges the wayward nations, the prophet announces He will raise up a remnant of the faithful who will continue to serve as His covenant people in the world. The book ends with a glorious promise for the future, a time when God will "quiet you in His love" and "rejoice over you with singing" (3:17).

ZERAH [ze'-rah] *(sprout)* — the name of seven men in the Old Testament but most notably one of the twins born to Judah by Tamar, his daughter-in-law (Gen. 38:30; 46:12, Zarah, KJV; Matt. 1:3, Zara, KJV). He founded a tribal family of Judah, the Zarhites (Num. 26:20).

ZERUBBABEL [ze-rub'-ba-bel] *(offspring of Babylon)* — head of the tribe of Judah at the time of the return from the Babylonian CAPTIVITY; prime builder of the second temple.

Zerubbabel is a shadowy figure who emerges as the political and spiritual head of the tribe of Judah at the time of the Babylonian Captivity. Zerubbabel led the first group of captives back to Jerusalem and set about rebuilding the temple on the old site. For some 20 years he was closely associated with prophets, priests, and kings until the new temple was dedicated and the Jewish sacrificial system was reestablished (Ezra 3:2–4:4; 5:2).

ZEUS [zoose] — the principal god of the ancient Greeks, considered ruler of the heavens and father of other gods. The Romans equated Zeus with their own supreme god, Jupiter. Barnabas was called Zeus by the people after the apostle Paul performed a miraculous healing at Lystra

ZEPHANIAH:
A Study and Teaching Outline

I. **The Judgment in the Day of the Lord** . . . . 1:1—3:8
  A. The Judgment on the Whole Earth 1:1–3
  B. The Judgment on the Nation of Judah . . . 1:4—2:3
    1. Causes of the Judgment 1:4–13
    2. Description of the Judgment. 1:14–18
    3. Call to Repentance 2:1–3
  C. The Judgment on the Nations Surrounding
    Judah 2:4–15
    1. Judgment against Gaza (West) 2:4–7
    2. Judgment against Moab and Ammon
      (East) 2:8–11
    3. Judgment against Ethiopia (South) 2:12
    4. Judgment against Assyria (North). 2:13–15
  D. The Judgment of Jerusalem 3:1–7
    1. Jerusalem's Wickedness 3:1–4
    2. The Lord's Justice. 3:5–7
  E. The Judgment on the Whole Earth 3:8
II. **The Salvation in the Day of the Lord** 3:9–20
  A. The Promise of Conversion 3:9–13
  B. The Promise of Restoration 3:14–20

(Acts 14:12–13; 19:35; Jupiter, KJV). The temple of Zeus at Athens was the largest in Greece. His statue at Olympia was one of the seven wonders of the ancient world.

ZILPAH [zil'-pah] — the mother of Gad and Asher (Gen. 30:9–13; 35:26). Zilpah was one of the female slaves of Laban, the father of Leah and Rachel. When Leah married Jacob, Laban gave her Zilpah to serve as her maid (Gen. 29:24; 46:18). Later, Leah gave Zilpah to Jacob as a CONCUBINE (Gen. 30:9).

ZION [zi'-un] — the city of David and the city of God. The designation of Zion underwent a distinct progression in its usage throughout the Bible.

The first mention of Zion in the Bible is in 2 Samuel 5:7: "David took the stronghold of Zion (that is, the City of David)." Zion, therefore, was the name of the ancient Jebusite fortress situated on the southeast hill of Jerusalem at the junction of the Kidron Valley and the Tyropoeon Valley. The name came to stand not only for the fortress but also for the hill on which the fortress stood. After David captured "the stronghold of Zion" by defeating the Jebusites, he called Zion "the City of David" (1 Kin. 8:1; 1 Chr. 11:5; 2 Chr. 5:2).

When Solomon built the temple on Mount Moriah (a hill distinct and separate from Mount Zion), and moved the ark of the covenant there, the word "Zion" expanded in meaning to include also the temple and the temple area (Ps. 2:6; 48:2, 11–12; 132:13). It was only a short step until Zion was used as a name for the city of Jerusalem, the land of Judah, and the people of Israel as a whole (Is. 40:9; Jer. 31:12). The prophet Zechariah spoke of the sons of Zion (Zech. 9:13). By this time the word "Zion" had come to mean the entire nation of Israel.

The most important use of the word "Zion" is in a religious or theological sense. Zion is used figuratively of Israel as the people of God (Is. 60:14). The spiritual meaning of Zion is continued in the New Testament, where it is given the Christian meaning of God's spiritual kingdom, the church of God, the heavenly Jerusalem (Heb. 12:22; Rev. 14:1; Sion, KJV).

ZIPPORAH [zip-po'-rah] *(female bird)* — a daughter of Jethro, priest of Midian, and wife of Moses (Ex. 2:21–22; 4:25; 18:2–4). Their sons were Gershom and Eliezer. When the Lord sought to kill Moses because Eliezer had not been circumcised, Zipporah grabbed a sharp stone and immediately circumcised the child. She and the two sons must have returned to Jethro rather than continuing on to Egypt with Moses, because she is not mentioned again until after the EXODUS. Along with Jethro, she and her two sons visited Moses in the wilderness after the Hebrew people left Egypt (Ex. 18:1–5).